A GUIDE
TO THE COLLEGE LIBRARY

A
GUIDE TO THE
COLLEGE LIBRARY

The Most Useful Resources
for Students and Researchers

CHRISTOPHER LEE PHILIPS

WALKER AND COMPANY
New York

First published in the United States of America in 1993 by Walker
Publishing Company, Inc.

Published simultaneously in Canada by Thomas Allen & Son Canada,
Limited, Markham, Ontario

Library of Congress Cataloging-in-Publication Data
Philips, Christopher Lee.
A guide to the college library : the most useful resources for
students and researchers / Christopher Lee Philips.
p.   cm.
Includes bibliographical references and indexes.
ISBN 0-8027-1283-5
1. Academic libraries—United States.   2. Academic libraries—
Canada.   3. Reference books—Bibliography.   I. Title.
Z675.U5P5   1993
025.5'2777'0973—dc20   93-17748
CIP

Grateful acknowledgment is made to OCLC,
the Online Computer Library Center, Inc.,
for permission to reprint materials from the Dewey Decimal Classification.
DDC and Dewey Decimal Classification are registered trademarks of
OCLC Online Computer Library Center, Incorporated.

Printed in the United States of America

2   4   6   8   10   9   7   5   3   1

To ALADIN

CONTENTS

Who this book is for, why this book was written, and how to use it,
  plus a discussion of information resources and ready reference
  materials and a list of what you can expect to find in the college
  library.

I

The Identification and Organization
of Information Resources   I

How librarians have identified and organized information resources
  and the tools you need to find and use these resources.

2

Ready Reference: Information Resources and How They Work   25

Definitions and descriptions of many types of information resources available in the college library, with examples of each and some discussion as to how to use them to your advantage.

3

Major Areas of Study   93

A directory of select information resources in some of the most popular major areas of study in colleges and universities.

4

Getting the Most from a College Library   325

What a college library has to offer for students and researchers.

PREFACE

THIS BOOK IS, in part, a product of my graduate education in Library and Information Science, an academic program I began at the Catholic University of America in 1988. In greater measure it is the result of a long fascination with libraries and how they work, and how librarians over the years have organized human knowledge and made it accessible for a variety of needs.

I owe a debt of gratitude to the college and university member libraries which make up the Washington Research Library Consortium, and to several other academic institutions in Washington, D.C. They include the Jack and Dorothy Bender Library and Learning Resources Center of The American University, the John K. Mullen Memorial Library of The Catholic University of America, the Merrill Learning Center of the Gallaudet University, the Fenwick Library of George Mason University, the Melvin Gelman Library of The George Washington University, the Joseph Mark Lauinger Library of Georgetown University, the Founders Library of Howard University, the Reinsch Library of Marymount University, the Sister Helen Sheehan Library of Trinity College, the Learning Resources Division of the University of the District of Columbia Library, and the Mount Vernon College Library.

Finally, my greatest debt of gratitude goes to my wife, Janet, who gave me the confidence and stability required to begin this project, and helped me find the time I needed to finish it.

INTRODUCTION

THROUGHOUT THE United States and Canada there are hundreds of colleges and universities with hundreds of thousands, even millions of books in their libraries. These numbers don't even begin to include all the other types of information resources available in the college library, such as microforms, periodicals, and CD-ROM and on-line data bases. Libraries are full of information, and all those millions of books and other information resources can be enormously useful to you in pursuing a quality education. But how do you decide which ones to use? How do you find them? And then, how do you use them?

If you're reading this book, chances are you're a student and you'd like some advice on how to use the information resources in your college library quickly and efficiently. The aim of *A Guide to the College Library* is to help you learn what types of information resources exist in most college libraries, help you learn to find them whenever you want, and help you learn to use them to your advantage. Written especially for undergraduates (and others as well), *A Guide to the College Library* will help you learn to weave your way through the library in whatever college or university you attend. And it's arranged by major areas of study, so that any student can use it.

Once you've learned about abstracts, the library catalog, encyclopedias, style books, and many other resources, you will find that the library is one of the greatest assets on campus. In fact, you'll probably spend more of your student career in the college library than you do in the classroom. You'll find that knowing how to use information resources will be extremely valuable to you for the rest of your life. Master your college library and the information resources in it, and you'll be able to use any library, anywhere.

When I was an undergraduate (let's just say that was pre-MTV), I wished I knew more about the library's information resources and how to use them in ways that would be informative and helpful to me for each of the areas of study I found interesting. I took lots of different classes, but I didn't really learn to use the library very well until I went to graduate school, and by then I had learned everything the hard way. Don't make the same mistake I made. You should learn to use your college library during the first week of the first semester of your first year; you don't have to learn the hard way.

Any student interested in any of the major areas of study in most colleges and universities can reap substantial rewards from this book, whether you've just signed up for freshman English, are finally completing your required hours in math, or are a continuing education student taking courses at night. The material is presented in a very straightforward manner, as in a reference book. It's something that you can refer to over and over again for the specific needs of each class you take.

First, you'll learn about how information resources are identified and organized. Then you'll learn about many different types of information resources available in college libraries. Next, all of these information resources will be defined for you in a clear and concise manner. You'll be given many examples of information resources that are specific to every major area of study, as well as suggestions on how to use them. Then we'll look at representative information resources for some of the most popular major areas of study in colleges and universities in the United States and Canada. The English section will help you get through freshman English. The biology section will help you get through biology, especially if you're an English major. That's why the book is arranged by major areas of study: you'll want to know which information sources apply to your favorite subjects, but each section will be especially helpful for courses in subjects you *don't* major in. This book is designed to help you get out of college by helping you get into the library.

What you need is something that'll help you get your homework done — tonight! Besides, you need to know what's in the library and how to use it the first week of classes. You don't want to wait until exams to learn how to use the library. Sometimes students go all the way through college trying to avoid ever having to go in the place. You might say, "Fine, like, I'll miss it," but in fact, you'll be using libraries and the information resources in them for the rest of your life, at one time or another, for one reason or another.

Too often some of the best things in libraries and some of the quickest and easiest information resources to use go unnoticed and undiscovered. Sometimes that happens because libraries and the information resources in them can be a little intimidating, even with the genuine and sincere help of librarians, who are generally helpful and knowledgeable. If you use this guide and apply what's in it to the classes you take, you'll have a road map to the college library, a road map you can use now and in the future. You'll save time and energy and prevent the aggravation of brain drain when it comes to doing library research. That way you'll have more time to do what students do best; I presume you all have your own opinions as to what students do best.

Finally, after you've become an expert at selecting, finding, and using information resources, you'll get a few suggestions on "the life of the library": using other library services, browsing the collection, library etiquette, and the Freedom of Information Act.

Try out these fun facts. I was crunching some numbers the other day. Did you know that the Harvard University libraries (there are more than one) have over eleven million volumes and counting? If each of those books were a pizza, we could feed every undergraduate student in the United States and Canada during the next Superbowl.

But seriously, the library in your school may have an enormous collection, one in which you may feel yourself totally lost even after diligent and repeated efforts by librarians and professors to get you acquainted with it. Don't panic. Read this book. It will help you work smarter rather than harder when you walk into the college library. And when you work smarter in the library, you can work harder elsewhere, in the classroom, for example. Work smarter in the library and you will get things done in a quicker, easier manner.

So, you're in college. You're a student embarking on the adventure of a lifetime and trying valiantly to choose an academic major. Let's say you've signed up for several classes, probably a lot of them required for your Bachelor of Arts or Sciences degree, and you want to find out what sort of information resources apply to your first semester classes. Your professor gives an assignment on the first day of class. Some of them do that just because it gives them that feeling we all know and love — power. Let's say you've got to do a term paper by the end of the semester, give a class presentation sometime during the semester, or do a lab project without blowing up the chemistry building. You're going to have to go to the library, find some information that will be buried deep inside some of the resources in the library, and then use that information in a quick and efficient manner. Amidst those millions of volumes of books and all those other information resources that don't relate to the present assignment, you're going to have to find some particular pieces of information that are specific to the current assignment, things that will help you do the work you need to do to get you the grade you want. Let's assume that's an A.

Maybe you need a book on abstract art or medieval drama, electrical engineering or voodoo economics. You might need to incorporate the results of a scientific experiment into a discussion of your lab project. You might need to check the value of the dollar against the rupee. You might need to figure out what the rupee is before you do that. Maybe you want to get a map of the city of Dunkirk. You might need to determine whether to use the French or the English spelling of the city. Maybe you'd like to know when your favorite actress was born or when your favorite actor made his first movie. You might just need to check the date someone became a member of Congress or confirm the citation to someone's book. Maybe you need to know the population of Kalamazoo in 1982. No matter what it is, your college library will probably have some kind of information resource that can help you with just about everything you want to learn (academically speaking) while you're a student. You can probably find everything your professors ever wrote, and maybe everything they ever read, in your college library.

The most basic resource in the college library is information, but information is packaged in so many different ways and presented in so many different formats. There is a vast amount of information available in the library, but sometimes the information you're after can be a little hard to find. Sometimes different information resources can be a little hard to use. You may be thinking, "Well, everybody knows how a book works." Maybe. Did you know that most books printed in Russia and many other countries, such as France and Spain, have the table of contents in the back of the book instead of the front? You wouldn't want to read a book from beginning to end just to figure that out, would you? This would be especially true if you just wanted to read one chapter or section of the book in the first place. So with that in mind, you should be aware of the many differences in information resources as you learn the best ways to use them.

Whatever college you attend, and whatever major area of study you choose, your college library will provide you with a wealth of information resources to use in pursuing your education. Each of the types of information resources, which we will discuss in chapter 2, "Ready Reference: Information Resources and How They Work," can be important to you because of the type of information provided, the format in which the information is presented, and the access that information gives you to other information. Look over this list and see if you're familiar with these types of information resources. See if you know how to use them.

Abstracts
Almanacs
Anthologies and collections
Archival materials
Atlases
Bibliographies
Biographical sources
Catalogs
CD-ROM data bases
Chronologies and histories
Codes and rules
Concordances
Dictionaries
Digests
Directories
Dissertations
Encyclopedias
Fact books
Government documents
Guides and handbooks
Indexes
Microforms
On-line data bases
Periodicals
Quote books
Reviews
Statistical sources
Style books
Thesauruses
Yearbooks

The arrangement of this book differs from other books on how to do research. Other research books often assume that you already know about the differences between the various types of information resources, that you already know what they're called and how to use them. They assume that you know the difference between newspapers and newsletters, abstracts and digests, almanacs and yearbooks, journals and magazines, and so on. I am confident that you know a lot of this already, but you could probably use a little guidance and advice on some of the subtle differences in information resources. You could certainly benefit from lots of examples. Furthermore, while I'm sure you know how to look up a book in the library catalog, I want to show you how to use many more of the tools in the library so that before your first semester is over, you'll be a master at working the library for all it's worth.

Finally, this book is for students, not the general public. All the information in this book is geared toward helping you learn to use the *college* library. Examples of information resources come from college libraries. Subjects covered are academic subjects, the major areas of study popular in most colleges and universities.

Chapter 1, "The Identification and Organization of Information Resources," is of primary importance. If you skip this and start thumbing through the book until you come to the major areas of study that you're most interested in, you'll miss a great deal of valuable information. While the book lists and describes a lot of information resources to use in the major areas of study, chapter 1 will help you learn how to decide which types of information resources are most suited to your needs, how to locate those information resources, and how to use them quickly and efficiently. Chapter 1 will also help you learn to devise your own research tactics and make your own research discoveries. So, begin at the beginning. That way, you will succeed in your research, no matter what the topic.

Chapter 2, "Ready Reference: Information Resources and How They Work," gives you general definitions, brief descriptions, and useful examples of the various information resources that are located in the ready reference section of your library. These are the information sources you're going to use more than once while you're in school. Go through this chapter before you go on to chapter 3, "Major Areas of Study," so that you'll understand the material in the major areas of study more quickly and easily. If you don't, you'll end up coming back to it.

Chapter 3 is not an exhaustive list of everything written on the major areas of study, but it does contain, in each instance, many representative information resources currently available in the ready reference section of many college and university libraries on the subject under consideration. Certainly you can skip the architecture section if you're a history major, and you can skip the engineering section if you're an architecture major. But take my word on this, the more time you spend in the college library, in the classroom, or in any learning environment, the more you'll come to understand the inherently interrelated nature of information. After all, one of the goals of a college degree is to get a well-rounded education.

Chapter 4, "Getting the Most from a College Library," includes hints on using other library services, browsing the collection, library etiquette, and the Freedom of Information Act, all of which are directly related to the "life of the library." Libraries have been around for thousands of years. Their mission has always been to preserve the heritage of their cultures and to provide information resources for their constituencies. The constituency in the college library is you. Understanding a little about the "life of the library" will help you appreciate it all the more. An understanding of the college library, its information resources, and how to use them will help you get through school with better grades and possibly make you a lifetime library user.

I

The Identification and Organization of Information Resources

ALL INFORMATION RESOURCES need some sort of key — an identification, a definition, a description, a finding device — so that their arrangement in libraries will make sense and so that they can be found by anyone who walks in the door. That's why information resources are cataloged and classified. In very simple terms, all information resources are cataloged for purposes of identification and classified for purposes of location. There are various types of cataloging and classification systems used in libraries throughout the world. Two prominent types of cataloging and classification systems with which you should at least be familiar are the Dewey Decimal Classification System, which we'll call Dewey, and The Library of Congress Classification System, which we'll call LC.

In most cases, smaller libraries, special libraries, and public libraries use Dewey, and colleges and universities use LC. Don't worry, you don't need to learn everything under the sun about cataloging and classification, but you should learn the difference between these two cataloging and classification systems. You'll want to learn a little bit about how Dewey works in case you need to visit the public library when you're home studying for exams. You'll want to learn a little bit more about how LC works because that is very likely the system used in your college library.

When librarians perform the tasks of cataloging and classifying information resources, they use huge sets of rules. One aspect of these rules is how to apply subject headings to information resources. For example, there are subject headings for Soviet Union with a variety of more closely defined subject breakdowns that follow. If you were looking in the library catalog under Russia, expecting to find information resources devoted to anything about the Soviet Union, you'd probably see a note reading See Soviet Union. We all know the Soviet Union used to be Russia and a bunch of other places, but when you are looking for information resources by subject, you need to know the actual subject under which the information resources have been cataloged and classified. Is what you're looking for cataloged and classified under Russia? Soviet Union? Commonwealth of Independent States? Subject headings are subject to change.

To make sure we all look under the right subject headings, librarians have for years used two distinct and agreed-upon lists of subject headings. One is the *Sears List of Subject Headings*, which is basically the appropriate list of subject headings to consult when researching information resources in the public library using Dewey. The other is the *Library of Congress Subject Headings*, which come in several huge red volumes that should be used when researching information resources in the college library that uses LC. The lesson here is that when you're researching by subject, as opposed to author or title, make sure you and the library agree on what the subject is called.

And if all that isn't enough, there are a few things you need to know about the alphabet. Now, I know you all know the alphabet. But have you ever had to put things in alphabetical order? Would you believe there are rules for this sort of thing? Well, there are, and it's a good thing there are rules, or you'd never be able to find anything when you look in the library catalog, in the dictionary, in the phone book, or in a bunch of other places. The section on filing rules will discuss two types of rules, The American Library Association Filing Rules and The Library of Congress Filing Rules. As I said before, you don't have to learn filing rules backward and forward. Just keep in mind the fact that they exist and be able to apply them when you're trying to find St. Louis and Saint Louis, MacArthur and McCarthy, *1984*, *Nineteen Eighty-Four*, *2001: A Space Odyssey*, and some other alphabetically tricky subjects.

Once you've learned a little about cataloging and classification, subject headings, and filing rules, you'll be able to use your library catalog much faster and with greater success. You'll be able to read bibliographic citations with ease and accuracy. You'll also be able to spot the call number and the other parts of a bibliographic citation and locate the information resource you want quickly and easily. After that,

Chapter 2, "Ready Reference: Information Resources and How They Work," will make much more sense to you. So will Chapter 3, "Major Areas of Study."

Cataloging and Classification

Cataloging and classification are among the most fundamental things librarians do so that library users can identify, find, and use information resources. Cataloging is a way of recording the descriptive elements of an information resource that can be identified by looking closely at the resource itself. Cataloging provides complete and concise identification of an information resource as it becomes part of the library collection. That identification is for inventory and retrieval purposes, but it also assists library users in determining whether or not the library resource in question is appropriate for their research. Catalogers look at everything about an information resource, starting first with the author, title, and subject. Those are the three fundamental reference points to any information resource. Cataloging lists the author or authors, the title and subtitle, and the subject or subjects that have been designated for the resource.

Cataloging also gives us some other valuable information about library resources. The catalog record will tell us if there is an index, a chronology, or a bibliography included in a book. The catalog record will tell us if there are any artistic works in the book, such as charts, diagrams, photographs, or maps. The catalog record will tell us the format of the library resource. If it's not a book but a pamphlet, the catalog record will tell us. If it's a microform, a photograph, a blueprint, or a drawing, the catalog record will tell us. That way you won't go trudging off to the periodical shelves looking for a journal that is available only on microform. The catalog record will also give the call number, usually in both Dewey and LC, and a series of subject headings under which you will find the book in question as well as other books on the same topic. Cataloging is like a checklist of information about an information resource. The standard checklist includes the three most basic elements of cataloging — author, title, and subject — but it includes other useful information as well.

Classification refers to the task of putting like materials together. I don't mean simply putting all the books and periodicals together; I mean putting all the books written on the concept of avant-garde theater together and putting all the books on molecular theory together.

In the college library, you will certainly find all the microforms together, all the periodicals and newspapers together, the government documents and the oversized atlases together, but you won't find the *Encyclopedia of Southern Culture* with the *Encyclopedia of Associations*, and you won't find the *Encyclopaedia Britannica* with either of those. While cataloging is pretty straightforward, classification can get a little tricky, even for librarians. That's why librarians have developed standard classification systems to identify and organize information resources.

THE DEWEY DECIMAL CLASSIFICATION

The Dewey Decimal Classification was created by Melvil Dewey, who lived from 1851 to 1931. Dewey helped establish the American Library Association, which is the main professional association for librarians in the United States. He also organized the first library school in the United States at Columbia University in 1887. The popularity and reliability of the Dewey Decimal System have kept it in constant use in small, public, and special libraries for over one hundred years.

Very simply, the Dewey Decimal System uses arabic numbers (as opposed to roman numerals) and decimals to catalog and classify books and to assign call numbers to them. There are ten main classes in the Dewey Decimal System and they are easy to remember. Each of the main classes covers a broad field of human knowledge. Each main class is further subdivided, going from the general to the specific, from broader concepts in human knowledge to more specific areas of study.

THE DEWEY DECIMAL CLASSIFICATION
The Ten Main Classes in Dewey
and Their Primary Subdivisions

000 ....**Generalities**

010	Bibliography
020	Library and Information Science
030	General Encyclopedic Works
040	
050	General Serials and Their Indexes
060	General Organizations and Museology
070	News Media, Journalism, Publishing
080	General Collections
090	Manuscripts and Rare Books

100 .... **Philosophy and Psychology**

    110   Metaphysics
    120   Epistemology, Causation, Humankind
    130   Paranormal Phenomena
    140   Specific Philosophical Schools
    150   Psychology
    160   Logic
    170   Ethics (Moral Philosophy)
    180   Ancient, Medieval, Oriental Philosophy
    190   Modern Western Philosophy

200 .... **Religion**

    210   Natural Theology
    220   Bible
    230   Christian Theology
    240   Christian Moral and Devotional Theology
    250   Christian Orders and Local Church
    260   Christian Social Theory
    270   Christian Church History
    280   Christian Denominations and Sects
    290   Other and Comparative Religions

300 .... **Social Sciences**

    310   General Statistics
    320   Political Science
    330   Economics
    340   Law
    350   Public Administration
    360   Social Services: Association
    370   Education
    380   Commerce, Communications, Transport
    390   Customs, Etiquette, Folklore

400 .... **Language**

    410   Linguistics
    420   English and Old English
    430   Germanic Languages: German
    440   Romance Languages: French
    450   Italian, Romanian, Rhaeto-Romanic
    460   Spanish and Portuguese Languages
    470   Italic Languages: Latin

480   Hellenic Languages: Classical Greek
490   Other Languages

500 ....Natural Sciences and Mathematics

510   Mathematics
520   Astronomy and Allied Sciences
530   Physics
540   Chemistry and Allied Sciences
550   Earth Sciences
560   Paleontology: Paleozoology
570   Life Sciences
580   Botanical Sciences
590   Zoological Sciences

600 ....Technology (Applied Sciences)

610   Medical Sciences: Medicine
620   Engineering and Allied Operations
630   Agriculture
640   Home Economics and Family Living
650   Management and Auxiliary Services
660   Chemical Engineering
670   Manufacturing
680   Manufacture For Specific Uses
690   Buildings

700 ....The Arts

710   Civic and Landscape Art
720   Architecture
730   Plastic Arts: Sculpture
740   Drawing and Decorative Arts
750   Painting and Paintings
760   Graphic Arts: Printmaking and Prints
770   Photography and Photographs
780   Music
790   Recreational and Performing Arts

800 ....Literature and Rhetoric

810   American Literature in English
820   English and Old English Literatures
830   Literatures of Germanic Languages
840   Literatures of Romance Languages

850	Italian, Romanian, Rhaeto-Romanic
860	Spanish and Portuguese Literatures
870	Italic Literatures: Latin
880	Hellenic Literatures: Classical Greek
890	Literatures of Other Languages

900 ....**Geography and History**

910	Geography and Travel
920	Biography, Genealogy, Insignia
930	History of Ancient World
940	General History of Europe
950	General History of Asia: Far East
960	General History of Africa
970	General History of North America
980	General History of South America
990	General History of Other Areas

The Dewey Decimal System is a very logical way of cataloging and classifying information resources using the basic principle of working from the general to the specific under ten main classes of human knowledge.

THE LIBRARY OF CONGRESS CLASSIFICATION SYSTEM

When the brand-new Library of Congress building opened in 1897 (the Jefferson Building behind the Capitol), the librarians there decided they needed a better way of cataloging and classifying books. They thought about using the Dewey Decimal Classification, but Melvil Dewey didn't like some of the changes they wanted to make in his system, so the Library of Congress developed its own system.

The Library of Congress Classification System, or LC for short, works a lot like Dewey. One difference is that LC uses letters with its call numbers whereas Dewey only uses numbers. But the idea is still the same: to catalog and classify information resources in an orderly fashion so that the user can find them. You're more likely to be using LC in your college or university library. Like Dewey, LC works from the general to the specific in organizing human knowledge.

THE LIBRARY OF CONGRESS CLASSIFICATION SYSTEM

A	General Works
B–BJ	Philosophy. Psychology
BL–BX	Religion
BL, BM, BP, BQ	Religion: Religions, Hinduism, Judaism, Islam, Buddhism
BX	Religion: Christian Denominations
C	Auxiliary Sciences of History
D	History: General and Old World (Eastern Hemisphere)
E–F	History: America (Western Hemisphere)
G	Geography. Maps. Anthropology. Recreation.
H–HJ	Social Sciences: Economics
HM–HX	Social Sciences: Sociology
J	Political Science
K	Law (General)
KD	Law of the United Kingdom and Ireland
KDZ, KG–KH	Law of the Americas, Latin America, and the West Indies
KE	Law of Canada
KF	Law of the United States
KK–KKC	Law of Germany
L	Education
M	Music
N	Fine Arts
P–PA	General Philology and Linguistics. Classical Languages and Literatures
PA Supplement	Byzantine and Modern Greek Literature. Medieval and Modern Latin Literature
PB–PH	Modern European Languages
PG	Russian Literature
PJ–PM	Languages and Literatures of Asia, Africa, Oceania. American Indian Languages. Artificial Languages
P–PM Supplement	Index to Languages and Dialects
PN, PR, PS, PZ	General Literature. English and American Literature. Fiction in English. Juvenile Belles Lettres
PQ, Part 1	French Literature
PQ, Part 2	Italian, Spanish, and Portuguese Literatures

PT, Part 1	German Literature
PT, Part 2	Dutch and Scandinavian Literatures
P–PZ	Language and Literature Tables
Q	Science
R	Medicine
S	Agriculture
T	Technology
U	Military Science
V	Naval Science
Z	Bibliography. Library Science

Let's take a closer look at one of the subdivisions in LC and see how it works. We'll use PN for Literature and see how LC works from the general to the specific in organizing human knowledge.

| PN, PR, PS, PZ | General Literature. English and American Literature. Fiction in English. Juvenile Belles Lettres |

PN .....1–6790 ....**Literary History and Collections (General)**

PN	80–99	Criticism
PN	101–245	Authorship
PN	441–1009.5	Literary History (including folk literature, fables, prose romances)
PN	1010–1551	Poetry
PN	1560–1590	The Performing Arts. Show Business

PN .....1600–3307 .....**Drama**

PN	1660–1693	Dramatic Composition
PN	1865–1999	Special Types of Drama (including tragedy, comedy, vaudeville, puppet plays, pantomimes, ballet, radio and television broadcasts, motion pictures)
PN	2000–3307	Dramatic Representation. The Theater (including management, the stage and accessories, amateur theatricals, tableaux, and pageants)
PN	3311–3503	Prose. Prose Fiction.
PN	4001–4355	Oratory. Elocution, Recitations, etc.

PN	4400	Letters
PN	4500	Essays
PN	4699–5650	Journalism. The Periodical Press, etc.

PN	**.....6010–6790**	**.....Collections of general literature**
PN	6080–6095	Quotations
PN	6099–6110	Poetry
PN	6110.5–6120	Drama
PN	6120.15–.95	Fiction
PN	6121–6129	Orations
PN	6130–6140	Letters
PN	6141–6145	Essays
PN	6147–6231	Wit and Humor. Satire
PN	6249–6790	Miscellaneous (Including anecdotes, aphorisms, maxims, mottoes, toasts, riddles, proverbs, comic books, comic strips)

The Library of Congress system is supported by an organizational and administrative behemoth called the federal government. There are librarians at work in the federal government whose jobs consist of deciding the rules by which books and other information resources will be cataloged and classified. You don't need to memorize all those call numbers, but you should remember the basics well enough so that you can recognize call number ranges in the library when you are searching for information resources.

Subject Headings

Using subject headings in your research can assist you in finding where we librarians have decided to put things. You should at least be familiar with and know how to use the *Sears List of Subject Headings*, for Dewey, and the *Library of Congress Subject Headings*, for LC.

Subject headings are important for the clear reading and tracing of information resources. When you want to search for information resources in the college library by subject, start with a quick look in the *LC Subject Headings*. For example, let's say you're a spy buff. Look up Spy in the *LC Subject Headings*. You'll find an entry for Spying, which directs you to look under Espionage. Then go to Espionage and see what's there.

Espionage (May Subd Geog)
  UF   Spying
    BT   Intelligence service
         Secret Service
         Sovereignty, Violation of
         Subversive activities
    SA   subdivision Secret service under names of wars, etc., e.g.
         World War, 1939–1945 — Secret service; United States
         — History — Civil War, 1861–1865 — Secret Service
    NT   Defense information, classified
         Ninjutsu
         Sex in espionage
         Trials (Espionage)

You're probably wondering what all the shorthand means. The abbreviations are called *scope notes*, and they are part of the guide in reading and understanding subject headings.

UF means Use For (don't look under Spying, look under
    Espionage)
BT means Broader Term (there's more general stuff here)
SA means See Also (there's more stuff here)
NT means Narrower Term (there's more specific stuff here)

One of the things about subject headings is that you can have several of them assigned to one book or information resource in the classification process. Each subject heading may have its own breakdown or several breakdowns. Each major area of study will have LC subject headings that will help direct you to information resources in the library. The most general information resources will be found at the beginning of each subject heading. At the beginning of most subject headings, you'll find breakdowns for general works such as dictionaries and encyclopedias, a history of the subject, study and teaching in the subject area, philosophy of the subject, technique in the subject area, and collected works in the subject area. Again, you don't have to learn all the subject headings. Just know how to use them.

Filing Rules

There are rules for filing things numerically and alphabetically. But don't worry. It's not as if you have to relearn the alphabet, and you don't have to memorize this stuff. The object here is for you to remember that there are rules and that depending on what you're looking for, you might have to put these rules to use.

The two basic types of filing rules are published by the Library of Congress and by the American Library Association. Let's say you're looking through your library catalog or some other numerical or alphabetical reference list, and you want to find something on the McCarthy hearings or on General Douglas MacArthur. Maybe you're looking for an author with a hyphenated name like Rhys-Davies or a publication entitled *These Times*. How about titles with nothing but numbers and letters in them? Where do you start to look for something on MTV or VH-1? Where do you find materials on St. Louis or Mount Saint Helens? Think about it. Where would you look for the title *1984*, that antiutopian novel by George Orwell? Is it spelled out, *Nineteen Eighty-Four*? What about *Fahrenheit 451* by Ray Bradbury? Sure, you can find them by looking under the author, but what if you didn't know the author? What about a title search? How would you look up a magazine like *The New Republic*? Do you look under The or New or under something else?

In order to find almost anything, almost anywhere, be it in an abstract, an index, the library catalog, an encyclopedia or a dictionary, even and especially in the telephone book, you need to know about the filing rules of numerical and alphabetical order and how they have been applied to the source you're looking through.

These things are all worth knowing because just a little time spent learning them will save you light-years in the library. Filing rules, like cataloging, classification, and subject headings, were created to help you find the things you're looking for without spending a whole semester in the process. You'll appreciate this when you arrive at the library fifteen minutes before closing time one evening, looking desperately for something that seems as if it would be easy to find but isn't.

Generally, *numerals* are filed first, in numerical order. Numbers spelled out as words are filed like any other words. That means that the title of a book like *1984* by George Orwell will be near the beginning of your library catalog. The novel *1985* by Anthony Burgess will be filed closely thereafter. *2001: A Space Odyssey* will follow. But *One Flew Over the Cuckoo's Nest* by Ken Kesey will be filed under the letter O for One. Numerals first. The exception to this is if it has been decided to interfile all numbers as if they were spelled out as words. *Letters* are filed letter by letter and then word by word. You can ignore articles like *a*, *an*, and *the* in the title of a book. *The Right Stuff* by Tom Wolfe will be filed under R for Right, and will come before *The Rights of Man* by Thomas Paine. Right before Rights. All *punctuation*, meaning hyphens, quotation marks, question marks, exclamation points, and even the colon and semicolon, is ignored in filing. *Abbreviations* are filed as if they were completely spelled out. This means that St. Louis will be filed as if it were spelled Saint Louis. Anything with Mc or Mac in it, like McCarthy or MacArthur, will be filed as Mac.

The point is that when you're looking up anything in the library catalog — a reference book, an index, an encyclopedia, or a dictionary — if you don't come to it right away, think about whether or not you're looking in the right place. The best example of this is that most wonderful reference book most of us have in our homes, the phone book. The phone book works on the principle of alphabetical and numerical filing rules. Otherwise, how would we be able to find 1-2-3 Printers or One-Two-Three Printing? Most reference books that employ long lists of information that must be alphabetized using some sort of rules usually give you directions at the beginning of the work on how the filing rules of alphabetical and numerical order apply to that particular reference.

The Library Catalog

Your library catalog may include a card catalog, an on-line catalog, or both. In most colleges, the main library collection is accessed through an on-line catalog, but older special collections still may be accessible only through an old card catalog. In card catalogs, information resources are filed by author, title, and subject. There are two types of card catalogs. A *divided* card catalog includes three separately labeled sets of drawers containing author, title, and subject cards, each in their own alphabetical sequence. An *integrated* card catalog contains all the author, title, and subject cards in one alphabetical sequence. Card catalogs have been around in libraries since the late nineteenth century. In fact, some reference books have been produced just by photocopying hundreds of thousands of library cards. Card catalogs are easy to use, but they're definitely the old technology. Still, they work. All the works by your favorite author will be listed alphabetically under the author's name. Titles of the author's books will be listed in alphabetical order by title. All the works about your favorite author, if that author is listed as a subject, will also appear in alphabetical order. All the works on agreed-upon subject headings will be listed alphabetically by those subject headings.

On-line catalogs reproduce on computer the same information found on catalog cards. Somewhere in your library there's probably a room full of computer terminals with little instruction pamphlets next to them explaining how to use the on-line catalog. You use the on-line catalog in the same basic way as you use the card catalog. You can search by author, title, or subject. Searching the on-line catalog is much faster than searching the card catalog, and you can usually sit down while you're doing it. You can also perform more sophisticated searches on an on-line catalog. For example, you can often search the on-line catalog by subject heading and by call number range. You can do things like keyword searches and Boolean searches (named for English mathematician and logician George Boole) while you're on-line. This means you can search a keyword like Soviet and come up with all occurrences of the word Soviet in titles, subject headings, or other parts of the on-line catalog record. You can use Boolean search terms (and, not, or) to find keywords in a record and their relation to other keywords. This is where the on-line catalog really comes in handy. You can do searches like "find Soviet and not military"; "find Soviet or Russian and not economy"; "find Russian ballet and not Soviet ballet." The way you do a search from the on-line catalog depends on the type of computer system you have in your college library. Each type of system has different commands, such as Find, Display, Search, Show, and Look. If you haven't tried an on-line system yet, don't worry. They're all so easy, even the computerphobic can learn to use them quickly and easily.

Learning the library catalog, whether it includes a card catalog or an on-line catalog or a little bit of both, is one of the most important things you can do to get acquainted with your college library. However it's set up, learn the library catalog during your first week of classes. You'll need to use it for the next four years and beyond, so why wait?

Bibliographic Citations and Call Numbers

When you search for information resources using the library catalog, you'll also find the bibliographic citations to those information resources. Bibliographic citations are the end result of cataloging and classification. They are the full-text, easy to read, ordinary English result of the cataloging and classification process. They are written to describe clearly and concisely the basic information about a book, a magazine, a government document, a report, a map, a photograph, or most any other type of information resource. Bibliographic citations will include all the information used to identify and locate an information resource during the process of cataloging and classification, beginning with the three fundamental reference points: author, title, and subject. A bibliographic citation is meant to help you not only identify and locate information resources but also understand, if only in the briefest manner, what the information resource can provide. That way you can more easily determine whether or not you really want to look at the resource before you go hunting for it.

Bibliographic citations also include call numbers to direct you to the information resource. When I refer to call numbers, I am referring to what is usually going to be a call number created by Dewey or a call number created by LC. You will recall from our discussion of these two classification systems that call numbers in Dewey use arabic numbers only and call numbers in LC start with letters but use both letters and numbers. Call numbers are part of the end result of cataloging and classification, but they aren't written in ordinary English. They've written in code, librarianese, if you will. Remember, LC is used in most college libraries, and when you want to find an information resource, you must first have a bibliographic citation with a call number.

It is easiest to get a citation first and *then* go looking for it — unless, of course, you want to go through the stacks until you get a warm, fuzzy feeling about which information resource is right for you. It's the citation in your library catalog that alerts you to the existence of the information resource in your college library and the call number that directs you to its location in the collection. In the library catalog, you will find a full bibliographic citation to all the information resources in your college library that have been cataloged and classified. Bibliographic citations include, but are not limited to, the following:

1. The title, subtitle, and sometimes the popular title
2. The name of the author, editor, compiler, etc.
3. The subject headings assigned to the book
4. The call number
5. The publisher and the publishing history

Now let's look at a bibliographic citation with all the information from cataloging and classification on it. We'll identify the parts of the bibliographic citation, including the subject headings and the call numbers, and discuss what they tell us and where they can lead us. We'll use the information from a Library of Congress catalog card.

Sheehy, Gail.
The man who changed the world : the lives of Mikhail S. Gorbachev / Gail Sheehy. -1st ed.- New York, NY: HarperCollins, c1990.
xiv, 401 p., [16] p. of plates : ill. ; 24 cm.
"Portions of this work originally appeared in Vanity fair" — T.p. verso. Includes bibliographical references (p. 385–387) and index.
ISBN 0-06-016547-2 (cloth) : $22.95 ($29.95 Can.)
1. Gorbachev, Mikhail Sergeevich, 1931– 2. Heads of state — Soviet Union — Biography. 3. Soviet Union — Politics and government — 1985–
I. Title.
DK290.3.G67S52 1991 90-55173
947.085'4'092 — dc20
[B] AACR 2 MARC

This is an *author* card with the author's name printed across the top. The *title* card would have all the same information, with the title printed across the top. For *subject* cards, each subject heading would also appear across the top, and there would be one card for each subject heading (Gorbachev, Heads of State, and so on). The information would be the same in an on-line catalog, but you would determine which access point retrieves the catalog record when you choose to search by author, title, or subject. The catalog record will look a little more like computerese on the screen, but it will provide you with the same important information.

The catalog card tells us that this book is a first edition, it was published in New York, and it was published by HarperCollins in 1990. What about the little section that begins with roman numerals? The "xiv" at the beginning of that line means that the preface or introduction — some part of the book before the actual text starts — is fourteen pages long. Then there are a total of 401 numbered pages to the book. Within those 401 pages there are sixteen [16] pages of plates, which refer to photographs. The abbreviation *ill.* means illustrated. The notation "24 cm." refers to the book's height on the shelf — about 9½ inches. If there were maps or charts or other diagrams or art, it would say so here. The notation "T.p. verso" refers to additional information about the contents of the book. That information is printed on the left-hand side (verso) of the title page (T.p.), indicating that portions of the book originally appeared in *Vanity Fair* magazine. The work has a bibliography on pages 385–87, which might be helpful to you in further research, even if you didn't need this book in particular; and there is an index. The ISBN (International Standard Book Number) and price are mostly for librarians' use.

The next segment of information is tremendously important and helpful in doing smart research. This segment contains the subject headings. There were three subject headings assigned to this book in the cataloging and classification process, each with their own subject breakdowns. Each subject heading is listed with an arabic number.

1. Gorbachev, Mikhail Sergeevich, 1931–
2. Heads of State — Soviet Union — Biography
3. Soviet Union — Politics and Government — 1985–

These three subject headings show that 1) Mikhail Gorbachev is important enough to be considered a subject, 2) Heads of State is a subject breakdown that can be applied to geographical regions such as the Soviet Union, and 3) the Soviet Union, as a subject, has a variety of breakdowns, one of which is Politics and Government for the years 1985 to the present.

Following these subject headings are additional entries, which give other locations where you can find a catalog card for this book. In this case, there is only "I. Title." Added entries, usually confined to the title, the author and additional authors, editors, contributors, translators, and other people involved in the creation of the book, are identified by Roman numerals. On the author card, there will be an additional entry for the title. On the title card, there will be an additional entry for the author. If there were two authors, there would be two additional author entries, one for each author. While searching author and title is easy enough, once you find a subject heading that is right on the mark in your research, you can trace that subject heading in the card catalog or on the on-line catalog for additional material. Each subject heading gives you an additional route to search for this book as well as for similar information resources.

On the lower left is the LC call number, written in letters and numbers. At the center is the Dewey call number, written in numerals. The call numbers are the key to finding the book or other information resource on the shelf, or wherever it's kept. On the far right is the Library of Congress catalog card number, which is for library reference purposes such as getting additional cards.

Subject Breakdowns and Call Numbers

People's names can be subjects, if they're important enough. Madonna, President Clinton, Michael Jackson, Bo Jackson, and many other familiar names among celebrities, politicians, and other public figures may get their own subject headings.

For major subjects, such as the Soviet Union, biology, chemistry, philosophy, dancing, or other countries or topics, there will be further subject breakdowns, going from the general to the specific. In chapter 3, you will see subject breakdowns and call number ranges reflecting some of the general works helpful for each major area of study. Listed below are some of the most basic subject breakdowns and LC call number ranges for general information resources applying to all major areas of study.

> Collections. Series. Collected Works (AC)
> Encyclopedias (AE)
> Dictionaries and General Reference Books (AG)
> Indexes (AI)
> Museums. Collectors and Collecting (AM)
> Newspapers (AN)
> Periodicals (AP)
> Academies and Learned Societies (AS)
> Yearbooks. Almanacs. Directories (AY)
> History of Scholarship and Learning (AZ)

Primary and Secondary Sources

There is a very important distinction between primary and secondary sources. Primary sources are those materials, in whatever format, that came directly from the individual, institution, or other entity that you're studying. An author's manuscript or book is a primary source. Einstein's notebooks are primary sources. Documents are primary sources. Archives store and maintain primary sources, be they letters, manuscripts, notebooks, or any other original source. A primary source is the first creation of information from which all other secondary discussion of that information flows.

Secondary sources are filters. Secondary sources are reviews of available resources, perhaps both primary and secondary. Secondary sources are dictionaries, encyclopedias, and the multitude of other information resources that have been condensed from primary sources to reflect available information on a given topic.

Information Old and New

Just because an information resource is old, that doesn't mean it's not important or not what you're looking for. Whether it's useful or not depends on the currency of the information you need. A scientific dictionary published in 1962 isn't going to give you much on computers, although it may provide you with some historical insight.

The more recent the resource, the more possibility it has for being up to date and accurate. A directory published in 1975 may list the names, addresses, and phone numbers of institutions or individuals you might want to contact, but phone numbers and addresses change.

When you're doing research with information resources, you should determine whether or not you need historical or current information, or both. Then you should select information resources that provide not only the type of information you're seeking but also the recency you require.

Publishers Large and Small

Throughout this book you will see some publishers mentioned over and over again, not as an endorsement of one publisher over another but because some publishers focus more often on reference works than others. Publishers like Bowker, Wilson, Gale, Facts on File, McGraw-Hill, and Libraries Unlimited have solid reputations in the publishing industry and produce dependable reference books year after year. When you're looking at an information resource, look at the publisher or vendor or whatever the information providers call themselves. Their institutional identity will give you some indication of the reliability of the information resource.

There are several types of publishing companies. Major firms like Bowker and Wilson focus on reference books. Trade publishers like Simon & Schuster, Random House, and Macmillan publish a little bit of everything, including reference works. University presses like Harvard, Oxford, and Cambridge usually focus on scholarly works written by academics. Finally, there are small and local publishers, which produce information resources geared to a local, regional, or subject-specific audience.

Traditional Academic Disciplines

Different major areas of study fall under different academic disciplines. Traditional distinctions in college courses are usually reflected in the types of degrees students seek.

The arts and humanities traditionally consist of subjects such as archaeology, classical studies, folklore, history, languages and literatures, performing arts, philosophy, religion, radio, film and television, theater and dance. The sciences traditionally consist of subjects including chemistry, engineering, geology, math, physics, and medicine. The social sciences include the study of anthropology, economics, geography, law, criminal justice, political science, psychology, public administration, and sociology.

These distinctions are reflected in the titles of various information resources you will use in the college library. Simply having arts, science, or humanities in the title of an abstract, an index, a dictionary, or encyclopedia should give a clue about whether or not that resource is going to have the type of information you're after.

Developing Research Strategies

When you walk into the college library, you become a hunter and a gatherer. But you don't use brute force; you use cunning. When you enter the college library, you've got to have a plan. Your best plan when doing research, especially in a topic that's new to you, is to work from the general to the specific — that is, if you're not an expert in the field, cast a big net.

If you're taking your first course in philosophy, and you think Nietzsche might be interesting, don't go digging up *Thus Spake Zarathustra* and wade through it expecting to become enlightened about Nietzsche and his philosophy. A better method is first to look up Nietzsche in a dictionary, encyclopedia, or biographical source. Find a digest of one of his works. Read an entry in the encyclopedia on the work itself.

I'm not suggesting you should use secondary sources such as dictionaries and encyclopedias instead of primary sources or the more sophisticated scholarship on a topic, and I do not suggest you cite dictionaries and encyclopedias or other general reference works when you're writing a term paper, but you will be better off if you familiarize yourself with much of the topic in a very general way before you go plunging head-long into long, heavy, difficult works. Until you get a command of your topic, whatever it is, try to work from the general to the specific. Then, by all means, tackle the difficult works.

A good research strategy is based on several fundamental activities: brainstorming; defining and limiting your topic; identifying, gathering, and collating materials; and reviewing and editing materials.

Brainstorming is one of the easiest and most stimulating aspects of a research project. When you brainstorm on a topic, write down all the words and phrases, subjects and names, places and dates, and any other relevant information that comes to mind. The purpose of brainstorming is simply to put what you know, or what you think you know, down on paper.

The next step is to take this information and give it shape. Define and limit your topic to fit the goal of your research, be it preparation for a term paper or plans for spring break. Eliminate those elements that are off the mark before you move on to the more time-consuming aspects of identifying, gathering, and collating materials. In defining and limiting your topic, it is useful to consult the most basic reference materials, such as dictionaries, encyclopedias, and lists of subject headings, to confirm that you are using the correct terms used in the topic under consideration and that you are approaching your topic in an appropriate manner.

Once you have defined and limited your topic, you will be ready to identify and gather research materials and collate them in a manner that will suit your needs. To identify the right materials for your research, you will refer to abstracts, catalogs, indexes, and other finding aids to lead you to the best books, periodical articles, and other materials on your topic. You will refer to directories for help in locating individuals who can provide you with additional assistance. In identifying the best materials for your research, you will use secondary sources, filters that guide you to the appropriate primary sources in your topic. You will use print-based reference materials as well as computer-based reference sources. In most instances, you will be searching by author, title, and subject. Some resources, such as on-line data bases and CD-ROM data bases will provide you with additional points of access, such as searching by call-number range, by subject heading, or by a variety of access points particular to the source material, such as geographical regions, political affiliations, or chemical product codes.

As you identify materials that appear to be appropriate to your research, maintain a bibliography of all your resources, including full citations for each item, written in the manner prescribed by the style manual required for your subject area. Your bibliography may include materials such as manuscripts, letters, books, and periodical and newspaper articles. Then use your bibliography to locate and gather together all the materials you have discovered.

When you have gathered your research materials, collate them in the manner best suited to the goal of your research or to your own study habits. You may find it useful to collate the material any number of ways: by author, by subject, in chronological order, in alphabetical or numerical order.

Reviewing and editing your research demands that you make a thorough assessment of each item under consideration. During the reviewing and editing process, you may discover that you need more material on one aspect of the topic. You may discover conflicting information. You may decide to eliminate some of the material you have gathered. As you continue your research you will inevitably have to repeat some of the processes (brainstorming, further limiting and redefining of your topic, identifying and gathering more material).

★ OUTSTANDING SOURCES ★

Some of the information sources in chapter 2 are preceded by a star (★). You should get to know these forty information sources no matter what your major area of study, no matter what your interests. They are easily among the most essential reference materials in the college library, or in any library for that matter, and they will serve you well throughout your college career and into your professional life. Master these "stellar" sources and you'll find yourself using them over and over again.

American Men and Women of Science (p. 39)
Arts and Humanities Citation Index (p. 71)
Bibliographic Index (p. 75)
Biography Index (p. 75)
Book Review Digest (p. 55)
Book Review Index (p. 69)
Books in Print (p. 36)
Chase's Annual Events (p. 91)
Dissertation Abstracts International (p. 27)

Encyclopaedia Britannica (p. 60)
Encyclopedia of Associations (p. 57)
Essay and General Literature Index (p. 76)
Facts on File (p. 63)
Familiar Quotations (p. 84)
Famous First Facts (p. 63)
General Science Index (p. 73)
Guide to Reference Books (p. 36)
Guinness Book of Records (p. 64)
Historical Statistics of the United States (p. 87)
Historic Documents (p. 31)
Humanities Index (p. 73)
A Manual For Writers of Term Papers (p. 89)
The National Newspaper Index (p. 72)
National Union Catalog (p. 44)
The New York Times Index (p. 71)
Oxford English Dictionary (p. 50)
Passenger and Immigration Lists Index (p. 77)
Public Affairs Information Service/PAIS International (p. 74)
Rand McNally Commercial Atlas and Marketing Guide (p. 34)
Readers' Guide to Periodical Literature (p. 74)
Roget's International Thesaurus (p. 90)
Science Citation Index (p. 71)
Social Sciences Citation Index (p. 71)
Social Sciences and Humanities Index (p. 75)
Statistical Abstract of the United States (p. 87)
U.S. Government Manual (p. 68)
Walford's Guide to Reference Material (p. 37)
Who's Who in America (p. 42)
The World Almanac and Book of Facts (p. 29)
A World Bibliography of Bibliographies (p. 35)

2

Ready Reference: Information Resources and How They Work

NOW I'M SURE some, if not most, of you know how many, if not all, of the following types of information resources work — that is, that they have a table of contents and an index and so forth. (Or that they're yellow and on the reference shelf or are never where they're supposed to be when you look for them.) The point of this chapter is to familiarize you with some of the real basics in information resources. The basics make up the *ready reference* section of the library, which contains the most general and frequently used information resources and is usually separate from the rest of the collection. Ready reference titles can be used by everyone, in every major area of study, at some time or another. Once you become familiar with them, chances are that you'll find more and more reasons to use them.

When looking at ready reference materials in general, you should first familiarize yourself with how they work. By that I mean how they're set up, how they're organized. Are they organized alphabetically, geographically, chronologically, or by some sort of subject heading? What type of reference are you looking at and in what format is the information presented? What, if any, links or access does this reference give you to other information resources?

Some ready reference materials use a lot of abbreviations. Some use sample entries to explain the format in which information is repeatedly presented. You'll recognize the table of contents and index, but some reference materials have specialized indexes, such as geographical indexes, personal-name indexes, corporate-author indexes, and subject-specific indexes. Some reference materials have bibliographies to direct you to other relevant works. Some have chronological tables to give you the scope of events through time. The better you understand the differences in how reference materials are organized, the better you'll be able to use them.

Different types of reference materials are used more often for certain areas of study. *Atlases* are common to the study of history and geography. *Manuscripts* are common in music and literature. *Concordances* are also common to the study of literature. There are indexes, abstracts, dictionaries, and encyclopedias for most of the major areas of study. As you spend more and more time in the library, you will find that different fields have different strengths and weaknesses in the types of ready reference materials and other information resources available. Some types of ready reference materials simply work better for some major areas of study than for others.

The following list briefly identifies and defines many ready reference materials that can be useful to every student, no matter what major area of study you choose. Examples are given as well as suggestions on how to use them to your advantage. See if you can think of a reason to use some or most of these materials for your current class assignments or your own personal interests.

Abstracts

Abstracts give brief summaries of books, dissertations, experiments, meetings, proceedings, procedures, reviews, and periodical and journal articles. They are often issued monthly or quarterly and then collected and bound together in books by year or copied on microform. Many abstracts are available through on-line data bases. There are several types of abstracts. Some simply indicate that something exists on your topic by giving you the citation to the work and a brief description of it. Others may evaluate the item under consideration. An evaluative abstract will be more helpful than an indicative abstract in determining the usefulness of a work.

An abstract gives you a brief description of the item under consideration so that you can decide whether or not it will be useful to you. Then, the citation directs you to the actual book, article, dissertation, or review itself. An abstract will help you find condensed, useful information on your subject in a quick and efficient manner. It will also help you figure out whether or not you want to read the full text of the item abstracted. Abstracts save time. Wouldn't you rather read one hundred words rather than one hundred pages to figure out whether the material is to the point?

EXAMPLES OF ABSTRACTS

Congressional Information Service Abstracts. Washington, D.C.: Congressional Information Service, annual. (KF 49 .C62)

Brief abstracts of hearings of the committees of the U.S. Congress, House and Senate documents, reports, and special publications.

★ **Dissertation Abstracts International.** Ann Arbor, Mich.: University Microfilms International, annual. (Z 5055 .U5)

You'll want to learn this one. This publication prints abstracts for dissertations of doctoral candidates in all fields from five hundred universities in the United States and abroad. With *DAI*, you can find and read the abstract of your professor's Ph.D. dissertation. You can also locate in-depth studies and substantial bibliographies on your topic with *DAI*.

Master's Abstracts International. Ann Arbor, Mich.: University Microfilms International, annual. (Z 5055 .U5 A6)

MAI provides the same sort of information as *DAI* above, only with these abstracts, you'll read what industrious students wrote to get their master's degrees.

Women Studies Abstracts. Littleton, Mass.: Rush Publishing Co., annual. (Z 7962 .W62)

A subject-specific abstracting service. This one focuses on women's issues in education, science, history, literature, biography, and other topics. The abstracting service includes book reviews and an annual index.

LOCATING ABSTRACTS

Bound abstracts are usually shelved with the subject to which they pertain and usually in the ready reference section of the library. They may also be available on microform and on CD-ROM or on-line data bases.

Almanacs

The word *almanac* is from medieval Latin *almanachus*. An almanac is an annual publication that lists enormous amounts of data, facts, and statistics, collected for the previous year and in retrospect. Almanacs *differ* from yearbooks in that they hold more historical data and statistics. The 1993 almanac will have plenty of data on 1992 and compare it to previous years. It will have endless lists of fun facts. Each major country usually publishes its own almanac. The American, British, and Canadian almanacs are generally available in most college libraries. There are several general reference almanacs on the market, which usually come out every January. States have almanacs too, which cover state history, statistics, and individual characteristics like the state bird, the state flower, the state motto, and other fun facts about the state.

A good almanac can help you give verifiable, quantifiable, factual information more accurately. When you're about to make some grand generalization about something that's quantifiable and verifiable, save face; look it up in an almanac or, better yet, in two almanacs.

EXAMPLES OF ALMANACS

Almanac of the 50 States: Basic Data Profiles with Comparative Tables, ed. by Edith R. Horner. Palo Alto, Calif.: Information Publications, 1992. (HA 203 .A5)

Contains statistics on demographics of population, health, education, government, housing, crime, the economy, communications, and transportation, for each of the fifty states.

The Canadian Almanac and Directory. Toronto: Copp Clark, annual. (AY 414 .C2)

Covers world news, current events, history, cultural events, business, and health with a primary focus on Canada and things Canadian.

Information Please Almanac. New York: Simon & Schuster, annual. (AY 64 .I55)

A popular almanac organized by subject. It has a chronology of the year, a list of records, and a "people" section, which highlights individuals in the news during the given year.

The People's Almanac, by David Wallechinsky and Irving Wallace. New York: Doubleday, 1975. (AG 106 .P46)

The People's Almanac is a different type of almanac. It covers fewer of the dull, statistical materials found in annual almanacs and relies on broader coverage of more interesting facts. *The People's Almanac* has gone through several editions since it came out, but, unlike other general reference almanacs, it is not published annually.

The Weather Almanac. Detroit: Gale, 1992. (QC 983 .R83)

This specialized-subject almanac covers U.S. weather data, including storms, air pollution, record-breaking weather, and round-the-world weather and climates. Includes section on weather fundamentals and glossary of weather-related terms.

Whitaker's Almanac. London: Whitaker, annual. (AY 754 .W5)

Whitaker's, published since 1868, is the almanac for the United Kingdom. *Whitaker's* may have better international coverage than U.S. almanacs, if that is what you need. It includes a yearbook and a reference book in one volume.

★ **The World Almanac and Book of Facts.** New York: World Almanac, annual. (AY 67 .N5 W7)

This almanac has been published in America since 1868, except for a ten-year break between 1876 and 1886. The index is in the front and lists all kinds of things from abbreviations to Zoroaster. In the almanac you'll find a chronology of events for the year, a summary of world history, a description of the countries of the world, and pictures of their flags. You'll also find the federal minimum hourly wage rates since 1950, tables of interrelation of measurement, the NCAA Division I women's champions since 1982, Academy Award winners, and a mountain of other fun facts.

LOCATING ALMANACS

Current-year general reference almanacs are either found with other ready reference materials or kept behind the reference desk. Older almanacs, if your library keeps them, will be shelved in the main collection under the appropriate call number. Subject-oriented almanacs are classed with the subject to which they pertain, be it politics, education, history, or science.

Anthologies and Collections

Anthologies and collections are usually selected works by an individual author or a group of authors, or selected articles or other writings by various authors on a specific subject. Anthologies and collections are also where you'll find materials that are simply too short to publish alone in book form. Anthologies and collections are often literary; there are many anthologies of articles, plays, poetry, and short stories. Some anthologies and collections are issued annually.

EXAMPLES OF ANTHOLOGIES AND COLLECTIONS

The Armchair Traveler, ed. by John Thorn and David Reuther. New York: Simon & Schuster, 1988. (G 465 .A75)

A collection of travel articles that have appeared in magazines, newspapers, and books. It includes articles by numerous authors on travel experiences in various places.

The Complete Short Stories of Ernest Hemingway. New York: Charles Scribner's Sons, 1987. (PS 3515 .E37 A15)

A complete collection of the short stories of Ernest Hemingway. The stories originally appeared in magazines and newspapers or were published in other collections of short stories.

The Great Documents of Western Civilization, by Milton Viorst. King of Prussia, Pa.: Chilton Book Company, 1965. (CB 245 .V5)

Includes the texts of many great documents that molded Western civilization, such as the Magna Carta, the Declaration of Independence, the Communist Manifesto, and the United Nations Charter.

★ **Historic Documents.** Washington, D.C.: Congressional Quarterly, Inc., annual. (E 839.5 .H57)

Since 1972, *Historic Documents* has collected and published the most significant and newsworthy documents of the year, every year. The 1990 volume included Barbara Bush's commencement speech at Wellesley and Octavio Paz's acceptance speech for the 1990 Nobel Prize in Literature. Includes index of names and subjects.

Irish Folk Tales, ed. by Henry Glassie. New York: Pantheon Books, 1985. (GR 153.3 I75)

A book of collected Irish tales by various authors, some handed down through generations by oral tradition. This collection prints tales that may never have been published before.

The Man From the U.S.S.R. and Other Plays, by Vladimir Nabokov. Trans. by Dmitri Nabokov. New York: Harcourt Brace Jovanovich, 1984. (PG 3476 .N3 A26)

A collection of plays and essays by the famous Russian novelist Vladimir Nabokov, collected and edited by his son, Dmitri Nabokov. The plays were originally published in Berlin, Paris, and New York during Vladimir Nabokov's lifetime.

LOCATING ANTHOLOGIES AND COLLECTIONS

Anthologies and collections will be shelved with the subjects to which they pertain, be they anthologies of journal articles, plays, poetry, music, short stories, or collections of documents and letters. Anthologies and collections are often assembled from documents, letters, and manuscripts in archival collections. The catalog record for anthologies and collections often gives only the editor's name, or the names of only a few contributors. To make up for this shortcoming, you must use an index to find materials that have been "buried in anthology."

Archival Materials

Archival materials are stored permanently in an archive where protective conditions exist for their management and preservation through time. Archives are akin to warehouse storage. We don't use the resources in an archive all the time, but when we want to use them, we need to be able to find what we're looking for in their recesses.

Archives and libraries are looked upon by researchers with a sort of reverence. There are national archives, state archives, municipal archives, university archives, newspaper archives, and corporate archives, just to name a few. Archives often coexist with libraries, because their missions are often complementary.

An archive is where you'll mine the riches of scholarship into primary sources — those documents, letters, manuscripts, and transcripts that came directly from the individual you're studying. Documents can take on most any form in most any medium. They are simply records that bear information. Manuscripts are usually considered something typed or written by hand, usually on paper. Literary manuscripts, like the handwritten or typewritten drafts of Hemingway's works, are most familiar. There was also a rough draft of the Constitution before it was printed, and that's a manuscript. Einstein's theory of relativity came out of his head and onto the page before it was published in a book. Documents, letters, and manuscripts are primary sources, as are any archival materials. They are the first tangible evidence of the creative process.

LOCATING ARCHIVAL MATERIALS

Many libraries and archives have substantial collections of archival materials of great value to scholars. To find archival materials, use a directory to the archives and a catalog or an index to the archival materials. There are also guides and handbooks for the use of archives and archival materials. Your college or university may have its own archive and may house the papers of famous graduates. The college may also publish a guide to doing a certain type of research in its archive.

Atlases

An atlas, named for the Titan of Greek mythology who carried the weight of the heavens on his shoulders, is a book, usually a folio or oversized book, of maps, charts, illustrations, statistics, and other geographical data. A good general-reference atlas will list maps of all the continents and countries, showing their capitals, regions, rivers, republics, populations, place names, and natural resources, among many other things.

There are atlases of subjects, cultural dynamics, physical and ecological characteristics, economic and political characteristics, wars and revolutions, and atlases of the solar system, to name just a few. There are also historical atlases, which will give you the lay of the land for a particular historical period. When using an atlas, don't forget that politics usually change the map every so many years. When Germany reunited, and when the Soviet Union ceased to exist, many mapmakers and atlas publishers found themselves with loads of new work to do. An atlas, like any good reference book, can go out of date with the passing of time.

EXAMPLES OF ATLASES

The Atlas of the Universe, by Patrick Moore. New York: Rand McNally, 1977. (QB 44 .M5425)

Though it's a little dated, this atlas covers the earth from space, the moon, the stars, and the solar system. Notice that this atlas is classed in QB for astronomy. Most atlases are classed under G for Geography. It's still likely to be with the rest of the atlases in an atlas case.

The Historical Atlas of United States Congressional Districts: 1789–1983, by Kenneth C. Martis. New York: Free Press, 1982. (G 1201 .F9 M3)

A political atlas for political scientists and others interested in the geographical distribution of statistical data on the American electorate. It includes sections on apportionment, roll-call voting behavior, and voting trends. It is an excellent example of an atlas geared to a particular subject, using geographical data to compile subject-specific information.

National Geographic Atlas of the World. 8th ed. Washington, D.C.: National Geographic Society, 1990. (G 1021 .N38)

The National Geographic Society has a solid reputation in the geography business, and the new atlas, which came out in the fall of 1990, is a testament to their commitment to the science. In short, it's a beauty and a wonder, with outstanding illustrations and sections that include country profiles with flags and key facts, geographic comparisons, airline distances, temperature and rainfall, foreign terms, abbreviations, and an index.

National Geographic Historical Atlas of the United States: Centennial Edition. Washington, D.C.: National Geographic Society, 1988. (G 1201 .S1 N3)

This thoroughly researched, beautifully illustrated atlas provides panoramic coverage of American civilization. Sections include chronological studies of the land, the people, the economy (agriculture and industry), and networks (transportation and communication).

★ **Rand McNally Commercial Atlas and Marketing Guide.** Skokie, Ill.: Rand McNally, annual. (G 1036 .R2)

This atlas, published annually, has an enormous amount of data on transportation and communications (airline, railroad, telephone, and postal systems), economic phenomena (population, income, manufacturing, military, and sales data), population figures for MSAs (Metropolitan Statistical Areas), and state maps that include indexes of statistics and places.

We the People: An Atlas of America's Ethnic Diversity, by James Paul Allen and Eugene James Turner. New York: Macmillan, 1988. (G 1201 .E1 A4)

This atlas reveals, through maps and statistics, the cultural diversity of America. It relies heavily on the 1980 Census. Look up your heritage here. Check out where your ancestors came from and what parts of the country they inhabit. It reveals all the human ingredients that make up the American "melting pot."

LOCATING ATLASES

Most atlases are oversized, or folios, and are usually stored in an atlas case or lying flat on a table. Smaller general atlases are usually shelved in the geography section. Subject-specific atlases are shelved with the subject to which they pertain. Atlases often are bulky and heavy. If you drop one, its own weight can break its spine and shorten its life span in the library.

Bibliographies

Bibliographies are not just for hard-core librarians. A bibliography is a listing of books, periodicals, and other useful sources of information. An annotated bibliography is a listing of books, articles, and other useful sources of information with a description of each work cited. There are bibliographies of works on particular subjects and bibliographies of bibliographies concerned with various areas of study. There are exhaustive bibliographies, which purport to list everything on the topic, and select bibliographies, which claim to leave a few things out.

One of the best ways to find out what's published in a major area of study is to consult a bibliography. A bibliography will give you brief citations to works in select areas of study. A bibliography can help point you in the direction of the right books and other materials for your field of inquiry. Some well-organized, subject-specific bibliographies are published under titles like "source book," "reference guide," or "information sources in . . ." a given subject.

EXAMPLES OF BIBLIOGRAPHIES

Bibliographies of Bibliographies

★ **A World Bibliography of Bibliographies,** by Theodore Besterman. 4th ed. Lausanne: Societas Bibliographica, 1965–66. (Z 1002 .B5684)

One of the best and most comprehensive bibliographies to be found in most college and university libraries. It's just old. So you have to keep in mind that decades of other stuff is now in print. *Besterman's* will give you a good look at how interesting and informative a really good bibliography can be.

General Bibliographies

Bibliographic Index.

See under Indexes in this chapter.

★ **Books in Print.** New York: Bowker, annual. (Z 1215 .P972)

Published annually since 1948, *Books in Print* is a catalog of books being published during the current year. It has separate volumes for author, title, and subject. Use *Books in Print* to determine what's being published in your major area of study now. Also included in the full set of *Books in Print* is a volume listing titles that have gone out of print, and a publisher's directory.

Canadian Books in Print. Toronto: University of Toronto Press, annual. (Z 1365 .S9)

A catalog of all the books being published in a given year in Canada. Emphasis is more on the English-language books published in Canada.

Cumulative Book Index. New York: Wilson, annual. (Z 1215 .U6)

Published since 1928, *CBI* is a world bibliography of books in English, organized alphabetically by author, title, and subject. It began as *The United States Catalog* in 1902. *CBI* is an index that directs you to the fact that certain books were published in English in a given year, but it serves the function of a bibliography by giving the author, title, publisher, and date of those books. Finally, it is a catalog of the books published in English each year, though it will not tell you what libraries have the books in their collections.

Guide to Reference Books, by Eugene P. Sheehy. 10th ed. Chicago: American Library Association, 1986. (Z 1035.1 .S43)

Referred to by librarians as "Sheehy," this is an exhaustive bibliographical reference to other reference works in all areas of the humanities, sciences, and social sciences.

International Bibliography of the Social Sciences. London and New York: Routledge, annual.

This collective, international multilanguage bibliography is published in four separate sets, covering economics, political science, social and cultural anthropology, and sociology. Each set has its own call number, covers materials in more than twenty-five languages, and includes indexes by author, subject, and place name.

MLA International Bibliography. New York: Modern Language Association, annual. (Z 7006 .M64)

Since 1921, the *MLA International Bibliography* has provided bibliographical reference to books and articles on the subject of modern languages and their study. It covers materials in English, French, German, Spanish, Italian, Portuguese, Romanian, Scandinavian, and selected eastern European languages.

Scientific and Technical Books and Serials in Print. New York: Bowker, annual. (Q 100 .S41)

Lists serials and books in print and currently available in science, technology, and engineering fields.

Serials and Newspapers in Microform. New York: Bowker, annual. (Z 6946 .S47)

A bibliography of newspapers and other periodicals available on microform, listing titles, date ranges, and the microform publishing company. It will tell you if your hometown paper or favorite magazine is available on microform.

Walford's Guide to Reference Material, by Albert John Walford, 5th rev. ed., 3 vols. London: Library Association, 1989. (Z 1035 .W17 G9)

Referred to by librarians as "Walford," this is an exhaustive bibliographical reference to English-language reference works in all areas of the humanities, sciences, and social sciences.

Whitaker's Books in Print. London: Whitaker, annual. (Z 2001 .R33)

Whitaker's is the English version of *Books in Print* and has been around just as long. It covers books in print anywhere in the United Kingdom.

Specialized Bibliographies

Bibliographic Guide to Conference Publications. 2 vols. Boston: G. K. Hall, annual. (Z 5051 .B5)

A bibliography of "proceedings, reports, and summaries of conferences, meetings, and symposia in all fields, as well as collections or partial collections of papers presented at conferences." Covers all countries in all languages.

Proceedings in Print. Halifax, Mass.: Proceedings in Print, Inc., annual. (Z 5063 .A2 P7)

Tells you if the proceedings of a conference are available in print. The index covers corporate authors, sponsoring agencies, editors, and subject headings for all topics.

LOCATING BIBLIOGRAPHIES

Bibliographies are usually shelved with ready reference materials at the end of the ready reference shelf in call number range Z or shelved with the subjects to which they pertain. Bibliographies are usually found at the back of most scholarly books and in anything that relies on other sources. There are probably bibliographies at the back of your textbooks, for example.

Biographical Sources

By biographical sources I do not mean single-volume biographies of your favorite baseball player, political maverick, or film star. These are reference works that collect biographical data on persons of some notoriety and present the information briefly and accurately. For dependable biographical sources, the data have usually been generated by researchers under certain guidelines. For vanity books, the data may be supplied by the subjects themselves.

Perhaps the most common title for biographical sources is *Who's Who.* You've heard the titles before: *Who's Who Among Sunburned Tourists from Bermuda to the Outer Banks* and that sort of thing. There are who's who books for countries, for states, for ethnic groups, for gender groups, for political, professional, and social groups, among others.

There are "who was who" books for those historical characters no longer with us.

The biographical source should, at the very least, list full name, date of birth, marriage and children, degrees, accomplishments, publications, awards, and occupations of the subject. Vanity books will give brief sketches of their subjects, all of which are likely to be flattering. People usually pay money to get their names put in vanity books. Reliable biographical sources are good for confirming verifiable data about people. Vanity biographical works will usually help you spell the names correctly.

EXAMPLES OF BIOGRAPHICAL SOURCES

★ **American Men and Women of Science: 1992–1993.** 18th ed. 8 vols. New York: Bowker, 1992. (Q 141 .A47)

Published every two years, this is a standard biographical dictionary of men and women in the physical and biological sciences, including chemistry, computers, engineering, mathematics, physics, astronomy, and medicine.

Biography and Genealogy Master Index.
Biography Index.

See under Indexes in this chapter.

Chambers Biographical Dictionary. New York: Chambers, 1984. (CT 103 .C4)

Chambers is a good one-volume biographical desk dictionary for brief biographical information on the world's most notable people.

Current Biography. New York: Wilson, annual. (CT 100 .C8)

Published since 1940, *Current Biography* provides "brief, objective, accurate, and well-documented biographical articles about living leaders in all fields of human accomplishment the world over." *Current Biography* is issued monthly in magazine format and annually in a bound volume.

Dictionary of American Biography. 17 vols. New York: Charles Scribner's Sons, 1964–81. (E 176 .D56)

A good source for prominent Americans. It includes bibliographies when appropriate. This scholarly work was based on the British *Dictionary of National Biography*, below.

Dictionary of National Biography. London: Oxford, annual. (DA 28 .D4)

A "who was who" of British subjects. The first volume was published in 1908. Each biography is written by a noted contributor and includes a brief bibliographical note. Currently, only those who have passed on are published in the *DNB*.

Dictionary of Scientific Biography. 16 vols. New York: Charles Scribner's Sons, 1970–80. (Q 141 .D5)

This international biography includes articles on scientists throughout history, covering individuals representing all areas of science and technology. It includes signed articles by scholars in the field.

The International Who's Who. London: Europa, annual. (CT 120 .I5)

International coverage with brief biographies of world figures, including their degrees, positions, honors, and awards. Focuses on world leaders and their accomplishments. Includes a section on reigning royal families.

Monarchs, Rulers, Dynasties and Kingdoms of the World, compiled by R. F. Tapsell. New York: Facts on File, 1983. (D 107 .T36)

A one-volume reference to the genealogy of the royal families of nations, including family trees, heirs, and pretenders. Organized by region and by period.

New York Times Biographical Service. Ann Arbor, Mich.: University Microfilms International. (CT 120 .N45)

Issued every month and made up of collected biographical articles and obituaries for names in the news that have appeared in *The New York Times* during the month.

Notable American Women, 1607–1950, ed. by Edward T. James. Supplemented by *Notable American Women, The Modern Period,* ed. by Barbara Sicherman and Carol Hurd Green. Cambridge: Harvard University Press, 1980. (CT 3260 .N57)

These two volumes provide extensive biographical sketches of American women and include bibliographies.

Who's Who. New York: St. Martin's Press, annual. (DA 28 .W6)

Since 1849, this British reference has included names of notables in the British Isles. They are living, as opposed to the folks in the *DNB*, who are not. Inclusion is by invitation.

Who's Who in Africa: Leaders for the 1990s, by Alan Rake. Metuchen, N.J.: Scarecrow, 1992. (DT 18 .R35)

Organized by African country, this is a biographical reference to African social and political leaders. It includes brief information on each country and biographies of each country's leaders.

Who's Who Among Black Americans, ed. by Christa Brelin. 7th ed. Detroit: Gale, 1992. (Z 39.48)

Now published every two years, this biographical reference gives personal and professional data, as well as obituaries, a geographic index, and an occupational index.

Who Was Who. London: A & C Black, annual. (DA 28 .W65)

Another reference for the British Isles. Published since 1897, it includes all those who have been published in the A. C. Black's *Who's Who* but have since died. Their biographies are now eliminated from the A. C. Black's *Who's Who* and updated posthumously.

Who Was Who in America. Chicago: Marquis. (E 176 .W64)

Covers 1607 to the present for the United States and includes most everyone who was anyone during that time. Marquis publishes many ''Who's Who'' titles providing biographical information on prominent Americans, including:

★ *Who's Who in America* (E 663 .W56)
Who's Who in the East (E 176 .W643)
Who's Who in the Midwest (E 176 .W644)
Who's Who in the South and Southwest (E 176 .W645)
Who's Who in the West (F 595 .W64)
Who's Who of American Women (E 663 .W5)
Who's Who of Emerging Leaders in America (CT 213 .W48)
Who's Who in the World (CT 120 .W5)

Who's Who in the Arab World. 8th ed. Beirut: Publitec Publications, 1992. (D 198.3 .W5)

An example of a who's who book for a particular region of the world. It has a biographical section, a survey of Arab countries, and an outline of the Arab world.

Who's Who in Japan: 1991–1992. Asia Press, 1991. (CT 1836 .W47)

Country-specific, with brief biographies including name, degrees, positions held, date of birth, education, career, honors, family, hobbies, address, and telephone number.

The World Who's Who of Women: 1992/1993. 11th ed. Cambridge, England: International Biographical Centre. (HQ 1123 .W65)

Includes biographical sketches of prominent women throughout the world in various professions.

LOCATING BIOGRAPHICAL SOURCES

Who's Who books and other biographical sources may be classed with the subjects to which they pertain. *Who's Who in America* will be classified with American history. A "who's who" of world figures will usually be classed with world history. Biographies of famous American politicians are classed with American politics. Biographies of musicians are classed with music.

Catalogs

Here I am referring to a printed catalog that lists all the books and other information resources available in a particular library, be it a college library or a special collection within a library. A catalog is different from a bibliography in that it is a list of books and other sources of information found in a specific library and usually has no annotations. The publication of bound catalogs was introduced before the advent of on-line catalogs for colleges and universities with large holdings of significant interest to other institutions and scholars. Often the bound catalog consists merely of 3×5 cards from the source library's card catalog, photocopied onto the page. Bound catalogs are usually oversize or folios.

A catalog will give you an access point to the collections of other institutions. It's also a great way to find items on your major area of study that you may not discover by looking through your own college library catalog. Some countries publish catalogs of all the books that enter the collection of their national library. These are generally called national union catalogs or national library catalogs or simply union catalogs. Remember, these are bound catalogs that list information resources in other libraries, not necessarily your college library.

EXAMPLES OF CATALOGS

Library Catalogs

Dictionary Catalog of the Henry W. and Albert A. Berg Collection of English and American Literature. 5 vols. and suppls. The New York Public Library Astor, Lenox & Tilden Foundations: The Research Libraries. Boston: G. K. Hall, 1969. (Z 2011 .N55)

The Bergs were serious book collectors. They donated their collection to the New York Public Library, which then cataloged the gift of first editions, rare books, letters, and manuscripts and had this catalog printed to reflect the entire collection.

Dictionary Catalog of the Jesse E. Moorland Collection of Negro Life and History. Howard University Library. 9 vols. Boston: G. K. Hall, 1970. (Z 1361 .N39 H82)

Moorland donated his library to Howard University, after which it was cataloged and became part of the collection. The university then had this catalog printed to reflect his gift to the library and to provide an access point to the collection, which covered his interests in masonry, religion, and history.

National Union Catalogs

★ **National Union Catalog: Pre-1956 Imprints.** 754 vols. Chicago and London: Mansell, 1968–81. (Z 881 .A1 U518)

The most significant bound catalog of books for the United States is *The National Union Catalog*. You can't miss it, because it takes up a whole wall in any academic library. Take a look at it: over 750 volumes containing copies of catalog cards. This huge undertaking collected all the cataloged holdings of the major research libraries in the U.S. and Canada, including the Library of Congress, for all items published before 1956. Includes books, pamphlets, maps, atlases, and music.

National Union Catalog of Manuscript Collections. Washington, D.C.: Cataloging Distribution Service of the Library of Congress, annual. (Z 6620 .U5 N3)

First published in 1962, this catalog covers manuscript collections in archives, libraries, and other manuscript repositories in cities, states, colleges, museums, and other institutions throughout the country. It covers all subjects for which manuscript collections exist, including art, astronomy, history, literature, music, psychology, and religion.

Locating Catalogs

Library catalogs are shelved with the subject to which they pertain, or shelved alone, if they are as voluminous as *The National Union Catalog*. They are often shelved at the end of the ready reference collection in the Z call number range.

CD-ROM Data Bases

Compact disks are not just for your basic easy-listening, country-western, heavy metal, or rap music. Compact disk technology (CD-ROM means Compact Disk Read Only Memory) now allows us to search through years of newspapers on CD-ROM data bases, even complete sets of encyclopedias. CD-ROM data bases are set up on desktop computers. They're as easy to use as changing a disk. You use the same types of commands searching a CD-ROM data base (find, look, display, search) as you use searching an on-line data base. You search using the same variables (author, title, subject) you use in print-based research. Many excellent library reference sources, traditionally found in print form, are now also available on CD-ROM data bases.

ABI/Inform indexes more than eight hundred journals in business, management, and economics. Business Index indexes more than eight hundred journals in business, management, and trade. It also includes indexing for business stories that appear in *The Wall Street Journal* and *The New York Times*. The 1990 Census is now available on CD-ROM. Compendex Plus indexes more than 4,500 journals and books in all major fields of engineering. *Dissertation Abstracts International* indexes abstracts of doctoral dissertations from more than five hundred colleges and universities. Coverage is from 1861 to the present. ERIC indexes more than seven hundred journals in education, from 1966 to the present. MEDLINE indexes more than three thousand journals and books in the physical and biological sciences, with coverage from 1983 to the present. PSYCLIT indexes more than fourteen hundred journals in psychology and related fields from 1974 to the present. PAIS indexes more than twelve hundred journals and eight thousand books in public affairs and the social sciences. Subject coverage includes business, economics, finance, government, international relations, law, and political science. PAIS coverage is from 1972 to the present.

LOCATING CD-ROM DATA BASES

This is an easy one, since you're not going to use a CD-ROM data base without a disk player hooked up to a computer. There will usually be a separate computer work station for CD-ROM data bases.

Chronologies and Histories

Chronologies list the dates that things happened, in sequence. They are often called date books or timetables. Chronologies may cover the entire expanse of recorded time, or the period specific to the historic events under consideration.

There are many times when you will wish you had some idea of the sequence in which things happened. Perhaps you'll want to check to see that you're writing a report that carries no chronological mistakes or anachronisms in it. The chronological boo-boo is embarrassing but easy to avoid. For example, when you're writing action and dialogue in a short story for English 101, you can't have a Civil War soldier talking on the telephone, but you can have him pose with a young lady for a photograph. Chronologies help you pinpoint time and events with greater accuracy. They can also give you a better grasp of the flow of events themselves. Almanacs, fact books, and yearbooks are also helpful in determining the chronological sequence of events.

Histories provide a broad sweep of information regarding a nation, a culture or civilization, or a sociological, economic, or political story. Histories are sometimes referred to as surveys, for example, a survey of Western civilization. Histories usually provide a very readable, general-interest approach to a topic.

EXAMPLES OF CHRONOLOGIES AND HISTORIES

Facts on File

See under Fact Books in this chapter.

A Chronology of the History of Science: 1450–1900, by Robert Mortimer Gascoigne. New York: Garland, 1987. (Q 125 .G39)

Covers the history of mathematics, astronomy, physics, chemistry, geology, botany, zoology, microbiology, and other branches of science during the era of the scientific revolution.

Holidays and Anniversaries of the World. Detroit: Gale, 1985. (GT 3930 .H65)

A chronological look at the special days of the year throughout the world. It includes notes on the development of the modern calendar, a perpetual calendar, a glossary of time words, Latin terms of time, anniversaries and suggested gifts, and an index of names, terms, and events. Details every month and day of the year.

The New York Public Library Book of Chronologies. New York: Prentice-Hall, 1990. (D 11 .W47)

A popular reference to chronological events that have been recorded in the popular era. It's very good for the twentieth century.

The Timetables of History, by Bernard Grun. New York: Simon & Schuster, 1979. (D 11 .G78)

This book, updated by Bernard Grun and based on Werner Stein's *Kulturfahrplan*, is a good reference for the major events of the world going back as far as 5000 B.C. It covers history, politics, literature and the arts, religion, philosophy, music, and daily life.

The Timetables of Science, by Alexander Hellemans and Bryan Bunch. New York: Simon & Schuster, 1988. (Q 125 .H557)

This is a good reference for the major scientific events of the world going back as far as 2.5 million years B.C. It covers science in general, astronomy, biology, chemistry, earth science, mathematics, medicine, physics and technology.

Watergate: Chronology of a Crisis. Washington, D.C.: Congressional Quarterly, Inc., 1975. (E 860 .C64)

An example of a chronology for a specific historical series of events, including chronological analysis of the Watergate break-in, the Senate inquiry, the White House tapes, and Nixon's impeachment, resignation, and pardon.

LOCATING CHRONOLOGIES

Subject oriented chronologies will be shelved with the subject to which they pertain. A chronology of world history will be shelved with other books on world history. Chronologies are often included as an element in a book devoted to a topic of historical consequence. A good study of the discovery of penicillin might have a chronology of events leading from early experiments to the discovery itself.

Codes and Rules

A code book, in this instance, is not what some spies use to relay messages on short-wave radio. Here we mean legal codes and codes of ethics for different professions. Also considered here are rules of procedure, standards of professional conduct, and proper etiquette.

EXAMPLES OF CODES AND RULES

Code of Federal Regulations. Washington, D.C.: Office of the Federal Register/National Archives and Records Administration. (JK 416 .C6)

CFR is the codification of "general and permanent regulations published in the Federal Register by the Executive Departments and Agencies of the Federal Government." It is organized by title, which in this case means subject. Title number 12, for example, is Banks and Banking. Title number 34 is Education. Individual CFR volumes are updated irregularly.

Codes of Professional Responsibility, ed. by Rena A. Gorlin. 2nd ed. Bureau of National Affairs, 1990. (BJ 1725 .C57)

A reference to codes of ethics and professional responsibilities, organized by profession. Includes codes that have often been written by the associations that represent the various professions. Check your own professional interest and see what your professional code of ethics entails.

Emily Post's Etiquette, by Elizabeth L. Post. 14th ed. New York: Harper & Row, 1984. (BJ 1853 .P6)

This is one of several well-known etiquette books that will help you behave yourself throughout most of your life, even if you have to follow certain codes, rules, and standards to do it.

Robert's Rules of Order: The Standard Guide to Parliamentary Procedure, by General H. M. Robert. (JF 515 .R692)

Any edition of *Robert's Rules of Order* is the kind of thing you ought to read if you ever plan to hold one of those high-powered jobs that require a knowledge of how to run a board meeting.

United States Code. Washington, D.C.: Government Printing Office, 1982. (K 44 .C4)

The *U.S. Code* is where you'll find the codification of federal laws. It's organized by title, which in this case again means subject. It includes tables of statutes, executive orders, presidential proclamations, and a general index. It also includes a popular-name index, which is an index to the names of legislation and other documents that have taken on popular names in the press, such as the Hatch Act or the Meese Commission Report.

LOCATING CODES AND RULES

Legal codes will be shelved with legal materials for the same jurisdiction. Professional codes will be shelved with the subject to which that profession pertains. Codes may be found in the yearbooks of many professional associations. Parliamentary rules will be found in politics. Rules of the game will be found with sports. Etiquette books will be found with materials on social customs.

Concordances

A concordance is a special kind of word book. Concordances are now produced by computer. They retrieve every word in a text and show how the word was used.

EXAMPLES OF CONCORDANCES

The NIV Exhaustive Concordance, by Edward W. Goodrick and John R. Kohlenberger III. Grand Rapids, Mich.: Zondervan Publishing House, 1990. (BS 425 .G62)

This concordance is based on the new international version of the Bible and includes an index of conjunctions, articles, prepositions, and pronouns, as well as language indexes in Hebrew, Aramaic, and Greek. Organized alphabetically by word and sequentially by book, chapter, and verse.

The Harvard Concordance to Shakespeare. Cambridge: Harvard University Press, 1973. (PR 2892 .S62)

Lists every word in Shakespeare's canon and where it appeared in his plays and poems. Each word is printed from the line where it appears.

LOCATING CONCORDANCES

Concordances will be shelved with the subjects to which they pertain. Concordances to the Bible will be shelved with religion. Concordances to Shakespeare will be shelved with other Shakespeare materials in English literature.

Dictionaries

Dictionaries are books that give you the various meanings of words, often their etymology (where they came from and/or their history), and a guide to their pronunciation. These rules apply more often to dictionaries of languages. Dictionaries of subjects like accounting, physics, or theater usually give the meaning of the word only as it is used in the profession or practice of the subject under consideration. There are also more specialized dictionaries, such as dictionaries of concepts, which offer definitions of phrases particular to certain areas of study. There are visual dictionaries that use illustrations to define graphic concepts. The word *dictionary* in the title of a book suggests that the contents are presented in strict alphabetical order.

EXAMPLES OF DICTIONARIES

Language Dictionaries

The American Heritage Dictionary of the English Language. Boston: Houghton Mifflin, 1992. (PE 1628 .A623)

The new *American Heritage Dictionary* includes word histories and notes on contemporary usage to help you write sentences with words that don't sound archaic or out of date. Illustrations are also featured.

★ **Oxford English Dictionary.** 2nd ed. London: Oxford University Press, 1989. (PE 1625 .O87)

The *OED* is perhaps the most extensive effort ever made at producing a dictionary of language. It has references to almost every English word you could ever think of. Even the section covering the word *of* is fairly extensive.

Oxford Latin Dictionary. London: Oxford University Press, 1982. (PA 2365 .E5 O9)

This dictionary of the mother tongue of romance languages covers the Latin language, Latin authors, and their works.

Partridge's Concise Dictionary of Slang and Unconventional English: From the Work of Eric Partridge, ed. by Paul Beale. New York: Macmillan, 1990. (PE 3721 .P3)

Partridge was a lexicographer who published several authoritative dictionaries of slang before his death. This is an updated volume. See if the slang you use is here.

Specialized Dictionaries

A Concise Dictionary of Indian Tribes of North America. Algonac, Mich.: Reference Publications, Inc., 1978. (E 76.2 .L44)

This dictionary defines, in lengthy essays and in alphabetical order, the various Indian tribes on the North American continent. Includes illustrations, bibliography, and index.

Acronyms, Initialisms and Abbreviations Dictionary, ed. by Jennifer Mossman. Detroit: Gale. (P 365 .A28)

If you've ever wondered what the ALA, an LLB, or the ed. after the name on the title page of a book stands for, look here. This reference is published every two years.

Bernstein's Reverse Dictionary, by Theodore M. Bernstein. 2nd ed. New York: Times Books, 1988. (PE 1591 .B45)

This is a great dictionary to use when you can think of the definition but can't think of the word. It is organized alphabetically by phrase or idea.

Dictionary of the History of Ideas: Studies of Selected Pivotal Ideas, ed. by Philip P. Wiener. 5 vols. New York: Charles Scribner's Sons, 1973. (CB 5 .D52)

A dictionary of concepts rather than mere word definitions, which includes signed articles on intellectual concepts, by scholars. Entries are both single words (Authority) and phrases (Art for Art's Sake). Includes cross-reference index and bibliography.

An Exaltation of Larks, by James Lipton. New York: Viking, 1990. (PE 1689 .L5)

You'd never know it, but this is a dictionary. It gives the collective nouns for hundreds of singular things. It's enough to make a shush of librarians cackle with laughter.

The Harper Dictionary of Modern Thought, ed. by Alan Bullock and Stephen Trombley. New York: Harper & Row, 1988. (AG 5 .H19)

A dictionary of ideas and concepts. When you want a definition of a phrase that has come into the language such as *free association* or *permanent revolution*, look here. It contains more than four thousand articles by more than one hundred contributors.

Pseudonyms and Nicknames Dictionary. 2nd ed. Detroit: Gale, 1982. (CT 120 .P8)

Lists nicknames and pen names of the famous and not so famous, with sources for verification. Has characteristics of a who's who and a proper-name dictionary.

Webster's New Dictionary of Synonyms. Springfield, Mass.: Merriam-Webster, 1984. (PE 1591 .W4)

A dictionary providing analysis and definitions of synonyms and antonyms along with examples of their use in English language and literature.

Subject Dictionaries

The American Heritage Dictionary of Science. Boston: Houghton Mifflin, 1986. (Q 123 .B35)

A standard science desk dictionary that includes a pronunciation guide, etymology, and tables of measures, units, signs, and symbols.

Chambers Science and Technology Dictionary. New York: Chambers, 1988. (Q 123 .C482)

A basic desk dictionary of scientific and technical terms, including tables on the plant and animal kingdoms, chemical elements, and geological tables. Includes explanation of the Greek alphabet.

Chambers World Gazetteer. New York: Chambers, 1988. (G 103.5 .C44)

A gazetteer is simply a geographical dictionary that defines geographical terms and places. A gazetteer differs from an atlas in that it is not an oversize or folio volume and has few if any maps.

Webster's New Geographical Dictionary. New York: Merriam-Webster, 1984. (G 103.5 .W42)

A geographical dictionary that defines place names, reveals their history, and provides a guide to their pronunciation. Like gazetteers, geographical dictionaries have few if any maps.

Visual Dictionaries

The Facts on File Visual Dictionary, by Jean-Claude Corbeil. New York: Facts on File, 1986. (AG 250 .C63)

This visual dictionary will help you "look up the word from the picture" and "find the picture from the word." It is a strictly diagrammatic dictionary of things visual, with general, thematic, and specialized indexes.

What's What: A Visual Glossary of the Physical World, by Reginald Bragonier, Jr., and David Fisher. Maplewood, N.J.: Hammond, 1981. (AG 250 .B7)

A unique work that explains, visually, what the subject is, how it works, and why, for things in the physical world, from living things to transportation to sports and recreation to signs and symbols. Illustrations range from the photographic to the artistic. Includes index.

The Woman's Dictionary of Symbols and Sacred Objects, by Barbara G. Walker. New York: Harper & Row, 1988. (CB 475 .W45)

An illustrated visual dictionary of symbols specific to women and women's studies, organized by shape, by type, and by broad topic. Includes bibliography and index.

LOCATING DICTIONARIES

Dictionaries of languages will be shelved with grammars of those languages. Dictionaries of subjects will be shelved with the subjects to which they pertain. Dictionaries of people's proper names should be considered biographical reference works, even if the publisher has chosen to put *dictionary* (of biography) in the title.

Digests

When you see *digest* in the title of something, it means that a publisher has taken certain information, perhaps bulky or highly dispersed information, and made it simpler and easier to access. It has been digested into manageable size. A variety of materials are digested: books, book reviews, periodical articles, statistics (thank goodness). Digests are akin to abstracts in that their object is to provide brief information about something more lengthy, so that a reader can decide from the digest whether or not to read the full text.

EXAMPLES OF DIGESTS

Congressional Research Service Bill Digest: Digest of Public General Bills and Resolutions. Washington, D.C.: Congressional Research Service, biannual. (KF 18 .L5)

Summarizes the "essential features of Public Bills and Resolutions and changes thereto made during the legislative process." Organized in three parts, it includes action taken during the congress, digests of public general bills and resolutions, and indexes to digested bills and resolutions.

★ **Book Review Digest.** New York: Wilson, annual. (Z 1219 .C95)

This is a good example of how a digest can help thin out your reading workload. *BRD* lists book reviews alphabetically by author of the book reviewed. The excerpts of reviews and their citations are valuable to give you brief, quick information on the book and then direct you to the review.

Dictionary of Historic Documents, by George C. Kohn. New York: Facts on File, 1991. (D 9 .K63)

Kohn's book digests some twenty-two hundred documents "which helped steer the course of human history." Includes an alphabetical document-and-title index and bibliography.

LOCATING DIGESTS

Digests are often printed in abstracts, indexes, and scholarly journals. Reference digests are usually shelved with the topics to which they pertain.

Directories

Directories are traditionally designed to help you get the name, address, and phone number of someone or some organization. There are directories of all kinds of things, from that great people directory known as the phone book to directories of periodicals, institutions, organizations, and individuals. If a reference book has *directory* in the title and doesn't give you a name, address, and phone number, then what on earth does it claim to direct you to? Directories are like specialized phone books. If you can't find the phone book that lists whom or what you want to contact, look for a directory of the appropriate subject. Most of the directories below give you names, addresses, and phone numbers.

EXAMPLES OF DIRECTORIES

Awards, Honors and Prizes: An International Directory of Awards and Their Donors. 9th ed. Detroit: Gale, 1992. (AS 8 .A87)

A directory of the honors and recipients of prizes in numerous fields of professional endeavor. Volume one covers the United States and Canada. Volume two covers international prizes.

Directory of Archive and Manuscript Repositories in the United States. 2nd ed. Oryx Press, 1988. (CD 3020 .D49)

A directory of archives, by state and then alphabetically by city, which includes a repository index and subject–proper name index.

Directory of Online Databases. Detroit: Cuadra/Gale, annual. (Z 674.3 .D47)

Provides information on data-base producers and on-line services with geographic, subject, and master indexes.

Directory of Published Proceedings. New York: InterDok, annual. (Z 7409 .D56)

This unique resource gives you access to the proceedings of various associations, learned societies, and other instructional or institutional bodies. The directory acts as a bibliography of printed and published proceedings of congresses, conferences, summer schools, symposia, meetings, and seminars. It covers all fields of study in three separate series. Series SEMT covers science, engineering, medicine, and technology. Series SSH covers the social sciences and humanities. Finally, Series PCE covers pollution control and ecology.

Editor and Publisher Yearbook. New York: Editor and Publisher, annual. (PN 4700 .E4)

Although it says *yearbook* in the title, this is a directory of all the newspapers in the country. It just happens to come out every year.

★ **Encyclopedia of Associations.** Detroit: Gale, annual. (HS 17 .G334)

This is a directory. It calls itself an encyclopedia, but it's really a directory providing encyclopedic information on associations. The *Encyclopedia of Associations* will tell you the essential name, address, phone, and fax number. Plus, you'll be able to find out who's in charge, when the organization was founded, its membership, staff, budget, publications, circulation, and when and where the next annual meeting or convention will take place. It's indexed by name and keyword. By the way, the index in this reference work directs you to an entry number, not a page number.

International Directory of Little Magazines and Small Presses, ed. by Len Fulton. 27th ed. Paradise, Calif.: Dustbooks, 1991–92. (Z 6944 .L5 D5)

Here's an example of a directory that acts as a reference to the not-so-mainstream press. It's indexed by region and by subject.

International Research Centers Directory: 1992–93. Detroit: Gale, 1992. (Q 179.98 .I58)

A directory, by country, covering more than seven thousand research programs and facilities. Includes master, subject, and country indexes.

Martindale-Hubbell Law Directory. Summit, N.J.: Martindale-Hubbell, Inc., annual. (JK 1517 .M37)

The standard directory for lawyers in the United States. It's arranged by state and then by city. You must first know the state in which the attorney practices. Then you must know the city where the attorney practices before you can find an entry. When you're searching Washington, D.C., this is no problem, but when you're looking for someone in New York or California, you'd better know the city.

Martindale-Hubbell gives the usual information lawyers want to know about a law firm and about the lawyers in the firm, such as when they were born, when they were admitted to the bar, where they can practice, where and when they went to college and law school, what law journal they may have edited, and what legal associations they belong to. It also may give a "legal ability rating" for the lawyer and "firm rating" for the firm.

National Faculty Directory. Detroit: Gale, annual. (L 901 .N34)

Lists all the professors teaching in colleges and universities in the United States and select Canadian schools and provides essential directory information.

National Five Digit Zip Code and Post Office Directory. 2 vols. Washington, D.C.: National Information Data Center, annual. (HE 6361 .N37)

A directory by state, giving postal addresses and zip codes for every place in the United States, right down to the street. By the way, North Pole, Alaska is 99705.

Standard Periodical Directory. New York: Oxbridge Communications, Inc., annual. (Z 6951 .S78)

Provides directory information on more than sixty thousand publications in the United States and Canada. The book is organized by some two hundred and fifty broad subject headings. The index gives titles and their page references (not entry numbers) for location in the book.

LOCATING DIRECTORIES

General directories will be shelved with ready reference materials. Subject-specific directories will be shelved with the subject to which they pertain. Remember, if you don't get names, addresses, and phone numbers out of these references, what kind of directories are they?

Dissertations

Academics research, write, and publish dissertations in microform (and scarcely anyplace else) in order to receive the Pretty heavy Degree, or Ph.D. Dissertations are often valuable contributions to the sum of knowledge and require an enormous amount of work. Dissertations are supposed to contain a substantial body of original research that makes a significant contribution to a particular major area of study. Dissertations themselves are very useful in doing research because they often have outstanding bibliographies and present substantial information on a focused topic.

In order to locate a dissertation on a particular area of study, use the *CDI*, the *Cumulative Dissertations Index*. Use the *DAI*, or *Dissertations Abstracts International*, to get an abstract of the dissertation so you can determine if you want to read the whole thing. Dissertations awarded by your college or university may be shelved together in one location.

Encyclopedias

General encyclopedias are usually alphabetically organized reference works designed to cover a broad range of topics in some detail. As with dictionaries, there are also subject encyclopedias, which are limited to coverage of specific topics. There are several general encyclopedias on the market. Each targets a specific audience. *The Book of Knowledge* is for children. *World Book* is aimed at high school students. *The Encyclopedia Americana* and *Encyclopaedia Britannica* are for the college and adult markets. But that doesn't mean you'll never use *The Book of Knowledge* or *World Book*. Their simplicity is often their best asset. Encyclopedias have long histories, and each one has its own track record for accuracy and comprehensiveness, which is judged again and again as new editions are published. The features that must be considered in evaluating an encyclopedia are its subject coverage and intended audience, reputation for accuracy and reliability, writing style, and currency, as well as whether it has a good index, graphics, and bibliographical references.

General Encyclopedias

Academic American Encyclopedia. Danbury, Conn.: Grolier, Inc., 1993. (AE 5 .A23)

A well-illustrated, general-interest encyclopedia intended for college use. The final volume is an index to the complete set.

Collier's Encyclopedia: With Bibliography and Index. New York: Macmillan, 1992. (AE 5 .C683)

Has black-and-white and color illustrations and added features such as pronunciation guides and bibliographies. The final volume contains bibliographies and an index.

Encyclopedia Americana. Danbury, Conn.: Grolier, Inc., 1992. (AE 5 .E333)

Encyclopedia Americana was first published in 1829. It is a well-illustrated, general-interest reference work. The final volume indexes the entire set.

Encyclopedia of Associations

See under Directories in this chapter.

★ **Encyclopaedia Britannica.** Chicago: Encyclopaedia Britannica, 1990. (AE 5 .E363)

Encyclopaedia Britannica has a long history. First published between 1768 and 1771, it set the standard for encyclopedias. Still rather British in its focus, the current edition is divided into a Micropaedia for ready reference and a Macropaedia for knowledge in depth. *Britannica* is updated annually with a general-interest yearbook and a science yearbook. *Encyclopaedia Britannica* also publishes *The Great Books of the Western World* (AC 1 .G7), a collection of what *Britannica*'s editorial board considers to be some of the Western world's most significant writings.

World Book Encyclopedia. Chicago: World Book, Inc., 1992. (AE 5 .W55)

Though intended for "younger readers," *World Book* has clear and accessible articles and illustrations. It's often simpler to consult than a more scholarly source when you just want the most basic information. Final volume includes brief bibliographies and index.

Subject Encyclopedias

The Canadian Encyclopedia. Edmonton: Hurtig Publishers, Inc., 1985. (AG 5 .C27)

A country-specific encyclopedia that focuses exclusively on the arts and sciences, the industries and employment, the history, politics, and culture of Canada.

Encyclopedia of Asian History. 4 vols. New York: Charles Scribner's Sons, 1988. (DS 31 .E53)

Prepared under the auspices of The Asia Society. It includes signed articles by scholars in the field, illustrations, maps, and an index.

Encyclopedia of Southern Culture, by Charles Reagan Wilson and William Ferris. Chapel Hill, N.C.: University of North Carolina Press, 1989. (F 209 .E53)

A cultural, regional encyclopedia covering southern states in the United States. Subjects include agriculture, education, geography, language, literature, politics, and religion.

Encyclopedia of Ukraine. 4 vols. and suppls. Toronto: University of Toronto Press, 1978. (DK 508 .E613)

Another country-specific encyclopedia, covering Ukraine from its earliest times through the Soviet period. The signed articles are indexed by name and subject and include bibliographies and illustrations.

International Encyclopedia of the Social Sciences. New York: The Free Press, 1968. (H40 .A215)

The scope of this encyclopedia is intentionally limited to disciplines acknowledged as belonging to the social sciences: anthropology, economics, geography, history, law, political science, psychiatry, psychology, sociology, and statistics. Although the *International Encyclopedia of the Social Sciences* is now dated, it does provide a useful and substantial background to topics in the social sciences.

McGraw-Hill Encyclopedia of Science and Technology. 7th ed. 20 vols. New York: McGraw-Hill, 1992. (Q 121 .M3)

A general-interest scientific encyclopedia produced by an international editorial advisory board. It includes over seven thousand entries and fifteen thousand illustrations. The encyclopedia is supplemented by yearbooks annually.

Van Nostrand's Scientific Encyclopedia. 7th ed. 2 vols. New York: Van Nostrand Reinhold, 1989. (Q 121 .V3)

A standard two-volume desk encyclopedia with "representative topical coverage" of major subjects, including animal life, chemistry, math, and physics.

LOCATING ENCYCLOPEDIAS

There are encyclopedias published by major countries that are specific to that country alone and encyclopedias published by various countries that claim to have world coverage. There are encyclopedias in Arabic, English, Hebrew, French, Chinese, Korean, German, Russian, and many other languages. Some examples of foreign-language encyclopedias are *Der Neue Brock Haus* in German, *Dizionario Enciclopedico Italiano* in Italian, *Enciclopedia de Mexico* in Spanish, *Enciclopedie Universal Ilustrada* in Spanish, *Encyclopaedia Universalis* in French, and the *Great Soviet Encyclopedia* in Russian and English. General encyclopedias in any language are usually classed in the A call number range of the ready reference section. Country-specific encyclopedias are usually classed with other materials on the history of the country.

Fact Books

Digging out facts can be a pretty difficult and drawn-out project. Wouldn't it be nice if there were some specific books that could tell you the facts, like world's records and famous firsts? There are, and they're often simply called fact books.

EXAMPLES OF FACT BOOKS

The Encyclopedia of American Facts and Dates, by Gorton Carruth. 8th ed. New York: Harper & Row, 1987. (E 174.5 .C3)

This book covers "all aspects of American History and popular culture." Includes "more than 15,000 facts and dates uniquely arranged side by side under topics and in chronological order." Includes index of names, places, and topics.

Facts about the Cities, comp. by Allan Carpenter. New York: Wilson, 1992. (HT 123 .C385)

Organized alphabetically by state, includes select major cities with population over seventy-five thousand. Includes information on cultural resources, climate, housing, transportation, and tourism, among other things.

Facts about the Presidents: From George Washington to George Bush, by Joseph Nathan Kane. 5th ed. New York: Wilson, 1989. (E 176.1 .K3)

This one's a little out of date, but it contains all the vitals you'd ever want to know about almost every president from birth through death, including career, family, terms in office, and life chronology. Also gives brief discussion of significant life events. Includes substantial tables of comparative data and index.

Facts about the States, ed. by Joseph Nathan Kane and others. New York: Wilson, 1989. (E 180 .K4)

Filled with coverage of the states, including comparative demographic and geographic tables.

★ **Facts on File.** New York: Facts on File. (D 410 .F3)

Published weekly and bound annually since 1940, *Facts on File* is a survey of world news that includes a news digest and a cumulative index. Organized by broad topic and country, then indexed chronologically. Annual volumes provide a chronological record of the year.

★ **Famous First Facts: A Record of First Happenings, Discoveries and Inventions in the United States,** by Joseph Nathan Kane. New York: Wilson, 1989. (AG 5 .K315)

Kane's *Famous First Facts* is one of the standard references in most any library. It answers the questions "who, what, when, or where was the first . . . ?" The arrangement is first by topic, with references to the appropriate subjects. Further arrangement is by year, day of the month, name, and place. Pick a first and check it out.

★ **The Guinness Book of Records.** New York: Facts on File, annual. (AG 243 .G87)

The Guinness Book of World Records is long on superlatives: the longest, the shortest, the smallest, the largest, the whateverest is in *Guinness*. A deservedly popular reference and compendium of amusing trivia.

Keesing's Record of World Events. Formerly *Keesing's Contemporary Archives*. Cambridge: Longman. (D 410 .K4)

Keesing's is the British *Facts on File*. Since 1931 it has provided "a unique contemporary record of modern history, and a factual, objective reference source on current affairs." Material is selected from "the world's press and information sources." Issued weekly and bound annually. It is organized by subject and by country and indexed monthly.

World Fact Book. Washington, D.C.: Government Printing Office, annual. (G 122 .U56)

Published annually by the Government Printing Office for U.S. government officials. It is researched, written, and compiled by the Central Intelligence Agency. Organized alphabetically by country, it also includes maps and statistics.

LOCATING FACT BOOKS

Fact books are usually international and historical in scope and content and are consequently found in the world history section of the ready reference area, although fact books on American history will be shelved with American history, and fact books on sports will be shelved with sports. Fact books bear similarities to almanacs and to chronologies, guides, handbooks, and yearbooks.

Government Documents

There's a certain sense of gratification you'll feel whenever you succeed in getting something done that involves the government. Dealing with government documents is no exception. You'll find that all governments have a strange way of making this sort of activity a uniquely painful experience, even if they don't mean to.

The good news is, there *are* ways of finding government documents. The bad news is, there are countless government documents and only so many indexes to them. In the federal government, there are two types of government documents, those which are published by the Government Printing Office (GPO), and those which are published by the federal agency that writes or produces them.

Many college libraries are federal depository libraries and keep select government documents in their collection. In most college libraries, government documents are shelved together, sometimes in a separate reading room for government documents. Of course, if the librarians at your college have decided to interfile the government documents with the subjects to which they pertain, you will get a call number when you look up the item in the library catalog.

The federal government also publishes many periodicals. There are two periodicals published by the federal government that are especially important to learn to use and understand. The *Congressional Record* (J 11 .R2), published each day one or both houses of Congress are in session, prints the text of all the proceedings and debates of the United States Congress. The *Federal Register* (J 1 .A2), published Monday through Friday, makes available to the public each of the public regulations, presidential proclamations, executive orders, and legal notices issued by the president and by the various federal government agencies.

LOCATING GOVERNMENT DOCUMENTS

To find most government documents, you need an index or a catalog or both. Each of the resources listed below will provide some instructions on how to locate government documents. Look at the sample entry at the beginning of the index for guidance.

Government Reports Annual Index. Springfield, Va.: U.S. Department of Commerce National/Technical Information Service, annual. (Z 7916 .B47)

An index to U.S. government–sponsored research, development, and engineering reports and foreign technical reports. There is a keyword index, an author index, and a corporate-author index. NTIS is the clearinghouse for scientific and technical information from the U.S. government.

Index to Publications of the United States Congress. Washington, D.C.: Congressional Information Service, annual. (KF 49 .C62)

This index to the United States Congress includes citations to committee hearings, House and Senate documents, and reports and treaties.

Index to U.S. Government Periodicals. Chicago: Infordata, quarterly. (Z 1223 .Z9 I5)

The U.S. government publishes many periodicals. The *Treasury Bulletin* and *The Monthly Labor Review* are only two examples. While many government periodicals are indexed in *The Reader's Guide to Periodical Literature*, many are not; these must be accessed through the *Index to U.S. Government Periodicals*.

Monthly Catalog of United States Government Publications. Washington, D.C.: Government Printing Office, monthly. (Z 1223 .A18)

The GPO has been printing this since 1895 and shows no sign of letting up. It's the essential bibliographic catalog and guide to government documents as they are published. It includes a user's guide and a sample entry at the beginning of each monthly issue. It is indexed by author, title, subject, and title keyword.

Monthly Checklist of State Publications. Washington, D.C.: Government Printing Office, monthly. (Z 1223.5 .A1 U5)

This publication does for the states what the *Monthly Catalog* does for the federal government. It's a listing of state publications that have been received and cataloged by the Library of Congress. It's organized by state and has an annual subject and issuing-agency index.

Guides and Handbooks

Guides and handbooks are written to help you get acquainted with a particular subject, be it an academic topic, a consumer interest, or a country on your vacation list. They are also written to teach you how to use something or how to get somewhere or find something. They're supposed to provide you with the basics of the subject under consideration. A good guide or handbook should have some instructional value, like a "how-to" book. Guides and handbooks can provide some of the same sorts of information found in directories, fact books, and bibliographies. They can be especially useful in planning your next spring break or your next term paper, whichever comes first.

EXAMPLES OF GUIDES AND HANDBOOKS

Guide to the Records of the United States House of Representatives at the National Archives, 1789–1989. Washington, D.C.: National Archives and Records Administration, 1989. (CD 3042 .H86 U55)

An example of a guide to materials on Congress housed in the National Archives. It will help you figure out how to access public records and archival resources of the legislative branch, including records of legislative committees. It includes a guide to researching Congress in general. There is a companion volume for the U.S. Senate (CD 3042 .S46 U54).

Handbook of American Popular Literature, ed. by M. Thomas Inge. New York: Greenwood, 1988. (PS 169 .P64 H26)

This subject-area handbook covers American popular fiction: bestsellers, children's literature, comic books, detective and mystery novels, dime novels, westerns, and science fiction.

The New York Public Library Desk Reference. New York: Simon & Schuster, 1989. (AG 6 .N49)

A guide to reference questions most frequently asked of the librarians at the New York Public Library. It includes sections on times and dates, weights and measures, signs and symbols, grammar and punctuation, forms of address, and sports and games.

The Reader's Adviser: A Layman's Guide to Literature. New York: Bowker, 1986. (Z 1035 .R42)

Any edition of *The Reader's Adviser* is a pleasure to browse and a good reference to better books. The arrangement is by broad subject area.

Each section begins with a brief description of the topic under consideration and lists bibliographies of the most significant books, old and new, that should be consulted for an appropriate reading of the topic. Brief excerpts of reviews from periodical literature are included.

★ **U.S. Government Manual.** Washington, D.C.: Government Printing Office, annual. (JK 421 .A32)

This is a government document, inasmuch as it's published by the federal government. If you learn to use one government document or even one handbook, *learn this one*. It is a guide and information directory to as much as you will be able to learn about the federal government without seeking office.

LOCATING GUIDES AND HANDBOOKS

Guides and handbooks will be shelved with the subjects to which they pertain. Guides to Bali or Bermuda will be shelved with those countries' reference materials, not in a separate travel section.

Indexes

Indexes provide you with alphabetical lists of books, articles, and other information sources by author, title, and subject but do not always give you substantive information on the work cited. They're not supposed to give you much information about something. They're supposed to direct you to it. It's very hard to find a book review, a periodical or journal article, a story or a poem in an anthology, or some other piece of information that is a part of a larger collection without using an index.

There are several distinctly different types of indexes. Book-review indexes give you information on where to find book reviews in other works, usually in periodicals. Citation indexes give you information on where a certain work was cited in another work, be it a book, an article, or a paper presented at a conference. Newspaper indexes give you the date certain stories appeared in the news. Periodical indexes give you information on where certain articles appeared in general-interest and scholarly periodicals. Specialized indexes give you information on where more specialized types of materials or information resources appeared. There are also subject indexes for different areas of study.

Whenever you use an index, make sure that the index does in fact index the subjects or the specific periodicals you're researching. Most indexes list at the beginning of the volume the subjects and the periodicals indexed, usually with a sample entry to show how much and what type of information is provided and in what format.

EXAMPLES OF INDEXES

Book-Review Indexes

Book-review indexes help you find book reviews. Of the thousands of books published each year, only a fraction get reviewed. Those reviews are cited in the various book-review indexes and can be consulted to help you determine the quality of a book and the reception it got from the scholarly community or the public at large. To use a book-review index, you obviously ought to know the author and the title of the book reviewed. It also helps to know the year the book was published because the main book-review indexes come out annually.

★ **Book Review Index.** Detroit: Gale, bimonthly. (Z 1035 .A1 B6)

Published since 1965, *Book Review Index* indexes reviews of fiction and nonfiction books that appear in hundreds of periodicals.

Combined Retrospective Index to Book Reviews in Humanities Journals: 1802–1974. Woodbridge, Conn.: Research Publications, Inc., 1982. (AI 3 .C65)

This index cites half a million reviews in more than 150 humanities journals. It indexes reviews in the humanities, including subjects such as archaeology, classical studies, folklore, history, language and literature, performing arts, philosophy, religion, film, television, radio, theater, and dance.

Combined Retrospective Index to Book Reviews in Scholarly Journals: 1886–1974. Arlington, Va.: Carrollton Press, Inc., 1979. (Z 1035 .A1 C64)

An index to scholarly reviews, organized by author, listing every review of each author's works. It covers works in all fields of inquiry, including the arts and humanities, the sciences, and the social sciences.

Index to Book Reviews in the Humanities. Williamston, Mich.: Philip Thomson, annual. (Z 1035 .A1 I63)

An index organized by author and title, which indexes reviews in the humanities, including subjects such as archaeology, classical studies, folklore, history, language and literature, performing arts, philosophy, religion, film, television, radio, theater, and dance.

Index to Scientific Reviews. Philadelphia: Institute for Scientific Information, monthly. (Q 1 .I381)

ISR indexes review articles from more than three thousand scientific journals and review sources. Arrangement is by subject, by country, by author, and by source publication. *ISR* indexes reviews in chemistry, earth sciences, engineering, mathematics, medicine, physics, and other topics in science.

Technical Book Review Index. Pittsburgh, Pa.: JAAD Publishing Co., annual. (Z 7913 .T36)

TBRI is an index to book reviews appearing in periodical literature devoted to the pure sciences, the life sciences, medicine, and technology.

Citation Indexes

A citation index helps you find where a work was cited in another work. Using a citation index will help you determine where material was cited, whether many writers in a field cited the work, and, to some degree, whether or not the work has credibility.

The citation indexes published by the Institute for Scientific Information are organized by author, title, and something ISI calls the "permuterm" index. In using the ISI citation indexes, you search for materials in three different arrangements, using the Citation Index, the Source Index/Corporate Index, and the Permuterm Subject Index.

The Citation Index lists citations, alphabetically by author, to works cited in other works. This can show you the number of times one of your professors' works has been cited and where. The Source Index/ Corporate Index is an index to works cited, arranged alphabetically by author, be it an individual author or a corporate author. The Permuterm Subject Index uses significant words from the titles of all works to index them as thoroughly as possible.

Publications by ISI require some diligence to use but yield lots of valuable, well-organized information. Examples of ISI indexes are listed below.

★ Arts and Humanities Citation Index. (AI 3 .A63)

An international index to the arts and humanities, including subjects such as art, dance, drama, film, literature, music, radio, television, and theater.

★ Science Citation Index. (Q 1 .S32)

An international index to the literature of science, medicine, agriculture, technology, and the behavioral sciences.

★ Social Sciences Citation Index. (Z 7161 .S65)

An international index to the social sciences, including such subjects as anthropology, criminal justice, economics, geography, law, political science, psychology, public administration, and sociology.

Newspaper Indexes

Use a newspaper index to get the news reporting of an incident as it happened. Many newspapers publish their own index or have another company do it for them. Below are examples of some newspaper indexes.

The Atlanta Journal-Constitution Index (AI 21 .A87)
The Boston Globe Index (AI 21 .B271)
The Chicago Tribune Index (AI 21 .C45)
The Christian Science Monitor Index (AI 21 .C46)
The Houston Post Index (AI 21 .H68)
The Los Angeles Times Index (AI 21 .L65)
The New York Times Index (AI 21 .N44)
The Times of London Index (AI 21 .T51)
The Washington Post Index (AI 21 .W2)

The best newspaper index for national and international events is ★**The New York Times Index** (AI 21 .N44). It's been around since 1851. Below are two general newspaper indexes that cover a variety of newspaper publications.

Alternative Press Index: An Index to Alternative and Radical Publications. Baltimore, Md.: Alternative Press Center, annual. (AI 3 .A4)

Published since 1969, *API* indexes materials not usually found at the grocery store or drugstore newsstands. It includes reviews of books, film, records, television, and theater.

★ **The National Newspaper Index.** Los Altos, Calif.: Information Access Corp. (AI 21 .N325)

Published since 1979, *The National Newspaper Index* provides an indexing service for five major newspapers: *The New York Times*, *The Wall Street Journal*, *The Washington Post*, the *Christian Science Monitor*, and *The Los Angeles Times*. The index is available on a data base, on microfiche, and in print.

Periodical Indexes

Periodical indexes give you access to articles, reviews, and other materials that appear in scholarly or mass-market periodicals. Most periodical indexes have author, title, and subject access.

Access: The Supplementary Index to Periodicals. New York: Gaylord, annual. (AI 3 .A23)

Access gives you access to periodical articles not indexed in other indexing services such as *Reader's Guide*. It includes indexing of materials from many regional and city magazines.

The American Humanities Index. New York: Whitston Publishing Company, annual. (AI 3 .A7)

AHI indexes close to five hundred scholarly journals in the arts and humanities and includes an author and subject index.

Applied Science and Technology Index. New York: Wilson, annual. (Z 7913 .I7)

Published since 1913, *ASTI* indexes more than three hundred English-language periodicals devoted to chemistry, earth sciences, engineering, mathematics, physics, space, telecommunications, and other topics.

British Humanities Index. London: Bowker-Saur, annual. (AI 3 .B7)

BHI has indexed British newspaper and journal articles in the humanities since 1962. Arrangement is by subject with an author index at the end of each bound annual volume.

Business Periodicals Index. New York: Wilson, annual. (Z 7164 .C81 B983)

Published since 1958, *BPI* indexes close to three hundred English-language periodicals devoted to business and economic issues by author and subject.

★ **General Science Index.** New York: Wilson, annual. (Q 1 .G46)

Indexes English-language periodical articles devoted to many fields of science, including astronomy, chemistry, medicine, mathematics, physics, and zoology. Book reviews are also indexed at the end of each volume.

Hispanic American Periodicals Index. UCLA: Latin American Center, annual. (F 1401 .H43)

A subject and author index to Hispanic periodicals with main subject headings in Spanish and in Portuguese. Includes index to book reviews.

★ **Humanities Index.** New York: Wilson, annual. (AI 3 .H85)

This is one offshoot of the *Social Sciences and Humanities Index*, which split into two parts in 1974 to accommodate two broad areas of study. The *Humanities Index* indexes close to three hundred English language periodicals in the areas of archaeology, classical studies, history, languages, literature, performing arts, philosophy, religion, and related topics.

Index to Black Periodicals. Boston: G. K. Hall, annual. (AI 3 .O4)

Indexes African-American periodicals with coverage beginning in 1950. Includes articles, reviews of books, film, music, records, and theater. Arrangement is by author and subject.

Nineteenth Century Readers' Guide to Periodical Literature. 2 vols. New York: Wilson, 1944. (AI 3 .R496)

Indexes nineteenth-century periodical literature by author, subject, and illustrator, covering the period 1890 to 1899. Indexes book reviews by author and poems by title.

Poole's Index to Periodical Literature. New York: Peter Smith, 1938. (AI 3 .P7)

Poole's covers 1802 to 1906. According to Poole himself, his is "an index to subjects and not to writers, except when writers are treated as subjects." All told, *Poole's*, during the period covered, indexes more than half a million articles from more than four hundred periodicals. After 1906, you get the same sort of indexing with the *Readers' Guide to Periodical Literature*, listed below.

★ Public Affairs Information Service: PAIS International. New York: Public Affairs Information Service, annual. (Z 7163 .P9)

Published since 1915, *PAIS International* is an index to periodical articles on socioeconomic topics such as economics, political science, and sociology.

★ Readers' Guide to Periodical Literature. New York: Wilson, annual. (AI 3 .R48)

Published since 1913, the *Readers' Guide to Periodical Literature* is the standard index to articles and reviews that appear in magazines. It picks up where *Poole's* left off. *Readers' Guide* indexes general-interest periodicals that are published in the United States. The indexing is by author and subject. At the end of the index to periodical articles are book reviews indexed by author.

★ **Social Sciences and Humanities Index.** New York: Wilson, 1907–74. (AI 3 .R49)

Indexes periodicals in subjects including anthropology, archaeology, classics, economics, geography, history, languages, literature, political science, religion, and sociology. It is organized by author and by subject. No reviews are indexed here. This index has gone through some name changes. The first eighteen volumes are called the *International Index to Periodicals*. In 1974, the index split into two separate publications, the *Social Sciences Index* and the *Humanities Index*.

Social Sciences Index. New York: Wilson, annual. (AI 3 .S62)

Published since 1974, *SSI* indexes, by author and subject, periodical literature devoted to the social sciences, including subjects such as anthropology, economics, geography, political science, sociology, and related topics.

Specialized Indexes

Specialized indexes give you information on and access to information that is hard to find, widely distributed, or not collected and indexed elsewhere.

★ **Bibliographic Index: A Cumulative Bibliography of Bibliographies.** New York: Wilson, 1937–   . (Z 1002 .B595)

This is one of those works that says it's two things. But it's primarily an index to bibliographies. When you want to find good bibliographies in your major area of study, consult this index.

★ **Biography Index.** New York: Wilson, quarterly. (Z 5301 .B5)

Published since 1947, the *Biography Index* provides access to biographical material on noted individuals that has been published in books and periodicals.

Comprehensive Dissertations Index. Ann Arbor, Mich.: University Microfilms International. (Z 5053 .C64)

Use *CDI* in conjunction with *Dissertation Abstracts International*. *CDI* indexes all dissertations awarded in the United States since 1861 and some awarded in Canada and other countries. The index will direct you to the abstracts.

Congressional Information Service Index. Washington, D.C.: Congressional Information Service, annual. (KF 49 .C62)

Indexes names and subjects that appear in committee hearings, House and Senate documents, reports, and special publications of the United States Congress.

Consumer Index to Product Evaluations and Information Sources. Ann Arbor, Mich.: Pierian Press, 1992. (TX 335 .C676)

An index to consumer information in periodicals and other consumer-information sources covering food, clothes, the home, transportation, education, and health.

★ **Essay and General Literature Index.** New York: Wilson, annual. (AI 3 .E752)

Published since 1934, this is an index to essays published in collections, collected works, and the like. Collected essays by different authors in one volume often show only the editor's name in the catalog record. Coverage begins in 1900 and indexes materials in the humanities and social sciences. Index is by author and subject.

Index Translationum. Paris: UNESCO, annual. (Z 6514 .T7 I42)

A unique resource that indexes more than fifty thousand books each year that have been translated to or from one or more foreign languages. It covers all subjects and has an index to authors.

Index to Scientific and Technical Proceedings. Philadelphia: Institute for Scientific Information, annual. (Q 101 .I5)

Index to Social Science and Humanities Proceedings. Philadelphia: Institute for Scientific Information, annual. (AI 3 .I53)

These indexes cover proceedings, conferences, congresses, conventions, seminars, and workshops of societies, associations, and publishers in the humanities, the sciences, and social sciences throughout the world. Papers and speeches given before proceedings are also indexed by category, contents, author/editor, sponsor, meeting location, and "permuterm" index.

★ **Passenger and Immigration Lists Index: A Guide to Published Arrival Records of about 500,000 Passengers Who Came to the United States and Canada in the Seventeenth, Eighteenth and Nineteenth Centuries.** 3 vols. Detroit: Gale, 1981. (CS 68 .P363)

A unique reference that acts as a guide to lists of passengers who came to the United States and Canada during the seventeenth, eighteenth, and nineteenth centuries. The index cites, with subsequent supplements, a million names and hundreds of sources.

Short Story Index. New York: Wilson. (Z 5917 .S7)

Short stories are usually found in periodicals and anthologies because they're too short to be published separately in books. To find them, you need an index. *SSI*, published in five-year cumulations, indexes thousands of short stories in hundreds of periodicals and collections. The arrangement is alphabetical by author, title, and subject. It includes a list of anthologies or collections indexed.

LOCATING INDEXES

Generally, newspaper indexes and periodical indexes will be found at the beginning of the ready reference collection in the A call number range. Subject-specific indexes will be shelved with those subjects. Don't forget that there's an index of some kind, be it a general alphabetical index or a specialized geographical or chronological index, in almost every nonfiction book.

Microforms

If there's such a thing as "new" technology, as distinguished from "old" technology, then this stuff is definitely the latter. Microfilm and microfiche, collectively called microforms, are still around and can be found in almost every library in the world. Microfilm comes in reels.

Microfiche comes in sheets. Newspapers are usually on microfilm, and journals and magazines are usually on microfiche. Even though I refer to microforms as "old" technology, you won't get a copy of anything from *The New York Times* during the Great Depression anyplace else.

Microfilm was first developed in the 1930s. The advent of microforms helped us document and store records in a space-saving manner. Microforms are a little awkward to use, but they hold vast treasures. Newspapers available on microfilm include *The New York Times*, *The Wall Street Journal*, *The Washington Post*, and probably your own hometown paper. Most major magazines are available on microfiche. Your library will probably have other information available on microforms, such as previous years of the U.S. Census. Microforms have helped us keep historical records intact. Find the microform room in your library and check a local or national newspaper for the day you were born.

LOCATING MICROFORMS

Microforms are usually stored in large metal cabinets in an area devoted exclusively to their use. They should be accompanied by several microform reader-printers so that you can read and photocopy what you find on microform.

o
On-line Data Bases

When you read the words on-line data base, think computers. On-line data bases store information that is accessed through computers, be they desktop computers in your home or dormitory or laptop computers that you carry on the road and connect to an on-line data base via modem and phone line.

There are on-line data-base vendors, such as the ones listed below, which provide access to on-line data bases for subscribers. On-line data-base subscribers may be corporations, libraries, schools, or individuals. There are also in-house on-line data bases that are available only to those within a given organization.

On-line data bases are distinguished from CD-ROM data bases by the fact that they are usually accessed from a desktop or laptop computer by dialing into a larger, main computer through a modem and phone line. On-line data bases are also updated regularly, sometimes daily, whereas CD-ROM data bases work on self-contained desktop computers and must be replaced each time new information needs to be added or when old information needs to be updated. Most on-line data bases cost money each time you use them. CD-ROM data bases, the disks carrying the information, are sold at a one-time cost. College and university libraries tend to provide students with access to CD-ROM data bases rather than the more expensive on-line data bases.

COMPUSERVE

CompuServe is a popular on-line data base for personal-computer users with about a million members nationwide. It can provide access to software, electronic bulletin boards, and shopping by computer. You can get CompuServe at home or in your dorm as long as you have a computer, a modem, a phone line, and a few bucks.

DATATIMES

Datatimes is a vendor that provides many of the nation's local newspapers on-line. Some of the newspapers available on Datatimes include *The Arizona Daily Star*, *The Boston Herald*, *The Denver Post*, *The Kansas City Star*, *The Oakland Tribune*, *The Omaha World Herald*, *The Peoria Journal Star*, and *The Tulsa Tribune*, to name just a few. Datatimes is generally marketed to media and other corporate clients.

DIALOG

Dialog is one of the earliest on-line data base vendors. Dialog has hundreds of separate data bases with a broad range of subjects and is especially strong in the sciences. Dialog is available in many public libraries for a fee. It too is usually marketed toward corporate and high-tech clients.

LEGISLATE

Legislate provides on-line data-base access to activities of Congress, as well as access to government publications like *The Congressional Record*. Legislate is marketed toward media, legal, and corporate clients.

LEXIS/NEXIS

Lexis/Nexis is the service provided by Mead Data Central. The Lexis part is a legal data base with federal and state case law as well as numerous specialized legal materials and university law journals. Nexis is for news. On Nexis, you can get many major newspapers, magazines, and specialized information sources. Lexis/Nexis is marketed to the legal, media, and corporate communities.

PRODIGY

Prodigy, a joint venture of Sears and IBM, is another of the major on-line data-base services marketed toward the home-computer user. You can get many services with Prodigy, including travel, bulletin boards, games, shopping, banking and finance, education, news, weather, sports, and other useful information. Like Compuserve, with Prodigy you just need a computer, a modem, a phone line, and a few bucks to use it.

REUTERS

Reuters is a vendor that provides on-line news and information with broad coverage of the world. Reuters also has reporters and photographers covering news events across the globe. Reuters is marketed primarily toward media clientele.

VU/TEXT

Vu/Text provides on-line access to many local newspapers. Some of the local newspapers available on Vu/Text include *The Annapolis Capital*, *The Evansville Courier*, *The Fort Lauderdale News & Sun Sentinel*, *The Fresno Bee*, *The Knoxville News-Sentinel*, *The Philadelphia Daily News*, *The St. Paul Pioneer Press Dispatch*, and *The Virginian-Pilot/Ledger-Star*. Vu/Text is similar in scope to Datatimes.

WESTLAW

Westlaw is a data-base service provided by the West Publishing Company, which is a very heavy hitter in the law-book business. Westlaw provides access to case law, law reviews, and other legal information. Westlaw is marketed to the legal community and is available on most law school campuses in the law library.

LOCATING ON-LINE DATA BASES

On-line data bases are accessed through computers, so look for the computer work stations in your college library. On-line data bases usually cost money, so check with a reference librarian on what, if any, types of on-line data bases are available to students. To find a particular on-line data base devoted to a particular subject, use a directory to on-line data bases.

Periodicals

Periodicals go by half a dozen or more different names (journals, magazines, weeklies, monthlies, etc.). The main distinction about a periodical, and the reason why things are called periodicals, is that they are published periodically. This means daily, weekly, monthly, quarterly, annually, or even irregularly.

Different periodicals serve different functions and audiences. One way to judge a periodical is by the circulation figures, which are usually available in a periodical index or directory. Circulation figures may represent paid subscription as well as membership in an institution that sends the periodical along to all who belong. The best way to search for periodicals in a particular subject area, even irregular periodicals, is to use an index to periodicals or a periodical directory. Abstracts, almanacs, digests, and indexes can be considered periodicals because they too are issued periodically, be it monthly, quarterly, or annually. Below are descriptions of several other types of periodicals.

BULLETINS

A bulletin is a periodical that prints news about an institution, professional association, government agency, or social organization. When you read *bulletin* in the title, think of a brief monthly or quarterly publication that gives the news of the day to members or others who are interested in the subject to which the bulletin is devoted. Some bulletins are well-established publications, for example, the *Bulletin of the Atomic Scientists*, published by the Educational Foundation for Nuclear Science. Others are perhaps as well established but with less circulation, for example, the *Bulletin Baudelairien*, published by Vanderbilt University's W. T. Bandy Center for Baudelaire Studies.

JOURNALS

A journal is a periodical that prints articles, reviews, reports, or proceedings, usually under the auspices of an institution, professional association, government agency, or social organization. The word *journal* in the title should suggest a periodical devoted to the ongoing record of the studies, affairs, and interests of the issuing agency. For example, the *Journal of Education Statistics* is published by the American Educational Research Association. *The Journal of Philosophy* is published through Columbia University in New York.

LOOSE-LEAF SERVICES

A loose-leaf service is a reference periodical that comes in a ring binder and is updated daily, weekly, or monthly by adding new pages and removing old, superseded pages. Loose-leaf services work well for information that changes frequently. Some of the most common loose-leaf services are devoted to business, law, and technology. Two publishers that flourish in this market are the Bureau of National Affairs (BNA) and Commerce Clearing House (CCH). For example, BNA publishes a loose-leaf service called the *Equal Employment Opportunity Commission Compliance Manual*. CCH publishes the *Federal Banking Law Reports*. Loose-leaf services often have *service* or *reporter* in the title.

MAGAZINES

A magazine is usually a glossy, four-color publication printed for mass consumption; a magazine usually attracts a large, general audience and can be found on the local newsstand. There are, however, examples of magazines devoted to very specific subjects, especially those subjects that have a large enough following to constitute a good subscription base. Most magazines are published by a for-profit publishing company, though some come from membership in an organization. *American Libraries* is a glossy magazine that comes with membership in the American Library Association.

NEWSLETTERS

Newsletters are similar to bulletins in that they are brief, focused news periodicals devoted to the subject interests of a particular group. The newsletter publishing industry took off with the advent of desktop publishing. Some newsletters are full of fun facts for people interested in certain subjects; some are published daily and contain up-to-the-minute information on topics. *Communications Daily*, for example, published by Warren Publishing, Inc., covers the telecommunications industry. *The Newsletter of Water Polo Canada* is published by the Canadian Water Polo Association.

NEWSPAPERS

There are newspapers published for national consumption and there are newspapers published for local consumption. *The Christian Science Monitor*, *USA Today*, and *The Wall Street Journal* are three papers published nationally. Newspapers with national reputations include *The Chicago Tribune*, *The Los Angeles Times*, *The Miami Herald*, *The New York Times*, and *The Washington Post*.

To find anything in the newspaper, be it a local or national paper, you have to use a newspaper index. Remember, for anything national or international in scope after 1851, use *The New York Times Index*. It's the best newspaper index there ever was.

PROCEEDINGS

Proceedings constitute the activities of an association or professional or social organization. They may be in the form of speeches, papers presented at conferences, the minutes of meetings, or votes on legislative activities. Proceedings are published irregularly, usually by the agency that holds them. For example, the *Proceedings of the Biological Society of Washington* are published by the Biological Society of Washington through the National Museum of Natural History. The *Proceedings of the National Academy of Science* are published by the National Academy of Science. In order to locate the proceedings of an organization, you must consult a directory or index to such proceedings.

LOCATING PERIODICALS

Periodicals are usually stored in a separate area in the library, though some older bound periodicals will be found in the book stacks. Periodicals on microforms will be in the microform reading rooms. Always use a directory of periodicals to find the right periodical to search for articles, reviews, or news. Then use an index to find the articles or reviews themselves, searching by author, title, or subject.

Quote Books

Quote books list quotations from the writings and speeches of the famous and the not so famous. There are general quote books covering broad topics, and there are quote books for certain subjects, such as politics, business, history, and literature. There are quote books devoted to famous people, such as Winston Churchill, William F. Buckley, and Ronald Reagan.

Use a quote book to confirm something you think someone famous once said. There are also books of misquotations, which can be very, very funny. Hamlet never said, "Alas, poor Yorick, I knew him well." Quotes sometimes add a flourish to your writing if used economically, carefully, and in the right context.

EXAMPLES OF QUOTE BOOKS

Dictionary of Biographical Quotation of British and American Subjects. New York: Knopf, 1978. (CT 773 .D38)

Uniquely arranged quote book that lists quotes by and about famous people. A subtitle might be "Who Said What About Whom."

★ **Familiar Quotations: A Collection of Passages, Phrases and Proverbs Traced to Their Sources in Ancient and Modern Literature,** by John Bartlett. 15th ed. Boston: Little, Brown, 1980. (PN 6081 .B27)

This book is universally referred to as *Bartlett's Quotations* or just plain *Bartlett's*. It has been around for over a hundred years (Bartlett died in 1905) and is a favorite among researchers, speakers, readers, and writers. It's organized chronologically by author with a subject index.

The Oxford Dictionary of Modern Quotations, ed. by Tony Augarde. London: Oxford, 1991. (PN 6080 .O94)

This dictionary of "modern" quotations helps to update some of the older quote books. It is organized alphabetically by author and has a subject index.

The Quotable Woman: 1800–1981, compiled and ed. by Elaine Partnow. New York: Facts on File, 1982. (PN 6081.5 .Q6)

A book of quotations by women "based on reputation, remarkability, quotability, and availability of their work," arranged chronologically by author. Includes author and subject index.

They Never Said It: A Book of Fake Quotes, Misquotes, and Misleading Attributions, by Paul F. Boller, Jr., and John George. New York: Oxford University Press, 1989. (PN 6081 .B635)

This is a book of misquotes. Arthur Conan Doyle's Sherlock Holmes never said, "Elementary, my dear Watson." Only the actor Basil Rathbone ever uttered that phrase, in a film about Sherlock Holmes.

What They Said: The Yearbook of World Opinion, compiled and ed. by Alan F. Pater and Jason R. Pater. Palm Springs, Calif.: Monitor Book Co., annual. (D 410 .W49)

Published since 1969, *What They Said* is an annual quote book that includes lengthy quotations from people in the news in national and international affairs. The national section is organized by broad subject areas. The international section is organized by geographic regions. Includes index of speakers and of subjects.

LOCATING QUOTE BOOKS

Quote books will be shelved with the subjects to which they pertain. They are most often considered part of the subjects of history and language. Quote books related to a major historical figure will be shelved with world history. Quote books useful to students of government and for politicians will be shelved with political science. Quote books useful for English majors will be shelved with literature.

Reviews

There are reviews of books, theatrical performances, museum exhibitions, concerts, experiments, software programs, and countless other things. Reviews are not all alike. It helps to know both the credentials of the reviewer and the type of review you're reading. Reviewers are usually identified in some manner at the beginning or the end of the review; "The reviewer is professor emeritus of geophysics at a major university." From that you might assume the reviewer is qualified and reputable. But what's the reviewer's angle? This requires further inquiry into the reviewer's background, a close reading of the review, and some knowledge of the publication's editorial policy.

The most common type of review is a book review. *The New York Times Book Review* and *The New York Review of Books* are two of the preeminent publications in America for mass market, general interest, and literary books. In these two periodicals, the form of the review can vary greatly. Reviews may often act as a platform for writers to make their own points about a topic. These are easily identified by the frequent digression of the reviewer from the actual book review. Popular magazines review books too, usually popular books. Scholarly reviews, be they reviews of technical or literary works, appear in scholarly journals.

LOCATING REVIEWS

Reviews are usually embedded in abstracts, newspapers, journals, and magazines. Use an index to book reviews or other types of reviews to locate the review. Use a digest to get the review in a brief format.

Statistical Sources

The best statistics are the ones that make your own argument work. But these statistics have to come from somewhere. They have to have some credibility. One of the best sources for statistics, at least in America, is the federal government. There are people in the United States Department of Commerce called statisticians who gather up all this stuff and then publish it all too often. States also compile statistics.

Use statistics to make your arguments stronger or to influence your audience, but above all, make sure you understand the currency, reliability, and integrity of the statistics you're using. Their reliability must be determined by the credibility of the collection process as well as the group or individual doing the analysis.

EXAMPLES OF STATISTICAL SOURCES

American Statistics Index. Washington, D.C.: Congressional Information Service, annual. (Z 7554 .U5 A46)

Published since 1974, *ASI* is an indexing and abstracting service for U.S. government statistical publications, organized by subject, name, demographic category, and title.

County and City Data Book. Washington, D.C.: U.S. Bureau of the Census, 1992. (HA 202 .A36)

The arrangement of this statistical guide leaves a bit to be desired. It is organized by tables of statistics on states, counties, cities, and places. When using the *County and City Data Book*, go first and most directly to the brief section called "Helpful Hints for Finding Information." It's too long to reproduce here, but it is essential in using the book, which has no index. This resource supplements the *Statistical Abstract*, listed below, for county and city statistical information.

★ **Historical Statistics of the United States, Colonial Times to 1970.** Washington, D.C.: U.S. Bureau of the Census, 1976. (HA 202 .B87)

The focus in this book is obviously on historical statistics and consequently it has broader chronological coverage than the annual statistics volumes listed above.

State and Metropolitan Area Data Book. Washington, D.C.: U.S. Bureau of the Census, 1987. (HA 205 .S72)

This resource supplements the *Statistical Abstract*, listed below, in terms of state and metropolitan area statistics.

★ **Statistical Abstract of the United States.** Washington, D.C.: U.S. Bureau of the Census, annual. (HC 202)

According to the preface, "The *Statistical Abstract of the United States*, published since 1879, is the standard summary of statistics on the social, political, and economic organization of the United States." If you want U.S. statistics, start here. One look at it and you'll agree it crunches numbers on most everything. The contents at the beginning give you page numbers for several dozen broad topics. The index in the back gives you citations to more narrowly focused "tables" of statistical data. The index cites table numbers, not page numbers.

Statistical Reference Abstracts. Washington, D.C.: Congressional Information Service, annual. (HA 202 .S7)

This publication of the Congressional Research Service provides abstracts of statistical publications of private organizations and state government sources.

Statistical Reference Index. Washington, D.C.: Congressional Information Service, annual. (HA 202 .S7)

This publication of the Congressional Information Service is an index to statistical publications from private organizations and state government sources.

Statistics Sources. 2 vols. Detroit: Gale, 1991. (HA 36 .S84)

This essential statistics reference includes select bibliographies of statistical sources, federal telephone contacts, federal statistical data bases, and a directory of statistical sources.

Style Books

Sometimes called a style manual, a style book is a set of rules for writers. These are rules that cover everything from capitalization and punctuation to sentence structure and word choice. The rules are usually made up by a publisher, an educational institution, a newspaper, or some other organization whose business is words and writing.

You should use whatever style book is recommended in your area of study. For many college freshmen, it may be the *Harbrace Handbook* or the *Little, Brown Handbook*. For law students, it's probably *The Blue Book: A Uniform System of Citation*. For psych majors, it's probably the *APA Guide*. For English majors, it's probably the *MLA Handbook* or the *Chicago Manual of Style*. If you're a newspaper reporter, it's either the AP or UPI manual or one published by your own newspaper.

EXAMPLES OF STYLE BOOKS

The Chicago Manual of Style. 13th ed. Chicago: University of Chicago Press, 1982. (Z 253 .U69)

One of the best and most frequently required manuals for writers, editors, and all those in the publishing business. It covers bookmaking, style, production, and printing. The shorter version of the manual, written for those who must write the inevitable term paper, is Turabian's, listed below.

The Elements of Style, by Strunk and White. 3rd ed. New York: Macmillan, 1979. (PN 1408 .S772)

This is a classic style manual for writers, which is brief and to the point. Gives clear rules and plain examples.

★ **A Manual For Writers of Term Papers, Theses, and Dissertations,** by Kate L. Turabian. 5th ed. Chicago: University of Chicago Press, 1987. (LB 2369 .T8)

Turabian, as it is called by all those countless undergraduates who have suffered through freshman composition, is one of a handful of books devoted to the topic of how to present your writing; that is, how to quote and footnote and dozens of other stylistic rules that you may as well learn now, while you're still patient, and while you have the time.

The MLA Style Manual. New York: Modern Language Association, 1985. (PN 147 .A28)

The MLA Style Manual is geared toward students writing papers in the humanities. This edition replaced the 1971 edition, which some people prefer. I had finally learned the old 1971 edition sometime in 1983. The next year my thesis adviser told me I would have to learn the new one to write my thesis.

Webster's Standard American Style Manual. Springfield, Mass.: Merriam-Webster, 1985. (PN 147 .W36)

This general style manual covers grammar, punctuation, abbreviations, math and science, documentation of sources, design and typography, printing and binding. Includes glossary of terms, bibliography, and index.

Thesauruses

A thesaurus is a word book that helps you identify the right words to use at the right time with the right subject. A general-language thesaurus will give you synonyms for words you know, thereby helping you learn new words. A subject-specific thesaurus will give you the right word to use when doing research in a certain topic and will show you the relationship between words in the subject under consideration.

★ **Roget's International Thesaurus,** ed. by Robert L. Chapman. 5th ed. New York: HarperCollins, 1992. (PE 1591)

This is a new thesaurus of English language words and their synonyms. Many editions of Roget's and several other thesauruses can be found in most college libraries.

A Women's Thesaurus: An Index of Language Used to Describe and Locate Information By and About Women, ed. by Mary Ellen S. Capek. New York: Harper & Row, 1987. (Z 695.1 .W65)

A subject-specific thesaurus that uses alphabetical and hierarchical displays and scope notes (BT for broader term; NT for narrower term) to identify the relationships among words. The thesaurus gives you the broader term, the narrower term, and the term related to the one you consider.

Yearbooks

Yearbooks are published every year, as you may have guessed. That's because publishers have found a good market for certain types of information that needs updating every year. Yearbooks provide some of the same types of information as almanacs, dictionaries, and encyclopedias, on an annual basis. Yearbooks that are published as supplements to encyclopedias provide excellent coverage of world events for the year under consideration. Many major organizations and professions publish yearbooks specific to their activities during the year. Yearbooks often go by obvious titles like *The Year in Underwater Basket Weaving* or *Clover Picker's Annual*.

EXAMPLES OF YEARBOOKS

The Annual Register: A Record of World Events. London: Longman, annual. (D 2 .A7)

The Annual Register was first published by British statesman Edmund Burke in 1758 and continues to come out every year. It is heavy on international coverage and lists obituaries, chronicles events, and provides maps to illustrate current news. Broken down by major countries and by major subjects, it also reproduces important documents of the year, each year.

The Book of the States. Lexington, Kentucky: Council of State Governments, annual. (JK 2403 .B62)

A good yearbook for state information that lists answers to questions about the state nickname, motto, flower, bird, tree, and a host of other things about the states. Not every state has everything. Vermont has a state insect, the honeybee. Virginia has no state insect but has a state shell, the oyster. Vermont has no state shell. No wonder.

★ Chase's Annual Events: The Day-by-Day Directory. Chicago: Contemporary Books, annual. (D 11.5 .C48)

Chase's Annual Events is a calendar of notable events for the year, including holidays, festivals, calendars for several years forward, universal, standard, and daylight times, and even leap seconds, during applicable years, of course.

The Europa World Yearbook. 2 vols. London: Europa, annual. (JN 1 .E85)

International in scope, *The Europa World Yearbook* provides an introductory summary of each country, a statistical survey, and a directory of significant government agencies and business, cultural, media, and religious organizations.

The Municipal Yearbook. Washington, D.C.: International City Management Association, annual. (JS 344 .C5 A24)

The Municipal Yearbook gives you the scoop on annual city data. Written essentially by and for city government executives, it starts out with some broad articles on cities as institutions and then crunches numbers, giving statistics and profiles on municipalities. Toward the end of the book are some valuable compilations of information such as a list of directories of agencies and associations of states and counties. It includes municipal officials in U.S. cities with a population of greater than twenty-five hundred. The final section lists a bibliography of sources of information particular to the organization, administration, and daily life of cities.

The Statesman's Yearbook: Statistical and Historical Annual of the States of the World, ed. by John Paxton. New York: St. Martin's Press, annual. (JA 51 .S7)

Published since 1864, this yearbook lists data, facts, and figures for all the states of the world, which includes states, international organizations, and countries.

Yearbook of the United Nations. New York: United Nations Department of Public Information, annual. (JX 1977 .A37)

Includes a directory of intergovernmental organizations related to the U.N., an analysis of U.N. structure, a roster of the U.N., and its charter. Includes indexes to subjects and an index to resolutions and decisions of the United Nations.

Yearbook of Science and the Future. Chicago: Encyclopaedia Britannica, Inc., annual. (Q 9 .B78)

Encyclopaedia Britannica supplements its full set with a general-interest yearbook as well as this science yearbook. The *Yearbook of Science and the Future* includes feature articles on important current topics, a "science update," and reprinted selections from a "science classic" each year. Organized by broad topic. It includes a list of award-winning scientists and obituaries.

LOCATING YEARBOOKS

Yearbooks that come with encyclopedias will be shelved at the end of those sets of encyclopedias. Scientific and cultural organizations often publish yearbooks, which will be shelved with the subjects to which they pertain.

3

Major Areas of Study

THE FOLLOWING IS a list of ready reference information sources to use when researching many of the major areas of study popular in colleges and universities. Each major area of study includes a section on ready reference materials, followed by a listing of select subject headings, breakdowns, and call number ranges. The major subject headings for each major area of study are listed alphabetically in the Appendix in the Subject–Call Number Index.

It would take hundreds of volumes to list every ready reference information source on every popular major area of study. As you read these words, there are librarians in your college or university library going through the collection, looking for damaged books to send to a bindery for repair, checking for dated reference books to renew or replace, and adding new books, microforms, CD-ROM disks, periodicals, and other new information sources to the collection. A good library collection grows and changes every day. Use the examples listed under the following major areas of study as a guide when considering what type of information you're looking for and what type of information resource is likely to have it. Your library may have newer editions of information resources in some areas or similar resources by different publishers in other areas. Books and other information resources are getting to be more and more expensive. Libraries sometimes purchase new encyclopedias or dictionaries less frequently than they would like to. Sometimes a library simply cannot afford to replace old information resources that wear out. Sometimes, for the sake of shelf space, libraries retain only the most up-to-date copy of an information resource. This is especially true of almanacs, directories, and yearbooks. If the dictionary or encyclopedia I list for your major area of study is not in your library collection, look in your library catalog and find a similar one that will provide the information you're after. Use the subject headings, breakdowns, and call numbers for your major areas of study and check out what's on the shelf in your college library in the same general call number range.

Many of the reference materials discussed in the previous chapter are valuable when researching these more specific areas of study. The sources preceded by an asterisk (*) are listed under their respective types in chapter 2. Each title discussed throughout the book is also listed in the Appendix in the Title–Call Number Index.

Applied Sciences

COMPUTER SCIENCE AND DATA PROCESSING

Abstracts and Indexes

Computer Abstracts. Birmingham, Ala.: MCB University Press, monthly. (QA 76.5 .C6126)

Abstracts of articles on computer theory, programming, systems organization, communications, and networks. Also abstracts conferences proceedings. Includes subject index.

Computer and Control Abstracts. Piscataway, N.J.: Institution of Electrical Engineers: INSPEC/IEEE, monthly. (QA 76.5 .C612)

A personal and corporate author and subject index to computer science literature. Includes list of acronyms and abbreviations.

Computer Literature Index. Phoenix, Ariz.: Applied Computer Research, Inc., monthly. (QA 76.5 .Q32)

A subject, author, and publisher index to computer science literature in periodicals, books, conference papers, and reports. Covers computers, the computer industry, education, hardware, and software.

Microcomputer Index. Medford, N.J.: Learned Information, Inc., quarterly. (QA 76.5 .M54)

Abstracts of over two thousand articles covering news in the industry, software, and hardware. Includes book reviews.

* *Applied Science and Technology Index.* (Z 7913 .I7)
* *Consumer Index to Product Evaluations.* (TX 335 .C676)
* *General Science Index.* (Q 1 .G46)
* *Index to Scientific Reviews.* (Q 1 .I381)
* *Index to Scientific and Technical Proceedings.* (Q 101 .I5)
* *Science Citation Index.* (Q 1 .S32)
* *Technical Book Review Index.* (Z 7913 .T36)

Bibliographies

An Annotated Bibliography on the History of Data Processing, compiled by James W. Cortada. New York: Greenwood, 1983. (QA 76.17 .C62)

Covers the early history of data processing in such areas as computer punch cards, early digital computers, and the dawning of the computer age.

* *Bibliographic Guide to Conference Publications.* (Z 5051 .B5)
* *Proceedings in Print.* (Z 5063 .A2 P7)
* *Scientific and Technical Books in Print.* (Q 100 .S41)

Biographical Sources

Who's Who in Computer Science and Data Processing. Chicago: Quadrangle Books, annual. (QA 76.2 .A1 W5)

A biographical directory of individuals in the computer science and electronic data processing field in the United States and Canada.

* *American Men and Women of Science.* (Q 141 .A47)
* *Dictionary of Scientific Biography.* (Q 141 .D5)

Chronologies and Histories

* *Chronology of the History of Science: 1450–1900.* (Q 125 .G39)
* *Timetables of Science.* (Q 125 .H557)

Dictionaries and Encyclopedias

Complete Multilingual Dictionary of Computer Terminology, compiled by George Nania. Chicago: Passport Books, 1984. (QA 76.15 .N37)

Dictionary of Computing. 2nd ed. New York: Oxford University Press, 1986. (QA 76.15 .D526)

The Historical Dictionary of Data Processing Technology, by James W. Cortada. New York: Greenwood, 1987. (QA 76.15 .C67)

The Illustrated Computer Dictionary, by Donald D. Spencer. 3rd ed. Columbus, Ohio: Merrill Publishing Co., 1986. (QA 76.15 .S67)

Macmillan Dictionary of Personal Computers and Communications, by Dennis Longley and Michael Shain. New York: Macmillan, 1986. (QA 76.5 .L682)

McGraw-Hill Dictionary of Information Technology and Computer Acronyms, Initials and Abbreviations, by Jerry M. Rosenberg. New York: McGraw-Hill, 1992. (QA 76.15 .R68)

Van Nostrand Reinhold Dictionary of Information Technology, ed. by Dennis Longley and Michael Shain. New York: Van Nostrand Reinhold, 1989. (QA 76.15 .L63)

These seven single-volume desk dictionaries in the area of computer and information science cover personal computers, foreign languages, historical terms, and abbreviations.

Encyclopedia of Computer Science and Technology, ed. by Belzer, Holzman, and Kent. 16 vols. and 10 supps. New York: Dekker, 1975– . (QA 76.15 .E5)

This encyclopedia of computer science is updated with supplemental volumes and includes signed articles by scholars in the field, illustrations, and bibliographies.

Macmillan Encyclopedia of Computers, ed. by Gary G. Bitter.
2 vols. New York: Macmillan, 1992. (QA 76.15 .M33)

This shorter computer science encyclopedia also includes signed articles by scholars in the field, illustrations, and bibliographies, as well as appendices listing computer associations, manufacturers, and telecommunications companies.

McGraw-Hill Personal Computer Programming Encyclopedia, ed. by William J. Birnes. 2nd ed. New York: McGraw-Hill, 1989. (QA 76.6 .M414)

Signed articles by scholars in the field on computer languages and operating systems, illustrations, a glossary of terms, bibliography, and index.

* *Acronyms, Initialisms and Abbreviations Dictionary.* (P 365 .A28)
* *Facts on File Visual Dictionary.* (AG 250 .C63)
* *McGraw-Hill Encyclopedia of Science and Technology.* (Q 121 .M3)

Directories

The following directories, published by Data Pro of Delran, New Jersey, are periodically updated loose-leaf directories of goods and services in the computer industry.

Data Pro Directory of Microcomputer Hardware. (QA 76.5 .D253)
Data Pro Directory of Microcomputer Software. (QA 76.6 .D37)
Data Pro Directory of Microcomputers. (QA 76.5 .D273)
Data Pro Directory of Minicomputers. (QA 76.5 .D27)
Data Pro Directory of Software. (QA 76 .D322)

Directory of Computer Facilities in Higher Education, ed. by Charles H. Warlick. Austin, Tex.: University of Texas at Austin, annual. (QA 76.215 .D57)

A directory of computing facilities in colleges and universities in Canada, Mexico, Puerto Rico, and the United States. Covers institutional budget, affiliations, and memberships.

Directory of Portable Databases. Detroit: Cuadra/Gale, annual. (QA 76.9 .D32 D57)

This directory covers CD-ROM data bases, diskettes, and magnetic tape–based data bases. Includes index to information providers, vendors, and distributors.

Online Database Search Services Directory. 2nd ed. Detroit: Gale, 1988. (QA 76.55 .O55)

Covers over seventeen hundred libraries and other information providers in the United States and Canada. Includes information on publicly available on-line data bases.

* *Directory of Online Databases.* (Z 674.3 .D47)
* *Encyclopedia of Associations.* (HS 17 .G334)
* *International Research Centers Directory.* (Q 179.98 .I58)

Guides and Handbooks

Computer Virus Handbook. Oxford: Elsevier, 1990. (QA 76.76 .C68)

A handbook to a hot new topic in computer science that includes a history of computer viruses, reports from "virus hunters," testing of antivirus products, and computer virus defense.

Periodicals

Byte
Computer
Computer Journal
Computers and Automation
Computers and People
Computerworld
Datamation
Interface Age
Journal of the Association for Computing Machinery
PC Magazine
PC World

Reviews

Software Reviews on File. New York: Facts on File. (QA 76.75 .S64)

A monthly accumulation of microcomputer software reviews in the areas of business, education, communications, data processing, entertainment, and word processing.

Statistical Sources

* *Statistics Sources.* (HA 36 .S84)

SELECT SUBJECT HEADINGS, BREAKDOWNS, AND CALL NUMBERS

Computer Science (QA 75.5 - QA 76.95)

Periodicals (QA 75.5)
General Works (QA 76)
Dictionaries, Encyclopedias (QA 76.15)
History (QA 76.17)
Biography (QA 76.2)
Directories (QA 76.215)
Vocational Guidance (QA 76.25)
Digital Computers (QA 76.5)
    Programming Languages (QA 76.7)
    Computer Software (QA 76.75)
    Special Computers (QA 76.8)

ENGINEERING

Abstracts and Indexes

Applied Mechanics Reviews. New York: American Society of Mechanical Engineers. (TA 1 .A6395)

Abstracts and reviews of mechanical engineering literature. Covers feature articles, book reviews, and journal literature.

ASCE Annual Combined Index. New York: American Society of Civil Engineers. (TA 1 .A58)

An annual index to ASCE publications, including papers, technical notes, feature articles, and reviews.

ASCE Publications Information. New York: American Society of Civil Engineers. (TA 1 .A58 A53)

Abstracts from journals and new books of the American Society of Civil Engineers by title, subject, and author.

Electrical and Electronics Abstracts. Piscataway, N.J.: INSPEC. (TK 7800 .E4383)

Abstracts to electrical engineering articles. Includes author index, bibliographical index, book and conference index, and corporate-author index.

The Engineering Index Monthly: The Index to the World's Engineering Developments. New York: Engineering Information, Inc. (Z 5851 .E62)

Published since 1884, this monthly index is organized by subject headings from the publisher's controlled list of indexing terms. Includes author index and editor index. Uses controlled vocabulary. Brief abstracts are included.

Energy Information Abstracts Annual. New York: Bowker, annual. (TJ 163.2 .E482)

An index and abstracts of articles from scientific and technical trade and scholarly journals by subject, geographic area, industry terms, author, and source.

Energy Research Abstracts. Springfield, Va.: U.S. Department of Energy/Office of Science and Technology, semimonthly. (TJ 163.2 .E484)

Abstracts to all scientific and technical reports and patent applications that originated through the U.S. Department of Energy labs, including theses and conference papers.

Environment Abstracts Annual. New York: Bowker, annual. (TD 172 .E5)

Abstracts and indexes information from journals, proceedings, and reports, representing the impact of technology on the environment.

Index to IEEE Publications. New York: Institute of Electrical and Electronics Engineers, Inc., monthly. (Z 5832 .I54)

Index to the publications of the Institute of Electrical and Electronics Engineers, their periodicals, proceedings, standards, and special issues. Published since 1951, it includes an author and subject index.

International Aerospace Abstracts. National Aeronautics and Space Administration, semimonthly. (TL 500 .I57)

Aeronautics, space science, and technology. Provides abstracts of journals, books, proceedings, and translations. Indexed by subject, author, meeting, and report number.

International Civil Engineering Abstracts. New York: CITIS, monthly. (TA 1 .I58)

Summarizes papers in building science and construction. Most documents abstracted are in English. Covers structural engineering, bridges, buildings, foundations, tunnels, highways, and airports. Includes keyword index.

Pollution Abstracts. Bethesda, Md.: Cambridge Scientific Abstracts, bimonthly (TD 172 .P65)

Noise, air and land pollution, marine pollution, freshwater pollution, sewage and wastewater treatment, waste management, toxicology, and health issues.

* *Applied Science and Technology Index.* (Z 7913 .I7)
* *General Science Index.* (Q 1 .G46)
* *Index to Scientific Reviews.* (Q 1 .I381)
* *Index to Scientific and Technical Proceedings.* (Q 101 .I5)
* *Science Citation Index.* (Q 1 .S32)
* *Technical Book Review Index.* (Z 7913 .T36)

Bibliographies

A Guide to the Literature of Electrical and Electronics Engineering, by Susan B. Ardis. Littleton, Colo.: Libraries Unlimited, 1987. (TK 145 .A72)

Bibliographies of ready reference materials, handbooks, journals, product literature, patents, and standards.

Information Sources in Engineering, edited by L. J. Anthony. 2nd ed. London: Butterworth's, 1985. (T 10.7 .I54)

Primary and secondary sources in engineering, including specialized subject areas such as stress analysis, fluid mechanics, marine technology, chemical and nuclear engineering.

* *Bibliographic Guide to Conference Publications.* Z 5051 .B5)
* *Proceedings in Print.* (Z 5063 .A2 P7)
* *Scientific and Technical Books in Print.* (Q 100 .S41)

Biographical Sources

American Engineers of the Nineteenth Century: A Biographical Record, by Christine Roysdon and Linda A. Khatri. New York: Garland, 1978. (TA 139 .R7)

An index to nineteenth-century engineers, their dates and professional contributions, as well as an index of citations to their work in engineering journals.

The Biographical Dictionary of Science: Engineers and Inventors, ed. by David Abbott. New York: Peter Bedrick Books, 1986. (TA 139 .B56)

An alphabetical listing of significant engineers and inventors and their contributions, including a glossary of terms and index.

Who's Who in Engineering. 8th ed. Washington, D.C.: American Association of Engineering Societies, 1991. (TA 139 .E37)

Biographical information on some fifteen thousand men and women in fifty-eight countries "whose dedication and achievements have earned the recognition and respect of their peers."

* *American Men and Women of Science.* (Q 141 .A47)
* *Dictionary of Scientific Biography.* (Q 141 .D5)

Chronologies and Histories

Dictionaries

* *Chronology of the History of Science: 1450–1900.* (Q 125 .G39)
* *Timetables of Science.* (Q 125 .H557)

Dictionary of Engineering Acronyms and Abbreviations, by Harald Keller and Ume Erb. New York: Neal-Schuman, 1989. (TA 11 .E73)

Dictionary of Mechanical Engineering, ed. by G. H. F. Nayler. 3rd ed. London: Butterworth's, 1985. (TJ 9 .N28)

The Illustrated Dictionary of Electronics, ed. by Rufus P. Turner and Stan Gibilisco. 5th ed. Blue Ridge Summit, Pa.: TAB Books, 1991. (TK 7804 .T87)

McGraw-Hill Dictionary of Engineering, ed. by Sybil P. Parker. New York: McGraw-Hill, 1984. (TA 9 .M35)

McGraw-Hill Dictionary of Mechanical and Design Engineering, ed. by Sybil P. Parker. New York: McGraw-Hill, 1984. (TJ 9 .M395)

The engineering dictionaries above are single-volume desk references to mechanical, electrical, and civil engineering, with illustrations, tables and formulas, and lists of acronyms and abbreviations.

* *Acronyms, Initialisms and Abbreviations Dictionary.* (P 365 .A28)
* *Facts on File Visual Dictionary.* (AG 250 .C63)
* *What's What: A Visual Glossary of the Physical World.* (AG 250 .B7)

Directories

The Blue Book of Building and Construction. New York: Contractors Register, Inc., annual. (HD 9715 .U53 W317)

The Blue Book provides directory information for architects, engineers, general contractors and subcontractors, major corporations, suppliers, and manufacturers in the building industry. There are different volumes covering select major metropolitan areas.

Directory of Engineering and Engineering Technology: Undergraduate Programs. Washington, D.C.: American Association for Engineering Education, 1992. (T 64 .D57)

This directory lists professional societies, honor societies, and financial aid sources, compares undergraduate degree programs, and includes alphabetical and geographical program indexes.

* *Directory of Online Databases.* (Z 674.3 .D47)
* *Encyclopedia of Associations.* (HS 17 .G334)
* *International Research Centers Directory.* (Q 179.98 .I58)

Encyclopedias

Encyclopedia of Fluid Mechanics, ed. by Nicholas P. Cheremisinoff. Houston, Tex.: Gulf Publishing Co., 1986.

Signed articles by scholars in the field on the phenomena and dynamics of the flow of liquids, gas-liquids, polymer flow, and surface and groundwater flow.

Encyclopedia of Materials Science and Engineering. 8 vols. Oxford: Pergamon, 1986. (TA 402 .E53)

Includes signed articles by scholars in the field, with author, citation, and subject indexes and a list of acronyms.

International Encyclopedia of Integrated Circuits, ed. by Stan Gibilisco. 2nd ed. New York: McGraw-Hill, 1992. (TK 7874 .G5)

Clocks, counters, timers, communications circuits, control circuits, data-conversion and processing circuits, logic circuits, microcomputer peripherals, power supplies, and test equipment.

Modern Plastics Encyclopedia. New York: McGraw-Hill, annual. (TP 986 .A1 M682)

A specialized encyclopedia covering resins and compounds, chemicals and additives, processing and components. Includes keyword index, advertiser's index, and buyer's guide.

The Water Encyclopedia, by Frits van der Leeden and others. 2nd ed. Chelsea, Mich.: Lewis Publishers, 1990. (TD 351 .V36)

Climate and precipitation, hydrological elements, surface and groundwater, water quality and use, environmental problems, resources management, laws, and treaties.

* *McGraw-Hill Encyclopedia of Science and Technology.* (Q 121 .M3)

Guides and Handbooks

Civil Engineer's Reference Book, ed. by L. S. Blake. 4th ed. London: Butterworth's, 1989. (TA 151 .C58)

This encyclopedic, illustrated handbook of signed articles by scholars in the field covers mathematics, statistics, and theory for civil engineers.

Electronic Engineer's Handbook, ed. by Donald G. Fink and Donald Christiansen. 3rd ed. New York: McGraw-Hill, 1989. (TK 7825 .E34)

Covers basic principles of electrical engineering, materials and devices, circuits and functions, systems and applications.

Engineering Formulas, by Kurt Gieck and Reiner Gieck. 6th ed. New York: McGraw-Hill, 1990. (TA 151 .G4713)

A handbook of formulas for analytical geometry, statistics, calculus, statics, kinemetrics, dynamics, hydraulics, and other engineering applications.

Eshbach's Handbook of Engineering Fundamentals, ed. by Byron D. Tapley. 4th ed. New York: Wiley, 1990. (TA 151 .E8)

Encyclopedic in scope, this handbook covers mathematics for engineers, mechanics, aerodynamics, computer science, electronics, and chemical engineering.

Marks' Standard Handbook for Mechanical Engineering, ed. by Eugene A. Avallone and Theodore Baumeister. 9th ed. New York: McGraw-Hill, 1987. (TJ 151 .M37)

Coverage of mathematics for mechanical engineering, materials, transportation, building construction, shop processes, electronics, industrial engineering, and environmental control.

Materials Handbook, ed. by George S. Brady and Henry R. Clauser. New York: McGraw-Hill, 1991. (TA 402 .B72)

Encyclopedic descriptions of minerals, chemicals, plant and animal substances, engineering and industrial materials, and the nature and properties of those materials.

Metals Handbook. 9th ed. 17 vols. Metals Park, Ohio: American Society for Metals, 1978–1989. (TA 459 .A5)

Cast irons, carbon and alloy steel, steel fabrication, and corrosion. Includes appendices of abbreviations and symbols.

Standard Handbook for Electrical Engineers, ed. by Donald G. Fink and H. Wayne Beaty. 12th ed. New York: McGraw-Hill, 1987. (TK 151 .S8)

Provides concise coverage of circuits, power systems, transmission systems, wiring, motors, electronics, lighting, and standards.

Standard Handbook of Hazardous Waste Treatment and Disposal, ed. by Harry M. Freeman. New York: McGraw-Hill, 1989.

Signed articles on the history, laws, and regulations that govern hazardous-waste treatment and disposal, including sections on recycling, thermal and biological processes of treatment, and facilities.

Structural Engineering Handbook, ed. by Edwin H. Gaylord, Jr., and Charles N. Gaylord. 3rd ed. New York: McGraw-Hill, 1990. (TA 635 .S77)

Structural analysis, computer applications in structural engineering, soil mechanics, design, and construction using various materials.

Periodicals

Engineer
Engineer and Surveyor
Engineering
Engineering News
Engineering News Record
International Journal of Engineering Science
Journal of Basic Engineering
Machine Design
Proceedings of the Institution of Civil Engineers
Proceedings of the Institution of Electrical Engineers
US Woman Engineer

Statistical Sources

* *Statistics Sources.* (HA 36 .S84)

Thesauruses

Thesaurus of Engineering and Scientific Terms. New York: Engineers Joint Council, 1967. (Z 695.1 .E5)

Covers engineering and related sciences. It is a thesaurus of terms with a permuted term index (made up of significant words from definitions themselves), a subject-category index, and a hierarchical index.

SELECT SUBJECT HEADINGS, BREAKDOWNS, AND CALL NUMBERS

Technology (General) (T 1 - T 995)

Industrial Safety (T 54 - T 55.3)
Industrial Engineering (T 55.4 - T 60.8)
Patents. Trademarks (T 201 - T 342)
Mechanical Drawing. Engineering Graphics (T 351 - T 385)
Exhibitions. World's Fairs (T 391 - T 995)

Engineering (General) (TA 1 - TA 2040)

Periodicals (TA 1 - TA 4)
Congresses (TA 5)
Exhibitions (TA 6)

Collected Works (TA 7)
Dictionaries and Encyclopedias (TA 9)
Symbols and Abbreviations (TA 11)
Directories (TA 12)
History (TA 15)
Country Divisions (TA 21 - TA 126)
Biography (TA 139)
Civil Engineering (General) (TA 144 - TA 156)
Human Engineering (TA 166 - TA 167)
Systems Engineering (TA 168)
Engineering Economy (TA 177.4 - TA 185)
Mechanics of Engineering (TA 349 - TA 359)
Materials of Engineering (TA 401 - TA 492)
Surveying (TA 501 - TA 625)
Structural Engineering (TA 630 - TA 695)
Engineering Geology (TA 705 - TA 710.5)
Earthwork. Foundations (TA 715 - TA 787)
Tunneling. Tunnels (TA 800 - TA 820)
Transportation Engineering (TA 1001 - TA 1280)
Applied Optics. Lasers (TA 1501 - TA 1820)
Plasma Engineering (TA 2001 - TA 2040)

Hydraulic Engineering (TC 1 - TC 1665)

Environmental Technology (TD 1 - TD 949)

Municipal Engineering (TD 159 - TD 167)
Environmental Protection (TC 169 - TC 171.5)
Environmental Pollution (TC 172 - TC 196)
Water Supply: Domestic and Industrial (TC 201 - TC 500)
Sewage Collection and Disposal Systems (TC 511 - TC 780)
Municipal Refuse. Solid Wastes (TC 785 - TC 812.5)
Street Cleaning. Litter (TC 813 - TC 870)
Special Types of Pollution (TC 878 - TC 894)
Industrial Sanitation. Industrial Wastes (TC 895 - TC 899)
Rural and Farm Sanitary Engineering (TC 920 - TC 931)

Highway Engineering. Roads and Pavements (TE 1 - TE 450)
Railroad Engineering and Operation (TF 1 - TF 1620)
Bridge Engineering (TG 1 - TG 470)
Building Construction (TH 1 - TH 9745)

Mechanical Engineering and Machinery (TJ 1 - TJ 1570)

Control Engineering (TJ 212 - TJ 225)
Steam Engineering (TJ 268 - TJ 740)
Machine Shops and Machine Shops Practice (TJ 1125 - TJ 1345)
Agricultural Machinery (TJ 1480 - TJ 1496)

Electrical Engineering. Nuclear Engineering (TK 1 - TK 9971)

Production of Electric Energy (TK 1001 - TK 1841)
Dynamoelectric Machinery (TK 2000 - TK 2891)
Distribution of Electric Power (TK 3001 - TK 3521)
Electric Lighting (TK 4125 - TK 4399)
Telecommunications (TK 5101 - TK 6720)
Electronics (TK 7800 - TK 8360)
Computer Engineering (TK 7885 - TK 7895)
Nuclear Engineering. Atomic Power (TK 9001 - TK 9401)
Electricity for Amateurs (TK 9900 - TK 9971)

Motor Vehicles. Aeronautics. Astronautics (TL 1 - TL 4050)

Motor Vehicles (TL 1 - TL 390)
Aeronautics (TL 500 - TL 778)
Rockets (TL 780 - TL 785.8)
Astronautics (TL 787 - TL 4050)

Mining Engineering. Metallurgy (TN 1 - TN 997)

Chemical Technology (TP 1 - TP 1185)

Chemical Engineering (TP 155 - TP 156)
Manufacture and Use of Chemicals (TP 200 - TP 248)
Fuel (TP 315 - TP 360)
Food Processing and Manufacture (TP 368 - TP 456)
Low Temperature Engineering. Refrigeration (TP 480 - TP 498)
Fermentation. Alcoholic Beverages (TP 500 - TP 660)
Petroleum Refining and Products (TP 690 - TP 692.4)
Gas Industry (TP 751 - TP 762)
Clay Industries. Ceramics. Glass. Cement (TP 785 - TP 888)
Textile Dyeing and Printing (TP 890 - TP 933)
Paints, Pigments, Varnishes, Etc. (TP 934 - TP 944)
Polymers, Plastics and Their Manufacture (TP 1080 - TP 1185)

Business and Financial Studies

ACCOUNTING, BANKING, AND FINANCE

Almanacs and Yearbooks

The Banker's Almanac and Yearbook. New York: IPC Press, Ltd., annual. (HG 2984 .B3)

Almanac of banks and banking that provides information on the principal banks of the world and the standards of international banking.

International Monetary Market Yearbook. Chicago: Chicago Mercantile Exchange, annual. (HG 3853 .F6 I58)

World Currency Yearbook. Brooklyn, N.Y.: International Currency Analysis, Inc. annual. (HG 219 .P5)

The two references above provide information on currency values and rates of foreign exchange for most currencies traded throughout the world.

* *Almanac of the 50 States.* (HA 203 .A5)
* *Annual Register.* (D 2 .A7)
* *Book of the States.* (JK 2403 .B62)
* *Information Please Almanac.* (AY 64 .I55)
* *Municipal Yearbook.* (JS 344 .C5 A24)
* *World Almanac and Book of Facts.* (AY 67 .N5 W7)

Atlases

* *Rand McNally Commercial Atlas and Marketing Guide,* annual. (G 1036 .R2)

Bibliographies

Accounting Articles, 1963– ; Describing and Indexing Accounting Articles Published in Accounting and Business Periodicals, Books, and Pamphlets. Chicago: Commerce Clearing House. (Z 7164 .C81 C78)

A loose-leaf periodical containing articles on accounting and accounting techniques that have been taken from other sources.

Accounting Literature in Non-Accounting Journals: An Annotated Bibliography, by Panadda Tantral. New York: Garland, 1984. (HF 5635 .T36)

Bibliography of significant articles, books, and other sources of information that appear outside the traditional accounting literature.

Management Accounting Research: A Review and Annotated Bibliography, by Charles F. Klemstine and Michael W. Maher. New York: Garland, 1984. (HF 5635 .C81 K72)

Bibliography of managerial accounting literature for those in the leadership and decision-making roles in accounting firms.

* *Books in Print.* (Z 1215 .P972)

Biographies

Who's Who in Finance and Industry. Chicago: Marquis, biennial. (HF 3023 .A2 W5)

Directory information and biographical sketches of capitalists and financiers in the United States and Canada.

* *Current Biography.* (CT 100 .C8)
* *Who's Who in America.* (E 663 .W56)

CD-ROM Data Bases

ABI / Inform
Business Index
Compendex Plus
PAIS International

Chronologies and Histories

* *Holidays and Anniversaries of the World.* (GT 3930 .H65)
* *New York Public Library Book of Chronologies.* (D 11 .W47)

Codes and Rules

AICPA Professional Standards. 2 vols. Chicago: Commerce Clearing House. (HG 5667 .A562)

This loose-leaf service, published by Commerce Clearing House for the American Institute of Certified Public Accountants, includes chapters on U.S. auditing standards, business ethics, and international accounting.

Miller's Comprehensive GAAS Guide: A Comprehensive Statement of Generally Accepted Auditing Standards. New York: Miller Accounting Publications. (HF 5667 .M52)

This loose-leaf service is a restatement of generally accepted auditing and accounting principles and practices.

SEC Accounting Rules. Chicago: Commerce Clearing House. (HF 5601 .C55)

This loose-leaf service contains information on accounting rules and regulations and rules on financial reporting and accounting as prescribed by the Securities and Exchange Commission. It is organized by subject headings, with topical lists, finding aids, and case tables.

* *Code of Federal Regulations.* (JK 416 .C6)
* *Codes of Professional Responsibility.* (BJ 1725 .C57)
* *Robert's Rules of Order.* (JF 515 .R692)
* *United States Code.* (K 44 .C4)

Dictionaries and Encyclopedias

Comparative Glossary of Accounting Terms in Canada, the United Kingdom and the United States. New York: Accountant's International Study Group, 1975. (HF 5621 .A24)

Dictionary of Accounting, by Ralph W. Estes. 2nd ed. Cambridge, Mass.: MIT Press, 1985. (HF 5621 .E77)

Kohler's Dictionary for Accountants, ed. by W. W. Cooper and Yuji Ifiri. 6th ed. Englewood Cliffs, N.J.: Prentice-Hall, 1983. (HF 5621 .K6)

Macmillan Dictionary of Accounting, by R. H. Parker. New York: Macmillan, 1984. (HF 5621 .P37)

The dictionaries listed above are single-volume desk dictionaries covering various principles and practices in the areas of accounting and auditing.

Accountant's Encyclopedia, ed. by Jerome K. Pescow. 2 vols. Englewood Cliffs, N.J.: Prentice-Hall, 1982. (HF 5635 .P93)

A basic encyclopedia of accounting, with signed articles by scholars in the field, representing broad coverage in conceptual and practical applications of accounting and auditing.

Encyclopedia of Accounting Systems, ed. by Jerome K. Pescow. 3 vols. Englewood Cliffs, N.J.: Prentice-Hall, 1975. (HF 5635 .E54)

In signed articles written by scholars in the field, this encyclopedia "describes and illustrates accounting systems for the broadest possible spectrum of industries, businesses, professions, and non-profit organizations."

The St. James Encyclopedia of Banking and Finance, ed. by Glenn G. Munn and others. 9th ed. Chicago: St. James Press, 1991. (HG 151 .M8)

This is a single-volume desk encyclopedia with substantial articles on every aspect of banking and finance on an international basis.

* *Acronyms, Initialisms and Abbreviations Dictionary.* (P 365 .A28)

Directories

Accounting Firms and Practitioners. New York: American Institute of Certified Public Accountants, annual. (HF 5601 .A8338)

An annual directory, organized by city and by state, of individual accountants and accounting firms, all of whom are members of the American Institute of Certified Public Accountants.

Investment Companies. New York: Weisenberger Financial Services, annual. (HG 4497.7 .W47)

This is an annual directory of investment companies that includes information on the fund directors, the fund policies, and their performance.

The National Directory of Certified Public Accountants. Princeton, N.J.: Norback Publishing Company, annual. (HF 5627 .N26)

An annual directory of certified public accountants in the United States that provides directory and specialization information.

* *Encyclopedia of Associations.* (HS 17 .G334)

Fact Books

* *Facts About the Cities.* (HT 123 .C395)
* *Facts About the States.* (E 180 .K4)
* *Facts on File.* (D 410 .F3)
* *Keesing's Record of World Events.* (D 410 .K4)
* *World Fact Book.* (G 122 .U56)

Guides and Handbooks

Accountant's Desk Handbook, by Albert P. Ameiss and Nicholas A. Kargas. 2nd ed. Englewood Cliffs, N.J.: Prentice-Hall, 1981. (HF 5635 .A474)

Accounting Desk Book: The Accountant's Everyday Instant Answer Book, by William J. Casey. 7th ed. Revised by Douglas L. Blensly and Tom M. Plank. Englewood Cliffs, N.J.: Institute for Business Planning, 1983. (HF 5635 .C33)

Accounting Handbook, by Joel G. Siegel and Jae K. Shim. New York: Barron's, 1990. (HF 5635 .S586)

Handbook of International Accounting, ed. by Frederick D. S. Choi. New York: Wiley, 1991. (HF 5686 .I56)

Handbook of Modern Accounting, ed. by Sidney Davidson. 3rd ed. New York: McGraw-Hill, 1983. (HF 5635 .H23)

Handbook of Model Accounting Reports and Formats, by Thomas M. Vickman. Englewood Cliffs, N.J.: Prentice-Hall, 1987. (HF 5635 .V53)

Mahon's Industry Guides for Accountants and Auditors, by James Joseph Mahon. New York: Warren, Gorham & Lamont, 1980. (HC 103 .M355)

Modern Accountant's Handbook, by James Don Edwards. Homewood, Ill.: Dow Jones–Irwin, 1976. (HF 5635 .M757)

Financial Mathematics Handbook, by Robert Muksian. Englewood Cliffs, N.J.: Prentice-Hall, 1984. (HF 5691 .M84)

Standard accounting desk books and handbooks that cover financial accounting, accounting mathematics, management accounting, income tax, and auditing. Some include signed articles by scholars in the field on accounting and accounting standards for international business enterprises, international analysis, financial reporting, and disclosure.

Indexes

Accountant's Index. New York: American Institute of Certified Public Accountants, annual. (Z 7164 .C81 A5)

An index to accounting articles by author and subject. Covers English-language periodicals only. Also includes books, pamphlets, and government documents relating to accounting, organized by author, title, and subject. This index continues the one below.

Accountant's Index: A Bibliography of Accounting Literature to December, 1920. New York: American Institute of Accountants, 1920. Reprint. New York: Garland, 1988. (HG 5635 .A23)

A bibliography of accounting articles covering reference books on accounting and allied topics. Provides historical basis for the literature of accounting.

Banking Literature Index. Washington, D.C.: American Bankers Association, annual. (HG 1501 .B268)

The *ABA Banking Literature Index* is an index to periodical literature covering issues in banking and finance.

* *Business Periodicals Index.* (Z 7164 .C81 B983)
* *Index to Social Science and Humanities Proceedings.* (AI 3 .I53)
* *Public Affairs Information Service.* (Z 7163 .P9)
* *Social Sciences Index.* (AI 3 .S62)

Periodicals

ABA Banking Journal
ABA Bankers Weekly
ABACUS
Accountancy
Accountant
Accountant's Journal
Accountant's Magazine
Accountant's Digest
Accounting and Business Research
Accounting Research
Accounting Review
Accounting Today
American Banker
Bank Management
Bank Administration
Banker
Banker's Magazine
Banker's Monthly
Barron's National Business and Financial Weekly
Certified Public Accountant
Commercial and Financial Chronicle
CPA Client Bulletin
CPA Journal
Finance
Financial Executive
Financial Times
Financial Planning
Financial Market Trends
Government Accountant's Journal

Institutional Investor
International Federation of Accountants Newsletter
International Journal of Accounting
Investor's Daily
Journal of Finance
Journal of Money, Credit and Banking
Journal of Banking Finance
Journal of Retail Banking
Journal of Accountancy
Journal of Accounting and Public Policy
National Public Accountant

Statistical Sources

* *American Statistics Index.* (Z 7554 .U5 A46)
* *County and City Data Book.* (HA 202 .A36)
* *Historical Statistics of the United States.* (HA 202 .B87)
* *State and Metropolitan Area Data Book.* (HA 205 .S72)
* *Statistical Abstract of the United States.* (HC 202)
* *Statistics Sources.* (HA 36 .S84)

SELECT SUBJECT HEADINGS, BREAKDOWNS, AND CALL NUMBERS

Accounting. Bookkeeping (HF 5601 - HF 5689)

Periodicals (HF 5601)
Congresses (HF 5603)
Collected Works (HF 5603.5)
Biography (HF 5604)
History (HF 5605 - HF 5616)
Dictionaries and Encyclopedias (HF 5621)
Theory. Methods (HF 5625)
Addresses. Essays. Lectures (HF 5629)
Study and Teaching (HF 5630)
General Works (HF 5631 - HF 5657)
Current Value Accounting (HF 5657.5)
Disclosure Accounting (HF 5658)
Inflation (HF 5667)
Auditing (HF 5667)
Installations of Accounts (HF 5669)
Special Forms (HF 5671 - HF 5679)

Machine Methods (HF 5679)
Accounts and Books (HF 5680 - HF 5681)
By Business Activity (HF 5686 - HF 5687)

Finance (HG 1 - HG 9999)

Dictionaries and Encyclopedias (HG 151)
Liquidity (HG 177)
Personal Finance (HG 179)
Money (HG 201 - HG 1496)

Banking (HG 1501 - HG 3550)

Periodicals (HG 1501 - HG 1505)
Societies (HG 1507 - HG 1515)
Congresses (HG 1521)
Collected Works (HG 1526)
Yearbooks (HG 1531)
Directories (HG 1536)
History (HG 1551 - HG 1573)
Statistics (HG 1576 - HG 1577)
Study and Teaching (HG 1581 - HG 1582)
Museums (HG 1584)
Theory (HG 1586 - HG 1588)
Addresses. Essays. Lectures (HG 1591)
General Works (HG 1601 - HG 1607)
Handbooks. Manuals (HG 1611)
Rate of Interest (HG 1621 - HG 1638)
Loans (HG 1641 - HG 1643)
Reserves. Liquidity (HG 1656)
Accounts and Deposits (HG 1660)
Insurance of Deposits (HG 1662)
Drafts. Checks (HG 1685 - HG 1703)
Mergers (HG 1722)
Bank Stocks (HG 1723)
Banks and the State (HG 1725 - HG 1778)
Special Classes of Banks (HG 1811 - HG 2351)
By Region or Country (HG 2401 - HG 3550)

Credit (HG 3691 - HG 3769)
Foreign Exchange (HG 3810 - HG 4000)
Finance Management (HG 4001 - HG 4280.7)
Trust Services (HG 4301 - HG 4480.9)

Investment (HG 4501 - HG 6051)
Lotteries (HG 6105 - HG 6270.9)
Thrift and Saving (HG 7920 - HG 7933)
Insurance (HG 8011 - HG 9999)

Public Finance (HJ 1 - HJ 9995)

Documents. By Country (HJ 9 - HJ 99.6)
History and Conditions (HJ 210 - HJ 1620)
Income and Expenditure (HJ 2005 - HJ 2347)
Revenue. Taxation (HJ 2240 - HJ 3192.7)
Taxation (HJ 3231 - HJ 5957)
Customs Administration (HJ 6603 - HJ - 7390)
Expenditure (HJ 7451 - HJ 7977)
Public Credit. Debts. Loans (HJ 8003 - HJ 8899)
Claims (HJ 8903 - HJ 8963)
Local Finance (HJ 9000 - HJ 9694.7)
Public Accounting (HJ 9701 - HJ 9995)

ECONOMICS AND GENERAL BUSINESS

Abstracts and Indexes

Business Index. Foster City, Calif.: Information Access Company, monthly. (HF 501 .B86)

A microform index to more than eight hundred periodicals, organized by author, title, and subject. Indexes articles on business, economics, and related matters in both mainstream and business-oriented periodicals.

Index of Economic Articles in Journals and Collective Volumes. Nashville, Tenn.: American Economic Association, annual. (Z 7164 .E2)

Indexes more than three hundred economic journals in English by subject and by author. Includes a list of journals indexed and a unique collective-author-volume index for things in anthologies.

Predicasts

Predicasts are indexes to business and industry data published in several series by Predicasts, Inc., of Cleveland, Ohio.

Predicasts F & S Index Europe. 1978– . (HG 1040.9 .E8 F14)

This *Predicasts* series indexes more than 750 business-related periodicals concentrating on articles dealing with European economic matters. Organized by industry, country, and company.

Predicasts F & S Index International. 1969– . (HG 4503 .F8)

This *Predicasts* series deals with all countries except the United States and Europe. It too indexes more than 750 periodicals and is organized by industry, country, and company.

Predicasts F & S Index United States. 1967– . (HG 4961 .F8)

Focuses on the United States, indexes hundreds of periodicals, and is organized by industry and company.

Predicasts Forecasts. 1984– . (HC 101 .P7)

Indexes articles that forecast business and economic activity among industries and companies in the United States.

Worldcasts. 1986– . (HF 1040 .P74)

Forecasts world business and economic activity, with the exception of the United States. It is arranged by industry and by country.

* *Business Periodicals Index.* (Z 7164 .C81 B983)
* *Index to Social Science and Humanities Proceedings.* (AI 3 .I53)
* *Public Affairs Information Service.* (Z 7163 .P9)
* *Social Sciences Index.* (AI 3 .S62)

Almanacs and Yearbooks

Annual Report of the President. Washington, D.C.: Government Printing Office, annual. (HC 106.5 .A272)

This report usually accompanies the president's budget report. Each year the *ERP* is transmitted to the Congress, together with the Annual

Report of the Council of Economic Advisors. It covers the American economy, the economic outlook, and the labor market. Includes statistical tables related to income, employment, and production.

Dow Jones–Irwin Business and Investment Almanac, by Sumner N. Levine. Homewood, Ill.: Dow Jones–Irwin, annual. (HF 5003 .D68)

This is an annual of business and investments covering corporations, finance, and economic conditions in the United States.

Everybody's Business: An Almanac—The Irreverent Guide to Corporate America, ed. by Milton Moskowitz and others. New York: Harper & Row, 1986. (HD 2785 .E88)

An all-encompassing almanac of American business, covering food, clothing, advertising, personal cash flow, industry, transportation, and other money matters.

* *Almanac of the 50 States.* (HA 203 .A5)
* *Annual Register.* (D 2 .A7)
* *Book of the States.* (JK 2403 .B62)
* *Europa World Yearbook.* (JN 1 .E85)
* *Information Please Almanac.* (AY 64 .I55)
* *Municipal Yearbook.* (JS 344 .C5 A24)
* *World Almanac and Book of Facts.* (AY 67 .N5 W7)

Atlases

* *Rand McNally Commercial Atlas and Marketing Guide.* (G 1036 .R2)

Bibliographies

International Bibliography of Economics. London and New York: Routledge, annual. (Z 7164 .E2)

One of four publications in the series *International Bibliography of the Social Sciences,* prepared by the British Library of Political and Economic Science of the London School of Economics. This multilanguage bibliography covers documents concentrating on twentieth-century economic history, theory, and policy. It is organized by author, subject, and place-name, and covers materials in more than twenty-five languages.

* *Books in Print.* (Z 1215 .P972)

Biographical Sources

Biographical Dictionary of American Business Leaders, by John N. Ingham. 4 vols. Westport, Conn.: Greenwood, 1983. (HC 102.5 .A2 153)

Includes appendices organized by industry, company, birthplace, religion, and ethnicity. It covers American business leaders from colonial times to the present.

* *Current Biography.* (CT 100 .C8)
* *Who's Who in America.* (E 663 .W56)

CD-ROM Data Bases

ABI / Inform
Business Index
Compendex Plus
PAIS International

Chronologies and Histories

* *Holidays and Anniversaries of the World.* (GT 3930 .H65)
* *New York Public Library Book of Chronologies.* (D 11 .W47)

Codes and Rules

* *Code of Federal Regulations.* (JK 416 .C6)
* *Codes of Professional Responsibility.* (BJ 1725 .C57)
* *Robert's Rules of Order.* (JF 515 .R692)
* *United States Code.* (K 44 .C4)

Dictionaries and Encyclopedias

The Dow Jones–Irwin Dictionary of Financial Planning, by Robert W. Richards. Homewood, Ill.: Dow Jones-Irwin, 1986. (HG 151 .R52)

A one-volume desk dictionary of personal finance and monetary planning for the individual investor and the general consumer.

Encyclopedia of American Economic History: Studies of the Principal Movements and Ideas, ed. by Glenn Porter. 3 vols. New York: Charles Scribner's Sons, 1979. (HC 103 .E52)

Begins with a chronological survey of American economic history and covers the social and institutional framework of the American economy from colonial times to the present.

* *Acronyms, Initialisms and Abbreviations Dictionary.* (P 365 .A28)

Directories

Brands and Their Companies/Companies and Their Brands. Detroit: Gale, annual. (T 223 .V4 A22)

Provides cross-reference from brands and the companies that own them to companies and the brands they own.

Directory of U.S. Labor Organizations: 1990–1991, ed. by Courtney D. Gifford. Washington, D.C.: Bureau of National Affairs, 1990. (HD 6504 .A15)

Information on nearly three hundred U.S. labor organizations representing some seventeen million U.S. workers. Also charts the structure of the AFL-CIO.

International Directory of Company Histories. 5 vols. Chicago: St. James Press, 1991. (HD 2721 .D36)

A directory to information about corporate headquarters of many significant companies; provides clearly written, signed articles that give histories of the companies concerned. Includes brief bibliographies and lists of subsidiaries.

National Directory of Corporate Public Affairs. Washington, D.C.: Columbia Books, annual. (HD 59 .N24)

The companies, the people, and the industries of corporate America in public relations, state and national lobbying, consumer affairs, and risk analysis.

Ward's Business Directory. Detroit: Gale, annual. (HG 4057 .A575)

Provides directory information to U.S. public and private companies with special sections including geographical listings and rankings by sales within Standard Industrial Classification (SIC) codes.

Dun's Directories.

Dun's Directories of Parsippany, New Jersey, listed below, provide directory information on America's corporate families, public and private businesses, and economic perspectives on each business by industry category and by state.

America's Corporate Families. (HG 4057 .A164)
Dun's Business Rankings. (HG 4057 .A253)
Dun's Regional Business Directory. (HG 4058 .W3 D86)
Million Dollar Directory. (HC 102 .D8)
Who Owns Whom. (HG 4538 .H423)

Moody's Manuals.

Moody's Manuals, published by Moody's Investors Service of New York and listed below, provide directory information and a guide to financial information on over-the-counter stocks, foreign companies, utilities and transportation stocks, and information on municipal bond yields.

Bank and Finance Manual. (HG 4961 .M65)
Industrial Manual. (HG 4961 .M67)
International Manual. (HG 4509 .M66)
Municipal and Government Manual. (HG 4931 .M58)
OTC Manual. (HG 4961 .M7237)
Public Utility Manual. (HG 4961 .M7245)
Transportation Manual. (HG 4971 .M73)

Standard & Poor's Directories.

Directory information on corporations, their directors and executives, and corporate families; economic perspectives on major corporations.

Standard & Poor's Corporation Records. (HG 4501 .S70)
Standard & Poor's 500 Directory. (HG 4501 .S366)
Standard & Poor's Register. (HG 4057 .A4)

World Business Associations. 4 vols. Detroit: Gale, 1992. (HG 4009 .W675)

Information on more than 100,000 companies throughout the world involved in international trade. Includes product and industry indexes.

* *Encyclopedia of Associations.* (HS 17 .G334)

Fact Books

* *Facts About the Cities.* (HT 123 .C395)
* *Facts About the States.* (E 180 .K4)
* *Facts on File.* (D 410 .F3)
* *Keesing's Record of World Events.* (D 410 .K4)

Guides and Handbooks

The Dow Jones–Irwin Guide to Personal Financial Planning, by Frederick Amling. Homewood, Ill.: Dow Jones–Irwin, 1986. (HG 179 .A554)

A single-volume desk reference to personal finance and financial planning for the investor and the general consumer.

The Dow Jones–Irwin Guide to the Wall Street Journal, by Michael B. Lehmann. Homewood, Ill.: Dow Jones–Irwin, 1990. (HB 3743 .L44)

A guide to the use of the Wall Street Journal in interpreting business cycles and economic indicators in the United States.

Standard Industrial Classification Manual. Springfield, Va.: National Technical Information Service, 1987. (HF 1042 .A55)

According to the preface, "the Standard Industrial Classification (SIC) is the statistical classification standard underlying all establishment-based Federal economic statistics classified by industry."

Periodicals

American Economic Review
American Economist
Barron's National Business and Financial Weekly
Brookings Review
Business
Business America
Business and Economic Review
Business Economics
Business International
Business Today
Business Week
Contemporary Economic Problems
Economic Indicators
Economist
Employment and Earnings
Federal Reserve Bulletin
The Financial Times
Forbes
Fortune
Harvard Business Review
Inc.
Industry Week
Journal of Business
Journal of Economic Literature
Journal of Economic Perspectives
Monthly Labor Review
Political Economy
Producer Prices and Price Indexes
Social Economy
Treasury Bulletin
The Wall Street Journal

Statistical Sources

Dow Jones Average: 1885–1985. New York: Dow Jones-Irwin, 1986. (HG 4519 .D59)

A statistical history of the Dow Jones record, with statistics showing the highs, lows, averages, and closings on the exchange.

Handbook of Basic Economic Statistics. Washington, D.C.: Government Statistics Bureau, annual. (HC 101 .H252)

An annual compilation of U.S. government statistics and basic economic data on agriculture, commerce, industry, and labor.

Handbook of Labor Statistics. Washington, D.C.: U.S. Department of Labor/Bureau of Labor Statistics. (HD 8064 .A3)

This periodical bulletin from the Bureau of Labor Statistics covers the employment and productivity statistics of labor in the United States.

U.S. Industrial Outlook: Business Forecasts for 350 Industries. Washington, D.C.: U.S. Department of Commerce, annual. (HC 106.5 .A17)

Natural resources, energy, industries, materials, production and manufacturing, information and communications, transportation, health care, financial and business services. Full of data and statistics generated by the U.S. government.

* *American Statistics Index.* (Z 7554 .U5 A46)
* *County and City Data Book.* (HA 202 .A36)
* *Historical Statistics of the United States.* (HA 202 .B87)
* *State and Metropolitan Area Data Book.* (HA 205 .S72)
* *Statistical Abstract of the United States* (HC 202)
* *Statistics Sources* (HA 36 .S84)

SELECT SUBJECT HEADINGS, BREAKDOWNS, AND CALL NUMBERS

Statistics (HA 1 - HA 4737)

Economic Theory (HB 1 - HB 3840)

Economics as a Science (HB 71 - HB 74)
History of Economics (HB 75 - HB 130)
Methodology (HB 131 - HB 145)
Value (HB 201 - HB 205)
Price (HB 221 - HB 236)
Competition (HB 238 - HB 251)

Capital (HB 501)
Income (HB 522 - HB 715)
Consumption (HB 801 - HB 843)
Welfare Theory (HB 846 - HB 846.8)
Demography (HB 848 - HB 3697)
Business Cycles (HB 3711 - HB 3840)

Economic History (HC 1 - HC 1085)

Special Topics (HB 79 - HC 90)
Economic Geography (HC 92)
By Region (HC 94 - HC 1085)

Economic History and Conditions (HD 1 - HD 9999)

Production (HD 28 - HD 69)
Economic Growth (HD 72 - HD 88)
Land Use (HD 101 - HD 1395)
Agriculture (HD 1401 - HD 2210)
Industry (HD 2321 - HD 4730.9)
Labor (HD 4801 - HD 8943)
Special Industries (HD 9000 - HD 9999)

Transportation and Communications (HE 1 - HE 9900)

Commerce (HF 1 - HF 6182)

Boards of Trade (HF 294 - HF 343)
Balance of Trade (HF 1014)
Commercial Geography (HF 1021 - HF 1027)
Commodities (HF 1040 - HF 1054)
Commercial Policy (HF 1401 - HF 1647)
Tariff Policy (HF 1701 - HF 2701)
By Region or Country (HB 3000 - HF 4050)
Business (HF 5001 - HF 6182)
  Vocational Guidance (HF 5381 - HF 5386)
  Business Ethics (HF 5387)
  Marketing (HF 5410 - HF 5417.5)
  Wholesale Trade (HF 5419 - HF 5422)
  Retail Trade (HF 5428 - HF 5429.6)
  Shopping Centers (HF 5429.7 - HF 5430.6)
  Buying (HF 5437 - HF 5444)
  Canvassing (HF 5446 - HF 5459)
  Stores (HF 5460 - HF 5469.5)

Markets (HF 5469.7 - HF 5481)
Secondhand Trade (HF 5482 - HF 5482.3)
Black Market (HF 5482.6 - HF 5482.65)
Warehousing and Storage (HF 5484 - HF 5495)
Personnel (HF 5500.2 - HF 5506)
Equipment (HF 5520 - HF 5541)
Office Organization (HF 5546 - HF 5548.6)
Industrial Psychology (HF 5548.7 - HF 5548.85)
Personnel Management (HF 5549 - HF 5549.5)

Business Mathematics (HF 5691 - HF 5716)
Business Communication (HF 5717 - HF 5746)
Shipping of Merchandise (HF 5761 - HF 5780)
Advertising (HF 5801 - HF 6182)

Communications and Media Studies

ADVERTISING, MARKETING, AND PUBLIC RELATIONS

Abstracts and Indexes

American Public Opinion Index. Louisville, Ky.: Opinion Research Service, annual. (HM 261 .I552)

An index to public opinion, collected by questions asked of individuals in scientifically administered surveys. The material is arranged by subject.

Index to International Public Opinion. Westport, Conn.: Greenwood Press/Survey Research Consultants International, annual. (HM 261 .I552)

Public opinion polls conducted in the United States and in the rest of the world. The material is arranged by subject and by country.

* *Business Periodicals Index.* (Z 7164 .C81 B983)
* *Consumer Index to Product Evaluations.* (TX 335 .C676)

Almanacs and Yearbooks

* *Almanac of the 50 States.* (HA 203 .A5)
* *Annual Register.* (D 2 .A7)
* *Book of the States.* (JK 2403 .B62)
* *Chase's Annual Events.* (D 11.5 .C48)
* *Information Please Almanac.* (AY 64 .I55)
* *Municipal Yearbook.* (JS 344. C5 A24)
* *World Almanac and Book of Facts.* (AY 67 .N5 W7)

Atlases

* *Rand McNally Commercial Atlas and Marketing Guide.* (G 1036 .R2)
* *We the People.* (G 1201 .E1 A4)

Bibliographies

American Advertising: A Reference Guide, by Emelda L. Williams and Donald W. Hendon. New York: Garland, 1988. (HF 5223 .W54)

The history of advertising, the institution of advertising, the creative process in advertising, and select advertising classics.

The Bibliography of Marketing Research Methods, ed. by John R. Dickinson. 3rd ed. Lexington, Mass.: Lexington Books, 1990.

This bibliographical resource includes more than fourteen thousand entries covering more than two hundred subject headings in advertising and marketing research.

* *Books in Print.* (Z 1215 .P972)

Biographical Sources

Who's Who in Advertising. Chicago: Marquis, 1989. (HF 6178 .W48)

Biographical information on advertising executives throughout the United States and Canada.

* *Current Biography.* (CT 100 .C8)
* *Who's Who in America.* (E 663 .W56)

CD-ROM Data Bases

ABI / Inform
Business Index
Compendex Plus

Chronologies and Histories

* *Holidays and Anniversaries of the World.* (GT 3930 .H65)
* *New York Public Library Book of Chronologies.* (D 11 .W47)
* *Timetables of History.* (D 11 .G78)

Codes and Standards

* *Code of Federal Regulations.* (JK 416 .C6)
* *Codes of Professional Responsibility.* (BJ 1725 .C57)
* *Robert's Rules of Order.* (JF 515 .R692)

Dictionaries and Encyclopedias

Advertising Slogans of America, by Harold E. Sharp. Metuchen, N.J.: Scarecrow Press, 1984. (HF 6135 .S53)

A unique reference book that provides the slogans for some of America's most popular products and traces their origin. Includes product index.

Macmillan Dictionary of Marketing and Advertising, ed. by Michael J. Boker. London: Macmillan, 1984. (HF 5412 .M32)

International in scope, this single-volume desk dictionary includes signed articles by scholars in the field of advertising and marketing.

The Marketing Glossary, by Mark N. Clemente. New York: AMACOM, 1992. (HF 5415 .C5414)

A dictionary of marketing, advertising, sales, public relations, direct marketing, and market research. Includes bibliography.

* *Acronyms, Initialisms and Abbreviations Dictionary.* (P 365 .A28)
* *Bernstein's Reverse Dictionary.* (PE 1591 .B45)
* *Facts on File Visual Dictionary.* (AG 250 .C63)
* *Partridge's Concise Dictionary of Slang.* (PE 3721 .P3)
* *Pseudonyms and Nicknames Dictionary.* (CT 120 .P8)
* *What's What: A Visual Glossary of the Physical World.* (AG 250 .B7)

Directories

The Directory of Management Consultants: 1993.
Fitzwilliam, N.H.: Kennedy Publications, 1992. (HD 69 .C6 D56)

Directory information on management consultants and consulting firms and their business affiliations. Includes index of services and industries represented.

Marketing News. Chicago: American Marketing Association, annual. (HF 5410 .A46)

An international directory of the American Marketing Association and Marketing Services Guide. Covers research services, consultants, communications, and software.

O'Dwyer's Directory of Public Relations Executives. New York: O'Dwyer, annual. (HD 59 .O353)

An alphabetical listing of directory information on public relations executives, including their name, title, career history, awards, education, address, and telephone.

O'Dwyer's Directory of Public Relations Firms. New York: O'Dwyer, annual. (HM 263 .O37)

Directory information on public relations firms with a cross index to their client companies, a list of firms ranked by fees, and an index to specialized public relations firms.

Direct Marketing Market Place. (HF 5415.1 .D57)
Standard Directory of Advertisers. (HF 5805 .S7)
Standard Directory of Advertising Agencies. (HF 5805 .S72)
Standard Directory of Worldwide Marketing. (HF 5804 .S73)

These four directories, published by Macmillan, provide information on corporations that have substantial advertising interests. They list basic directory information, including names and addresses of key advertising and marketing personnel.

Business Publication Rates and Data. (HF 5905 .S792)
Consumer Magazine and Agri-Media Rates and Data. (HF 5905 .S794)
Print Media Production Data. (HF 5905 .P7)
Spot Radio Rates and Data. (HF 5905 .S74)
Spot Television Rates and Data. (HF 5905 .S745)

These five directories, published by the Standard Rate and Data Service, give advertising rates, circulation figures, and publishing or broadcasting specifications for a variety of media, as well as basic directory information to key advertising and marketing personnel.

* *Awards, Honors and Prizes.* (AS 8 .A87)
* *Editor and Publisher Yearbook.* (PN 4700 .E4)
* *Encyclopedia of Associations.* (HS 17 .G334)
* *National Five Digit Zip Code and Post Office Directory.* (HE 6361 .N37)
* *Standard Periodical Directory.* (Z 6951 .S78)

Fact Books

* *Encyclopedia of American Facts and Dates.* (E 174.5 .C3)
* *Facts About the Cities.* (HT 123 .C385)
* *Facts About the Presidents.* (E 176.1 .K3)
* *Facts About the States.* (E 180 .K4)
* *Facts on File.* (D 410 .F3)
* *Famous First Facts.* (AG 5 .K315)
* *Keesing's Record of World Events.* (D 410 .K4)

Guides and Handbooks

The Dartnell Public Relations Handbook, by Robert L. Dilenschneider and Dan J. Forrestal. Chicago: Dartnell, 1987. (HD 59 .D28)

Essays on public relations, public relations and the marketplace, internal and corporate public relations, case studies, and a public relations bibliography.

International Marketing Handbook, ed. by Frank E. Bair. 3 vols. Detroit: Gale, 1988. (HF 1416 .I63)

Arranged alphabetically by country, this resource provides access to information on the trade practices, taxation, transportation and distribution, and credit policies of other countries.

Lesly's Handbook of Public Relations and Communications, by Philip Lesly. 4th ed. Chicago: Probus, 1991. (HM 263 .L46)

Lesly's and *Dartnell,* above, are classic handbooks that include essays, case studies, and a public relations bibliography.

Madison Avenue Handbook: The Image Makers Source. New York: Peter Glenn, 1990. (HF 5805 .M3)

This handbook covers production, music and sound, props, stages, studios, film and print media, fashion, and other areas of the advertising and marketing industry.

Publicity and Public Relations, by Dorothy I. Doty. New York: Barron's, 1990. (HD 59 .D68)

Part of the Barron's Business Library, this is a handbook primarily for business executives on public relations and its uses. Includes bibliography.

Periodicals

AD
AD Forum
Advances in Marketing and Public Policy
Advertising Age: The International Newspaper of Marketing
Advertising Age Magazine
Adweek
Adweek's Market Guide to Media
American Demographics
Folio
Gallup Report
Graphis

Industrial Distribution
Industrial Marketing Journal
Journal of Advertising
Journal of Advertising Research
Journal of Marketing
Journal of Consumer Marketing
Journal of Marketing Research
Marketing
Marketing Communications
Media Decisions
Media News
Media Science
Mediaweek
Potentials in Marketing
Print
Printers Inc.
Public Relations Journal
Public Relations Quarterly
Public Relations Review
Sales and Marketing Management
Survey of Buying Power
Survey of Industrial and Commercial Buying Power
Transportation and Distribution Management
Visual Merchandising and Store Design

Quote Books

* *Familiar Quotations.* (PN 6081 .B27)
* *Oxford Dictionary of Contemporary Quotations.* (PN 6080 .094)

Statistical Sources

Mediamark Research Reports. New York: Mediamark Research Reports, Inc., annual. (HF 5415.3 .M43)

A statistical resource for demographic and marketing data on different media group audiences and markets.

* *American Statistics Index.* (Z 7554 .U5 A46)
* *County and City Data Book.* (HA 202 .A36)
* *Historical Statistics of the United States.* (HA 202 .B87)

* *State and Metropolitan Area Data Book.* (HA 205 .S72)
* *Statistical Abstract of the United States.* (HC 202)
* *Statistics Sources.* (HA 36 .S84)

SELECT SUBJECT HEADINGS, BREAKDOWNS, AND CALL NUMBERS

Public Relations (HD 59)

   Corporate Image (HD 59.2)
   Social Responsibilities (HD 60)
   General Works (HD 60.5)
   By Region or Country (HD 60.5)

Marketing (HF 5410 - HF 5417.5)

   Periodicals (HF 5410)
   Congresses (HF 5411)
   Dictionaries and Encyclopedias (HF 5412)
   General Works by Region or Country (HF 5415)
   Marketing Research (HF 5415.2)
   Customer Service (HF 5415.5)
   Product Coding (HF 5416)
   Pricing Policy (HF 5416.5)

Advertising (HF 5801 - HF 6182)

   Periodicals (HF 5801)
   Yearbooks (HF 5802)
   Dictionaries and Encyclopedias (HF 5803)
   Directories (HF 5804)
   Biography (HF 5810)
   History (HF 5811)
   Study and Teaching (HF 5813)
   Competition. Prizes (HF 5816)
   General Works (HF 5821 - HF 5827)
   Consumer Education (HF 5832)
   Regulation (HF 5833)
   Methods (HF 5837 - HF 6141)
      Outdoor Advertising (HF 5841)
      Direct Mail (HF 5856)
      Newspapers and Magazines (HF 5871)

COMMUNICATIONS AND JOURNALISM

Abstracts and Indexes

Alternative Press Index: An Index to Alternative and Radical Publications. Baltimore, Md.: Alternative Press Center, annual. (AI 3 .A4)

API indexes materials not usually found at the grocery store or on drugstore newsstands. It includes reviews of books, film, records, television, and the theater. Published since 1969.

Communications Abstracts: An International Information Source. Newberry Park, Calif.: Sage Periodicals Press, quarterly (P 87 .C6)

Abstracts of journals, books, and book chapters in communications. Includes source, author, title, and subject index.

Journalist Biographies Master Index, ed. by Alan E. Abrams. Detroit: Gale, 1979. (PN 4820 .J68)

An index to some nine thousand biographies of journalists in more than two hundred biographical directories and other resources.

Television News Index and Abstracts. Nashville, Tenn.: Vanderbilt Television News Archive. (PN 4784 .T4)

Published since 1968, this index is arranged chronologically by date down to the minutes and seconds of TV news broadcasting. Gives synopses of programs, participants, channels, and even commercial breaks.

* *National Newspaper Index.* (AI 21 .N325)
* *New York Times Index.* (AI 21 .N44)
* *Public Affairs Information Service.* (Z 7163 .P9)
* *Readers' Guide to Periodical Literature.* (AI 3 .R48)
* *Wall Street Journal Index.* (HG 1 .W26)
* *Washington Post Index.* (AI 21 .W22)

Almanacs and Yearbooks

* *Almanac of the 50 States.* (HA 203 .A5)
* *Annual Register.* (D 2 .A7)
* *Book of the States.* (JK 2403 .B62)
* *Chase's Annual Events.* (D 11.5 .C48)
* *Editor and Publisher Yearbook.* (PN 4700 .E4)
* *Information Please Almanac.* (AY 64 .I55)
* *Municipal Yearbook.* (JN 1 .E85)
* *World Almanac and Book of Facts.* (AY 67 .N5 W7)

Anthologies and Collections

* *Historic Documents.* (E 839.5 .H57)

Atlases

* *Rand McNally Commercial Atlas and Marketing Guide.* (G 1036 .R2)
* *We the People.* (G 1201 .E1 A4)

Bibliographies

American Journalism History: An Annotated Bibliography, by David Sloan. New York: Greenwood, 1989. (PN 4731 .S56)

A general history from 1690 to the present, covering the colonial, revolutionary, and party press, freedom of the press, the Civil War press, the industrial age, the New Journalism, the frontier and regional press, modern journalism, and broadcasting.

Black Media in America: A Resource Guide, by George H. Hill. Boston: G. K. Hall, 1984. (P 94.5 .A37 H54)

Books, monographs, dissertations, theses, and journal articles in advertising, broadcasting, communications, and public relations, consumerism, journalism, and marketing.

Communications and the Mass Media: A Guide to the Reference Literature, by Eleanor S. Black and James K. Bracken. Littleton, Colo.: Libraries Unlimited, 1991. (P 90 .B57)

Citations to bibliographies, dictionaries, encyclopedias, indexes and abstracts, catalogs, directories, and yearbooks for the study of mass communications, public relations, advertising, and journalism.

Mass Media Bibliography: An Annotated Guide to Books and Journals for Research and Reference, by Eleanor Blum and Frances Goins Wilhoit. Urbana: University of Illinois Press, 1990. (P 90 .B58)

Coverage of broadcasting media, print media, film, advertising, and public relations. Cites bibliographies, directories, yearbooks, journals. Includes author, title, and subject indexes.

Radio: A Reference Guide, by Thomas Allen Greenfield. New York: Greenwood, 1989. (PN 1991.3 .U6)

A bibliography covering the history of radio, networks and stations, radio drama, news music, comedy, variety, and sports. Also covers advertising, women in radio, religious radio, and armed-forces radio.

Television: A Guide to the Literature, by Mary Cassata and Thomas Skill. Phoenix, Ariz.: Oryx Press, 1985. (PN 1992.5 .C37)

A bibliography covering mass communications, historical development of television, reference sources, effects of television on society, television news, and television criticism. Includes author, title, and subject indexes.

* *Books in Print.* (Z 1215 .P972)

Biographical Sources

Biographical Dictionary of American Journalism ed. by Joseph P. McKerns. New York: Greenwood, 1989. (PN 4781 .B5)

A biographical directory of journalists, with appendices on columnists, cartoonists, humorists, editors, war correspondents, Washington correspondents, awards and prizes, and women in journalism.

Encyclopedia of Twentieth Century Journalists, by William H. Taft. New York: Garland, 1986. (PN 4871 .T34)

Lengthy biographies of significant journalists throughout the world, giving name, important dates, columns, awards, and prizes.

* *Current Biography.* (CT 100 .C8)
* *Who's Who in America.* (E 663 .W56)

Chronologies and Histories

* *New York Public Library Book of Chronologies.* (D 11 .W47)

Dictionaries and Encyclopedias

The Broadcast Communications Dictionary, revised and expanded by Lincoln Diamant. 3rd ed. New York: Greenwood, 1989. (PN 1990.4 .D5)

A subject dictionary of radio, television, programming and production, network and station operation, broadcast equipment and engineering, audio and video recording, advertising, and media usage.

Encyclopedia of American Journalism, by Donald Paneth. New York: Facts on File, 1983. (PN 4728 .P35)

Encyclopedic coverage of names and subjects in journalism. Includes subject index to awards, book critics, columnists, editors, and foreign correspondents.

International Encyclopedia of Communications, produced jointly by the Annenberg School of Communications and the University of Pennsylvania. 4 vols. New York: Oxford University Press, 1989. (P 87.5 .I5)

Signed articles by scholars in the field on diverse topics in communications. Includes bibliographies, illustrations, topical guide, and index.

NTC's Mass Media Dictionary, by R. Terry Ellmore. Lincolnwood, Ill.: National Textbook Company, 1991. (P 87.5 .E45)

Television, radio, newspapers, magazines, film, graphic arts, books, billboards, public relations, and advertising.

Webster's New World Dictionary of Media and Communications, by Richard Weiner. New York: Webster's New World/ Prentice-Hall, 1990. (P 87.5 .W45)

A standard desk dictionary covering names and subjects in media and communications. Includes explanation of abbreviations.

World Press Encyclopedia, ed. by George Thomas Kurian. 2 vols. New York: Facts on File, 1982. (PN 4735 .K87)

Sections covered include the international press, the world's developed press systems, smaller and developing press systems, and minimal and underdeveloped press systems. Includes appendices on the world's fifty great daily papers and press organizations.

* *Acronyms, Initialisms and Abbreviations Dictionary.* (P 365 .A28)
* *Bernstein's Reverse Dictionary.* (PE 1591 .B45)
* *Facts on File Visual Dictionary.* (AG 250 .C63)
* *Partridge's Dictionary of Slang.* (PE 3721 .P3)
* *Pseudonyms and Nicknames Dictionary.* (CT 120 .P8)

Directories

Benn's Media Directory. Kent, England: Benn Business Information Services Limited, annual. (P 88.8 .B462)

Three separate volumes in this directory cover the United Kingdom, Europe, and the world, providing information on publishing houses, national newspapers, periodicals, television, radio and cinema, and media organizations.

Repap Media Guide. Morristown, N.J.: Polyconomics, annual. (PN 4888 .P6 M37)

Annual coverage of print media and broadcast news, individual publishers, newspapers and magazines, and appendices on topics such as the year's highest-rated journalists.

Working Press of the Nation. Burlington, Ia.: National Research Bureau, annual. (PN 4875 .W6)

This four-volume directory of media and journalism covers newspapers, periodicals, and broadcast journalism in the United States and Canada.

* *Awards, Honors and Prizes.* (AS 8 .A87)
* *Encyclopedia of Associations.* (HS 17 .G334)
* *Standard Periodical Directory.* (Z 6951 .S78)

Fact Books

* *Encyclopedia of American Facts and Dates.* (E 174.5 .C3)
* *Facts About the Cities.* (HT 123 .C385)
* *Facts About the Presidents.* (E 176.1 .K3)
* *Facts About the States.* (E 180 .K4)
* *Facts on File.* (D 410 .F3)
* *Famous First Facts.* (AG 5 .K315)
* *Keesing's Record of World Events.* (D 410 .K4)
* *World Fact Book.* (G 122 .U56)

Guides and Handbooks

Guide to Sources in American Journalism History, ed. by Lucy Shelton Caswell. New York: Greenwood, 1989. (PN 4731 .G84)

Information on research strategies in journalism, research methods, and discussion of archives and manuscript collections and sources in the United States.

The Magazine: Everything You Need to Know to Make It in the Magazine Business, by Leonard Mogel. 2nd ed. Chester, Conn.: Globe Pequot Press, 1988. (Z 286 .P54 M63)

Handbook for those interested in breaking into and surviving in the periodical publishing business.

On-Line Data Bases

CompuServe
Datatimes
Dialog
Legislate
Lexis / Nexis
Prodigy

Reuters
Vu/Text

Periodicals

Accuracy in Media (AIM) Report
The Atlanta Journal-Constitution
The Boston Globe
The Chicago Tribune
The Columbia Journalism Review
The Christian Science Monitor
Editor and Publisher
Hometown Daily
The Houston Post
Journalism Quarterly
The Los Angeles Times
The New York Times
Nieman Reports
Quill
The Times of London
USA Today
The Wall Street Journal
Washington Journalism Review
The Washington Post

Quote Books

* *Familiar Quotations.* (PN 6081 .B27)
* *Oxford Dictionary of Modern Quotations.* (PN 6080 .O94)
* *What They Said.* (D 410 .W49)

Statistical Sources

* *American Statistics Index.* (Z 7554 .U5 A46)
* *County and City Data Book.* (HA 202 .A36)
* *Historical Statistics of the United States.* (HA 202 .B87)
* *State and Metropolitan Area Data Book.* (HA 205 .S72)
* *Statistical Abstract of the United States.* (HC 202)
* *Statistics Sources.* (HA 36 .S84)

Style Manuals

The Associated Press Stylebook and Libel Manual: The Journalist's Bible, ed. by Christopher W. French. 3rd ed. Reading, Mass.: Addison-Wesley, 1987. (PN 4783 .A8)

A basic style book for reporters, covering capitalization, abbreviation, punctuation, spelling, numerals, and usage. Includes guidelines for sports and business writing and a guide to computer terms as well as a libel manual and sections covering the right to privacy.

The UPI Stylebook: A Handbook for Writers and Editors, by Bobby Ray Miller. New York: United Press International, 1977. (PN 4783 .U24)

Handbook for journalists, covering topics such as editing, practical style matters, printing, authorship, and news reporting.

* *Elements of Style.* (PN 1408 .S772)

SELECT SUBJECT HEADINGS, BREAKDOWNS, AND CALL NUMBERS

Journalism (PN 4699 - PN 5650)

Periodicals (PN 4699 - PN 4705)
Yearbooks (PN 4709)
Congresses (PN 4717)
Exhibitions (PN 4720)
Collections (PN 4722)
Encyclopedias. Dictionaries (PN 4728)
General Works (PN 4731)
Addresses, Essays (PN 4733)
Periodical and Newspaper Publishing (PN 4734)
Technique (PN 4771)
Study and Teaching (PN 4785)
Amateur Journalism (PN 4825)
Magazines (PN 4832)
By Region or Country (PN 4840)
   America (PN 4841 - 5110)
   Europe (PN 5110 - 5359)

Near East (PN 5359 - 5365)
Asia. Far East (PN 5366 - 5449)
Africa (PN 5450 - 5510)

Earth Sciences

GEOGRAPHY AND OCEANOGRAPHY

Abstracts and Indexes

Geographical Abstracts. New York: Elsevier, bimonthly. (G 1 .G952)

Physical and human geography. Physical geography includes sedimentology, hydrology, climatology, meteorology, remote sensing, photogrammetry, and cartography. Human geography includes studies of history, populations, people and regions, rural and urban studies, agriculture, industry, transportation, and communications.

Index to Maps in Books and Periodicals. American Geological Society of New York. 10 vols. Boston: G. K. Hall, 1968. (GA 105 .A54)

An index of maps in the world's major cartographic publications. Entries are organized by subject and geopolitical division.

Oceanographic Abstracts. New York: Pergamon Press. (GC 1 .O24)

Abstracts in the study of marine biology and oceanography, including topics such as environmental protection and pollution.

* *Applied Science and Technology Index.* (Z 7913 .A7)
* *General Science Index.* (Q 1 .G46)
* *Science Citation Index.* (Q 1 .S32)
* *Social Sciences Index.* (AI 3 .S62)
* *Social Sciences Citation Index.* (Z 7161 .S65)

Almanacs and Yearbooks

* *Almanac of the 50 States.* (HA 203 .A5)
* *Information Please Almanac.* (AY 64 .I55)
* *Weather Almanac.* (QC 983 .R83)
* *World Almanac and Book of Facts.* (AY 67 .N5 W7)

Atlases

The Rand McNally Atlas of the Oceans, ed. by Martyn Bram-
well. New York: Rand McNally, 1977. (G 2800 .R3)

An atlas of the world's oceans in maps, charts, and diagrams, including sections on the ocean realm, life in the oceans, and an encyclopedia of marine life.

The Times Atlas and Encyclopedia of the Sea, ed. by A. D.
Couper. New York: Times Books, 1990. (G 2800 .T5)

Maps, charts, and diagrams of the seas; includes sections on marine
life and fishing and shipping industries.

* *Historical Atlas of U.S. Congressional Districts.* (G 1201 .F9 M3)
* *National Geographic Atlas of the World.* (G 1021 .N38)
* *National Geographic Historical Atlas of the U.S.* (G 1201 .S1 N3)
* *Rand McNally Commercial Atlas and Marketing Guide.* (G 1036 .R2)
* *We the People.* (G 1201 .E1 A4)

Bibliographies

Current Geographical Publications. Milwaukee, Wisc.: University of Wisconsin, Milwaukee/American Geographical Society,
monthly. (Z 6009 .A47)

This collection, begun in 1938, is a printed bibliography to books,
periodical articles, pamphlets, government documents, maps, and atlases, all of which are found in the University of Wisconsin at Milwaukee library. The bibliography is arranged by topic, by region, by new
maps and by new books.

A Guide to Information Sources in the Geographical Sciences, ed. by Stephen Goddard. London: Croom Helm, 1983. (G 116 .G84)

A bibliographical guide to geography, covering historical geography, agriculture, industrial geography, and geomorphology.

* *Scientific and Technical Books in Print.* (Q 100 .S41)

Biographical Sources

* *American Men and Women of Science.* (Q 141 .A47)
* *Dictionary of Scientific Biography.* (Q 141 .D5)

Dictionaries

The Dictionary of Human Geography, by R. J. Johnson. 3rd ed. London: Blackwell, 1986. (GF 4 .D52)

Longman Dictionary of Geography: Human and Physical, by Audrey N. Clark. London: Longman, 1985. (G 63 .C56)

The Penguin Dictionary of Physical Geography, by John B. Whittow. London: Allen Lane, 1984. (GB 10 .W48)

The single-volume subject dictionaries above cover subjects, names, places, terms, and concepts in the study of geography.

The Columbia Lippincott Gazetteer of the World. New York: Columbia University Press, 1962. (G 103 .7)

The Statesman's Yearbook World Gazetteer, ed. by John Paxton. 3rd ed. London: Macmillan, 1986. (G 103.5 .P38)

The two reference sources listed above are gazetteers that identify geographical places. A gazetteer generally defines place-names only. A geographical dictionary generally defines subjects and concepts as well as place-names.

Countries and Islands of the World: A Guide to Nomenclature, by Julie Wilcocks. 2nd ed. London: Clive Bingley, 1985. (G 103.5 .W54)

A concise guide to national and governmental name changes in states throughout the world during modern times.

A Dictionary of Toponyms, by Nigel Viney. London: The Library Association, 1986. (G 103.5 .V56)

Viney defines toponyms as "place-names which have come to mean something more than a place." This dictionary provides some insight as to why people meet their Waterloo, drive a sedan, and eat turkey at Thanksgiving.

The Facts on File Dictionary of Marine Science, ed. by Barbara Charton. New York: Facts on File, 1988. (GC 9 .F28)

Well-illustrated single-volume desk dictionary that focuses on the study of oceanography and marine science.

Names and Nicknames of Places and Things, ed. by Laurence Urdang. Boston: G. K. Hall, 1986. (G 105 .N36)

This dictionary, organized alphabetically with geographic and subject indexes, will tell you where to find places like the cowboy capital (Prescott, Arizona) and the cradle of civilization (ancient Greece).

Place-Name Changes Since 1900: A World Gazetteer, by Adrian Room. Metuchen, N.J.: Scarecrow Press, 1979. (G 103.5 .R66)

A unique resource that gives the history of place-name changes since the turn of the century. All entries are "official" or governmentally instituted place-name changes.

Provinces and Provincial Capitals of the World, ed. by Morris Fisher. 2nd ed. Metuchen, N.J.: Scarecrow Press, 1985. (G 103.5 .F57)

An alphabetical list of the provinces in different countries and their capitals throughout the world. Includes index.

* *Chambers World Gazetteer.* (G 103.5 .C44)
* *Webster's New Geographical Dictionary.* (G 103.5 .W42)

Directories

World Directory of Geography. Stuttgart: Franz Steiner Verlag, 1992. (G 64 .07)

A directory of geographers and geographical organizations and associations, organized alphabetically by country.

The World Map Directory 1992–1993. Santa Barbara, Calif.: Maplink, 1992. (GA 300 .W67)

Organized by continent, this directory provides access to publishers of maps throughout the world, including maps of countries, specific geographic regions, and cities.

Encyclopedias

McGraw-Hill Encyclopedia of Ocean and Atmospheric Sciences, ed. by Sybil P. Parker. New York: McGraw-Hill, 1980. (GC 9 .M32)

A single-volume desk dictionary for the study of oceanography and the atmosphere. It includes bibliographies and an index.

Standard Encyclopedia of the World's Mountains, ed. by Anthony Huxley. New York: G. P. Putnam's Sons, 1962. (GB 501 .H8)

Standard Encyclopedia of the World's Oceans and Islands, ed. by Anthony Huxley. New York: G. P. Putnam's Sons, 1962. (GB 471 .H9)

Standard Encyclopedia of the World's Rivers and Lakes, ed. by R. Kay Gresswell and Anthony Huxley. New York: G. P. Putnam's Sons, 1966. (GB 1203 .G73)

These three encyclopedias, though somewhat dated, contain introductions, descriptions, maps, and a gazetteer of rivers, lakes, mountains, oceans, and islands.

Cities of the World. 4 vols. Detroit: Gale, 1982. (G 153.4 .C57)

Covers the geographical, cultural, social, political, and economic aspects of the major cities of the world. Based on State Department reports.

Worldmark Encyclopedia of Nations. 7th ed. 5 vols. New York: Worldmark Press, 1988. (G 103 .W65)

Covers the geographical, historical, social, political, and economic aspects of the countries of the world.

Fact Books

* *Facts About the Cities.* (HT 123 .C385)
* *Facts About the States.* (E 180 .K4)
* *World Fact Book.* (G 122 .U56)

Guides and Handbooks

Practical Handbook of Marine Science, by Michael J. Kennish. Boca Raton, Fla.: CRC Press, 1989. (GC 11.2 .K46)

An alphabetically organized handbook in the study of oceanography and marine biology that includes bibliographies and index.

Periodicals

Applied Geography
Bulletin of Marine Science
Bulletin of the American Geographical Society
Canadian Geographical Journal
Canadian Geographer
Deep Sea Research
Focus
Geo
Geoforum
Geographic Notes
Geographic Journal
Geographic Review
Geography

Journal of Geography
Journal of Physical Oceanography
National Geographic
NOAA
Oceanography and Marine Biology
Oceanology
Oceans
Professional Geographer
Progress in Oceanography
Sea Frontiers
Sea Technology
Soviet Oceanography
Soviet Geography
Undersea Technology
Underwater Journal

Statistical Sources

Direct-Line Distances, by Gary L. Fitzpatrick and Marilyn J. Modlin. 2 vols. Metuchen, N.J.: Scarecrow Press, 1986. (G 109 .F 53)

A chart of geographical distances among one thousand and one cities, states, countries, and islands.

* *County and City Data Book.* (HA 202 .A36)
* *State and Metropolitan Area Data Book.* (HA 205 .S72)
* *Statistical Abstract of the United States.* (HC 202)
* *Statistics Sources.* (HA 36 .S84)

SELECT SUBJECT HEADINGS, BREAKDOWNS, AND CALL NUMBERS

Geography (G1 - G 9980)

Geography (General) (G 1 - G 142)

Periodicals (G 1)
Societies (G 2)
Congresses (G 56)
Collected Works (G 58)

Individual Authors (G 59)
Addresses, Essays, Lectures (G 62)
Dictionaries. Encyclopedias (G 63)
Directories (G 64)
Geographers (G 65)
Philosophy (G 70)
Study and Teaching (G 72)
Museums. Exhibitions (G 77)
History of Geography (G 80)
Toponymy (G 100.5 - G 108.5)
Great Cities (G 140)
Historical Geography (G 142)

Voyages and Travels (General) (G 149 - G 570)

Travel (G 149 - G 180)
History of Discoveries (G 200 - G 336)
Special Voyages (G 369 - G 503)
Adventures, Shipwrecks, Buried Treasure (G 521 - G 539)
Seafaring Life, Ocean Travel (G 540 - G 550)

Polar Regions (G 575 - G 890)
Tropics (G 905 - G 910)
Northern and Southern Hemispheres (G 912 - G 922)
Atlases (G 1000 - G 3122)
Globes (G 3160 - G 3182)
Maps (G 3190 - G 9980)
Mathematical Geography. Cartography (GA 1 - GA 1776)
Physical Geography (GB 3 - GB 5030)
Oceanography (GC 1 - GC 1581)

Oceanography (General) (GC 1 - GC 103)

Periodicals (GC 1)
Congresses (GC 2)
Collected Works (GC 3 - GC 8)
Dictionaries. Encyclopedias (GC 9)
Directories (GC 10)
Philosophy. Relation to Other Topics (GC 10 - GC 29)
Study and Teaching (GC 30 - GC 34)
Museums and Exhibitions (GC 35 - GC 41)
Oceanographic Research (GC 57 - GC 63)
Underwater Exploration (GC 65 - GC 78)

Submarine Topography (GC 83 - GC 89)
Estuarine Oceanography (GC 96 - GC 97)
Seawater (GC 100 - GC 103)

Chemical Oceanography (GC 109 - GC 117)
Salinity (GC 120 - GC 149)
Physical Oceanography (GC 149 - GC 181)
Ocean-Atmosphere Interaction (GC 181 - GC 190)
Dynamics of the Ocean (GC 200 - GC 376)
Marine Sediments (GC 376 - GC 603)
Oceanography (By Region) (GC 611 - GC 881)
Marine Resources (GC 1000 - GC 1023)
Marine Pollution (GC 1080 - GC 1581)

GEOLOGY

Abstracts and Indexes

Geological Abstracts. London: Elsevier, monthly. (QE 75 .G41)

Abstracts in mineralogy, geochemistry, stratigraphy, paleontology, geophysics, and extraterrestrial geology.

The Geological Society of America Abstracts with Programs. Boulder, Colo.: Geological Society of America, monthly. (QE 1 .G2143)

Abstracts of papers presented at meetings of various sections of the Geological Society of America.

Mineralogical Abstracts. New York and London: The Mineralogical Societies of America and Great Britain, monthly. (QE 351 .M421)

A cooperative abstracting service covering the areas of mineralogy, geochemistry, and petrology.

New Publications of the U.S. Geological Survey. Reston, Va.: Department of the Interior. (QE 75 .A1)

Coverage of new publications by the USGS and outside organizations, including books, maps, topographic maps, articles, and proceedings.

* *Applied Science and Technology Index.* (Z 7913 .I7)
* *General Science Index.* (Q 1 .G46)
* *Index to Scientific and Technical Proceedings.* (Q 101 .I5)
* *Index to Scientific Reviews.* (Q 1 .I381)
* *Proceedings in Print.* (Z 5063 .A2 P7)
* *Science Citation Index.* (Q 1 .S32)
* *Scientific and Technical Books in Print.* (Q 100 .S41)
* *Technical Book Review Index.* (Z 7913 .T36)

Atlases

* *National Geographic Atlas of the World.* (G 1021 .N38)
* *Rand McNally Commercial Atlas and Marketing Guide.* (G 1036 .R2)

Bibliographies and Catalogs

Bibliography and Index of Geology. Alexandria, Va.: American Geological Institute. (Z 6031 .G41)

This index, prepared by AGI geologists, includes books, serials, reports, and maps in all fields of geology. Organized in four sections, including serials, specific geological fields of interest, subject index, and author index.

Information Sources in the Earth Sciences, ed. by David N. Wood. 2nd ed. London: Bowker-Saur, 1989. (QE 26.2 .I53)

Primary and secondary literature on the earth sciences, computer literature, data bases, paleontology, petrology, geomorphology, and hydrology.

Subject Catalog of the Arthur Lakes Library of the Colorado School of Mines. 6 vols. Boston: G. K. Hall, 1977. (TN 145 .A77)

An extensive catalog of an ongoing collection of materials, including subjects such as chemicals, petroleum, refining engineering, chemistry and geochemistry, geology and geological engineering, geophysics, and mathematics. Includes materials in many languages.

* *Bibliographic Guide to Conference Publications.* (Z 5051 .B5)
* *Scientific and Technical Books in Print.* (Q 100 .S41)

Biographical Resources

* *American Men and Women of Science.* (Q 141 .A47)
* *Dictionary of Scientific Biography.* (Q 141 .D5)

Chronologies

* *Chronology of the History of Science: 1450–1900.* (Q 125 .C482)
* *Timetables of Science.* (Q 125 .H557)

Dictionaries and Encyclopedias

Concise Dictionary of Earth Sciences, ed. by Ailsa and Michael Allaby. New York: Oxford University Press, 1990. (QE 5 .C66)

Dictionary of Geological Terms, ed. by Robert L. Bates and Julia A. Jackson. 3rd ed. New York: Doubleday, 1984. (QE 5 .D55)

McGraw-Hill Dictionary of Earth Sciences, ed. by Sybil P. Parker. New York: McGraw-Hill, 1984. (QE 5 .M365)

These three single-volume dictionaries cover geology and the earth sciences, including topics in petrology, paleontology, geomorphology, and hydrology.

Encyclopedia of Minerals, by Willard Lincoln Roberts and others. 2nd ed. New York: Van Nostrand Reinhold, 1990. (QE 355 .R6)

An illustrated encyclopedia covering mineral names and formulas, as well as statistics regarding habit, color-luster, and mode of occurrence.

McGraw-Hill Encyclopedia of the Earth Sciences. New York: McGraw-Hill, 1978. (QE 5 .M29)

This illustrated encyclopedia includes signed articles by scholars in the field and tables of accepted mineral species.

The Story of the Earth, by Peter John Cattermole. New York: Cambridge University Press, 1985. (QE 26.2 .C384)

An encyclopedic dictionary of the earth throughout geological history, including illustrations, maps, bibliographies, and index.

Directories

Directory of Geoscience Departments: United States and Canada. 27th ed. Alexandria, Va.: American Geological Institute, 1988. (QE 1 .A391)

Provides directory information on departments in colleges and universities, faculties and degrees, geoscience fields, courses, and faculty specialties.

* *Encyclopedia of Associations.* (HS 17 .G334)
* *International Research Centers Directory.* (Q 179.98 .I58)

Guides and Handbooks

Geology for Civil Engineers, by A. C. McLean. 2nd ed. London: Allen & Unwin, 1985. (QE 33 .M375)

A civil engineer's handbook on engineering geology that includes bibliographical references and an index.

A Sourcebook in Geology: 1400–1900, by Kirtley F. Mather. Cambridge: Harvard University Press, 1970. (QE 3 .M298)

A handbook to the history of geology throughout its formative years as a scientific discipline. Includes illustrations, diagrams, and index.

Periodicals

Bulletin of the Geological Society of America
Earth

Earth Science
Earth Science Reviews
Environmental Geology
Geological Magazine
Geological Survey Resources
Geology
Geology Studies
Geotimes
Journal of Geological Education
Journal of Geology
Journal of the Geological Society
Quarterly Journal of the Geological Society

Statistical Sources

* *Statistics Sources.* (HA 36 .S84)

SELECT SUBJECT HEADINGS, BREAKDOWNS, AND CALL NUMBERS

Geology (QE 1 - QE 999)

Geology (General) (QE 1 - QE 350)

Study and Teaching (QE 40 - QE 61)
Geological Divisions (QE 65 - QE 70)
America (QE 71 - QE 258)
Europe (QE 261 - QE 287)
Asia (QE 289 - QE 319)
Africa (QE 320 - QE 339)
Australia (QE 340 - QE 350)

Mineralogy (QE 351 - QE 399)

Determinative Mineralogy (QE 367 - QE 371)
Descriptive Mineralogy (QE 372 - QE 388)
Special Groups of Minerals (QE 389 - QE 391)
Precious Stones (QE 392 - QE 399)

Petrology (QE 420 - QE 499)

Geographical Divisions (QE 443 - QE 456)
Igneous Rocks, Volcanic Ash, Tuff, Etc. (QE 461 - QE 462)
Sedimentary Rocks (QE 471 - QE 473)

Metamorphic Rocks (QE 475 - QE 499)

Dynamic and Structural Geography (QE 500 - QE 625)

Geochemistry (QE 514 - QE 516)
Dynamic Geology (QE 517 - QE 520)
Volcanoes and Earthquakes (QE 521 - QE 545)
Coral Islands and Reefs (QE 565 - QE 570)
Sedimentation (QE 571 - QE 597)
Earth Movements (QE 598 - QE 600)
Structural Geology (QE 601 - QE 625)

Stratigraphy (QE 640 - QE 699)

Paleozoic (QE 654 - QE 674)
Mesozoic (QE 675 - QE 688)
Cenozoic (QE 690 - QE 699)

Paleontology (QE 701 - QE 760)
Paleozoology (QE 760 - QE 899)
Paleobotany (QE 901 - QE 999)

Fine Arts

ARCHITECTURE

Almanacs and Yearbooks

The Architectural Annual. Philadelphia, Pa.: The Architectural League of America, annual. (NA 9 .A4)

This yearbook of the Architectural League of America has been published since 1900 and includes illustrations and articles on contemporary architecture.

Bibliographies and Catalogs

Architecture: A Bibliographic Guide to Basic Reference Works, Histories, and Handbooks, by Donald L. Ehresmann. Littleton, Colo.: Libraries Unlimited, 1984. (NA 2520 .E37)

A basic bibliography of building technology, building types, city design, and landscape architecture, covering primitive and prehistoric, ancient, early Christian and Byzantine, medieval, renaissance, baroque and rococo, and modern architecture.

Bibliography of Early American Architecture: Writings on Architecture Constructed Before 1860 in Eastern and Central United States, by Frank J. Roos, Jr. Urbana: University of Illinois Press, 1968. (NA 707 .R6)

A regional historic bibliography of architectural writings covering the Colonial period, New England, and the South. Includes list of historic architects.

* *Books in Print.* (Z 1215 .P972)

Biographical Sources

Contemporary Architects. Chicago: St. James Press, 1987. (NA 680 .C625)

This standard biographical reference lists the works and publications of significant architects. Includes illustrations and bibliography.

Macmillan Encyclopedia of Architects, ed. by Adolf K. Placzek. 4 vols. New York: The Free Press, 1982. (NA 40 .M25)

A biographical reference that includes selected illustrations, chronological tables, general bibliographies, a glossary, and indexes of architects' names and works.

* *Who's Who in America.* (E 663 .W56)

Dictionaries and Encyclopedias

A Dictionary of Architectural and Building Technology, by Henry J. Cowan. New York: Elsevier, 1986. (NA 31 .C63)

A Dictionary of Architecture, by Nicholaus Pevsner. Woodstock, N.Y.: Overlook Press, 1976. (NA 31 .P4)

The two single-volume subject dictionaries above list names and subjects in architecture and include some illustrations.

The Builder's Dictionary: or, Gentleman and Architect's Companion. 2 vols. Washington, D.C.: Association for Preservation Technology, 1981. (NA 31 .B85)

A classic illustrated dictionary of architecture, originally published in 1734, reprinted here as it originally appeared.

A Dictionary of Architecture and Building. 3 vols. Detroit: Gale, 1966. (NA 31 .S84)

Another classic illustrated architectural dictionary, this three-volume work was originally published by Macmillan in 1902.

Encyclopedia of American Architecture, by William Dudley Hunt. New York: McGraw-Hill, 1980. (NA 705 .H86)

A one-volume illustrated encyclopedia that briefly covers the profession and names and subjects in architecture.

Encyclopedia of Architecture, Design, Engineering and Construction, ed. by Joseph A. Wilkes. 6 vols. New York: Wiley/AIA, 1988. (NA 31 .E59)

Signed articles by scholars in the field on names and subjects in architecture, including tables of conversion factors, acronyms and abbreviations, and select illustrations.

Historic Architecture Sourcebook, ed. by Cyril M. Harris. New York: McGraw-Hill, 1976. (NA 31 .H56)

Alphabetical dictionary of the various attributes of architectural design, including illustrations of doors and windows, accolades, and sills.

* *Acronyms, Initialisms and Abbreviations Dictionary.* (P 365 .A28)
* *Facts on File Visual Dictionary.* (AG 250 .C63)
* *What's What: A Visual Glossary of the Physical World.* (AG 250 .B7)

Directories

Guide to Architectural Schools in North America.
Washington, D.C.: ACSA Press, 1989. (NA 2105 .G85)

Directory of information for the study of architecture, including sections on the history of architectural education in North America, suggested high school preparation, organizations in architecture, and descriptions of schools, colleges, departments, and faculty.

Sweet's Catalog File. New York: McGraw-Hill, annual. (TH 455 .S9)

Sweet publishes indexes to the catalogs of products sold by hundreds of companies in several different areas, including architecture and engineering. These include volumes devoted to general building and renovation, industrial construction and renovation, home building and remodeling, and contract interiors. Catalogs cover site work, concrete, metals, woods and plastics, doors and windows, finishes and specialties.

Thomas Register. New York: Thomas Publishing Co., annual. (T 12 .T46)

Thomas Register is similar to *Sweet's* in providing catalog information on different companies' products and services. *Thomas Register* also provides good directory information. The volumes cover 1) products and services, 2) company profiles and 3) catalog files. Includes trademark index.

* *Awards, Honors and Prizes.* (AS 8 .A87)
* *Encyclopedia of Associations.* (HS 17 .G334)

Guides and Handbooks

Architect's Handbook of Professional Practice, by David S. Haviland. Washington, D.C.: American Institute of Architects, 1988. (NA 2570 .A7)

A one-volume handbook to the study of architecture and architectural construction for the student and the practitioner. Includes bibliographies and index.

Indexes

The Architectural Index. Boulder, Colo.: Architectural Index, monthly. (NA 9 .A67)

Covers all aspects of architecture and the architecture profession as discussed in the periodical literature.

Avery Index to Architectural Periodicals. Boston: G. K. Hall, 1973–90. (Z 5945 .C649)

A continuous citation to periodicals on architecture organized in a single alphabetical sequence by author, architect, topic, geographical region, and architectural firm. Includes obituaries, book, and exhibition reviews. Indexed by author and name.

Periodicals

AIA Journal
American Architect
Architect
Architectural Design
Architectural Digest
Architectural Record
Architectural Review
Architecture: The American Institute of Architects Journal
Builder
Building Design Construction
Design Quarterly
Domus

Harvard Architecture Review
Historic Preservation
Journal of Architectural Education
Journal of Architectural Planning and Research
Journal of the Society of Architectural Historians
Landscape Architecture
National Cities Weekly
Pencil Points
Progressive Architecture
Zodiac

Thesauruses

Art and Architecture Thesaurus. 3 vols. The Getty Art History Information Program. New York: Oxford University Press, 1990. (Z 695.1 .A7)

A thesaurus of documents, terms, concepts, styles, periods, and people in the arts and fine arts throughout the world.

ART AND ART HISTORY

Abstracts and Indexes

Art and Archaeology Technical Abstracts. London: The Getty Conservation Institute, semiannual. (AM 1 .A7)

Begun in 1960, these are abstracts of books, articles, and reports on the study, conservation, and preservation of artistic and historic works throughout the world.

Art Index. New York: Wilson, annual. (N 23 .A78)

Published since 1935, the *Art Index* is an author and subject index to more than two hundred periodicals in such fields as architecture, art, archaeology, city planning, crafts, graphic design, industrial design, interior design, landscape architecture, museology, photography, film, and related subjects.

Index to Artistic Biography, by Patricia Pate Havlice. 3 vols. Metuchen, N.J.: Scarecrow Press, Inc., 1973. (N 40 .H38)

An index to biographical works on artists covering sixty-four works in ten languages. Gives artist's name, dates of birth and death, nationality, and media the artist employed.

World Painting Index, by Patricia Pate Havlice. 2 vols. Metuchen, N.J.: Scarecrow Press, 1977. (ND 45 .H38)

An index to painters, titles of their works, and paintings by unknown authors. Two supplemental volumes bring the index up to date to 1980.

* *American Humanities Index.* (AI 3 .A7)
* *Arts and Humanities Citation Index.* (AI 3 .A63)
* *British Humanities Index.* (AI 3 .B7)
* *Humanities Index.* (AI 3 .H85)

Bibliographies and Catalogs

250 Years of Afro-American Art: An Annotated Bibliography, by Lynn Moody Igoe and James Igoe. New York: Bowker, 1981. (N 6538 .N5 I35)

Includes a bibliography of basic sources and bibliographies by subject and by artist, as well as appendices of works by anonymous artists and art by groups.

Art Books. 2 vols. New York: Bowker, 1981. (N 7425 .A66)

A bibliography covering the periods 1876 to 1949 and 1950 to 1979. Arrangement is by subject, author, and title. Includes subject and title index to serials in art.

Art Books: A Basic Bibliography of Monographs on Artists, by Wolfgang M. Freitag. New York: Garland, 1985. (N 40 .F73)

A bibliographic reference to biographical sources on artists, mainly biographical dictionaries and encyclopedias. Alphabetical by artist, international in scope, it also includes an author index.

Arts in America: A Bibliography, ed. by Bernard Karpel. 4 vols. Washington, D.C.: Smithsonian Institution Press, 1979. (NX 503 .A1)

A bibliography covering art, architecture, decorative arts, sculpture, design, painting, and graphic arts. Includes sections on photography, film, theater, dance, and music.

BHA: Bibliography of the History of Art. Williamstown, Mass.: The Getty Art History Information Program, annual. (N 23.3 .B53)

Arranged chronologically, *BHA* is a bibliography of art history in the Western tradition, reflecting materials housed in Western libraries and institutions. *BHA* includes author, subject, and journal indexes and abstracts on general art history.

Guide to the Literature of Art History, by Etta Arntzen and Robert Rainwater. Chicago: American Library Association, 1980. (N 380 .A75)

A bibliography with international coverage of general works, directories, auction sales records, and other resources. Covers architecture, sculpture, drawing, painting, printing, photography, decorative and applied arts.

The Metropolitan Museum of Art Library Catalog. 25 vols. and suppls. Boston: G. K. Hall, 1960– . (Z 881 .N6622)

An all-encompassing catalog of one of America's great art libraries. It catalogs and classifies materials representing five thousand years of art and archaeology in the library's holdings.

RILA: International Repertory of the Literature of Art. Williamstown, Mass.: The Getty Art History Information Program, annual. (N 1 .R5)

RILA, published since 1975, is a bibliography of art literature covering reference and general works and specific materials on various periods in art history. Covers architecture, sculpture, pictorial and decorative arts, photography, and new media. Includes author and subject indexes.

* *Books in Print.* (Z 1215 .P972)

Biographical Sources

Contemporary American Women Sculptors. Phoenix, Ariz.: Oryx Press, 1986. (NB 212 .W37)

Biographical information on women sculptors, including name, maiden or family name, life dates, education and training, exhibitions, collections, preferred media, teaching, and bibliography.

Contemporary Artists. Chicago: St. James Press, 1989. (N 6490 .C65)

Biographical information on artists, including exhibitions of their work, collections, illustrations, and bibliographies.

Contemporary Graphic Artists: A Biographical, Bibliographical and Critical Guide to Current Illustrators, Animators, Cartoonists, Designers, and Other Graphic Artists. Detroit: Gale, 1987. (NC 45 .C6)

Personal biographical information, career, awards, writings, films, exhibitions, and critical sources for graphic artists.

Dictionary of Women Artists: An International Dictionary of Women Artists Born Before 1900, by Chris Petteys. Boston: G. K. Hall, 1985. (N 43 .P47)

Biographical source with signed articles by scholars in the field on women artists. Includes bibliography.

Folk Artists Biographical Index, ed. by George H. Meyer. Detroit: Gale, 1987. (NK 805 .F63)

Biographical source with biographies, bibliographies, and indices by ethnicity, geographical region, media, and type of art work.

Who's Who in American Art: 1991–92. 19th ed. New York: Bowker, 1991. (N 6536 .W5)

Reference giving biographical information on American artists, including a geographical index and list of recently deceased artists.

Who's Who in Art. 25th ed. Havart, Hants: The Art Trade Press, 1992. (N 40 .W6)

International reference on artists, designers, craftsmen, critics, writers, teachers, and curators. Includes an appendix on monograms and signatures.

* *Current Biography.* (CT 100 .C8)

Chronologies

Calendar of Creative Man, by John Paxton and Sheila Fairfield. New York: Facts on File, 1979. (NX 447.5 .P38)

Illustrated chronology of the arts, including literature, dance and drama, music, architecture, and three-dimensional arts.

* *Timetables of History.* (D 11 .G78)

Dictionaries and Encyclopedias

The Classified Directory of Artists' Signatures, Symbols and Monograms, by H. H. Caplan. Detroit: Gale, 1982. (N 45 .C36)

Covers signatures, symbols, and monograms in English, French, German, Spanish, and Italian. Provides brief biographical information including surname, first name, birthplace and dates, and the media the artist employed.

Encyclopedia of World Art. 15 vols. New York: McGraw-Hill, 1959. (N 31 .E56)

An older but comprehensive encyclopedia of art, edited by an international council of scholars with signed articles on topics covering the range of artistic expression throughout history. Recently published supplemental volumes update the set.

History of Art, by H. W. Janson. 3rd ed. revised and ed. by Anthony F. Janson. New York: Abrams, 1986. (N 5300 .J3)

Popular and authoritative reference covering artistic expression during the ancient world, the Middle Ages, the Renaissance, and the modern world. Includes chronological tables, glossary, bibliographies, and index.

History of Modern Art, by H. H. Arnason. 2nd ed. New York: Abrams, 1977. (N 6490 .A713)

Popular and authoritative reference covering painting, sculpture, architecture, designers, and photographers. Includes illustrations, bibliographies, and indexes.

McGraw-Hill Dictionary of Art, ed. by Bernard S. Myers. 5 vols. New York: McGraw-Hill, 1969. (N 33 .M23)

This encyclopedic dictionary of world art includes signed articles by scholars in the field on artists, subjects, concepts, and schools, with illustrations.

The Oxford Dictionary of Art, ed. by Ian Chilvers and Harold Osborne. New York: Oxford University Press, 1988. (N 33 .O93)

The Penguin Dictionary of Art and Artists, by Peter and Linda Murray. 5th ed. London: Penguin Books, 1983. (N 31 .M8)

The Thames and Hudson Dictionary of Art and Artists, ed. by Herbert Read. London: Thames and Hudson, 1985. (N 31 .T4)

The three dictionaries listed above are one-volume subject dictionaries for the study of art. They cover names and subjects in art and provide some illustrations.

A Visual Dictionary of Art. Greenwich, Conn.: New York Graphic Society, Ltd., 1974. (N 33 .B56)

A thoroughly illustrated visual dictionary of art by one of America's artistic societies, it includes signed articles by scholars in the field, covering world art by era and by region. Includes chronological table, bibliographies, and index.

* *Dictionary of the History of Ideas.* (CD 5 .D52)
* *Harper Dictionary of Modern Thought.* (AG 5 .H19)

* *Symbols: Signs and Their Meaning and Uses in Design.* (CB 475 .W48)
* *What's What: A Visual Glossary of the Physical World.* (AG 250 .B7)

Directories

American Art Directory: 1991–92. 54th ed. New York: Bowker, 1992. (N 50 .A54)

Directory information on museums, art schools, art organizations, and related information in the United States and Canada. Includes coverage of art magazines, newspapers, critics, exhibits, and scholarships.

American Artist Directory of Art Schools and Workshops. Nashville, Tenn.: Amusement Business, annual. (N 328 .A52)

Directory information on educational resources for artists, including public and art schools and teachers, workshops, tours, and other programs.

Art Museums of the World. 2 vols. New York: Greenwood, 1987. (N 410 .A78)

Signed articles by scholars in the field list alphabetically by country the major museums of the world, providing directory information on each museum, its history, significant events, and collections.

The Cambridge Guide to the Museums of Europe, by Kenneth Hudson and Ann Nichols. New York: Cambridge University Press, 1991. (AM 40 .H83)

Geographical guide to Europe's art museums from Austria to Italy to Switzerland, providing directory information and descriptions of each.

The Directory of Museums and Living Displays, by Kenneth Hudson and Ann Nichols. 3rd ed. New York: Stockton Press, 1985. (AM 1 .H78)

The authors conduct a tour of thirty-five thousand museums throughout the world, providing directory information and descriptions of each.

Guide to American Art Schools, ed. and compiled by John D. Werenko. Boston: G. K. Hall, 1987. (N 328 .W47)

Directory information for U.S. art schools, including degrees, majors, location, history, preparation, portfolio requirements, and undergraduate and graduate admissions requirements.

International Directory of Arts: 1991–1992. 2 vols. 20th ed. Frankfurt: Art Address, 1992. (N 50 .I6)

Directory information to the arts and artists of the world alphabetically by country in the language of the host country. Includes advertisements.

The Official Museum Directory. Washington, D.C.: The American Association of Museums, annual. (AM 10 .A204)

Institutional and biographical directory of all the museums in America and their related agencies, professional organizations, and staff.

* *Awards, Honors & Prizes.* (AS 8 .A87)

Guides and Handbooks

The Oxford Companion to Art, ed. by Harold Osborne. New York: Oxford University Press, 1970. (N 33 .09)

Signed articles by scholars in the field, illustrations, and names, subjects, schools, and concepts in art.

The Oxford Companion to the Decorative Arts, ed. by Harold Osborne. London: Oxford University Press, 1975. (NK 30 .093)

A companion to the decorative arts, such as furniture, glassmaking, and other arts; includes names and subjects and substantial bibliography.

Periodicals

American Artist Magazine
Art and Archaeology

Art Bulletin
Art Digest
Art Gallery
Art in America
Art International
Art Journal
Art Today
Artforum
Artnews
Arts
Arts Magazine
Artists Magazine
Connoisseur
Graphics
ID (Industrial Design)
Museum Studies
Parnassus
Portfolio
Sculpture Magazine
Smithsonian
Studio International

Thesauruses

Art and Architecture Thesaurus. 3 vols. The Getty Art History Information Program. New York: Oxford University Press, 1990. (Z 695.1 .A7)

A thesaurus of documents, terms, concepts, styles, periods, and people in the arts and fine arts throughout the world.

SELECT SUBJECT HEADINGS, BREAKDOWNS, AND CALL NUMBERS

Fine Arts (N 1 - NX 820)

Visual Arts (N 1 - N 9165)

Periodicals (N 1 - N 8)
Yearbooks (N 9)
Societies (N 10 - N 17)

Congresses (N 21 - N 23)
Collected Writings (N 25 - N 27)
Encyclopedias (N 31)
Dictionaries (N 33)
Terminology (N 34)
Biography (N 45)
Artists' Marks and Monograms (N 45)
Directories (N 50)
Theory. Philosophy (N 61 - N 72)
Study and Teaching (N 81 - N 390)
Art Museums, Galleries (N 400 - N 4040)
Exhibitions (N 4390 - N 5098)
Private Collections (N 5200 - N 5299)
History (N 5300 - N 7418)
General Works (N 7420 - N 7525)
Special Subjects (N 7560 - N 8266)
Art as a Profession (N 8350 - N 8356)
Art Studios, Materials, Etc. (N 8510 - N 8553)
Examination and Conservation (N 8555 - N 8580)
Economics of Art (N 8600 - N 8675)
Art and the State (N 8700 - N 9165)

Architecture (NA 1 - NA 9425)

Architecture (General) (NA 1 - NA 60)
Periodicals (NA 1 - NA 6)
Yearbooks (NA 9)
Societies (NA 10)
Congresses (NA 21)
Collected Writings (NA 25 - NA 27)
Encyclopedias and Dictionaries (NA 31)
Biographies (NA 40)
Directories (NA 50 - NA 55)
Architecture and the State (NA 100 - NA 130)
History (NA 200 - NA 1613)
Architecture as a Profession (NA 1995 - NA 1997)
Study and Teaching (NA 2000 - NA 2320)
Competitions (NA 2335 - NA 2360)
Museums (NA 2400 - NA 2460)
General Works (NA 2500 - NA 2599)
Architectural Design (NA 2700 - NA 2800)
Details and Decorations (NA 2810 - NA 4050)

Special Classes of Buildings (NA 4100 - NA 8480)
Aesthetics of Cities (NA 9000 - NA 9425)

Sculpture (NB 1 - NB 1952)

General (NB 1 - NB 50)
History (NB 60 - NB 1115)
Study and Teaching (NB 1120 - NB 1133)
General Works (NB 1135 - NB 1150)
Design and Technique (NB 1160 - NB 1195)
Restoration of Sculptures (NB 1199)
Special Materials (NB 1208 - NB 1270)
Motion, Color, Etc. (NB 1272 - NB 1291)
Special Forms (NB 1293 - NB 1310)

Drawing. Design. Illustration (NC 1 - NC 1940)

General (NC 1 - NC 45)
History of Drawing (NC 50 - NC 376)
Study and Teaching (NC 390 - NC 670)
General Works (NC 703 - NC 725)
Technique (NC 730 - NC 757)
Special Subjects (NC 760 - NC 825)
Graphic Art Materials (NC 850 - NC 915)
Conservation and Restoration (NC 930)
Illustration (NC 950 - NC 995)
Commercial Art (NC 997 - NC 1003)
Imagerie Populaire (NC 1280)
Pictorial Humor, Caricature, Etc. (NC 1300 - NC 1766)
Posters (NC 1800 - NC 1855)
Greeting Cards, Invitations, Etc. (NC 1860 - NC 1890)
Copying, Enlarging, and Reduction (NC 1920 - NC 1940)

Painting (ND 1 - ND 3416)

General (ND 25 - ND 47)
History (ND 49 - ND 1113)
Study and Teaching (ND 1115 - ND 1120)
General Works (ND 1130 - ND 1156)
Special Subjects (ND 1290 - ND 1460)
Technique and Materials (ND 1470 - ND 1660)
Watercolor Painting (ND 1700 - ND 2495)
Mural Painting (ND 2550 - ND 2888)
Illumination of Manuscripts and Books (ND 2890 - ND 3416)

Print Media (NE 1 - NE 2890)

Printmaking and Engraving (NE 1 - NE 978)
Wood Engraving (NE 1000 - NE 1352)
Metal Engraving (NE 1400 - NE 1879)
Etching and Aquatint (NE 1940 - NE 1975)
Serigraphy (NE 2236 - NE 2240)
Monotype (Printmaking) (NE 2242 - NE 2246)
Lumiprints (NE 2685)
Engravings on Glass (NE 2690)
Printing of Engravings (NE 2800 - NE 2890)

Decorative Arts (NK 1 - NK 9955)

Decorative Arts (NK 1 - NK 1133)
Arts and Crafts Movement (NK 1135 - NK 1149)
Decoration and Ornament (NK 1160 - NK 1678)
Interior Decoration (NK 1700 - NK 3505)
Other Art and Art Industries (NK 3600 - NK 9955)

Arts in General (NX 1 - NX 820)

Religious Arts (NX 654 - NX 694)
Patronage of the Arts (NX 700 - NX 750)
Special Art Centers (NX 798 - NX 820)

Humanities

HISTORY

Abstracts/Digests and Indexes

America: History and Life. Santa Barbara, Calif.: ABC-Clio, quarterly. (E 178 .A48)

Abstracts on the study of the United States and its immediate neighbors. North America, Canada, and all the regions of the United States.

Historical Abstracts. Santa Barbara, Calif.: ABC-Clio, quarterly. (D 299 .H52)

Historical Abstracts comes in two parts. Part A covers modern history from 1450 to 1914. Part B covers twentieth-century history from 1914 to the present. The abstracts are arranged generally by topic and by country.

* *American Humanities Index.* (AI 3 .A7)
* *Arts and Humanities Citation Index.* (AI 3 .A63)
* *Book Review Digest.* (Z 1210 .C95)
* *British Humanities Index.* (AI 3 .B7)
* *Dictionary of Historic Documents.* (D 9 .K63)
* *Dissertation Abstracts International.* (Z 5055 .U5)
* *Humanities Index.* (AI 3 .H85)
* *Index to Book Reviews in the Humanities.* (Z 1035 .A1 I63)
* *New York Times Index.* (AI 21 .N44)

Almanacs and Yearbooks

The Almanac of American History, ed. by Arthur M. Schlesinger, Jr. New York: G. P. Putnam's Sons, 1983. (E 174.5 .A45)

A chronologically arranged almanac that provides facts and dates for some of the most significant cultural, political, and socioeconomic events in the history of the United States. Includes index.

* *Annual Register: A Record of World Events.* (D 2 .A7)
* *Chase's Annual Events: The Day-by-Day Directory.* (D 11.5 .C48)
* *Information Please Almanac.* (AY 64 .I55)
* *World Almanac and Book of Facts.* (AY 67 .N5 W7)

Anthologies and Collections

* *Great Documents of Western Civilization.* (CB 245 .V5)
* *Historic Documents.* (E 839.5 .H57)

Atlases

The Atlas of Archaeology, ed. by K. Branigan. London: St. Martin's Press, 1982. (CC 165 .A83)

An atlas of maps covering archaeological discoveries organized by continent; includes a gazetteer, a glossary, and an index.

Atlas of Medieval Europe, by Donald Matthew. New York: Facts on File, 1983. (CB 351 .M293)

An atlas of maps and explanatory text on the history of medieval Europe, including chronological tables, a gazetteer, and an index.

Historical and Cultural Atlas of African Americans, by Molefi K. Asante and Mark T. Mattson. New York: Macmillan, 1991. (E 185 .A8)

Covers African origins, slavery, the Civil War, reconstruction, segregation, and the civil rights era. Includes chronology, bibliography, a graphics directory, and an index.

The World Atlas of Archaeology. London: Mitchell Beazley International, 1985. (G 1046 .E15 W613)

Archaeological discoveries organized by geographical regions and historical epochs, including a bibliography, a glossary, and an index.

* *National Geographic Historical Atlas of the U.S.* (G 1201 .S1 N3)
* *We the People.* (G 1201 .E1 A4)

Bibliographies

American Studies: An Annotated Bibliography, ed. by Jack Salzman. New York: Cambridge University Press, 1986. (E 169.1 .A486)

Bibliographies on United States studies in anthropology and folklore, art and architecture, history, literature, music, political science, popular culture, psychology, religion, science, and sociology.

Annual Bibliography of Victorian Studies. Edmonton, Alberta: Literary Information and Retrieval Database, annual. (CB 417 .A52)

Computer-generated bibliography of Victorian studies, focusing on history, literature, and individual authors. Author, title, and review indexes.

Archaeology: A Bibliographical Guide to the Basic Literature, by Robert F. Heizer, Thomas R. Hester, and Carol Graves. New York: Garland, 1980. (CC 165 .H44)

A bibliography (no annotations) covering broad topics in archaeology, such as field work and dating methods. Includes author index.

Asian American Studies: An Annotated Bibliography and Research Guide, ed. by Hyung-chan Kim. New York: Greenwood, 1989. (E 184 .06 K55)

General works and specific works on marriage and the family, culture, business, law, immigration and naturalization, and religion. Includes author and subject indexes.

Historiography: An Annotated Bibliography of Journal Articles, Books, and Dissertations, ed. by Susan K. Kinnell. 2nd ed. Santa Barbara, Calif.: ABC-Clio, 1987. (D 13 .H58)

Annotated bibliography of materials organized by broad topics, including economic history, social and intellectual history, and political history.

International Bibliography of Historical Sciences. New York and London: K. G. Saur, annual. (Z 6205 .I61)

Covers historical periodicals and significant aspects of historical inquiry. Includes name and geographical indexes.

Medieval Studies: A Bibliographical Guide, by Everett U. Crosby, C. Julian Bishko, and Robert L. Kellogg. New York: Garland, 1983. (CB 351 .C76)

An annotated bibliography of general works, encyclopedias, and dictionaries, translations, and biographical works. Includes a guide to scholars and learned societies.

Reference Sources in History: An Introductory Guide, by Ronald H. Fritze and others. Santa Barbara, Calif.: ABC-Clio, 1990. (D 20 .F74)

Bibliographic essays on reference works in history, focusing on secondary materials available in many libraries.

Writings on American History: A Subject Bibliography of Articles. Washington, D.C.: American Historical Society, annual. (E 178 .D61)

Articles on the colonial period, the American Revolution, the Civil War, the industrial era, and the twentieth century. Includes geographic and subject indexes.

* *Books in Print.* (Z 1215 .P972)
* *Cumulative Book Index.* (Z 1215 .U6)

Biographical Sources

The Blackwell Dictionary of Historians, ed. by John Cannon. London: Blackwell Reference, 1988. (D 14 .B58)

An international biographical dictionary of historians from earliest times to the present. Includes bibliographical references.

* *Dictionary of American Biography.* (E 176 .C8)
* *Monarchs, Rulers, Dynasties and Kingdoms of the World.* (D 107 .T36)
* *Who Was Who.* (DA 28 .W65)
* *Who Was Who in America.* (E 663 .W56)

Chronologies and Histories

The Cambridge Ancient History. New York: Macmillan/Cambridge University Press, 1927. (D 57 .C252)

A survey of history before human beings and the history of recorded civilizations from primitive times through the fourth century A.D. Includes maps, chronologies, illustrations, and historical tables.

The Cambridge Medieval History. New York: Macmillan/Cambridge University Press, 1967. (D 117 .C3)

Survey of history covering the Christian Roman Empire, Eastern and Western Europe, the Roman Empire, and the Byzantine Empire. Includes maps, chronologies, illustrations, and historical tables.

The New Cambridge Modern History. New York: Macmillan/ Cambridge University Press, 1979. (D 208 .N4)

Survey of modern history, beginning with the Renaissance, the Reformation, and the discovery of America and concluding with World War II. Includes maps, chronologies, illustrations, and historical tables.

* *Timetables of History.* (D 11 .G78)

Dictionaries and Encyclopedias

The Cambridge Encyclopedia of Archaeology, ed. by Andrew Sherratt. New York: Crown Publishers, 1980. (CC 165 .C3)

An illustrated encyclopedia covering broad archaeological concepts; includes a bibliography and index.

Dictionary of Historical Terms, by Chris Cook. New York: Macmillan, 1983 (D 9 .C67)

This is "a guide to the main themes, cliques, and innuendoes of over 1000 years of world history." Includes list of acronyms.

Dictionary of Medieval Civilization, by Joseph Dahmus. New York: Macmillan, 1984. (CB 351 .D24)

A one-volume dictionary of cultural and historical terms and proper names encountered in medieval studies.

Dictionary of the Middle Ages, ed. by Joseph R. Strayer. 13 vols. New York: Charles Scribner's Sons, 1983. (D 114 .D5)

Signed articles on subjects and proper names in the study of the Middle Ages, covering A.D. 500 to 1500. Covers the cultures of the Latin West, Asia Minor, the Near East, the Slavic states, and Muslim and Christian North Africa.

The Encyclopedia of Historic Places, ed. by Courtlandt Canby. 2 vols. New York: Facts on File, 1984. (D 9 .C29)

Places of historic importance throughout the world. Gives place-name, alternate spellings, modern name of the country where the place is located, its history, and significant events associated with the locale.

Encyclopedia of the Renaissance, ed. by Thomas G. Bergin. New York: Facts on File, 1987. (CB 361 .B43)

An illustrated encyclopedia of the European Renaissance, covering names and subjects in the era. Includes bibliography and chronological table.

The Macmillan Dictionary of Archaeology, ed. by Ruth D. Whitehouse. New York: Macmillan, 1983. (CC 70 .M33)

A dictionary of terms and place-names in archaeology with subject index and bibliography for further reading.

* *Dictionary of the History of Ideas.* (CB 5 .D52)
* *Harper Dictionary of Modern Thought.* (AG 5 .H19)

Directories

Directory of History Departments and Organizations in the United States and Canada: 1990–1991. Washington, D.C.: American Historical Association, 1990. (D 16.3 .G83)

A directory of schools offering degrees in history and historical organizations in the U.S. and Canada. Includes index of historians.

Grants, Fellowships, and Prizes of Interest to Historians: 1991–1992. Washington, D.C.: American Historical Association, 1991. (D 16.3 .G7)

Grants for degree-related research, prizes awarded for books, essays, articles, and dissertations. Includes bibliography. Alphabetical by school, agency, or award.

Hispanic Resource Directory: 1992–1994. Juneau, Alaska: Denali Press, 1992. (E 184 .S75 S27)

National, state and local Hispanic associations, educational institutions, bilingual education, Hispanic chambers of commerce, media, and statistics.

Historical Periodicals Directory. 5 vols. Santa Barbara, Calif.: ABC-Clio, 1981. (D 20 .H57)

A directory of historical periodicals oriented toward Western civilization, with volumes covering the United States and Canada, Europe, Russia, and Latin America.

* *Awards, Honors and Prizes.* (AS 8 .A87)
* *Directory of Archive and Manuscript Repositories.* (CD 3020 .D49)
* *Encyclopedia of Associations.* (HS 17 .G334)

Dissertations

Dissertations in History: An Index to Dissertations Completed in History Departments of United States and Canadian Universities: 1873–1980, by Warren F. Kuehl. 3 vols. University of Kansas Press, 1980. (D 21.3 .K83)

Numerical statistics on dissertations by school. Gives title of dissertation, author, and school accepting dissertation for degree. Indexed by name and subject.

Fact Books

* *Encyclopedia of American Facts and Dates.* (E 174.5 .C3)
* *Facts on File.* (D 410 .F3)
* *Famous First Facts.* (AG 5 .K315)
* *Keesing's Record of World Events.* (D 410 .K4)

Guides and Handbooks

The American Heritage Guide to Archaeology, by Warwick Bray and David Trump. New York: American Heritage Press, 1970. (CC 70 .B7)

A dictionary-handbook of place-names and terms in the study of archaeology. Illustrated, with maps and regional index.

Archives and Manuscript Repositories in the USSR: Moscow and Leningrad, by Patricia Kennedy Grimstead. Princeton, N.J.: Princeton University Press, 1972. (CD 1711 .G7)

Archives and Manuscript Repositories in the USSR: Estonia, Latvia, Lithuania, and Belorussia, by Patricia Kennedy Grimstead. Princeton, N.J.: Princeton University Press, 1981. (CD 1735 .B34 G74)

These two guides provide annotated bibliographies and directory information on archives containing cultural and political records. Both include author, title, and subject indexes.

British Archives: A Guide to Archive Resources in the United Kingdom, by Janet Foster and Julia Sheppard. Detroit: Gale, 1982. (CD 1040 .F67)

An alphabetical directory of archives in the U.K. Lists historical background, major collections, and description of facilities.

The Library of Congress: A Guide to Genealogical and Historical Research, by James C. Neagles. Salt Lake City, Utah: Ancestry Publishing, 1990. (E 180 .N43)

A handbook to doing genealogical research at the Library of Congress, with bibliographies and sections on different categories of research and resources by region and by state.

The New Guide to the Diplomatic Archives of Western Europe, ed. by Daniel H. Thomas and Lynn M. Case. Philadelphia: University of Pennsylvania Press, 1975. (CD 1001 .T4)

A list of archives by country; gives a brief history of the diplomacy and diplomatic organization of each country. Includes select bibliography.

Periodicals

American Historical Review
Current History
English History
Historian: A Journal of History
Historical Journal
History
History Today

Journal of Historical Studies
Journal of Modern History

Quote Books

* *Dictionary of Biographical Quotation.* (CT 773 .D38)
* *Familiar Quotations.* (PN 6081 .B27)
* *What They Said.* (D 410 .W49)

Statistical Sources

Statistical Handbook on U.S. Hispanics, compiled by Frank L. Schick and Renee Schick. Phoenix, Ariz.: Oryx Press, 1991. (E 184 .S75 S27)

Statistical data on demographics, immigration and naturalization, health, education, politics, economic conditions, and religion.

Statistical Record of Black America, compiled and ed. by Carrell Peterson Horton and Jessie Carney Smith. Detroit: Gale, 1990. (E 185.5 .S7)

Statistical data on demographics, business, economics, crime, education, the family, health, politics, and religion.

* *Historical Statistics of the United States.* (HA 202 .B87)

SELECT SUBJECT HEADINGS, BREAKDOWNS, AND CALL NUMBERS

Auxiliary Sciences of History (General) (C 1 - C 51)

History of Civilization (CB 3 - CB 481)

Archaeology (CC 1 - CC 960)

  Periodicals (CC 1 - CC 13)
  Yearbooks (CC 15 - CC 19)
  Societies (CC 20 - CC 39)
  Congresses (CC 51 - CC 64)
  Collected Works (CC 65 - CC 69)

Dictionaries. Encyclopedias (CC 70 - CC 72)
Philosophy. Theory (CC 72 - CC 81)
Study and Teaching (CC 93 - CC 97)
History of Archaeology (CC 100 - CC 106)
Archaeology as a Profession (CC 107 - CC 109)
Biography (CC 110 - CC 119)
Directories (CC 120 - CC 129)
Laws, Regulations, Etc. (CC 130 - CC 139)

Diplomatics. Archives. Seals (CD 1 - CD 6471)
Technical Chronology. Calendar (CE 1 - CD 97)
Numismatics (CJ 1 - CJ 6661)
Inscriptions. Epigraphy (CN 1 - CN 1355)
Heraldry (CR 1 - CR 6305)
Genealogy (CS 1 - CS 3090)
Biography (CT 21 - CT 9999)

History (General and Old World) (D 1 - D 1075)

Ancient History (D 51 - D 95)
Medieval History (D 111 - D 203)
Modern History (D 204 - D 475)
World War I (D 501 - D 680)
World War II (D 731 - D 838)
Post-War History, 1945 (D 839 - D 850)
Developing Countries (D 880 - D 888)
Eastern Hemisphere (D 890 - D 893)
Europe (General) (D 901 - D 1075)

Great Britain (DA 1 - DA 995)
Austria (DB 1 - DB 879)
France (DC 1 - DC 947)
Germany (DD 1 - DD 905)
Mediterranean Region (DE 1 - DE 100)
Greece (DF 10 - DF 951)
Italy (DG 11 - DG 999)
Netherlands (Low Countries) (DH 1 - DH 925)
Netherlands (Holland) (DJ 1 - DJ 500)
Eastern Europe (DJK 1 - DJK 77)
Soviet Union (DK 1 - DK 873)
Northern Europe (DL 1 - DL 1180)
Spain (DP 1 - DP 402)
Switzerland (DQ 1 - DQ 851)
Balkan Peninsula (DR 1 - DR 2285)
Asia (DS 1 - DS 937)

Africa (DT 1 - DT 995)
Oceania (South Seas) (DU 1 - DU 950)
Gypsies (DX 101 - DX 301)

America (E 11 - E 740)
America (General) (E 11 - E 29)
North America (E 31 - E 46)
Indians (E 51 - E 99)
Discovery of America (E 101 - E 135)

United States (General) (E 151 - E 740)

   Elements in the Population (E 184 - E 185.98)
   Colonial History (E 186 - E 199)
   Revolution (E 201 - E 298)
   Revolution to the Civil War (E 300 - E 453)
   Civil War (E 456 - E 655)
   Late Nineteenth Century (E 661 - E 738)
   Twentieth Century (E 740)

United States Local History (F 1 - F 975)

LITERATURE

Abstracts, Digests, and Indexes

The Columbia Granger's Index to Poetry. 9th ed. New York: Columbia University Press, 1990. (PN 1021 .G7)

A list of poetry anthologies where the poems it indexes can be found. The main sections consist of a title and first-line index, an author index, and a subject index. The new *Columbia* edition indexes more than 100,000 poems. Older editions are just called *The Granger's Index to Poetry*.

Index to Plays in Periodicals, by Dean H. Keller. Metuchen, N.J.: Scarecrow, 1990. (PN 1721 .K44)

Indexes thousands of plays that have appeared in more than one hundred periodicals. Different volumes cover different periods. Includes author and title index.

Magill's Masterplots Series.

The *Magill's Masterplots Series,* edited by Frank N. Magill and published by the Salem Press, provide essay reviews, character analysis, plot summaries, and digests of the world's literatures.

Masterplots. (PN 44 .M33)
Masterplots II: Non-fiction. (PN 44 .M345)
Masterplots II: American Fiction Series. (PN 846 .M37)
Masterplots II: Short Story Series. (PN 3326 .M27)
Masterplots II: World Fiction Series. (PN 3326 .M28)
Masterplots II: Drama Series. (PN 6112.5 .M37)

Ottemiller's Index to Plays in Collections: An Author and Title Index to Plays Appearing in Collections Published Between 1900 and 1985, revised and enlarged by Billie M. Connor and Helene G. Mochedlover. Metuchen, N.J.: Scarecrow, 1988. (PN 1631 .O77)

Organized alphabetically by author, including a list of collections indexed and a title index.

Poetry Index Annual. New York: Poetry Index Press. (PN 1022 .P6)

Since 1982 this index has provided access to poems in anthologies; listed by author, title, first line, and keyword.

Play Index. New York: Wilson. (PN 1631 .P34)

Published since 1949, the *Play Index* provides indexing to plays by author, title, and subject. Each volume includes plot and cast analysis for plays. Now published in five-year cumulations.

The Reader's Digest of Books, by Helen Rex Keller. New York: Macmillan, 1929. (PN 44 .K4)

Though obviously dated, this digest provides plot summaries to hundreds of works in world literature. Organized alphabetically by title, it includes the author's dates and major characters.

* *American Humanities Index.* (AI 3 .A7)
* *Arts and Humanities Citation Index.* (AI 3 .A63)

* *Book Review Digest.* (Z 1219 .C95)
* *Book Review Index.* (Z 1035 .A1 B6)
* *British Humanities Index.* (AI 3 .B7)
* *Dissertation Abstracts International.* (Z 5055 .U5)
* *Essay and General Literature Index.* (AI 3 .E752)
* *Humanities Index.* (AI 3 .H85)
* *Readers' Guide to Periodical Literature.* (AI 3 .R48)
* *Short Story Index.* (Z 5917 .S7)

Almanacs and Yearbooks

Magill's Literary Annual, ed. by Frank N. Magill. Englewood Cliffs, N.J.: Salem Press, annual. (PN 44 .M332)

Like Magill's *Masterplots,* this literary annual provides essay reviews of more than two hundred outstanding books that have published during the year under consideration.

Anthologies and Collections

The Norton Anthology of American Literature. 2 vols. New York: Norton. (PS 507 .N65)

The Norton Anthology of English Literature. 2 vols. New York: Norton. (PR 1105 .A2)

It doesn't matter which editions you have, these classic textbooks contain some of the acknowledged great works in American and English Literature, including poetry, prose, and drama. I wouldn't sell these at the end of the semester.

Bibliographies and Catalogs

Bibliographical Guide to the Study of the Literature of the USA, by Clarence Gohdes and Sanford E. Marovitz. Durham, N.C.: Duke University Press, 1984. (PS 88 .G6)

Poetry, fiction, and drama by region and ethnicity. Includes appendices on language and folklore.

Guide to American Literature, by Valmai Kirkham Fenster. Littleton, Colo.: Libraries Unlimited, 1983. (PS 88 .F46)

This guide provides bibliographical access to primary and secondary sources and guides to literature by genre, region, and ethnicity.

Key Sources in Comparative and World Literature: An Annotated Guide to Reference Materials, by George A. Thompson, Jr. New York: Ungar, 1980. (PN 523 .T56)

World literature organized by period, country and by genre, including sections on the classical and romantic periods.

Magill's Bibliography of Literary Criticism, ed. by Frank N. Magill. 4 vols. Englewood Cliffs, N.J.: Salem Press, 1979. (PN 523 .M29)

Bibliographies for the study of hundreds of literary works by thousands of authors in the Western literary tradition.

* *Books in Print.* (Z 1215 .P972)
* *Cumulative Book Index.* (Z 1215 .U6)
* *MLA International Bibliography.* (Z 7006 .M64)
* *National Union Catalog.* (Z 881 .A1 U518)

Biographical Sources

African American Writers, ed. by Valerie Smith. New York: Charles Scribner's Sons, 1991. (PS 153 .N5)

Signed biographical articles by scholars in the field include the writer's significant dates and works and bibliographical references.

American Women Writers: A Critical Reference Guide From Colonial Times to the Present, ed. by Lina Mainiero. 4 vols. New York: Ungar, 1979. (PS 147 .A4)

Signed biographical articles by scholars in the field include the writer's significant dates and works as well as bibliographical references.

British Writers, ed. by Ian Scott-Kilvert. New York: Charles Scribner's Sons, 1979. (PR 85 .B688)

A biographical reference to significant British authors and their works. Includes substantial bibliographies and index.

Contemporary Authors. Detroit: Gale. (PS 129 .C6)

Biographical information on living authors, summaries of their works and select criticism. Published irregularly in several different series.

Contemporary Dramatists. (PR 737 .C57)
Contemporary Novelists. (PR 883 .V55)
Contemporary Poets. (PN 603 .C6)

These three biographical sources, published by St. James Press of Chicago, provide biographical information on writers in each form, and information on their significant works, their education, and their careers.

Cyclopedia of Literary Characters, ed. by Frank N. Magill. New York: Harper & Row, 1963. (PN 44 .M34)

Includes some sixteen thousand characters from more than thirteen hundred works of world literature. Organized by title, with description of the work and its principal characters.

Dictionary of Literary Biography. Detroit: Gale. (PS 21 .D52)

The *DLB,* organized by period and by genre, is a voluminous reference to both famous and lesser-known writers of all periods and in all forms. New volumes are published irregularly.

An Encyclopedia of Continental Women Writers, ed. by Katharina M. Wilson. 2 vols. New York: Garland, 1991. (PN 481 .E5)

Signed biographical articles by scholars in the field on women writers in Eastern and Western European countries.

The International Authors and Writers Who's Who: 1991/ 92, edited by Ernest Kay. 12th ed. Cambridge: International Biographical Centre, 1991. (PN 451 .I8)

Biographical information on world authors. Includes appendices on literary agents and organizations, pseudonyms, literary awards, and prizes.

Latin American Writers, ed. by Carlos A. Sole. 3 vols. New York: Charles Scribner's Sons, 1989. (PQ 7081 .A1 L37)

Signed articles by scholars in the field on individual writers from Spanish- and Portuguese-speaking countries.

The Originals: Who's Really Who in Fiction, by William Amos. London: Jonathan Cape, 1985. (PN 56.4 .A46)

Organized alphabetically by fictional character, this unique reference includes discussion of the works different fictional characters appeared in as well as the author's models for those characters.

Wilson Biographical Reference Books.

The H. W. Wilson Company of New York publishes several biographical reference works devoted to writers. They provide basic biographical information on the author under consideration as well as a list of their works:

Greek and Latin Authors: 800 BC–AD 1000. (PA 31 .G7)
European Authors: 1000–1900. (PN 451 .K8)
British Authors Before 1800. (PR 105 .K9)
British Authors of the Nineteenth Century. (PR 451 .K8)
American Authors: 1600–1900. (PS 128 .K96)
Twentieth Century Authors. (PN 451 .K84)
World Authors: 1950–1970. (PN 451 .W3)
World Authors: 1970–1975. (PN 451 .W67)
World Authors: 1975–1980. (PN 451 .W672)

Chronologies and Histories

A Chronological Outline of American Literature, by Samuel J. Rogal. New York: Greenwood, 1987. (PS 92 .R67)

Organized by century, this chronology covers births, deaths, and significant events and literary works in American literary history. Includes index of authors and events.

Literary History of the United States, ed. by Robert E. Spiller and others. 2 vols. New York: Macmillan, 1974. (PS 88 .L522)

This two-volume history provides substantial essays and bibliographies on the most significant authors and periods of American literary history. Volume one provides the histories and volume two provides the bibliographies.

Dictionaries and Encyclopedias

Allusions—Cultural, Literary, Biblical and Historical: A Thematic Guide, ed. by Laurence Urdang and Frederick G. Ruffner. 2nd ed. Detroit: Gale, 1986. (PN 43 .A4)

Includes 8,700 entries within 712 thematic categories such as acting, chance, error, honesty, satire, and youth. Includes bibliography and index.

Benét's Reader's Encyclopedia. New York: Harper & Row, 1987. (PN 41 .B4)

Benét's is a standard one-volume reference to the world's great authors and their literary works, literary characters, and literary themes.

Benét's Reader's Encyclopedia of American Literature, ed. by George Perkins and others. New York: HarperCollins, 1991. (PN 41 .B4)

A one-volume reference that covers American authors and American literature, literary characters, and literary themes.

Brewer's Dictionary of Phrase and Fable, ed. by Ivor H. Evans. 14th ed. New York: Harper & Row, 1989. (PN 43 .B65)

The first edition of *Brewer's* was published in 1870. Now an acknowledged classic, it is a dictionary of names, words, and phrases, often taken from literature, with cites to the works themselves.

The Concise Oxford Dictionary of Literary Terms, by Chris Baldick. New York: Oxford University Press, 1990. (PN 41 .C67)

A brief dictionary of terms used in literature and literary study, from aleatory to onomatopoeia to Zeitgeist.

Dictionary of American Literary Characters, ed. by Benjamin Franklin V. New York: Facts on File, 1991. (PS 374 .C43 D5)

An alphabetic listing of characters from American literature that cites to works in which they appeared and describes the real characters on which they were based.

A Dictionary of Literary Terms and Literary Theory, by J. A. Cuddon. 3rd. ed. London: Blackwell, 1991. (PN 41 .C83)

Covers technical terms in literature, as well as literary forms, genres, groups, schools and movements, phrases, motifs, themes, personalities, and concepts.

The Drama Dictionary, by Terry Hodgson. New York: New Amsterdam Books, 1988. (PN 1625 .H62)

A dictionary of subject terms that are used in dramatic literature and in literary and professional life of the theater.

Encyclopedia of World Literature in the 20th Century, ed. by Leonard S. Klein. 4 vols. New York: Ungar, 1981. (PN 771 .E5)

Signed articles by scholars in the field on the literature of each country, its major authors, and their major works.

European Writers, ed. by George Stade. 14 vols. New York: Charles Scribner's Sons, 1983. (PN 501 .E9)

Encyclopedic coverage of European writers by period, including the Middle Ages, the Age of Reason and Enlightenment, the Renaissance, the romantic century, and the twentieth century. Includes biographies, criticism, and bibliographies.

Longman Dictionary and Handbook of Poetry, by Jack Myers and Michael Simms. New York: Longman, 1985. (PN 1021 .M94)

Alphabetic list of terms in poetry, such as dithyramb and spondee. Includes appendices of rhetorical and poetical devices and topical bibliography.

McGraw-Hill Encyclopedia of World Drama, ed. by Stanley Hochman. 5 vols. New York: McGraw-Hill, 1984. (PN 1625 .M3)

Contains signed articles by scholars in the field on names and subjects in world drama, with illustrations and bibliographies.

Twentieth-Century American Literature, ed. by Harold Bloom. 7 vols. New York: Chelsea House, 1985. (PS 221 .T834)

Encyclopedic coverage of American literature listed by author, including an author biography, discussion of the author's works, and selected criticism.

* *Bernstein's Reverse Dictionary.* (PE 1591 .B45)
* *Dictionary of the History of Ideas.* (CB 5 .D52)
* *Exaltation of Larks.* (PE 1689 .L5)
* *Oxford English Dictionary.* (PE 1625 .087)
* *Partridge's Concise Dictionary of Slang.* (PE 3721 .P3)
* *Pseudonyms and Nicknames Dictionary.* (CT 120 .P8)

Directories

Literary Market Place. New York: Bowker, annual. (PN 161 .L5)

LMP lists book publishers, editorial services, literary agents, book manufacturers, and other sources of information and expertise for people in the book trade. Bowker also publishes an international volume, called the *ILMP*.

* *Awards, Honors and Prizes.* (AS 8 .A87)
* *Directory of Archive and Manuscript Repositories in the U.S.* (CD 3020 .D48)
* *International Directory of Little Magazines and Small Presses.* (Z 6944 .L5 D5)
* *Standard Periodical Directory.* (Z 6951 .S78)

Guides and Handbooks

The Art of Literary Research, by Richard D. Altick. New York: Norton, 1975. (PR 56 .A68)

Altick's book provides fundamental instruction in literary research and covers literary scholarship, research materials, manuscripts, libraries, and archives.

Drury's Guide to Best Plays, by James M. Salem. Metuchen, N.J.: Scarecrow, 1987. (PN 1655 .D78)

Organized alphabetically by playwright, this guide provides notes on plot, characters, and production for hundreds of plays, both historical and contemporary.

The Feminist Companion to Literature in English: Women Writers From the Middle Ages to the Present, by Virginia Blain and others. New Haven, Conn.: Yale University Press, 1990. (PR 111 .F45)

Biographical information on women writers, their significant dates, and discussion of their works.

Literary Research Guide, ed. by Margaret C. Patterson. 2nd ed. New York: Modern Language Association, 1983. (PN 43 .P37)

This research guide is published by MLA, the association that represents America's English professors and other researchers and writers. It includes sections on the literature of the classical world, Afro-American, Scottish, Indian, and Welsh literatures, among others.

The New Guide to Modern World Literature, by Martin Seymour-Smith. London: Peter Bedrick Books, 1985. (PN 771 .S4)

This guide provides an alphabetical reference to modern literature, organized by country, which includes bibliographies and an index.

The Oxford Companions to Literature.

The works listed below are part of the *Oxford Companion* series, which provides a substantial introduction to the literature of other cultures in one volume and in dictionary form. Each volume is carefully edited by literary scholars:

The Oxford Companion to American Literature. (PS 21 .H3)
The Oxford Companion to Canadian Literature. (PR 9180.2 .O94)
The Oxford Companion to Canadian Theater. (PN 2301 .O94)
The Oxford Companion to Children's Literature. (PN 1008.5 .C37)
The Oxford Companion to Classical Literature. (PA 31 .H69)
The Oxford Companion to French Literature. (PQ 41 .H3)

The Oxford Companion to German Literature. (PT 41 .G3)
The Oxford Companion to Spanish Literature. (PQ 6006 .O93)
The Oxford Companion to the Theater. (PN 2035 .09)

The Oxford Guide to the English Language, ed. by E. S. C. Weiner and Joyce Hawkins. New York: Oxford University Press, 1984. (PE 1628 .O87)

Essential articles on the history, literature, and contemporary usage of the English language.

* *The Reader's Advisor.* (Z 1035 .R42)

Periodicals

The American Book Review
Bloomsbury Review
Cambridge Quarterly
Criterion
Criticism
The Hungry Mind Review
Literary Journal
The New York Review of Books
The New York Times Book Review
San Francisco Review of Books
Washington Post Bookworld
World Literature Today

Quote Books

* *Dictionary of Biographical Quotation.* (CT 773 .D38)
* *Familiar Quotations.* (PN 6081 .B27)

Reviews and Criticism

The Gale Literary Criticism Series.

Gale Research of Detroit publishes several guides to literary criticism that come out every year and cover the entire history of literature. Each series is devoted to a particular aspect or period of literary criticism:

CLC: Contemporary Literary Criticism. (PN 771 .C61)
TCLC: Twentieth-Century Literary Criticism. (PN 771 .C27)
NCLC: Nineteenth-Century Literary Criticism. (PN 761 .N5)
LC: Literature Criticism from 1400 to 1800. (PN 701 .L52)
SC: Shakespearean Criticism. (PR 2965 .S43)
CMLC: Classical and Medieval Literature Criticism. (PN 610 .C53)
Children's Literature Review. (PN 1009 .A1)
Short Story Criticism. (PN 3373 .S56)
Poetry Criticism. (PN 1010 .P449)
Drama Criticism. (PN 1625 .D72)

Magill's Critical Surveys.

Salem Press also publishes *Magill's Critical Surveys.* These reference works provide critical essays and bibliographies of the authors represented and their works:

Critical Survey of Drama. (PN 1625 .C74)
Critical Survey of Literary Theory. (PN 45 .C74)
Critical Survey of Long Fiction. (PN 3451 .C75)
Critical Survey of Poetry. (PN 1111 .C7)
Critical Survey of Short Fiction. (PN 3373 .C75)
Survey of Contemporary Literature. (PN 44 .M34)
Survey of Modern Fantasy Literature. (PN 56 .F34)
Survey of Science Fiction Literature. (PN 3448 .S45)

Style Books

* *Chicago Manual of Style.* (Z 253 .U69)
* *Elements of Style.* (PN 1408 .S772)
* *Manual for Writers of Term Papers.* (LB 2369 .T8)
* *MLA Style Manual.* (PN 147 .A28)

SELECT SUBJECT HEADINGS, BREAKDOWNS, AND CALL NUMBERS

Literature (General) (PN 1 - PN 6790)

Periodicals (PN 1 - PN 9)
Societies (PN 20 - PN 30)
Theory. Philosophy (PN 45 - PN 57)
Study and Teaching (PN 59 - PN 72)

Criticism (PN 80 - PN 99)
Authorship (PN 101 - PN 245)
Literary History (PN 441 - PN 1009.5)
Poetry (PN 1010 - PN 1525)
The Monologue (PN 1530)
The Dialogue (PN 1551)
The Performing Arts. Show Business (PN 1560 - PN 1590)
Drama (PN 1600 - PN 3307)
Prose (PN 3311 - PN 3503)
Oratory. Elocution, Etc. (PN 4001 - PN 4355)
Journalism (PN 4699 - PN 5650)
Collections of General Literature (PN 6010 - PN 6790)

English Literature (PR 1 - PR 9680)

Literary History and Criticism (PR 1 - PR 56)
Criticism (PR 57 - PR 78)
Women Authors (PR 111 - PR 116)
Relations to Other Literatures (PR 125 - PR 138)
By Period (PR 161 - PR 479)
Poetry (PN 500 - PR 681)
Drama (PR 641 - PR 739)
Prose (PR 750 - PR 888)
Oratory (PR 901 - PR 907)
Diaries (PR 908)
Letters (PR 911 - PR 917)
Essays (PR 921 - PR 927)
Wit and Humor (PR 931 - PR 937)
Folk Literature (PR 951 - PR 981)
Collections of English Literature (PR 1098 - PR 1369)
Anglo-Saxon Literature (PR 1490 - PR 1799)
Anglo-Norman Period (PR 1803 - PR 2165)
English Renaissance (1500–1640) (PR 2199 - PR 3195)
17th and 18th Centuries (PR 3291 - PR 3785)
19th Century (PR 3991 - PR 5990)
1900–1960 (PR 6000 - PR 6049)
1961– (PR 6050 - PR 6076)
English Literature: Provincial/Local. (PR 8309 - PR 9680)

American Literature (PS 1 - PS 3576)

Biography, Memoirs, Letters (PS 126 - PS 138)
Women Authors (PS 147 - PS 152)
By Period (PS 185 - PS 228)

Special Regions, States, Etc. (PS 241 - PS 286)
Poetry (PS 301 - PS 325)
Drama (PS 330 - PS 352)
Prose (PS 360 - PS 379)
Oratory (PS 400 - PS 408)
Diaries (PS 409)
Letters (PS 410 - PS 418)
Essays (PS 420 - PS 428)
Wit and Humor. Satire (PS 430 - PS 438)
Folk Literature (PS 451 - PS 478)
Collections of American Literature (PS 501 - PS 688)
Individual Authors (PS 700 - PS 3576)

Canadian Literature (PS 8001 - PS 8599)

Fiction and Juvenile Belles Lettres (PZ 1 - PZ 90)

Fiction in English (PZ 1 - PZ 4)
Juvenile Belles Lettres (PZ 5 - PZ 90)

PHILOSOPHY

Abstracts and Indexes

The Philosopher's Index. Bowling Green, Ohio: Philosophy Documentation Center, 1980. (B 53 .P4)

Indexes and abstracts "major philosophy journals" in English, French, German, Spanish, Italian, and other languages by author and by subject. Indexes book reviews.

* *American Humanities Index.* (AI 3 .A7)
* *Arts and Humanities Citation Index.* (AI 3 .A63)
* *British Humanities Index.* (AI 3 .B7)
* *Dissertation Abstracts International.* (Z 5055 .U5)
* *Humanities Index.* (AI 3 .H85)
* *Index to Book Reviews in the Humanities.* (Z 1035 .A1 I63)

Bibliographies

A Bibliography of Philosophical Bibliographies, ed. by Herbert Guerry. Westport, Conn.: Greenwood, 1977. (B 53 .G84)

A bibliography of bibliographies, including bibliographies of individual philosophers and historical and contemporary philosophical subjects.

The History of Ideas: A Bibliographical Introduction, ed. by Jeremy L. Tobey. 2 vols. Santa Barbara, Calif.: CLIO Press, 1975. (B 52 .T65)

An annotated bibliography of resources in the study of philosophy and the history of ideas from ancient times through early modern Europe.

Mythologies of the World: A Guide to Sources, by Ron Smith. Urbana, Ill.: National Council of Teachers of English, 1981. (BL 311 .S63)

These bibliographical essays on world mythology are organized by geographic region, representing Eastern, Western, and various other mythological cultures.

Philosophy Journals and Serials: An Analytical Guide, compiled by Douglas H. Ruben. Westport, Conn.: Greenwood, 1985. (B 72 .R72)

A descriptive bibliography of journal publications in philosophy, including their history, their audience, and where they are indexed and abstracted.

* *Books in Print.* (Z 1215 .P972)

Biographical Resources

Thinkers of the Twentieth Century, ed. by Roland Turner. Chicago: St. James Press, 1987. (CT 120 .T45)

Biographical sketches with bibliographical references to the major philosophers and other thinkers of the century. Articles signed by scholars in the field.

Women of Classical Mythology: A Biographical Dictionary, by Robert E. Bell. Santa Barbara, Calif.: ABC-Clio, 1991. (BL 715 .B445)

Biographical dictionary of women in Greek and Roman mythology, which also provides a list of the men in their lives.

Women Philosophers: A Bio-critical Sourcebook, by Ethel M. Kersey. New York: Greenwood, 1989. (B 105 .W6 K47)

A biographical reference to women in philosophy, by historical period, country, and discipline or principal subject of writings. Includes name index.

Chronologies and Histories

* *Timetables of History.* (D 11 .G78)

Dictionaries and Encyclopedias

A Concise Dictionary of Indian Philosophy: Sanskrit Terms Defined in English, by John Grimes. State University of New York Press, 1989. (B 131 .G67)

Philosophical terms, translated and transliterated from Sanskrit to English, with pronunciation guide.

Dictionary of Philosophy and Psychology, ed. by James Mark Baldwin. 3 vols. Reprint. New York: Peter Smith, 1960. (B 41 .B3)

A dated but durable dictionary of two related subjects in the social sciences that includes signed articles by scholars in the field on philosophy and religion.

Dictionary of Philosophy and Religion, by William L. Reese. Atlantic Highlands, N.J.: Humanities Press, 1980. (B 41 .R43)

This subject-specific dictionary includes coverage of individuals, subjects, and concepts.

The Encyclopedia of Eastern Philosophy and Religion, ed. by Stephan Schuhmacher and Gert Woerner. Boston: Shambala, 1989. (BL 1005 .L4813)

An encyclopedia of the major eastern religions and philosophies, including Buddhism, Hinduism, Taoism, and Zen. Includes bibliographies.

The Encyclopedia of Philosophy, ed. by Paul Edwards. New York: Macmillan, 1977. (B 41 .E5)

Contains signed articles by scholars in the field with bibliographies of works by and about significant philosophers.

The Mythology of All Races, ed. by Louis Herbert Gray. 13 vols. Reprint. New York: Cooper Square Publishers, Inc., 1964. (BL 25 .M8)

A dated but useful general reference to world mythologies; includes an index and bibliographies for each volume, covering Greek and Roman, Celtic, Semitic, Oceanic, and other mythological cultures.

Plato Dictionary, ed. by Morris Stockhammer. New York: Philosophical Library, 1963. (B 351 .S7)

A dictionary of terms as they are used in the text of Plato's works, taken from the Jowett translation.

The Woman's Encyclopedia of Myths and Secrets, by Barbara G. Walker. New York: Harper & Row, 1983. (BL 458 .W34)

An encyclopedia of mythology in which "the complex subject of sexism is approached from both the historical and the mythic viewpoints." Includes cross-references and marginal notes.

* *Dictionary of the History of Ideas.* (CB 5 .D52)
* *Harper Dictionary of Modern Thought.* (AG 5 .H19)

Directories

Directory of American Philosophers. Bowling Green, Ohio: Philosophical Documentation Center, biennial. (B 935 .D5)

A directory by state of philosophers in the United States and Canada. Includes notes on universities, assistantships, philosophical societies, and journals.

Guides and Handbooks

Bulfinch's Mythology, by Thomas Bulfinch. New York: Thomas Y. Crowell, 1970. (BL 310 .B82)

This single-volume work includes three classic Bulfinch studies of mythology from the mid-nineteenth century, *The Age of Fable, The Age of Chivalry,* and *The Age of Charlemagne.*

The Greek Myths, by Robert Graves. New York: George Braziller, 1957. (BL 781 .G65)

The Greek Myths is an illuminating and literate retelling of the greatest stories in Greek mythology by one of England's great twentieth-century poets.

Guide to Chinese Philosophy, by Charles Wei-Hsun Fu and Wing-Tsit Chan. Boston: G. K. Hall, 1978. (B 126 .F8)

A handbook for the study of Chinese philosophy with an overview of its history and annotated bibliographies of significant works.

The Handbook of Western Philosophy, ed. by G. H. R. Parkinson. New York: Macmillan, 1989. (B 804 .H17)

An encyclopedic treatment of Western philosophy covering broad topics such as theory of knowledge, metaphysics, and moral philosophy. Includes glossary of terms, chronology, index of names and subjects, and notes on contributors.

Research Guide to Philosophy, by Terrence N. Tice and Thomas P. Slavens. Chicago: American Library Association, 1983. (B 52 .T5)

A guide to the history of philosophy and particular areas of philosophical study. Includes bibliography of reference works.

Periodicals

American Philosophical Quarterly
History of Philosophy Quarterly

Idealist Studies
Inquiry
International Philosophical Quarterly
Journal of Philosophical Logic
Journal of Philosophy Studies
Journal of Philosophy
Journal of the History of Ideas
Journal of the History of Philosophy
Mind
New Scholasticism
Philosophical Quarterly
Philosophical Review
Philosophy East and West
Philosophy Today
Proceedings of the Aristotelian Society
Review of Metaphysics
Undergraduate Journal of Philosophy

Quote Books

* *Dictionary of Biographical Quotation.* (CT 773 .D38)
* *Familiar Quotations.* (PN 6081 .B27)

Reviews

World Philosophy: Essay-Reviews of 225 Major Works, ed.
by Frank N. Magill. 5 vols. Salem Press, 1982. (B 29 .W68)

Provides historical coverage of major philosophical works from the
sixth century B.C. to the late twentieth century. Includes brief bibliographies of "recommended reading" following each work.

SELECT SUBJECT HEADINGS, BREAKDOWNS, AND CALL NUMBERS

Philosophy (B 1 - B 5739)

Periodicals (B 1 - B 8)
Societies (B 11 - B 35)
Dictionaries (B 40 - B 52)
Methodology (B 53 - B 68)

General Works (B 69 - B 105)
Ancient; 600 B.C.–A.D. 430 (B 108 - B 708)
Medieval; 430–1450 (B 720 - B 765)
Renaissance (B 770 - B 785)
Modern; 1450/1600–   (B 790 - B 5739)

RELIGION

Abstracts and Indexes

Index Islamicus: Current Books, Articles and Papers on Islamic Subjects. London: Mansell. (Z 7835 .M6 L62)

This index covers a wide range of studies in Islamic subjects including education, law, and philosophy. Organized by subject and by Islamic country. Published quarterly with five-year cumulations.

Religious and Theological Abstracts. Myerstown, Pa.: Religious and Theological Abstracts, Inc., quarterly. (BR 1 .R286)

First published in 1956, these are "nonsectarian" abstracts of books and journal articles on biblical, theological, historical, and practical aspects of religion.

* *American Humanities Index.* (AI 3 .A7)
* *British Humanities Index.* (AI 3 .B7)
* *Humanities Index.* (AI 3 .H85)

Almanacs and Yearbooks

The Bible Almanac, ed. by James I. Packer and others. Nashville, Tenn.: Thomas Nelson Publishers, 1980. (BS 635.2 .B4)

A fact and date reference to studies of biblical times, including art, archaeology, government, laws, and music.

Atlases

Historical Atlas of the Religions of the World, ed. by Ismail Ragi al Farugi. New York: Macmillan, 1974. (BL 80.2 .F28)

Covers all the religions of the world in maps and pictures and identifies origins and distribution of religious belief across the world.

Zondervan NIV Atlas of the Bible, by Carl G. Rusmussen. Grand Rapids, Mich.: Zondervan, 1989. (BS 630 .R37)

Geographical and historical atlas of the Bible and biblical lands, with chronology, bibliography, gazetteer, and index.

Oxford Bible Atlas, ed. by Herbert G. May. 3rd ed. New York: Oxford, 1984. (BS 630 .O96)

Maps with descriptive text and archaeological notes covering the lands of the Bible. Includes gazetteer and index.

Bibliographies

The Book of Jewish Books: A Reader's Guide to Judaism, by Ruth S. Frank and William Wollheim. New York: Harper & Row, 1986. (BM 561 .B66)

An annotated bibliography of Jewish books, including children's books, history, and literature. Organized by subject and alphabetical by author.

Buddhism: A Subject Index to Periodical Articles in English: 1728–1971, by Yushin Yoo. Metuchen, N.J.: Scarecrow Press, 1973. (Z 7860 .Y65)

Bibliographical guide to the study of Buddhism that provides author and subject indexes to periodical literature in English.

Guide to Islam, by David Ede. Boston: G. K. Hall, 1983. (BP 161.2 .G84)

Annotated bibliographies on Islam, including the early, medieval, and modern periods of Islamic civilization. Includes bibliographies of social and cultural aspects as well as religion.

The Howard University Bibliography of African and Afro-American Religious Studies, compiled by Ethel L. Williams and Clifton F. Brown. Scholarly Resources, Inc., 1977. (BR 563 .N4)

A bibliography of African heritage, Christianity and slavery, religious life and the civil rights movement. Includes manuscript index and autobiographical and biographical notes.

Judaism and Christianity: A Guide to the Reference Literature, by Edward D. Starkey. Littleton, Colo.: Libraries Unlimited, 1991. (BM 45 .S83)

Information on reference literature, including bibliographies, indexes, dictionaries, encyclopedias, and biographical works, covering Judaism and Christianity in religious studies.

Religion and Society in North America: An Annotated Bibliography, ed. by Robert Brunkow. Santa Barbara, Calif.: ABC-Clio, 1983.

Annotated bibliography of broad topics in religion in the United States and Canada. Indexed by author and subject. Includes list of periodicals.

Religious Books: 1876–1982. 4 vols. New York: Bowker, 1983. (BL 48 .R44)

A bibliography by author, title, and subject and an index to currently available religious books in print.

Research Guide to Religious Studies, by John F. Wilson and Thomas P. Slavens. Chicago: American Library Association, 1982. (BL 41 .W5)

A handbook on religious scholarship with an annotated reference bibliography and an author, title, and subject index.

Theological and Religious Reference Materials, ed. by G. E. Gorman and Lyn Gorman. 3 vols. Westport, Conn.: Greenwood, 1984. (BS 511.2 .G67)

An annotated bibliography of bibliographies, dictionaries, handbooks, and general reference works in the area of religious studies.

Biographical Sources

The Biographical Directory of Negro Ministers, by Ethel L. Williams. 3rd ed. Boston: G. K. Hall, 1975. (BF 563 .N4 W5)

A biographical source for African-American clergy in the United States with a geographical index. Lists vital statistics, education, and service in the ministry.

Butler's Lives of the Saints, ed. by Herbert Thurston and Donald Attwater. 4 vols. New York: P. J. Kenedy & Sons, 1956. (BX 4654 .B8)

First published in 1756–59 by Alban Butler, *Butler's Lives* is arranged chronologically, covering all saints by their days. Each volume covers three months.

A Dictionary of Angels: Including the Fallen Angels, by Gustav Davidson. New York: Free Press, 1967. (BL 477 .D3)

A biographical dictionary of angels, whose names are explained, translated, and discussed in terms of origin. Entries come mostly from literary works, which are listed in the substantial bibliography.

Dictionary of American Religious Biography, ed. by Henry Warner Bowden. Westport, Conn.: Greenwood, 1977. (BL 72 .B68)

Biographical sketches and brief bibliographies of more than four hundred historical and contemporary American religious figures.

Dictionary of Christian Biography: Literature, Sects and Doctrines, ed. by William Smith and Henry Wace. 4 vols. London: John Murray, 1877. (BR 97 .S65)

A who's who of Christianity from earliest times. Dated but exhaustive. Includes substantial biographies and articles on religious terms and subjects.

The Oxford Dictionary of Saints, by David Hugh Farmer. 2nd ed. New York: Oxford University Press, 1987. (BR 1710 .F34)

This is a who's who of saints; includes biographical sketches, legends, martyrdom, and canonization. Includes a list of "unsuccessful English candidates for canonization."

Who's Who in the New Testament, by Ronald Brownrigg. New York: Holt, Rinehart and Winston, 1971. (BS 2430 .B67)

Proper names of individuals who appear in the New Testament; includes maps and illustrations.

Chronologies and Histories

The Cambridge History of the Bible, ed. by P. R. Ackroyd and C. F. Evans. 3 vols. New York: Cambridge University Press, 1970. (BS 445 .C26)

History of biblical languages, texts, the Old and New Testaments, and "the bible in the early church." Includes bibliography and index.

Concordances

The Complete Concordance to the Bible: New King James Version. Nashville, Tenn.: Thomas Nelson Publishers, 1983. (BS 425 .C65)

A concordance to the New King James Version, listing word occurrence sequentially by book, chapter, and verse.

The Eerdmans Analytical Concordance to the Revised Standard Version of the Bible, compiled by Richard E. Whitaker. Grand Rapids, Mich.: William B. Eerdmans Publishing Company, 1988. (BS 425 .W48)

Includes concordance of proper names, concordance of numbers, and indexes in Hebrew, Aramaic, Greek, and Latin.

The NIV Exhaustive Concordance, by Edward W. Goodrick and John R. Kohlenberger III. Grand Rapids, Mich.: Zondervan Publishing House, 1990. (BS 425 .G62)

Based on the New International Version, this concordance includes an index of conjunctions, articles, prepositions, and pronouns, as well as language indexes in Hebrew, Aramaic, and Greek. Alphabetical by word and sequential by book, chapter, and verse.

Nelson's Complete Concordance of the Revised Standard Version, ed. by John W. Ellison. 2nd ed. Nashville, Tenn.: Thomas Nelson Publishers, 1984. (BS 425 .E4)

A concordance to the Revised Standard Version, arranged alphabetically by word and sequentially by book, chapter, and verse. This concordance was computer-generated.

Dictionaries and Encyclopedias

Dictionary of the Bible, ed. by James Hastings. New York: Charles Scribner's Sons, 1963. (BS 440 .H5)

Based on the Revised Standard Version, this Bible dictionary includes signed articles by scholars in the field and maps of biblical places.

A Dictionary of Comparative Religion, ed. by S. G. F. Brandon. Charles Scribner's Sons, 1970. (BL 31 .D54)

A one-volume reference to prehistoric, classical, and Eastern religions including Buddhism, Christianity, Hinduism, and Islam.

Dictionary of Proper Names and Places in the Bible, by O. Odelain and R. Seguinear. New York: Doubleday, 1981. (BS 435 .Q3313)

Includes lists of proper names, tribes, genealogy, and indexes and chronologies. References are from The Jerusalem Bible.

The Eerdmans Bible Dictionary, ed. by Allen C. Myers. Grand Rapids, Mich.: William B. Eerdmans Publishing Company, 1987. (BS 440 .G7613)

"Based on the Revised Standard Version of the Bible, with attention to alternate readings in the King James Version, New International Version, Jerusalem Bible and others." Includes maps of biblical areas.

The Facts on File Dictionary of Religion, ed. by John R. Hinnells. New York: Facts on File, 1984. (BL 31 .F33)

Brief definitions of religious terms and concepts. Includes substantial bibliography and synoptic index.

The Interpreter's Dictionary of the Bible: An Illustrated Encyclopedia. 4 vols. plus suppl. Nashville, Tenn.: Abingdon Press, 1962. (BS 440 .I63)

A dictionary of proper names and subjects in the Revised Standard Version; signed articles by scholars in the field. Includes quotations, bibliographies, illustrations, and maps.

Modern Catholic Dictionary, by John A. Hardon. New York: Doubleday, 1980. (BX 841 .H36)

A dictionary of words, proper names, and subjects, the sources of which include documents from Vatican II.

The Vocabulary of Jewish Life, by Abraham Mayer Heller. New York: Hebrew Publishing Company, 1967. (BM 50 .H4)

A dictionaries, in English and in Hebrew, of the language of Jewish life as it is spoken in the home and in the synagogue.

Directories

Directory of Departments and Programs of Religious Studies in North America, ed. by Watson E. Mills. Council of Societies for the Study of Religion, 1990. (BL 41 .D46)

A directory of schools in the United States and Canada that offer undergraduate degrees in religion and graduate degrees based on teaching and research in religious studies.

The Directory of Religious Organizations in the United States. McGrath Publishing Company, 1982. (BL 2530 .U6 D57)

A directory of religious organizations throughout the United States, with subject coverage in education, the media, and evangelism.

Religious Periodicals Directory, ed. by Graham Cornish. Santa Barbara, Calif.: ABC-Clio, 1986. (BL 48 .C6)

A directory of religious periodicals in countries throughout the world, including directory information, title, subjects, and a geographical index.

Women's Religious History Sources: A Guide to Repositories in the United States, ed. by Evangeline Thomas. New York: Bowker, 1983. (BX 4220 .U6 W65)

A directory of archival and other resources for the study of women in religious history, organized by state and including bibliography, biographical register, glossary, and index.

Encyclopedias

The Encyclopedia of American Religions: Religious Creeds, ed. by J. Gordon Melton. Detroit: Gale, 1988. (BT 990 .E58)

More than four hundred fifty creeds and summaries of religious doctrines for churches and other religious groups in the United States and Canada. Includes name and keyword index.

Encyclopedia of the American Religious Experience: Studies of Traditions and Movements, ed. by Charles H. Lippy and Peter W. Williams. New York: Charles Scribner's Sons, 1988. (BL 2525 .E53)

Signed articles by scholars in the field. Includes coverage of the Native American, the Spanish empire, and religion in mass communications.

Encyclopedic Dictionary of Religion, ed. by Paul Kevin Meagher and others. 3 vols. Washington, D.C.: Corpus Publishing, 1979. (BL 31 .E42)

Signed articles by scholars in the field and a substantial list of reference works. Includes citations to Vatican II documents in the articles.

The Encyclopedia of Eastern Philosophy and Religion, ed. by Stephan Schuhmacher and Gert Woerner. Boston: Shambala, 1989. (BL 1005 .L4813)

An encyclopedia of the major Eastern religions and philosophies including Buddhism, Hinduism, Taoism, and Zen. Includes bibliographies.

The Encyclopedia of Judaism, ed. by Geoffrey Wigoder. New York: Macmillan, 1989. (BM 50 .E63)

Signed articles by scholars in the field, as well as a glossary of terms and word histories in the study of Judaism.

The Encyclopedia of Religion, ed. by Mircea Eliade. 16 vols. New York: Free Press, 1986. (BL 31 .E46)

An up-to-date encyclopedia of religion from earliest times to the present, with signed articles by scholars in the field and brief bibliographies.

Encyclopedia of Religion and Ethics, ed. by James Hastings. 12 vols. New York: Charles Scribner's Sons, 1922. (BF 31 .E4)

A dated but exhaustive treatment; contains signed articles by scholars in the field on religions and their ethical bases.

The Encyclopedia of Unbelief, ed. by Gordon Stein. 2 vols. New York: Prometheus Books, 1985. (BL 2705 .E53)

An encyclopedia of concepts, elements, and traditions focusing on nonbelief. Includes bibliography, lists of organizations, and publishers.

The Golden Bough, by Sir James George Frazer. 12 vols. New York: Macmillan, 1935. (BL 310 .F7) and *The New Golden Bough: A New Abridgement of the Classic Work by Sir James George Frazer,* ed. by Dr. Theodor H. Gaster. Criterion Books, 1959. (BL 310 .F72)

A classic study of folklore, religion, and society, covering topics including the magic art and spirits of the corn and of the wild. Includes bibliography and index. The abridgement has been updated.

The International Standard Bible Encyclopedia, ed. by Geoffrey W. Bromiley. 4 vols. Grand Rapids, Mich.: Eerdmans Publishing Company, 1979. (BS 440 .I6)

Based on the Revised Standard Version, this encyclopedia includes signed articles by scholars in the field and is organized by proper name and subject.

New Catholic Encyclopedia. 15 vols and suppls. New York: McGraw-Hill, 1967. (BX 841 .N44)

Signed articles on the teachings, history, organization, and activities of the Catholic Church. Includes illustrations, bibliographies, and an index.

Guides and Handbooks

Eerdmans Handbook to the Bible, ed. by David and Pat Alexander. Grand Rapids, Mich.: William B. Eerdmans Publishing Company, 1973. (BS 417 .A55)

Illustrated handbook with charts, maps, a gazetteer of places, and a brief who's who for proper names of individuals who appear in the Bible.

Handbook of Denominations in the United States, by Frank S. Mead. Rev. ed. by Samuel S. Hill. Nashville, Tenn.: Abingdon Press, 1984. (BR 516.6 .M38)

An alphabetical list of religious denominations in America, with brief discussion of the history, doctrine, and membership of each denomination.

Harper Bible Pronunciation Guide, ed. by William O. Walker, Jr. New York: Harper & Row, 1989. (BS 435 .H35)

A pronunciation guide to biblical and nonbiblical terms, subjects, and names, which are often made up of foreign, transliterated languages.

An Introduction to Buddhism: Teachings, History and Practice, by Peter Harvey. New York: Cambridge University Press, 1990. (BQ 4022 .H37)

A single-volume handbook on Buddhism, covering its history and philosophy as well as providing bibliographies for further readings.

Profiles in Belief: The Religious Bodies of the United States and Canada, by Arthur Carl Piepkorn. 2 vols. New York: Harper & Row, 1977. (BR 510 .P53)

An alphabetical list of religious denominations in the United States and Canada, with brief discussions of each denomination. Includes notes and bibliography.

A Reader's Guide to the Great Religions, ed. by Charles J. Adams. New York: Free Press, 1965. (BL 80.2 .A35)

Bibliographical essays on each of the major religions, acquainting the reader with some of the primary texts that provide the basis for study.

Periodicals

Journal for the Scientific Study of Religion
Journal of Religious Studies
Journal of the American Academy of Religion
Parabola
Religion
Religious Studies
Review of Religious Research
Theology Today

Quote Books

The Home Book of Bible Quotations, selected and arranged by Burton Stevenson. New York: Harper & Brothers, 1949. (BS 432 .S667)

Bible quotes, taken from the King James Version, arranged alphabetically by subject. Includes an index of proper names.

* *Familiar Quotations.* (PN 6081 .B27)

SELECT SUBJECT HEADINGS, BREAKDOWNS, AND CALL NUMBERS

Religion (BL 1 - BL 2790)

General (BL 1 - BL 150)
Religion in Relation to Special Subjects (BL 51 - BL 65)
Sacred Books (BL 70 - BL 71)
Biography (BL 71 - BL 72)
Religions of the World (BL 74 - BL 98)
Natural Theology (BL 175 - BL 290)
The Myth; Comparative Mythology (BL 300 - BL 325)
Classification of Religions (BL 350 - BL 385)

Religious Doctrines (BL 425 - BL 490)
Eschatology (BL 500 - BL 547)
Worship (BL 550 - BL 619)
Religious Life (BL 624 - BL 627)
Religious Organizations (BL 630 - BL 632)
History and Principles of Religions (BL 660 - BL 2670)

Judaism (BM 1 - BM 990)

General (BM 1 - BM 449)
Pre-Talmudic Jewish Literature (BM 480 - BM 488)
Sources of Jewish Religion (BM 495 - BM 532)
Relation of Judaism to Special Subjects (BM 534 - BM 538)
Principles of Judaism (BM 545 - BM 582)
Controversial Works Against the Jews (BM 585)
Jewish Works Against Christianity and Islam (BM 590 - BM 591)
Dogmatic Judaism (BM 600 - BM 645)
Heresy, Heresies (BM 646)
Apologetics (BM 648)
Practical Judaism (BM 650 - BM 747)
Biography (BM 750 - BM 755)
Samaritans (BM 900 - BM 990)

Islam (BP 1 - BP 610)

General (BP 1 - BP 68)
Biography (BP 70 - BP 80)
Islamic Literature (BP 87 - BP 89)
Sacred Books (BP 100 - BP 137)
General Works on Islam (BP 160 - BP 165)
Dogma (BP 165.5)
Theology (BP 166)
Heresy, Heresies (BP 167.5)
Apostasy from Islam (BP 168)
Works Against Islam and the Koran (BP 169)
Works in Defense of Islam (BP 170)
Benevolent Work (BP 170.2)
Missionary Work of Islam (BP 170.3 - BP 170.5)
Relation of Islam to Other Religions (BP 171 - BP 173)
Islamic Sociology (BP 173.25 - BP 173.45)
The Practice of Islam (BP 174 - BP 190)
Branches, Sects, Etc. (BP 191 - BP 253)

Buddhism (BQ 1 - BQ 9800)

Periodicals (BQ 1 - BQ 10)
Societies (BQ 12 - BQ 93)
Financial Institutions (BQ 96 - BQ 99)
Congresses (BQ 100 - BQ 102)
Directories (BQ 104 - BQ 105)
Museums (BQ 107 - BQ 109)
General Collections (BQ 115 - BQ 126)
Encyclopedias (BQ 128)
Dictionaries (BQ 130)
Terminology (BQ 133)
Questions and Answers (BQ 135)
Religious Education (BQ 141 - BQ 209)
Research (BQ 210 - BQ 219)
Antiquities (BQ 221 - BQ 249)
History (BQ 257 - BQ 799)
Persecutions (BQ 800 - BQ 829)
Biography (BQ 840 - BQ 858)
Buddhist Literature (BQ 1001 - BQ 1045)
Tripitaka (BQ 1100 - BQ 3340)
General Works (BQ 4000 - BQ 4060)
Doctrinal and Systematic Buddhism (BQ 4061 - BQ 4570)
Relations to Other Religions (BQ 4600 - BQ 4610)
Buddhist Pantheon (BQ 4620 - BQ 4905)
Practice of Buddhism (BQ 4620 - BQ 5720)

Christianity (BR 1 - BR 1725)

Early Christian Literature (BR 60 - BR 67)
Christianity in Relation to Special Subjects (BR 115)
Christian Antiquities (BR 130 - BR 133)
History (BR 140 - BR 1500)
Persecution. Martyrs. (BR 1600 - BR 1609)
Biography (BR 1690 - BR 1725)
The Bible (BS 1 - BS 2970)
Early Versions (BS 11 - BS 115)
Modern Texts and Versions (BS 125 - BS 355)
Works About the Bible (BS 410 - BS 680)
Old Testament (BS 701 - BS 1830)
New Testament (BS 1901 - BS 2970)
Doctrinal Theology (BT 10 - BT 1480)
Doctrine and Dogma (BR 19 - BT 33)

Divine Law (BT 95 - BT 97)
God (BT 98 - BT 180)
Christology (BT 198 - BT 590)
Mary, Mother of Jesus Christ (BT 595 - BT 680)
Creation (BT 695 - BT 748)
Salvation (BT 750 - BT 810)
Eschatology (BT 819 - BT 891)
Future State (BT 899 - BT 940)
Invisible World (BT 960 - BT 985)
Creeds, Confessions, Covenants, Etc. (BT 990 - BT 1010)
Catechisms (BT 1029 - BT 1040)
Apologetics (BT 1095 - BT 1255)
History of Specific Doctrines (BT 1313 - BT 1480)
Practical Theology (BV 1 - BV 5099)
Worship (BV 5 - BV 530)
Ecclesiastical Theology (BV 590 - BV 1652)
Missions (BV 200 - BV 3705)
Evangelism (BV 3750 - BV 3799)
Pastoral Theology (BV 4000 - BV 4470)
Practical Religion (BV 4485 - BV 5099)

Christian Denominations (BX 1 - BX 9999)

Church Unity (BX 1 - BX 9)
Eastern Churches (BX 100 - BX 189)
Orthodox Eastern Church (BX 200 - BX 745)
Roman Catholic Church (BX 800 - BX 4795)
Protestantism (BX 4800 - BX 9999)

Life and Health Sciences

BIOLOGY, BOTANY, AND ZOOLOGY

Abstracts and Indexes

Animal Behavior Abstracts. Bethesda, Md.: Cambridge Scientific Abstracts, monthly. (QL 750 .A598)

Abstracts from more than five thousand periodicals covering topics such as neurophysiology, ecology, genetics, and social anthropology.

Biological Abstracts. Philadelphia: BIOSIS, semimonthly. (QH 301 .B37)

BIOSIS is a not-for-profit abstracting service that provides biological abstracts in four major categories: by author, by subject, by "biosystematic" entry (taxonomic category), and by generic entry (by genus or genus-species).

Biological and Agricultural Index. New York: Wilson, monthly. (QH 301 .B434)

A subject index to periodicals, including the biological, agricultural, environmental, marine, and zoological sciences.

Current Contents: Agriculture, Biology and Environmental Sciences. Philadelphia: Institute for Scientific Information, monthly. (QH 301 .B374)

Indexes tables of contents for more than nine hundred journals covering agronomy, ecology, marine biology, zoology, and other topics in the life sciences.

Ecological Abstracts. New York: Elsevier, annual. (QH 540 .A66)

Published since 1974, these abstracts cover more than six hundred publications. There is an annual index by author, geographical region, and subject organism.

Ecology Abstracts. Bethesda, Md.: Cambridge Scientific Abstracts, monthly. (QH 540 .A66)

More than one thousand abstracts appear in each issue. Abstracts deal with "the interactions between microbes, plants and animals, and their environments." Includes sections on legislation, education, and conferences.

Genetics Abstracts. Bethesda, Md.: Cambridge Scientific Abstracts, monthly. (QH 431 .G322)

Published since 1968, each issue carries some twelve hundred abstracts from thousands of different journals and includes author and subject indexes.

Index to Illustrations of Living Things Outside North America: Where to Find Pictures of Flora and Fauna, by Lucile Thompson Munz and Nedra G. Slauson. (QL 46 .M85) and **Index to Illustrations of the Natural World: Where to Find Pictures of the Living Things of North America,** by John W. Thompson. (QL 151 .T46) Hamden, Conn.: Archon Books, 1981.

These indexes to visual information list sources for illustrations of flora and fauna and include index by scientific name and bibliographies.

Microbiology Abstracts: Section C: Algology, Mycology and Protozoology. Bethesda, Md.: Cambridge Scientific Abstracts. (QK 564 .M5)

A monthly abstracting service monitoring over five thousand journals. Abstracts are arranged in taxonomical order, including algae, fungi, lichens, and protozoa.

Taxonomic Literature. 7 vols. Utrecht: Bohn, Scheltema & Holkema, 1976. (QK 97 .S7)

Provides a title and name index to taxonomic literature, arranged alphabetically by author. Gives authors and author biographies as well as the titles of their writings.

* *General Science Index.* (Q 1 .G46)
* *Index to Scientific Reviews.* (Q 1 .I381)
* *Index to Scientific and Technical Proceedings.* (AI 3 .I53)
* *Science Citation Index.* (Q 1 .S32)

Bibliographies

Guide to Information Sources in the Botanical Sciences, by Elisabeth B. Davis. Littleton, Colo.: Libraries Unlimited, 1987. (QK 45.2 .D38)

Abstracts, indexes, data bases, dictionaries and encyclopedias, handbooks, and textbooks. Includes section on key publishers in the botanical sciences.

Information Sources in the Life Sciences, ed. by H. V. Wyatt. 3rd ed. London: Butterworths, 1987. (QH 303.6 .I54)

Books, journals, primary and secondary sources, and governmental information sources on biochemistry, biotechnology, genetics, zoology, ecology, botany, and the history of biology.

* *Scientific and Technical Books in Print.* (Q 100 .S41)

Biographical Sources

* *American Men and Women of Science.* (Q 141 .A47)
* *Dictionary of Scientific Biography.* (Q 141 .D5)

Chronologies and Histories

* *Chronology of the History of Science: 1450–1900.* (Q 125 .G39)
* *Timetables of Science.* (Q 125 .H557)

Dictionaries and Encyclopedias

Chambers Biological Dictionary. New York: Chambers, 1989. (QH 302.2 .C33)

A Concise Dictionary of Biology. New York: Oxford University Press, 1990. (QH 302.5 .C66)

A Dictionary of Botany, by R. John Little and C. Eugene Jones. New York: Van Nostrand Reinhold, 1979. (QK 9 .L735)

A Dictionary of Zoology, by A. W. Leftwich. New York: D. Van Nostrand, 1967. (QL 9 .L49)

The Facts on File Dictionary of Biology. New York: Facts on File, 1981. (QH 13 .C66)

Henderson's Dictionary of Biological Terms. 10th ed. New York: Wiley, 1989. (QH 302.5 .H65)

These are several representative subject dictionaries in the life sciences. A good dictionary in the life sciences will include an outline of the plant and animal kingdoms, tables for units of measure and conversion, a Greek alphabet and a list of common Latin and Greek noun endings.

Encyclopedia of Bioethics, ed. by Warren T. Reich. 4 vols. New York: Free Press, 1978. (QH 332 .E52)

Signed articles by scholars in the field, covering ethical and legal problems, ethical theories, religious traditions, and historical perspectives. Includes bibliographies.

Encyclopedia of Human Biology, ed. by Renato Dulbecco. 8 vols. New York: Academic Press, 1991. (QP 11 .E53)

Signed articles by scholars in the field on the full range of studies in human biology. Includes illustrations and bibliographies.

Encyclopedia of Plant Physiology, ed. by A. Pirson and M. H. Zimmermann. New York: Springer-Verlag, 1975. (QK 711.2 .E5)

Signed articles by scholars in the field on plant pathology, photosynthesis, plant ecology, and photomorphogenesis. Includes author index.

Grzimek's Encyclopedia of Mammals. 5 vols. New York: McGraw-Hill, 1990. (QL 701 .G79)

Grzimek's covers the different members of the mammal kingdom, including monotremata, marsupialia, primates, carnivora, cetacea, proboscidea, sirenia, and others. Includes black-and-white and color illustrations.

The Mammals of North America, ed. by E. Raymond Hall, New York: Wiley, 1981. (QL 715 .H15)

A well-illustrated encyclopedia of mammals, organized by family, covering both the United States and Canada.

Walker's Mammals of the World. 4th ed. 2 vols. Baltimore, Md.: Johns Hopkins University Press, 1983. (QL 703 .W222)

This encyclopedia covers more than one thousand genera; organized by family, genera, and species. Includes illustrations, bibliography, and index.

Wildflowers of the United States. 6 vols. New York: New York Botanical Garden/McGraw-Hill, 1966. (QK 115 .R53)

Includes volumes on the Southeastern states, Texas, the Southwestern states, the Northwestern states, the Central Mountain and Plains states. Includes glossary and color photos. Wildflowers are grouped by family.

Directories

* *Encyclopedia of Associations.* (HS 17 .G334)

Guides and Handbooks

Gray's Anatomy, 37th ed. London: Churchill Livingstone, 1989. (QM 23.2 .G731)

The first edition of this classic work was published in 1858. It covers cytology, embryology, osteology, arthrology, myology, angiology, neurology, and splanchnology and includes bibliographies and index.

Gray's Manual of Botany, by Merritt Lyndon Fernald. 8th ed. New York: D. Van Nostrand, 1970. (QK 117 .G75)

Arranged by order and family of vascular plants, this manual of botany includes an index to the Latin names of plants.

Guide to the Standard Floras of the World, by D. G. Frodin. London: Cambridge University Press, 1984. (QK 45.2 .F76)

Geographically arranged, this guide includes bibliographies pertaining to the world's flora as well as geographical and author indexes.

Handbook of Biochemistry and Molecular Biology, ed. by Gerald D. Fasman. 9 vols. Cleveland, Ohio: CRC Press, 1975. (QH 345 .H347)

Encyclopedic information on proteins, nucleic acids, lipids, carbohydrates, steroids, and physical and chemical data.

The Oxford Companion to Animal Behavior, ed. by David McFarland. New York: Oxford University Press, 1981. (QL 751 .O930)

A handbook to ethology with illustrations and bibliographies, as well as indexes of English and scientific names for animals.

Periodicals

Advances in Applied Biology
American Horticulturist
American Zoologist
American Naturalist
American Journal of Botany
Annals of Botany
The Auk
Biological Bulletin
Biological Journal of the Linnean Society
Biologist
Bioscience
BioTechnology
Botany Gazette
Botany Review
Current Awareness in Biological Sciences
Developmental Biology
Evolutionary Biology
Human Biology
Journal of Experimental Zoology
Journal of Zoology
Journal of Experimental Botany
Journal of Experimental Biology
Journal of Molecular Biology
Journal of Theoretical Biology
Marine Biology
Physiological Zoology
Plant Science
Quarterly Review of Biology
Systematic Zoology
Systematic Biology
Zoological Journal of the Linnean Society

Statistics

Biology Databook. Bethesda, Md.: Federation of American Societies for Experimental Biology, 1972. (QH 310 .A392)

Quantitative and descriptive tables of information on genetics, cytology, reproduction, parasites, nutrition, metabolism, respiration, and circulation.

SELECT SUBJECT HEADINGS, BREAKDOWNS, AND CALL NUMBERS

Natural History (General) (QH 1 - QH 278.5)

Nature Conservation. Landscape Protection (QH 75 - QH 77)
Microscopy (QH 201 - QH 278.5)

Biology (General) (QH 301 - QH 705)

Study and Teaching (QH 315 - QH 320)
Biological Laboratories (QH 320 - QH 323)
Methods of Research (QH 324 - QH 344)
Evolution (QH 359 - QH 390)
Variation (QH 401 - QH 411)
Hybridization (QH 421 - QH 425)

Genetics (QH 426 - QH 470)

General Works (QH 430 - QH 439)
Study and Teaching (QH 440 - QH 442)
Recombination Mechanisms (QH 443 - QH 457)
Mutations (QH 460 - QH 470)
Reproduction (QH 471 - QH 499)
Life (QH 501 - QH 531)

Ecology (QH 540 - QH 559)
Cytology (QH 473 - QH 671)

Physical and Chemical Properties (QH 611 - QH 630)
Physiological Properties (QH 631 - QH 647)

Botany (QK 1 - QK 989)

Botanical Gardens (QK 63 - QK 73)
Herbariums (QK 75 - QK 89)

Classification (QK 91 - QK 100)
Geographical Distribution (QK 101 - QK 474)

Spermatophyta. Phanerogams (QK 474 - QK 495)

Trees and Shrubs (QK 474 - QK 495)
Gymnosperms (QK 494)
Angiosperms (QK 495)

Cytogams (QK 504 - QK 638)

Local (QK 509 - QK 519)
Pteridophyta (QK 520 - QK 532)
Bryophyta (QK 532 - QK 533)
Algae. Algology (QK 564 - QK 580)
Lichens (QK 580 - QK 597)
Fungi (QK 600 - QK 638)

Plant Anatomy (QK 640 - QK 707)

Plant Physiology (QK 710 - QK 899)

Plant Ecology (QK 900 - QK 977)

Zoology (QL 1 - QL 991)

Collecting and Preserving (QL 61 - QL 100)
Geographical Distribution (QL 101 - QL 355)

Invertebrates (QL 362 - QL 599)

Insects (QL 461 - QL 599)

Chordates (QL 605 - QL 739)

Fishes (QL 614 - QL 639)
Reptiles and Amphibians (QL 640 - QL 669)
Birds (QL 671 - QL 699)
Mammals (QL 700 - QL 739)

Animal Behavior (QL 750 - QL 795)

Stories and Anecdotes (QL 791 - QL 795)

Morphology (QL 799)

Anatomy (QL 801 - QL 950)
Embryology (QL 851 - QL 991)
Human Anatomy (QM 1 - QM 981)
Physiology (QP 1 - QP 981)
Microbiology (QR 1 - QR 500)

NURSING

Almanacs

The Nurse's Almanac. Rockville, Md.: Aspen Systems Corp., 1984. (RT 41 .N85)

An almanac of nursing and the nursing profession, covering nursing instruction, assessment, diagnostics, and practices.

Bibliographies

Author's Guide to Journals in Nursing and Related Fields, by Steven D. Warner and Kathryn D. Schweer. New York: Haworth Press, 1982. (RT 24 .A97)

Directory and bibliographic information on nursing periodicals and nursing literature, as well as how to write and submit materials to journals in nursing.

Biographical Sources

American Nursing: A Biographical Dictionary, ed. by Vern L. Bullough and others. New York: Garland, 1988–92. (RT 34 .A44)

Biographical information on individuals who have made a significant contribution to the profession of nursing in the United States and historical background on nurses and the nursing profession.

Dictionary of American Nursing Biography, by Martin Kaufman. New York: Greenwood, 1988. (RT 34 .D53)

A biographical history of nurses and the nursing profession in the United States. Includes bibliography and index.

Who's Who in American Nursing. Washington, D.C.: Society of Nursing Professionals, biennial. (RT 34 .W5)

Biographical and directory information on nurses in the United States, including positions held, educational background, and professional specialties.

CD-ROM Data Bases

Medline

Dictionaries and Encyclopedias

Black's Medical Dictionary. New York: Barnes & Noble, 1990. (R 121 .T486)

Blakiston's Gould Medical Dictionary. New York: McGraw-Hill, 1979. (R 121 .B62)

Churchill's Illustrated Medical Dictionary. New York: Churchill Livingstone, 1989. (R 121 .I58)

Dorland's Illustrated Medical Dictionary. 27th ed. Philadelphia: W. B. Saunders, 1988. (R 121 .D73)

Stedman's Medical Dictionary. 25th ed. Baltimore, Md.: Williams & Wilkins, 1990. (R 121 .S8)

Taber's Cyclopedic Medical Dictionary. Philadelphia: F. A. Davis, 1989. (R 121 .T11)

Urdang Dictionary of Current Medical Terms. New York: Wiley, 1980. (R 121 .L33)

Webster's Medical Desk Dictionary. Springfield, Mass.: Merriam-Webster, 1986. (R 121 .W357)

The medical references above represent the many types of medical dictionaries available from different publishers, some of which have been in print for over a century. A good medical dictionary will include a glossary of medical signs and symbols, anatomical tables, a table of the elements, an explanation of the Greek alphabet, and substantial illustrations of the human body.

McGraw-Hill Nursing Dictionary. New York: McGraw-Hill, 1979. (RT 21 .M33)

A single-volume desk dictionary that covers nursing, medicine, and the health care profession in general.

Mosby's Medical, Nursing, and Allied Health Dictionary, ed. by Walter D. Glanze and others. St. Louis: Mosby, 1990. (R 121 .M89)

A standard desk dictionary with broad coverage of medicine, nursing, and the health care industry. Includes illustrations.

Directories

Guide to Programs in Nursing in Four-Year Colleges and Universities: Baccalaureate and Graduate Programs in the United States and Canada, by Barbara Klug Redman and others. New York: American Council on Education, 1987. (RT 79 .G85)

Information on undergraduate and graduate programs in nursing and information on the study and teaching of nursing in higher education in the United States and Canada.

The National Nursing Directory, by Kenneth E. Lawrence. Rockville, Md.: Aspen Systems Corp., 1982. (RT 25 .U5)

This directory provides information on medicine, nursing, voluntary health agencies, and information services for nurses in the United States.

* *Encyclopedia of Associations.* (HS 17 .G334)

Guides and Handbooks

Gray's Anatomy, 37th ed. London: Churchill Livingstone, 1989. (QM 23.2 .G731)

The first edition of this classic work was published in 1858. It covers cytology, embryology, osteology, arthrology, myology, angiology, neurology, and splanchnology. Includes bibliographies and index.

Assessment. (RT 48 .A87)
Diagnostics. (RT 48 .D5)
Nurse's Legal Handbook. (RT 86.7 .N88)
Practices. (RT 86.7 .P7)

The Springhouse Corporation publishes the four guides listed above in their Nurse's Reference Library series; they cover nurses' instructions in diagnosis, patient relations, patient assessment, and medical history.

Indexes

Cumulative Index to Nursing and Allied Health Literature. Glendale, Calif.: CINAHL, annual. (Z 6675 .N7 C8)

Published since 1961, this is an index of journals, books, and pamphlets by author and subject, covering nursing and specialized positions, such as cardiopulmonary technician, emergency services, health education, occupational therapy, radiological and surgical technology.

Hospital Literature Index. Chicago: American Hospital Association, annual. (Z 6675 .H76 A5)

Covers periodical literature on hospitals and management and administration of health care facilities.

Index Medicus. Washington, D.C.: National Library of Medicine, annual. (Z 6660 .I42)

This is actually a government document in the sense that it's published by the federal government. It is one of the fundamental indexes to medical and public health information and publications in the United States.

Periodicals

American Journal of Nursing
American Nurse
Advances in Nursing Science
Current Concepts in Clinical Nursing
Holistic Nursing Practice
Hospital Progress
International Journal of Nursing Studies
International Nursing Review
Journal of Advanced Nursing
Journal of Professional Nursing
Nurse Practitioner
Nursing
Nursing Digest
Nursing Times
RN

Statistical Sources

Measurement of Nursing Outcomes, by Carolyn Feher Waltz and Ora Strickland. New York: Springer, 1988. (RT 85.5 .M434)

The four volumes in this study cover measuring client outcomes, measuring nursing performance, measuring clinical skills, measuring client self-care and coping skills, and professional development for nurses. Includes bibliographies and indexes.

SELECT SUBJECT HEADINGS, BREAKDOWNS, AND CALL NUMBERS

Nursing (RT 1 - RT 120)

Periodicals. Societies. Serials. (RT 1)
Congresses by Region or Country (RT 3 - RT 20)
Dictionaries and Encyclopedias (RT 21)
Directories (RT 25)
Placement Agencies (RT 27)

Statistics and Surveys (RT 29)
History (RT 31)
Biography (RT 34 - RT 37)
General Works (RT 40 - RT 42)
Instruments (RT 44 - RT 47)
Observation (RT 48)
Nursing Care Plans (RT 49)
Nursing Records (RT 50)
Handbooks, Manuals, Etc. (RT 51)
Outlines, Syllabi, Etc. (RT 55 - RT 60)
Popular Works (RT 61)
Practical Nursing (RT 62)
Hygiene for Nurses (RT 67)
Mathematics for Nurses (RT 67)
Textbooks (RT 69 - RT 70)
Study and Teaching (RT 71)
Nursing as a Profession (RT 82)
Nursing Ethics (RT 85)
Special Topics (RT 87)

PREMED

Abstracts and Indexes

Biophysics, Bioengineering and Medical Instrumentation. Netherlands: Elsevier/Excerpta Medica, annual. (QH 505 .B473)

Abstracts in subjects pertaining to medical instrumentation and bioengineering, including therapeutics and computer automation, surgery and endoscopy, prostheses and artificial organs.

Hospital Literature Index. Chicago: American Hospital Association, annual. (Z 6675 .H76 A5)

Covers periodical literature on hospitals and management and administration of health care facilities.

Index Medicus. Washington, D.C.: National Library of Medicine, annual. (Z 6660 .I42)

A government document in the sense that it's published by the federal government, it is one of the fundamental indexes to medical and public health information and publications in the United States.

Bibliographies and Catalogs

Bibliography of Bioethics. Washington, D.C.: Georgetown University Kennedy Institute of Ethics, annual. (R 724 .B42)

Annual bibliography of writings on some of the difficult issues in bioethics, such as animal experimentation, capital punishment, euthanasia, and reproductive technologies.

Encyclopedia of Health Information Sources, ed. by Paul Wasserman. Detroit: Gale, 1986. (R 129 .E56)

This bibliography covers abstracting and indexing services, yearbooks, dictionaries and encyclopedias, periodicals and reviews.

Federal Information Sources in Health and Medicine: A Select Annotated Bibliography, by Mary Glen Chitty. New York: Greenwood, 1988. (R 129 .C45)

Bibliography for finding guides and subject-area bibliographies in the health sciences, health care administration, and medicine.

Medical and Health Care Books and Serials in Print. New York: Bowker, annual. (Z 6658 .65)

An annual bibliography that provides author, title, and subject access to current medical and health care literature.

Dictionaries and Encyclopedias

Black's Medical Dictionary. New York: Barnes & Noble, 1990. (R 121 .T486)

Blakiston's Gould Medical Dictionary. New York: McGraw-Hill, 1979. (R 121 .B62)

Churchill's Illustrated Medical Dictionary. New York: Churchill Livingstone, 1989. (R 121 .I58)

Dorland's Illustrated Medical Dictionary. 27th ed. Philadelphia: W. B. Saunders, 1988. (R 121 .D73)

Stedman's Medical Dictionary. 25th ed. Baltimore, Md.: Williams & Wilkins, 1990. (R 121 .S8)

Taber's Cyclopedic Medical Dictionary. Philadelphia: F. A. Davis, 1989. (R 121 .T11)

Urdang Dictionary of Current Medical Terms. New York: Wiley, 1980. (R 121 .L33)

Webster's Medical Desk Dictionary. Springfield, Mass.: Merriam-Webster, 1986. (R 121 .W357)

The references listed above represent some of the many types of medical dictionaries available from different publishers, some of which have been in print for over a century. A good medical dictionary will include a glossary of medical signs and symbols, anatomical tables, a table of the elements, an explanation of the Greek alphabet, and substantial illustrations of the human body.

The CIBA Collection of Medical Illustrations, ed. by Frank H. Netter. West Caldwell, N.J.: CIBA, 1983. (QM 25 .N47)

The CIBA Collection is a voluminous encyclopedia of highly detailed medical illustrations covering every aspect of the human body.

Dictionary of Medical Eponyms, by Barry G. Firkin. Parkridge, N.J.: Parkridge Publishing Group, 1987. (R 121 .F535)

A dictionary of proper names that have come to be associated with certain diseases, symptoms, diagnoses, and treatments.

Encyclopedia of Medical Devices and Instrumentation, ed. by John G. Webster. 4 vols. New York: Wiley, 1988. (R 856 .A3 E53)

Signed articles by scholars in the field on the machinery of health care. Includes illustrations, bibliographies, and index.

The Facts on File Dictionary of Health Care Management, ed. by Joseph C. Rhea and others. New York: Facts on File, 1988. (RA 393 .R48)

A dictionary for ethical issues, labor relations, management, personnel, program evaluation, and public relations in health care.

International Dictionary of Medicine and Biology. 3 vols. New York: Wiley, 1986. (R 121 .I58)

An encyclopedic dictionary organized by major subject areas, such as anatomy, dentistry, hematology, mycology, pediatrics, and radiology.

Logan's Medical and Scientific Abbreviations, by Carolynn M. Logan and M. Katherine Rice. Philadelphia: Lippincott, 1987. (R 123 .L8)

Medical abbreviations as well as Greek letters, medical symbols, Latin terms, and the elements. Includes bibliography.

The Medical Word Finder: A Reverse Medical Dictionary, by Betty Hamilton and Barbara Guidos. New York: Neal-Schuman, 1986. (R 121 .H232)

A useful reference for finding the right word when you can think of the symptom, the area of the body, or a phrase but can't think of the word for it all.

Textbook of Medicine, ed. by James B. Wyngaarden and others. Philadelphia: Saunders, 1988. (RC 46 .T35)

A classic primary textbook of internal medicine, which includes substantial illustrations, bibliographies, and index.

Directories

American College of Health Care Executives 1992 Directory. Chicago: American College of Health Care Executives, 1992. (RA 977 .A57)

Biographical information on hospital executives, including the positions they have held, their educational background, membership, awards, authorship, and community service.

Directory of Medical Specialists: 1991–1992. 25th ed. Chicago: Marquis Who's Who, 1991. (R 712 .A1 D5)

Directory information for individuals in the medical profession who have demonstrated a medical specialization in their work, research, and writing.

Medical and Health Information Directory: 1992–1993, ed. by Karen Backus. 6th ed. Detroit: Gale, 1992. (R 118.4 .V6 M43)

A directory of close to fifty thousand information resources in the medical profession and medical services and industries, including organizations, agencies, institutions, libraries, and health services.

Guides and Handbooks

Gray's Anatomy, 37th ed. London: Churchill Livingstone, 1989. (QM 23.2 .G731)

The first edition of this classic work was published in 1858. It covers cytology, embryology, osteology, arthrology, myology, angiology, neurology, and splanchnology. Includes bibliographies and index.

The Merck Manual of Diagnosis and Therapy. 15th ed. Rahway, N.J.: Merck & Company, Inc., 1987. (RC 55 .M4)

A standard desk manual in the medical profession, listing and explaining the symptoms, diagnosis, and treatment of disease in the human body.

The Oxford Companion to Medicine, ed. by John Walton and others. 2 vols. New York: Oxford University Press, 1986. (R 121 .O88)

Broad coverage of medicine in terms of its history and development, covering the subjects and significant individuals in the study of medicine.

Physician's Desk Reference. Montvale, N.J.: Medical Economics Data, annual. (RS 75 .P5)

A guide to pharmaceutical and diagnostic products by manufacturer, generic and chemical names, and category. Includes directory information on poison control centers.

Periodicals

American Journal of Medicine
Boston Medical and Surgical Journal
Consultant
Health
Health Services Research
Hospital Medicine
Hospital Practice
Journal of the American Medical Association
Journal of Experimental Medicine
Journal of Health and Human Behavior
Journal of Health and Social Behavior
Journal of Laboratory and Clinical Medicine
Journal of Medical Education
Lancet
Medical World News
New England Journal of Medicine

Quotations

Familiar Medical Quotations, ed. by Maurice Benjamin Strauss. Boston: Little, Brown, 1968. (R 707 .S91 F2)

Modeled on Bartlett's *Familiar Quotations,* this book of quotes is taken from the speeches and writings of the world's great men and women in medicine.

Statistical Sources

Health United States. Washington, D.C.: Department of Health and Human Services, annual. (RA 407.3 .U58)

Statistical data on diseases and disease prevention and a description of the ongoing goals of the Department of Health and Human Services.

World Health Statistics Annual. Geneva: World Health Organization, annual. (RA 651 .A485)

Statistical tables on world health in a global overview, including vital statistics, life expectancy tables, and causes of death.

SELECT SUBJECT HEADINGS, BREAKDOWNS, AND CALL NUMBERS

Medicine (General) (R 5 - R 920)

    History of Medicine (R 131 - R 684)
    Medical Education (R 735 - R 847)
    Medical Physics (R 895 - R 920)

Public Aspects of Medicine (RA 1 - RA 1270)
Pathology (RB 1 - RB 214)
Internal Medicine (RC 31 - RC 1245)
Surgery (RD 1 - RD 811)
Ophthalmology (RE 1 - RE 994)
Otorhinolaryngology (RF 1 - RF 991)
Gynecology and Obstetrics (RG 1 - RG 991)
Pediatrics (RJ 1 - RJ 570)
Dentistry (RL 1 - RL 715)
Dermatology (RL 1 - RL 803)
Therapeutics. Pharmacology (RM 1 - RM 931)
Pharmacy and Materia Medica (RS 1 - RS 441)
Nursing (RT 1 - RT 120)
Botanic, Thomsonian, and Eclectic Medicine (RV 1 - RV 431)
Homeopathy (RX 1 - RX 681)
Other Systermms of Medicine (RZ 201 - RZ 999)

Natural Sciences

ASTRONOMY AND PHYSICS

Abstracts and Indexes

Current Contents: Physical, Chemical and Earth Sciences. Philadelphia, Pa.: Institute for Scientific Information, monthly. (Q 1 .S322)

Current Contents prints the tables of contents of the most recent journal articles in the physical, chemical, and earth sciences. The "Current Book Contents" format includes a title word index, an author index, and a publishers' access directory.

Meteorological and Geoastrophysical Abstracts. Boston: American Meteorological Society, monthly. (QC 851 .A62)

An index and abstracts to journal articles, books, and conference publications both foreign and domestic.

Physics Abstracts. New York: Institution of Electrical Engineers, semimonthly. (Q 1 .S3)

Abstracts in physics, including materials that appear in "journals, reports, books, dissertations, and conference papers published in all countries and languages of the world." Approximately 150,000 items are abstracted each year. Arrangement is by author and subject.

* *Applied Science and Technology Index.* (Z 7913 .I7)
* *General Science Index.* (Q 1 .G46)
* *Index to Scientific and Technical Proceedings.* (Q 101 .I5)
* *Index to Scientific Reviews.* (Q 1 .I381)
* *Science Citation Index.* (Q 1 .S32)
* *Technical Book Review Index.* (Z 7913 .T36)

Almanacs and Yearbooks

Annual Review of Astronomy and Astrophysics. Palo Alto, Calif.: Annual Reviews, Inc. (QB 1 .A2884)

A cumulative review of the year's most significant articles and papers in the study of astronomy and astrophysics.

The Astronomical Almanac. Washington, D.C.: U.S. Government Printing Office, annual. (QB 8 .U1)

The movements of the sun, moon, stars, planets, and planetary satellites. Information on observatories; tables and statistical data for the year.

Yearbook of Astronomy. New York: W. W. Norton, annual. (QB 1 .Y4)

Significant articles and reviews as well as notable astronomical occurrences in astronomical studies each year.

* *Annual Register.* (D 2 .A7)
* *Chase's Annual Events.* (D 11.5 .C48)
* *Information Please Almanac.* (AY 64 .I55)
* *Weather Almanac.* (QC 983 .R83)
* *World Almanac and Book of Facts.* (AY 67 .N5 W7)

Atlases

The Cambridge Atlas of Astronomy. Middlesex: Newnes Books, 1985. (QB 65 .G6813)

An atlas of the sun, the solar system, the stars, the galaxy, and the "extragalactic" domain. Includes illustrations, bibliographies, glossary, and index.

* *Atlas of the Universe.* (QB 44 .M5425)

Bibliographies

Astronomy and Astronautics: An Enthusiast's Guide to Books and Periodicals, by Andy Lusis. London: Mansell, 1986. (QB 43.2 .L87)

Subject coverage includes general and practical astronomy, the history of astronomy, astrophysics, and the solar system. Includes author, title, and subject index.

The History of Physics: An International Bibliography, by Stephen G. Brush and Lanfranco Belloni. New York: Garland, 1983. (QC 7 .B78)

A bibliography covering various topics in physics, mechanics, relativity, quantum theory, and atomic and nuclear physics in their historical development.

Information Sources in Physics, ed. by Dennis F. Shaw. 2nd ed. London: Butterworths, 1985. (QC 21.2 .I53)

A bibliography of physics literature organized by subject, which also lists science libraries, abstracting and indexing services, and on-line information sources.

* *Scientific and Technical Books in Print.* (Q 100 .S41)

Biographical Sources

The Biographical Dictionary of Scientists: Astronomers. London: Blond Educational, 1985. (QB 35 .B56)

The Biographical Dictionary of Scientists: Physicists. London: Blond Educational, 1985. (QC 15 .B56)

The two biographical sources above are part of a series that provides biographical references to significant individuals in various branches of the sciences. Coverage is international.

* *American Men and Women of Science.* (Q 141 .A47)
* *Dictionary of Scientific Biography.* (Q 141 .D5)

Chronologies and Histories

* *Chronology of the History of Science: 1450–1900.* (Q 125 .G39)
* *Timetables of Science.* (Q 125 .H557)

Dictionaries and Encyclopedias

A Concise Dictionary of Astronomy, by Jacqueline Mitton. New York: Oxford University Press, 1991. (QB 14 .M58)

A Concise Dictionary of Physics. New York: Oxford University Press, 1985. (QC 5 .C66)

Dictionary of Astronomy, Space, and Atmospheric Phenomena, by David F. Tver. New York: Van Nostrand Reinhold, 1979. (QB 14 .T83)

McGraw-Hill Dictionary of Physics, ed. by Sybil P. Parker. New York: McGraw-Hill, 1984. (QC 5 .M424)

Macmillan Dictionary of Astronomy, ed. by Valerie Illingworth. 2nd ed. London: Macmillan, 1985. (QB 14 .M33)

Macmillan Dictionary of Physics, ed. by M. P. Lord. London: Macmillan, 1986. (QC 5 .L67)

Listed above are several dictionaries of astronomy and physics. Each covers basic terms and specific subjects and concepts. A good astronomy dictionary should include appendices of astronomical tables. A good physics dictionary should have tables of symbols, fundamental constants, conversion factors, and the Greek alphabet.

The Astronomy and Astrophysics Encyclopedia, ed. by Stephen P. Maran. New York: Van Nostrand Reinhold, 1992. (QB 14 .A837)

Signed articles by scholars in the field of astronomical topics, with a focus on discovery, study, and interpretation.

Encyclopedic Dictionary of Physics, ed. by J. Thewlis. 9 vols. and 4 supps. Oxford: Pergamon Press, 1971. (QC 5 .E53)

This encyclopedia has subject and author indexes and a multilingual glossary in English, French, German, Spanish, Russian, and Japanese.

Encyclopedia of Physics, ed. by Rita G. Lerner and George L. Trigg. 2nd ed. New York: VCH Publishers, 1991. (QC 5 .E546)

The Encyclopedia of Physics, ed. by Robert M. Besancon. 3rd ed. New York: Van Nostrand Reinhold, 1990. (QC 5 .E545)

The two single-volume encyclopedias listed above include signed articles by scholars in the field and select bibliographies on physics information sources.

International Encyclopedia of Astronomy. New York: Orion, 1987. (QB 14 .I58)

This single-volume illustrated encyclopedia of signed articles by scholars in the field covers seven major areas: the universe, the big bang, exploring space, interstellar matter, moons, pulsars, and super-clusters.

LB (Landolt-Bornstein) Numerical Data and Functional Relationships in Science and Technology. Berlin: Springer-Verlag. (QC 61 .L332)

LB is a voluminous continuing series of works on the scattering of elementary particles, molecular constants, magnetic properties, structural data, metals, semiconductors, geophysics, and meteorology. Look for the comprehensive index volume covering 1950 to 1985 and the subsequent annual index volumes when using *LB.*

PH (Handbuch der Physik) Encyclopedia of Physics. Berlin: Springer-Verlag. (QC 21 .H33)

Another multivolume continuing series covering mathematics, mechanics of solids, fluid dynamics, acoustics, light and matter, atoms, nuclear reactions, geophysics, and astrophysics.

Directories

World Nuclear Directory. 7th ed. London: Longman, 1985. (QC 774.2 .W67)

Information on institutions, organizations, and research centers involved in nuclear research and operations. Arranged by country.

* *Encyclopedia of Associations.* (HS 17 .G334)
* *International Research Centers Directory.* (Q 179.98 .I58)

Fact Books

* *Facts on File.* (D 410 .F3)
* *Keesing's Record of World Events.* (D 410 .K4)

Guides and Handbooks

CRC Handbook of Chemistry and Physics: 1992–1993, ed. by David R. Lide. 73rd ed. Boca Raton, Fla.: CRC Press, 1992. (QD 65 .H5)

A handbook including index and tables covering chromatography, spectrophotometry, spectroscopy, and qualitative tests.

American Institute of Physics Handbook. 3rd ed. New York: McGraw-Hill, 1972. (QC 61 .A5)

A handbook covering subjects in physics such as mechanics, acoustics, optics, atomic and molecular physics, and nuclear physics.

Periodicals

Advances in Physics
American Journal of Physics
Annals of Physics
Applied Physics
Astronomical Journal
Astronomy Quarterly
Astronomy and Astrophysics
Astronomy Magazine
Bulletin of the American Physical Society
Bulletin of the American Astronomical Society
Contemporary Physics
Essays in Physics
Foundations of Physics
International Journal of Theoretical Physics
International Comet Quarterly
Journal of Applied Physics
Journal of the American Association of Variable Star Observers
Journal of Physics
Journal of Chemical Physics

Physical Review
Physics Today
Planetary Report
Reviews of Modern Physics
Sky and Telescope

Statistical Sources

* *Statistics Sources.* (HA 35 .S84)

SELECT SUBJECT HEADINGS, BREAKDOWNS, AND CALL NUMBERS

Astronomy (QB 1 - QB 991)

Ephermerides (QB 7 - QB 14)
History (QB 15 - QB 55)
Study and Teaching (QB 61 - QB 70)
Observatories (QB 81 - QB 84)
Astronomical Instruments (QB 85 - QB 139)

Practical and Spherical Astronomy (QB 140 - QB 237)

Correction and Reduction of Observation (QB 151 - QB 185)
Geodetic Astronomy (QB 201 - QB 207)
Time (QB 209 - QB 224)
Longitude and Latitude (QB 225 - QB 237)

Geodesy (QB 275 - QB 343)

Geodetic Surveying (QB 301 - QB 328)
Gravity Determinations (QB 330 - QB 343)

Theoretical Astronomy and Celestial Mechanics (QB 349 - QB 488)

Perturbations (QB 361 - QB 410)
Theory of Tides (QB 414 - QB 450)
Astrophysics (QB 460 - QB 466)
Nonoptical Methods of Astronomy (QB 468 - QB 488)

Descriptive Astronomy (QB 495 - QB 991)

Universe. Space (QB 495 - QB 500)
Solar System (QB 501 - QB 991)
  Sun (QB 520 - QB 540)
  Moon (QB 580 - QB 595)
  Planets (QB 595 - QB 701)
  Comets (QB 717 - QB 732)
  Meteors (QB 740 - QB 753)
  Stars (QB 799 - QB 991)

Physics (QC 1 - QC 999)

Periodicals (QC 1)
Collected Works (QC 3)
Dictionaries and Encyclopedias (QC 5)
Philosophy (QC 5.5)
Nomenclature (QC 5.8)
History (QC 5.9)
Biography (QC 9)
Directories (QC 16.2)
Early Works (QC 17 - QC 19)
Mathematical Physics (QC 19.2 - QC 19.85)
Study and Teaching (QC 30 - QC 47)
Laboratories (QC 51)
Data Processing (QC 52)
Instruments and Apparatus (QC 53)
Museums (QC 60)
Handbooks, Tables, Formulas (QC 61)
Addresses. Essays. Lectures (QC 71)
Force and Energy (QC 72 - QC 75)
Weights and Measures (QC 81 - QC 114)
Descriptive and Experimental Mechanics (QC 120 - QC 168)
Atomic Physics (QC 170 - QC 197)
Acoustics. Sound (QC 221 - QC 246)
Heat (QC 251 - QC 338.5)
Optics. Light (QC 350 - QC 467)
Radiation Physics (QC 474 - QC 496.9)
Electricity and Magnetism (QC 501 - QC 766)
Nuclear and Particle Physics (QC 770 - QC 798)
Geophysics (QC 801 - QC 809)

Geomagnetism (QC 811 - QC 849)
Meteorology (QC 851 - QC 999)

CHEMISTRY

Abstracts and Indexes

Chemical Abstracts. Columbus, Ohio: American Chemical Society, weekly. (QD 1 .A51)

Abstracts of molecular chemistry, applied chemistry, chemical engineering, physical, inorganic, and analytical chemistry. Includes author, keyword, and patent indexes.

* *Applied Science and Technology Index.* (Z 7913 .I7)
* *General Science Index.* (Q 1 .G46)
* *Index to Scientific and Technical Proceedings.* (Q 101 .I5)
* *Index to Scientific Reviews.* (Q 1 .I381)
* *Science Citation Index.* (Q 1 .S32)
* *Technical Book Review Index.* (Z 7913 .T36)

Bibliographies

How to Find Chemical Information: A Guide for Practicing Chemists, Teachers and Students, by Robert E. Maizell. New York: Wiley, 1979. (QD 8.5 .M34)

A bibliographical guide to chemical literature, providing access to books, articles, patents, documents, and reviews in chemistry, chemical marketing, and business.

* *Scientific and Technical Books in Print.* (Q 100 .S41)

Biographical Sources

* *American Men and Women of Science.* (Q 141 .A47)
* *Dictionary of Scientific Biography.* (Q 141 .D5)

Chronologies and Histories

* *Chronology of the History of Science: 1450–1900.* (Q 125 .G39)
* *Timetables of Science.* (Q 125 .H557)

Dictionaries and Encyclopedias

The Concise Dictionary of Chemistry. New York: Oxford University Press, 1985. (QD 5 .C66)

The Facts on File Dictionary of Chemistry, ed. by John Daintith. New York: Facts on File, 1981. (QD 5 .D26)

The two chemistry dictionaries listed above provide definitions for chemical terms and concepts and tables of chemical elements.

Beilstein Handbook of Organic Chemistry. Berlin: Springer-Verlag. (QD 251 .B42)

This encyclopedic work, now in its fifth continuing series, contains "information and data relating to the structure, preparation and properties of organic compounds reported in the primary literature."

Comprehensive Biochemistry. 37 vols. Amsterdam: Elsevier, 1962–1990. (QD 415 .F63 C7)

Comprehensive encyclopedia of biological compounds, biochemical reaction mechanisms, and biochemical metabolism. Also covers the history of biochemistry.

Comprehensive Inorganic Chemistry. 5 vols. Oxford: Pergamon, 1973. (QD 151.2 .C73)

Comprehensive encyclopedia of inorganic chemistry, organized by chemical element; includes a master index.

Comprehensive Organic Chemistry: The Synthesis and Reaction of Organic Compounds, ed. by J. F. Stoddart. 6 vols. Oxford: Pergamon, 1979. (QD 245 .C65)

Stereochemistry, hydrocarbons, acids, organometallics, and biological compounds. Includes indexes by author, formula, subject, reagent, and reaction.

Comprehensive Organometallic Chemistry, ed. by Sir Geoffrey Wilkinson. 9 vols. Oxford: Pergamon, 1982. (QD 411 .C65)

Signed articles by scholars in the field. Includes subject, author, and formula indexes and an index of review articles and books.

Dictionary of Organic Compounds. 4th ed. 5 vols. New York: Oxford University Press, 1965. (QD 251 .D69)

An encyclopedic dictionary with long principal entries, formulas, functional derivations, and bibliographies.

Encyclopedia of Chemical Technology. 3rd ed. 24 vols., suppls., and index. New York: Wiley, 1978–84. (TP 9 .E685)

Signed articles by scholars in the field on chemical technology and industrial processes; covers the relationship of chemistry to subjects including energy, health, safety, and toxicology.

The Encyclopedia of Chemistry, ed. by Clifford A. Hampel and Gessner G. Hawley. 3rd ed. New York: Van Nostrand Reinhold, 1973. (QD 5 .E56)

Signed articles by scholars in the field on the various aspects of chemical science, including organic, inorganic, and analytical chemistry.

Gardner's Chemical Synonyms and Trade Names. 9th ed. Brookfield, Vt.: Gower Publishing Co., 1987. (TP 9 .G286)

A two-part chemical dictionary; includes an alphabetical list of trade names and their synonyms and a list of names and addresses of manufacturers and suppliers.

Hawley's Condensed Chemical Dictionary, rev. ed. by N. Irving Sax and Richard J. Lewis, Sr. 11th ed. New York: Van Nostrand Reinhold, 1987. (QD 5 .C5)

Hawley's gives definitions of terms and concepts in chemistry with appendices on the origin of chemical terms, the history of chemistry, chemical manufacturers, and trademarks.

MTP International Review of Science. London: Butterworths.

Three continuing multivolume encyclopedias in the study of chemistry: the *Inorganic Chemistry Series* (QD 151.2 .I58), the *Organic Chemistry Series* (QD 251.2 .O69), and the *Physical Series* (QD 453.2 .P57).

Mellor's Comprehensive Treatise on Inorganic and Theoretical Chemistry. New York: Longman's, 1922–67. (QD 31 .M52)

A multivolume encyclopedia covering the evolution and methodology of chemistry and the classification and study of the chemical elements.

The Thesaurus of Chemical Products. 2 vols. New York: Chemical Publishing Co., 1986. (TP 202 .A83)

Access to trade names under which chemicals are sold; cross-references generic chemical names with their trade names.

Treatise on Analytical Chemistry, ed. by Philip J. Elving. 14 vols. New York: Wiley, 1978–86. (QD 75.2 .K64)

Comprehensive encyclopedia of analytical chemistry with substantial bibliographies and subject indexes.

* *Acronyms, Initialisms and Abbreviations Dictionaries.* (P 365 .A28)

Directories

* *Encyclopedia of Associations.* (HS 17 .G334)
* *International Research Centers Directory.* (Q 179.98 .I58)

Guides and Handbooks

CRC Handbook of Basic Tables for Chemical Analysis. Boca Raton, Fla.: CRC Press, 1989. (QD 78 .B78)

Includes an index and tables covering chromatography, spectrophotometry, spectroscopy, and qualitative tests.

Chemical Engineer's Handbook. 5th ed. New York: McGraw-Hill, 1973. (TP 151 .C51)

Covers fundamental tables, the handling of fluids and solids, heat generation and transfer, and allied areas of engineering.

Handbook of Analytical Chemistry, ed. by Louis Meites. New York: McGraw-Hill, 1963. (QD 71 .M51)

Tables of fundamental data and qualitative analysis, discussion of techniques and methods, statistics in chemistry, and definitions of terms and symbols.

Lange's Handbook of Chemistry, ed. by John A. Dean. 13th ed. New York: McGraw-Hill, 1985. (TP 151 .H23)

Includes tables of mathematics, atomic and molecular structure, inorganic, organic, and analytical chemistry, electrochemistry, and spectroscopy.

Periodicals

Analytical Chemistry
Biochemistry
Canadian Journal of Chemistry
Chemical Bulletin
Chemical Communications
Chemical Reviews
Chemical Week
Chemist
Chemistry
Chemtech
Essays in Chemistry
Inorganic Chemistry
Journal of the American Chemical Society
Journal of Chemical Documentation
Journal of Chemical Education
Journal of Chemical Physics
Journal of Organic Chemistry
Today's Chemist
Topics in Current Chemistry

Statistical Sources

* *Statistics Sources.* (HA 36 .S84)

SELECT SUBJECT HEADINGS, BREAKDOWNS, AND CALL NUMBERS

Chemistry (QD 1 - QD 999)

History (QD 11 - QD 23)
Alchemy (QD 23 - QD 39)
Study and Teaching (QD 40 - QD 49)
Laboratories (QD 51 - QD 60)
Techniques and Operations (QD 63 - QD 70)

Analytical Chemistry (QD 71 - QD 142)

Quantitative Analysis (QD 81 - QD 96)
Qualitative Analysis (QD 101 - QD 121)
Technical Analysis (QD 130 - QD 142)

Inorganic Chemistry (QD 146 - QD 197)

Nonmetals (QD 161 - QD 169)
Metals (QD 171 - QD 197)

Organic Chemistry (QD 241 - QD 441)

Operations in Organic Chemistry (QD 257 - QD 315)
Carbohydrates (QD 320 - QD 327)
Aromatic Compounds (QD 327 - QD 341)
Antibiotics (QD 375 - QD 377)
Polymers (QD 380 - QD 388)
Organometallic Chemistry (QD 410 - QD 412)
Biological Chemistry (QD 415 - QD 441)

Physical and Theoretical Chemistry (QD 450 - QD 899)

Quantum Chemistry (QD 452 - QD 481)
Thermochemistry (QD 508 - QD 655)
Photochemistry (QD 701 - QD 731)

Crystallography (QD 901 - QD 999)

Geometrical/Mathematical Crystallography (QD 911 - QD 932)
Physical Properties of Crystals (QD 931 - QD 999)

MATHEMATICS

Abstracts and Indexes

Current Mathematical Publications. Providence, R.I.: American Mathematical Society, monthly. (QA 1.3)

An index to periodical literature and new books in mathematics published by the American Mathematical Society.

Mathematical Reviews. Providence, R.I.: American Mathematical Society, monthly. (QA 1 .M76)

Index and abstracts to articles on subjects for which mathematics provides the basis for understanding, including astronomy, economics, and biology.

* *Applied Science and Technology Index.* (Z 7913 .I7)
* *General Science Index.* (Q 1 .G46)
* *Index to Scientific and Technical Proceedings.* (Q 101 .I5)
* *Index to Scientific Reviews.* (Q 1 .I381)
* *Science Citation Index.* (Q 1 .S32)
* *Technical Book Review Index.* (Z 7913 .T36)

Bibliographies

Library Recommendations for Undergraduate Mathematics, by Lynn Arthur Steen. Washington, D.C.: Mathematical Association of America, 1992. (Z 6651 .L697)

A bibliography prepared by the Mathematical Association of America, which recommends specific texts and reference works for undergraduate mathematics libraries.

Use of Mathematical Literature, ed. by A. R. Darling. London: Butterworths, 1977. (QA 41.7 .U83)

The role of journals and reference materials in the study of mathematics, as well as sections on mathematical history and mathematical education.

* *Scientific and Technical Books in Print.* (Q 100 .S41)

Biographical Sources

The Biographical Dictionary of Scientists: Mathematicians. London: Blond Eduational, 1985. (QA 28 .B565)

Part of a series of biographical references on significant scientists, this Blond Educational title covers mathematicians on an international and historical basis.

* *American Men and Women of Science.* (Q 141 .A47)
* *Dictionary of Scientific Biography.* (Q 141 .D5)

Chronologies and Histories

* *Chronology of the History of Science: 1450–1900.* (Q 125 .G39)
* *Timetables of Science.* (Q 125 .H557)

Dictionaries and Encyclopedias

The Facts on File Dictionary of Mathematics, ed. by Carol Gibson. New York: Facts on File, 1981. (QA 5 .G52)

Mathematics Dictionary, by Glenn James and Robert C. James. New York: Van Nostrand Reinhold, 1992. (QA 5 .J33)

Webster's New World Dictionary of Mathematics, by William Karush. New York: Webster's New World, 1989. (QA 5 .K27)

A good mathematics dictionary will cover subjects in math as well as names if the name defines a mathematical concept, such as Kepler's Laws. A good mathematics dictionary should have appendices on symbols, notation, and conversion factors.

Encyclopedic Dictionary of Mathematics. Cambridge: MIT Press, 1987. (QA 5 .I8313)

This four-volume dictionary of mathematics is translated from the Japanese. It includes tables of formulas, statistical and numerical tables, and a name and subject index.

Encyclopedia of Mathematics. Holland: Reidel, 1987. (QA 5 .M3713)

This nine-volume encyclopedia of mathematics, translated from the Russian, has long survey articles, shorter, detailed problem articles, and brief definitions of mathematical concepts.

The VNR Concise Encyclopedia of Mathematics, by Walter Gellert. 2nd ed. New York: Van Nostrand Reinhold, 1989. (QA 40 .V18)

A one-volume illustrated encyclopedia of mathematics, which provides brief articles on subjects in mathematics, formulas, tables, and bibliographical references.

Guides and Handbooks

CRC Standard Mathematical Tables and Formulae, ed. by William H. Beyer. Boca Raton, Fla.: CRC Press, 1991. (QA 47 .M315)

Tables of constants and conversion factors and sections on algebra, geometry, trigonometry, analytical geometry, calculus, and differential equations. Includes appendix of mathematical symbols and notations.

Handbook of Applied Mathematics: Selected Results and Methods, by Carl E. Pearson. 2nd ed. New York: Van Nostrand Reinhold, 1983. (QA 40 .H34)

Provides formulas and tables as well as bibliographical references and an index.

Handbook of Mathematics, ed. by I. N. Bronshtein and K. A. Semendyayev. New York: Van Nostrand Reinhold, 1985. (QA 40 .B71)

Sections on mathematical tables, graphic representations, elementary mathematics, algebra, geometry, and calculus. Also includes bibliography and index.

An Index of Mathematical Tables, ed. by A. Fletcher and others. 2 vols. 2nd ed. Reading, Mass.: Addison-Wesley, 1962. (QA 47 .F55)

Volume one of this index of mathematical tables is arranged according to mathematical functions. Volume two provides a bibliography and index.

Periodicals

Advances in Applied Mathematics
American Journal of Mathematics
American Mathematical Monthly
Analyst
Annals of Mathematics
Applied Mathematics and Computation
Bulletin of the American Mathematical Society
College Mathematics Journal
Communications on Pure and Applied Mathematics
International Journal of Mathematical Education
Journal of the American Mathematical Society
Mathematics Magazine
National Mathematics Magazine
Proceedings of the American Mathematical Society
Studies in Applied Mathematics

Statistical Sources

* *Statistics Sources.* (HA 36 .S84)

SELECT SUBJECT HEADINGS, BREAKDOWNS, AND CALL NUMBERS

Mathematics (General Works) (QA 1 - QA 7)

Philosophy (QA 7 - QA 10)
Study and Teaching (QA 11 - QA 20)
History (QA 21 - QA 35)
General Works (QA 36 - QA 63)
Instruments and Machines (QA 64 - QA 74)

Arithmetic (QA 101 - QA 145)

Textbooks (QA 101 - QA 119)
Study and Teaching (QA 119 - QA 139)
Numeration (QA 139 - QA 145)

Algebra (QA 150 - QA 299)

Textbooks (QA 152 - QA 172)
Linear and Multilinear Algebra (QA 184 - QA 205)
Theory of Equations (QA 211 - QA 224)
Theory of Numbers (QA 224 - QA 255)
Machine Theory (QA 255 - QA 272)
Probabilities (QA 273 - QA 275)
Mathematical Statistics (QA 276 - QA 299)

Analysis (QA 299 - QA 433)

Calculus (QA 302 - QA 316)
Functional Analysis (QA 319 - QA 329)
Theory of Functions (QA 331 - QA 360)
Differential Equations (QA 370 - QA 387)

Geometry (QA 440 - QA 699)

Elementary Geometry (QA 451 - QA 477)
Special Topics in Plane Geometry (QA 481 - QA 497)
Descriptive Geometry (QA 497 - QA 529)
Trigonometry (QA 531 - QA 538)
Analytical Geometry (QA 551 - QA 563)
Algebraic Geometry (QA 564 - QA 581)
Topology (QA 611)
Algebraic Topology (QA 612)
Manifolds and Cell Complexes (QA 613)
Infinitesimal Geometry (QA 615 - QA 640)
Differential Geometry (QA 641 - QA 699)

Analytical Mechanics (QA 801 - QA 939)

Performing Arts

DANCE

Almanacs and Yearbooks

Dance World. New York: Crown, annual. (GV 1580 .D335)

Performance and production notes and details of cast, choreographers, and principal dancers of dance troupes and their performances throughout the year.

World Ballet and Dance: An International Yearbook. London: Dancebooks, annual. (GV 1580 .W89)

Covers ballet and modern dance throughout the world, as well as the traditional and ethnic dances of the nations of the world.

Bibliographies and Catalogs

Bibliographic Guide to Dance. Boston: G. K. Hall, annual (GV 1594 .N4)

Published since 1976, this bibliographic resource supplements the *New York Public Library Dictionary Catalog,* listed below.

The New York Public Library Dictionary Catalog of the Dance Collection. 10 vols. Boston: G. K. Hall, 1974. (GV 1593 .N48)

This catalog covers books, articles, prints, photographs, manuscripts, drawings, motion pictures, musical scores, and tape recordings that make up the library's dance collection.

Dance: An Annotated Bibliography, by Fred R. Forbes. New York: Garland, 1986. (GV 1594 .F58)

This bibliography of dance covers the period 1965 to 1982 and includes bibliographies of reference sources, reviews, and criticism.

Modern Dance and Ballet on Film and Video: A Catalog, by Susan Braun. New York: Dance Films Associates, 1986. (GV 1595 .B68)

A catalog of dance, including modern, ballet, and other forms, that has been captured in performance on film or video.

* *Books in Print.* (Z 1215 .P972)

Biographical Resources

Biographical Dictionary of Dance, by Barbara Naomi Cohen-Stratyner. New York: Schirmer Books, 1982. (GV 1785 .A1 C58)

Four hundred years of European and American dance history with entries on nearly three thousand artists of the dance, including dancers and choreographers, their careers, writings, and performances.

* *Current Biography.* (CT 100 .C8)

Dictionaries and Encyclopedias

The Concise Oxford Dictionary of Ballet, by Horst Koegler. 2nd ed. New York: Oxford University Press, 1982. (GV 1585 .K6313)

A brief dictionary of the dance, including ballet, dancers, choreographers, and the terms of their art.

The Dance Encyclopedia, ed. by Anatole Chujoy and P. W. Manchester. New York: Simon & Schuster, 1967. (GV 1585 .C5)

Includes signed articles by scholars and artists covering names and subjects in all aspects of dance.

Dictionary of the Dance, by W. G. Raffe. New York: A. S. Barnes, 1964. (GV 1585 .R3)

A standard dictionary with bibliographies and a geographical index as well as an index to subjects related to the dance.

The Encyclopedia of Dance and Ballet, ed. by Mary Clarke and David Vaughan. New York: G. P. Putnam's Sons, 1977. (GV 1585 .E53)

This is an illustrated encyclopedia of dance, dancers, and choreographers, with a glossary of technical terms.

Directories

Dance Directory: Programs of Professional Preparation in American Colleges and Universities. Washington, D.C.: National Dance Association, biennial. (GV 1754 .A1 D3)

A directory of the educational resources available in dance in the United States. Includes information on cost, facilities, auditions and admissions, and financial aid.

Stern's Performing Arts Directory. New York: DM, Inc., annual. (GV 1580 .D247)

This directory covers dance and music, including performers, schools, services, periodicals, sponsors, and government arts agencies.

* *Awards, Honors and Prizes.* (AS 8 .A87)

Guides and Handbooks

The Complete Guide to Modern Dance, by Don McDonagh. New York: Doubleday, 1976. (GV 1783 .M26)

Brief biographies of dancers and choreographers with a "choreo-chronicle" for each individual listed.

The Dancer's Survival Manual, by Marian Horosko. New York: Harper & Row, 1987. (GV 1597 .H67)

A practical and motivational how-to book for dancers, including tips on auditions, dancers' health, and career choices.

Indexes

Ballet Plot Index: A Guide to Locating Plots and Descriptions of Ballets and Associated Material, by William E. Studwell and David A. Hamilton. New York: Garland, 1987. (GV 1790 .A1 S77)

An index to books and collections in the study of ballet and dance. Includes ballet and composer index.

* *New York Times Index.* (AI 21 .N44)
* *Readers' Guide to Periodical Literature.* (AI 3 .R48)

Periodicals

Dance
Dance and Dancers
Dance Chronicle
Dance Life
Dance Magazine
Dance News
Dance Perspectives
Dancing

SELECT SUBJECT HEADINGS, BREAKDOWNS, AND CALL NUMBERS

Dancing   (GV 1580 - GV 1799)

Periodicals (GV 1580)
Congresses (GV 1583)
Dictionaries. Encyclopedias (GV 1585)
Terminology (GV 1587)
Philosophy (GV 1588)
General Works (GV 1590 - GV 1594)
Dancing as a Profession (GV 1597)
Addresses. Essays. Lectures (GV 1599)
Dance Criticism (GV 1600)
History (GV 1601 - GV 1743)
Social Dancing (GV 1746 - GV 1779)
Theatrical Dancing (GV 1781 - GV 1785)
   Ballet (GV 1786 - GV 1799)

DRAMATIC ARTS

Abstracts, Digests, and Indexes

The Film Index: A Bibliography. 3 vols. White Plains, N.Y.: Kraus International Publishers, 1985. (PN 1993.45 .W74)

Originally produced as a project of the Works Progress Administration in New York City, these three volumes, reprinted in 1985, cover the film as art, the film as industry, and film in society. Coverage is up to the late 1930s.

Film Literature Index. New York: Film and Television Documentation Center. (Z 5784 .M9 F45)

Quarterly index by author and subject to international periodical literature on film, television, and video. Indexes three hundred periodical titles covering more than one thousand subject headings.

Film Review Index: 1882–1985, ed. by Patricia King Hanson and Stephen L. Hanson. Phoenix, Ariz.: Oryx Press, 1986. (PN 1995 .F54)

An index to film reviews by director, by year produced, by country, and by film title. Includes extensive bibliography.

International Index to Film Periodicals: An Annotated Guide. London: International Federation of Film Archives, annual. (Z 5784 .M9 I49)

An index to the world's major film publications; includes an author, title, and subject index of reviews and biographies of noted people in film.

Magill's Survey of Cinema: English Language Films. Englewood Cliffs, N.J.: Salem Press, 1981. (PN 1993.45 .M3)

Magill's Survey of Cinema: Foreign Language Films. Englewood Cliffs, N.J.: Salem Press, 1985. (PN 1993.45 .M34)

Magill's Survey of Cinema: Silent Films. Englewood Cliffs, N.J.: Salem Press, 1982. (PN 1995.75 .M25)

Magill's Survey of Cinema is a digest covering English-language, foreign-language, and silent films. It is supplemented annually by *Magill's Cinema Annual*. Information for each film includes release date, production, direction, screenplay, cinematography, editing, art direction, costume, music, running time, cast, and synopsis.

* *Arts and Humanities Citation Index.* (AI 3 .A63)
* *American Humanities Index.* (AI 3 .A7)
* *British Humanities Index.* (AI 3 .B7)
* *Humanities Index.* (AI 3 .H85)
* *New York Times Index.* (AI 21 .N44)
* *Readers' Guide to Periodical Literature.* (AI 3 .R48)

Almanacs and Yearbooks

Film Review: 1991–92, Including Video Releases, by F. Maurice Speed and James Cameron-Wilson. London: Virgin, 1991. (PN 1993 .F624)

An international yearbook on the cinema, including coverage of the top ten films, new stars and new films, reviews, quotes, and a bibliography of books on film published during the year.

International Motion Picture Almanac. New York: Quigley Publishing Company, Inc., annual. (PN 1993.3 .I55)

International Television and Video Almanac. New York: Quigley Publishing Company, Inc., annual. (PN 1992.1 .I55)

These two almanacs contain sections on the industry year in review, statistics, awards, festivals, services, and a brief who's who in the entertainment industry.

Magill's Cinema Annual. Englewood Cliffs, N.J.: Salem Press. (PN 1993.45 .M33)

Published since 1982, this annual supplement to *Magill's Survey of Cinema* includes each film's release date, production, direction, screenplay, cinematography, editing, art direction, costume, music, running time, cast, and synopsis.

Theatre World. New York: Theatre World, annual. (PN 2277 .N5 A17)

Published since 1945, *Theatre World* is the yearbook of the American theater. It carries production photos, cast lists, running dates, and brief biographies of actors and directors.

Bibliographies and Catalogs

The American Film Institute Catalog of Motion Pictures Produced in the United States. 4 vols. New York: Bowker, 1976. (PN 1998 .A57)

A continuing set that covers feature films from 1921 through 1970. Includes information on cast, credits, and synopsis.

Blacks in American Films and Television, by Donald Bogle. New York: Garland, 1988. (PN 1995.9 .N4 B58)

A bibliography and index to movies, television series, miniseries, and specials featuring African-Americans. Entries are alphabetical by film title and include credits, cast, synopsis, and reviews.

The British Film Catalog: A Reference Guide, by Denis Gifford. London: David & Charles, 1986. (PN 1993.5 .G7 G53)

Covers one hundred years of British film, including information on titles, length, censor's certification, production and distribution, direction, the screenplay, cast and characters, and a plot summary. Includes title, and British/American alternate title index.

Ethnic and Racial Images in American Film and Television: Historical Essays and Bibliography, by Allen L. Woll and Randall M. Miller. New York: Garland, 1987. (PN 1995.9 .M56 W65)

Covers African-Americans, Arabs, Asians, Eastern Europeans and Russians, Germans, Hispanic Americans, Irish, Italians, Jews, and Native Americans. Includes author, film, and subject index.

Film Study: An Analytical Bibliography, by Frank Marchel. 4 vols. Madison, N.J.: Fairleigh Dickinson University Press, 1990. (PN 1994 .M36)

International in scope, this substantial bibliography covers the industry, film criticism, audiences, Hollywood, literature and film, film history, and film in other countries.

The Macmillan Film Bibliography: A Critical Guide to the Literature of the Motion Picture, by George Rehrauer. 2 vols. New York: Macmillan, 1982. (PN 1993.5 .A1 R44)

Reviews of motion pictures, books, periodicals, films, songs, television programs, stage plays, and screen plays. Includes notes on content, quality, availability, format, and subject matter.

On the Screen: A Film, Television, and Video Resource Guide, by Kim N. Fisher. Little, Colo.: Libraries Unlimited, 1986. (PN 1994 .F57)

Lists bibliographical guides, dictionaries, encyclopedias, indexes, abstracts, data bases, biographies, catalogs, directories and yearbooks, research centers, and societies.

* *Books in Print.* (Z 1215 .P972)

Biographical Sources

The Post-Feminist Hollywood Actress: Biographies and Filmographies of Stars Born After 1939, by Kerry Seagrave and Linda Martin. Jefferson, N.C.: McFarland, 1990. (PN 1998.2 .S44)

Discussion of the modern film actress with material organized in groups, such as superstars, leading ladies, new screen stars, and up-and-coming actresses.

Who's Who in Entertainment. Chicago: Marquis, 1988. (PN 1583 .W46)

Biographical sketches and directory information on performing artists and entertainers in the United States and Canada.

Who Was Who on Screen, by Evelyn Mack Truitt. 3rd ed. New York: Bowker, 1983. (PN 1998 .A2 T73)

Lists alphabetically by name many of the great stars of the early film days. Includes credits and awards.

Who's Who in American Film Now, by James Monaco. New York: New York Zoetrope, 1987. (PN 1993.5 .U6)

Covers current writers, producers, directors, actors, designers, cinematographers, choreographers, stunt people, musicians, special-effects wizards, and editors.

* *Current Biography.* (CT 100 .C8)

Dictionaries and Encyclopedias

The Complete Film Dictionary, by Ira Konigsberg. New York: New American Library, 1987. (PN 1993.45 .K66)

A one-volume dictionary of practical terms, technical terms, historical terms, and the language of business, production, criticism, and theory.

The Great Spanish Films: 1950–1990, by Ronald Schwartz. Metuchen, N.J.: Scarecrow, 1991. (PN 1993.5 .S7 S29)

Organized by decade, this reference work presents films alphabetically by title. Includes information on directors, credits, cast, commentary, and plot summary. Includes chronology, index, and bibliography.

Les Brown's Encyclopedia of Television, by Les Brown. New York: New York Zoetrope, 1982. (PN 1992.18 .B7)

Illustrated encyclopedia of names and subjects in television, including bibliographical and statistical appendices.

The Complete Actor's Television Credits, 1948–1988, by James Robert Parish and Vincent Terrace. 2nd ed. Metuchen, N.J.: Scarecrow Press, 1989. (PN 1992.4 .A2)

This reference work comes in two volumes, one for actors and one for actresses, covering every show or series appearance. Includes show title, dates, and channels.

The Complete Encyclopedia of Television Programs: 1947–1979, by Vincent Terrace. 2 vols. New York: A. S. Barnes, 1979. (PN 1992.3 .U5 T46)

A description of every show, its cast, stock performers, music, hosts, number of episodes, and running dates.

Encyclopedia of Television: Series Plots & Specials, 1937–1984, by Vincent Terrace. 2 vols. New York: New York Zoetrope, 1985. (PN 1992.3 .T46)

An update of the encyclopedia listed above, which gives a description of every show, its cast, stock performers, music, hosts, number of episodes, and running dates. Includes both serials and special shows.

International Dictionary of Films and Filmmakers. 4 vols. Chicago: St. James Press, 1984. (PN 1997.8 .F55)

Films, directors and filmmakers, actors and actresses, and writers and artists in the cinema. Includes bibliographies.

Directories

AFI Guide to College Courses in Film and Television. New York: Simon & Schuster, 1990. (PN 1993.8 .U5 A45)

This directory by The American Film Institute is a guide to undergraduate and graduate courses and schools. Includes index of degrees.

* *Awards, Honors and Prizes.* (AS 8 .A87)

Guides and Handbooks

Halliwell's Filmgoer's Companion, by Leslie Halliwell. 9th ed. London: Grafton Books, 1988. (PN 1993.45 .H35)

An alphabetical listing of movies and a bibliography of books. Includes index of films, fictional characters, series, and themes and index of alternative British/American titles.

Handbook of Soviet and East European Films and Filmmakers. New York: Greenwood, 1992. (PN 1993.5 .R9 H28)

Covers Russia, Poland, Czechoslovakia, Yugoslavia, Hungary, East Germany, Romania, and Bulgaria. Includes long essays on each country's film history and significant contributors. Includes chronology of major film events 1890–1990, and a subject and film index.

The Motion Picture Guide, by Jay Robert Nash and Stanley Ralph Ross. 12 vols. Chicago: Cinebooks, 1985. (PN 1995 .N346)

Organized alphabetically by film, this guide provides film titles, ratings, cast, synopsis, and notes on remakes and sequels.

The Oxford Companion to Film, by Liz-Anne Bawden. New York: Oxford University Press, 1976. (PN 1993.45 .O9)

This single-volume reference covers significant films and filmmakers, actors and actresses, and terminology in cinema.

Periodicals

American Theatre
Back Stage
Billboard
Drama
Drama Review
Film Comment
Film Quarterly
New Theatre Quarterly
Theater
Theatre Arts
Theatre Arts Monthly
Theatre Crafts
Theatre Journal
Theatre Survey
Variety

Reviews

Landers Film and Video Reviews. Escondido, Calif.: Landers Associates. (PN 1995 .L27)

Provides current reviews of current films alphabetically by film title, including credits, ratings, subject area, and commentary.

The New York Times Film Reviews: 1913–1982. 10 vols. New York: Times Books. (PN 1995 .N4)

This continuing series contains the reviews that ran in *The New York Times* during the dates specified. Includes reviews, a list of the best films of the year, and an index.

SELECT SUBJECT HEADINGS, BREAKDOWNS, AND CALL NUMBERS

The Performing Arts (PN 1560 - PN 1590)

    Periodicals (PN 1560 - PN 1569)
    Societies (PN 1570)
    Congresses, Conferences (PN 1574)
    Expositions (PN 1575)
    Study and Teaching (PN 1576)
    Dictionaries. Terminology (PN 1579)
    Performing Arts as a Profession (PN 1580)
    History (PN 1581)
    Biography (PN 1583)
    General Works (PN 1584)
    Centers for the Performing Arts (PN 1585 - PN 1589)
    Special Topics A–Z (PN 1590)

Drama (PN 1600 - PN 3307)

    Special Subjects (PN 1635 - PN 1650)
    Technique of Dramatic Composition (PN 1660 - PN 1693)
    History (PN 1720 - PN 1861)
    Special Types (PN 1865 - PN 1988)
    Broadcasting (PN 1990 - PN 1992.92)
      Radio Broadcasts (PN 1991 - PN 1991.9)
      Television Broadcasts (PN 1992 - PN 1992.92)
    Nonbroadcast Video Recordings (PN 1992.93 - PN 1992.95)
    Motion Pictures (PN 1993 - PN 1999)
    Dramatic Representation (PN 2000 - PN 3307)
      Art of Acting (PN 2061 - PN 2071)
      The Stage and Accessories (PN 2085 - PN 2091)
      By Period (PN 2131 - PN 2193)
      Ancient (PN 2131 - PN 2193)
      Medieval (PN 2152 - PN 2160)
      Renaissance (PN 2171 - PN 2179)

Modern (PN 2181 - PN 2193)
Special Regions or Countries (PN 2219.3 - PN 3030)
The Jewish Theater (PN 3035)
Amateur Theatricals (PN 3151 - PN 3171)
College and School Theatricals (PN 3175 - PN 3191)
Tableaux, Pageants (PN 3203 - PN 3299)

MUSIC

Abstracts and Indexes

The Music Index. Madison Heights, Mich.: Harmonie Park Press, monthly. (ML 118 .M84)

A subject and author guide to music periodical literature, covering hundreds of periodicals worldwide. Includes citations to book reviews.

RILM: Abstracts of Music Literature. New York: RILM Abstracts, quarterly. (ML 1 .I83)

Since 1967, the International Repertory of Music Literature has published these abstracts of secondary music literature covering approximately one hundred categories, including reference materials, historical musicology, ethnomusicology, theory, and related disciplines.

* *Arts and Humanities Citation Index.* (AI 3 .A63)
* *American Humanities Index.* (AI 3 .A7)
* *British Humanities Index.* (AI 3 .B7)
* *Humanities Index.* (AI 3 .H85)
* *New York Times Index.* (AI 21 .N44)
* *Readers' Guide to Periodical Literature.* (AI 3 .R48)

Bibliographies

Music: A Guide to the Reference Literature, by William S. Brockman. Littleton, Colo.: Libraries Unlimited, 1987. (ML 113 .G85)

A bibliography of general reference sources, bibliographical sources, music literature, and discographies. Includes supplemental sources on music societies, institutes, organizations, and associations.

Music Reference and Research Materials: An Annotated Bibliography, by Vincent H. Duckles and Michael A. Keller. 4th ed. New York: Schirmer Books, 1988. (ML 133 .D83)

An annotated bibliography covering dictionaries and encyclopedias, histories and chronologies, guides, catalogs, discographies, yearbooks, directories, and indexes.

Popular Music: A Reference Guide, by Roman Iwaschkin. New York: Garland, 1986. (ML 128 .P63 I95)

A bibliography of popular music, including Cajun, rap, and hip-hop, country, folk, jazz, and music from the stage and screen. Also covers music education, instruments, business, and careers.

* *Books in Print.* (Z 1215 .P972)

Biographical Sources

Baker's Biographical Dictionary of Musicians, ed. and revised by Nicolas Slonimsky. 7th ed. New York: Schirmer Books, 1984. (ML 105 .B16)

Biographical information on men and women composers and musicians, with dates of their first performances of major works, bibliography, and index.

Biographical Dictionary of Afro-American and African Musicians, by Eileen Southern. Westport, Conn.: Greenwood, 1982. (ML 105 .S67)

Provides biographical information, bibliographies and discographies, with appendices by period of birth, place of birth, and musical occupation.

Biographical Directory of Russian/Soviet Composers, ed. by Allan Ho and Dmitry Feofanov. New York: Greenwood, 1989. (ML 106 .S68 B56)

Includes signed articles by scholars in the field covering Russian/Soviet composers and musicians. Includes discography, index, and a list of compositions for each composer.

Blues Who's Who: A Biographical Dictionary of Blues Singers, by Sheldon Harris. New York: Arlington House, 1979. (ML 102 .B6)

Biographies and select bibliographies on blues singers. Includes indexes to film, radio, television, theater, songs, names, and places. Coverage is from 1900 through 1977.

A Dictionary of American Composers. New York: Garland, 1984. (ML 106 .U3 B87)

Biographies of composers, including their major works, education, and professional life. Includes appendix on teachers and their students.

Greene's Biographical Encyclopedia of Composers, by David Mason Greene. New York: Doubleday, 1985. (ML 390 .G85)

Biographical information on composers and their works. Organized chronologically with an index to composers.

International Encyclopedia of Women Composers, by Aaron I. Cohen. 2nd ed. 2 vols. New York: Books & Music, 1987. (ML 105 .C7)

Biographical information on women composers with appendices on music key signatures in twenty-five languages, lists of pseudonyms, composers by instrument, calling, occupation, and profession. Includes bibliography and discography.

International Who's Who in Music and Musicians' Directory: 1992/93, by David M. Cummings. Cambridge, England: International Who's Who in Music, 1992. (ML 106 .G7 W45)

Biographical information; includes appendices on orchestras, opera companies, music organizations, major competitions and awards, music libraries, and conservatories.

The Piano in Concert, by George Kehler. Metuchen, N.J.: Scarecrow Press, 1982. (ML 42 .A357)

A unique resource, giving biographical information of pianists and their programs in public performances. Includes citations to reviews and a biographical sketch of each pianist.

Wilson Biographical Reference Books.

The H. W. Wilson Company of Bronx, New York, publishes several biographical reference books devoted to composers and musicians. Each provides authoritative information on the lives and careers of many of the world's most noted composers and musicians.

Great Composers: 1300–1900. (ML 105 .E944)
Composers Since 1900. (ML 390 .E833)
Musicians Since 1900. (ML 105 .E97)

* *Current Biography* (CT 100 .C8)

Chronologies and Histories

The World Chronology of Music History, compiled and ed. by Paul E. Eisler. New York: Oceana, 1972–   . (ML 161 .E4)

A chronological record by day, month, and year of significant events in the world of music. Includes illustrations.

Dictionaries and Encyclopedias

Dictionary of Music, ed. by Alan Isaacs and Elizabeth Martin. New York: Facts on File, 1983. (ML 100 .D56)

The Harper Dictionary of Music, ed. by Christine Ammer. 2nd ed. New York: Harper & Row, 1987. (ML 100 .A48)

The New American Dictionary of Music, by Philip D. Morehead and Anne MacNeil. New York: Dutton, 1992. (ML 100 .M857)

The New Harvard Dictionary of Music, by Don Michael Randel. Cambridge: Belknap Press, 1986. (ML 100 .R3)

The Oxford Dictionary of Music, by Michael Kennedy. New York: Oxford, 1985. (ML 100 .K35)

Each of the five dictionaries listed above is a single-volume subject dictionary devoted to the study of music. Each covers subjects and names in music and provides some illustrations.

American Song: The Complete Musical Theatre Companion, by Ken Bloom. 2 vols. New York: Facts on File, 1985. (ML 128 .M78 B6)

Alphabetical listing of American musicals, including the title, date the show opened, cast, composer, lyricists, producers, songs, and choreographers.

The Dictionary of Opera, by Charles Osborne. New York: Simon & Schuster, 1983. (ML 102 .O6 O8)

A dictionary of opera titles, composers, characters, plot synopses, singers and their major roles. Includes illustrations.

The Encyclopedia of Folk, Country and Western Music, by Irvin Stambler and Grelun Landon. New York: St. Martin's, 1983. (ML 102 .F66)

An encyclopedia of a popular musical form. Coverage includes name entries with substantial bibliographical information, lists of awards, illustrations, and bibliographies.

Encyclopedia of the Musical Theater, by Stanley Green. New York: Dodd, Mead & Co., 1976. (ML 102 .M88)

Names, subjects, plays and musicals, with sections on awards, prizes, and long runs. Includes bibliography and discography.

The New Grove Dictionary of American Music, ed. by H. Wiley Hitchcock and Stanley Sadie. 4 vols. London: Macmillan, 1986. (ML 101 .U6 N48)

The entries in this dictionary of music are taken from *The New Grove Dictionary of Music and Musicians* and *The New Grove Dictionary of Musical Instruments,* both of which are listed below. Includes signed articles by scholars in the field, bibliographies, illustrations, and lists of works in libraries.

The New Grove Dictionary of Jazz, ed. by Barry Kernfeld. 2 vols. London: Macmillan, 1988. (ML 102 .J3 N48)

The entries in this dictionary of music are taken from *The New Grove Dictionary of Music and Musicians* and *The New Grove Dictionary of Mu-*

sical Instruments, listed below, and includes signed articles by scholars in the field, bibliographies, illustrations, and lists of works in libraries.

The New Grove Dictionary of Music and Musicians, ed. by Stanley Sadie. 20 vols. London: Macmillan, 1980. (ML 100 .N48)

Sir George Grove's dictionary was first published in 1878. It now includes signed articles by over twenty-five hundred contributors and a hundred editors. The articles include bibliographies, cross-references, lists of musical works, and libraries throughout the world holding scores in their collections.

The New Grove Dictionary of Musical Instruments, ed. by Stanley Sadie. 3 vols. London: Macmillan, 1984. (ML 102 .I5)

Selections are taken from *The New Grove Dictionary of Music and Musicians,* above. The signed articles include bibliographies, cross-references, lists of musical works, and institutions holding examples of the instruments.

The New Oxford History of Music, ed. by Egon Wellesz. 10 vols. London: Oxford University Press, 1957. (ML 160 .N44)

The world's major historical periods in music, including ancient and Oriental music, medieval music, the Renaissance, opera and church music, romanticism, and modern music. Includes illustrations, chronological tables, and index.

Directories

Directory of Music Faculties in Colleges and Universities: U.S. and Canada: 1990–1992. Missoula, Mont.: CMS Publications, 1990. (ML 13 .D57)

Directory information for institutions and faculty members. Includes index by area of teaching interest and index of faculty and graduate degrees. Institutions are listed alphabetically.

Musical America: International Directory of the Performing Arts. New York: Musical America Publishers, annual. (ML 12 .M88)

A directory of music, musicians, and dance in the United States and Canada, with some international coverage. Includes orchestras, opera companies, festivals, music schools and departments, record companies, publishers, and periodicals.

The New York Philharmonic Guide to the Symphony, by Edward O. D. Downes. New York: Walker and Company, 1976. (MT 125 .D68)

A one-volume guide to symphonic music, written by a well-known music historian with the cooperation of one of the world's foremost symphonies.

Opera Companies of the World, ed. by Robert H. Cowden. New York: Greenwood, 1992. (ML 12 .O63)

Profiles of the world's major opera companies, listed alphabetically by country. Includes brief history of the company, directory information, and brief bibliography.

The Schirmer Guide to Schools of Music and Conservatories Throughout the World, by Nancy Uscher. New York: Schirmer Books, 1988. (ML 12 .U8)

International directory to music schools, alphabetically by country. Includes indexes by program area and musical instrument. Covers academic information such as facilities and financial aid.

* *Awards, Honors and Prizes.* (AS 8 .A87)

Guides and Handbooks

The New Kobbe's Complete Opera Book, ed. and revised by the Earl of Harewood. New York: Putnam, 1976. (MT 95 .K52)

A classic handbook for opera lovers, organized chronologically by composer and country. Good synopses of opera plots.

The New Oxford Companion to Music, ed. by Denis Arnold. New York: Oxford University Press, 1983. (ML 100 .S37)

This two-volume work, composed of signed articles by scholars in the field, is arranged in two broad topics. The section called "The Human Element" covers composers, geography, and history. The music section covers musical works, musical instruments, form, sound, notation, and musical theory.

The Oxford Companion to Popular Music, by Peter Gammond. London: Oxford University Press, 1991. (ML 102 .P66)

A reference source for pop music with entries by name and subject. Includes indexes by people and groups, shows and films, and songs and albums.

Periodicals

Bach Jahrbuch
Beethoven Jahrbuch
Billboard
Choral Journal
Clavier
Down Beat
Early Music
Etude
Fanfare
Guitar
International Review of Music Aesthetics
Journal of Music Theory
Journal of Music and Musicology
Journal of Research in Music Education
Modern Drummer
Music and Musicians
Music Journal
Music Review
Musical Quarterly
Notes
Opera News
Piano Quarterly
Symphony Magazine
Tempo

SELECT SUBJECT HEADINGS, BREAKDOWNS, AND CALL NUMBERS

Music (General) (M 1 - M 3)

Instrumental Music (M 1 - M 1490)

Solo Instruments (M 6 - M 175)
Instrumental Music for Motion Pictures (M 176)
Instrumental Music for Radio and Television (M 176.5)
Music for Two or More Solo Instruments (M 177 - M 990)
Orchestra (M 1000 - M 1075)
String Orchestra (M 1100 - M 1160)
Band (M 1200 - M 1269)
Fife (M 1270)
Reduced Orchestra (M 1350 - M 1353)
Mandolin (M 1360)
Accordion Music (M 1362)
Minstrel Music (M 1365)
Jazz Ensembles (M 1366)
Instrumental Music for Children (M 1375 - M 1420)
Dance Music (M 1450)
Electronic Music (M 1473)
Music with Color Apparatus (M 1480)

Vocal Music (M 1 - M 5000)

Secular Vocal Music (M 1497 - M 1998)
Sacred Vocal Music (M 1999 - M 2199)
Unidentified Compositions (M 5000)

Music Literature (ML 1 - ML 3930)

Festivals. Congresses (ML 35 - ML 38)
Programs (ML 40 - ML 44)
Librettos (ML 48 - ML 54.8)
Writings of Musicians (ML 90)
Manuscripts, Autographs, Etc. (ML 93 - ML 97)
Dictionaries. Encyclopedias (ML 100 - ML 109)
Bibliography (ML 111 - ML 158)
History and Criticism (ML 159 - ML 3797)
Philosophy and Physics of Music (ML 3800 - ML 3923)
Literature on Music for Children (ML 3930)

Music Instruction and Study (MT 1 - MT 949)

History and Criticism (MT 2 - MT 5)
Music Theory (MT 6 - MT 7)
Special Methods (MT 20 - MT 32)
Composition (MT 40 - MT 67)
Improvisation. Accompaniment (MT 68)
Orchestra and Orchestration (MT 70 - MT 71)
Band and Instrumentation for Band (MT 73)
Analytical Guides (MT 90 - MT 145)
Guides (MT 150)
Instrumental Techniques (MT 170 - MT 810)
Singing and Voice Culture (MT 820 - MT 949)

Social Sciences

ANTHROPOLOGY AND SOCIOLOGY

Abstracts and Indexes

Abstracts in Anthropology. Westport, Conn.: Greenwood, quarterly (GA 1 .A2)

Abstracts to thousands of articles on anthropology organized by author and by subject. International in scope.

American Public Opinion Index. Tallahassee, Fla.: Opinion Research Service, annual. (HM 261 .A463)

Organized by subject, *POI* "actually lists the questions asked in national, state and local surveys and opinion polls."

Combined Retrospective Index to Journals in Sociology: 1895–1974. Arlington, Va.: Carrollton Press, 1978. (HM 1 .A11 C75)

This is an author-subject index to more than five hundred journals in the fields of anthropology and sociology.

Criminal Justice Periodicals Index. Ann Arbor, Mich.: University Microfilms International. (HV 8138 .C74)

An index to more than one hundred U.S., British, and Canadian journals in corrections, criminology, police studies, and prison administration and rehabilitation. Published three times a year.

Criminology and Penology Abstracts. Amsterdam, Netherlands: Kugler Publications, bimonthly. (HV 6001 .E9)

Abstracts on crime and juvenile delinquency, treatment of offenders, criminal procedure, and administration of justice. International in scope.

Current Contents: Sociological and Behavioral Sciences. Philadelphia, Pa.: Institute for Scientific Information, monthly. (Z 5851 .E623)

Current Contents indexes and reprints the tables of contents from hundreds of journals in the social and behavioral sciences.

Index to International Public Opinion. New York: Greenwood, annual. (HM 261 .I552)

Information on polls from "over 145 countries and geographical regions throughout the world." Analysis by age, sex, economic and educational levels, and religions.

Sage Abstracts. Sage Publications, Inc.

Sage publishes several quarterly abstracts on important issues in sociology. These include:

Sage Family Studies Abstracts. (HQ 536 .S23)
Sage Public Administration Abstracts. (JA 1 .S27)
Sage Urban Studies Abstracts. (HT 51 .S2)

Social Work Research Abstracts. Washington, D.C.: National Association of Social Workers, quarterly. (HV 91 .S52)

Editorials on research in social work and an author-subject index to abstracts from social work journals.

Sociological Abstracts. San Diego, Calif.: Sociological Abstracts, Inc. (HM 1 .S6)

Abstracts include author, subject, and source indexes and cover anthropology, economics, education, medicine, philosophy, statistics, and political science. International in scope.

* *Index to Social Science and Humanities Proceedings.* (AI 3 .I53)
* *Public Affairs Information Service: PAIS International.* (Z 7163 .P9)
* *Social Science Citation Index.* (Z 7161 .S65)
* *Social Sciences and Humanities Index.* (AI 3 .R49)
* *Social Sciences Index.* (AI 3 .S62)

Almanacs and Yearbooks

The Gallup Poll: Public Opinion Annual. Wilmington, Del.: Scholarly Resources, Inc., annual. (HN 90 .P8 G34)

This annual by the well-known American polling organization represents the results of polls conducted in person and over the telephone on various subjects.

* *Chase's Annual Events.* (D 11.5 .C48)

Atlases

* *We the People.* (G 1201 .E1 A4)

Bibliographies

Catalog of Manuscripts at the National Anthropological Archives. Department of Anthropology, National Museum of Natural History, Smithsonian Institution. 4 vols. Boston: G. K. Hall, 1975. (GN 24 .N34)

A catalog of manuscripts, mostly documents collected by the Bureau of American Ethnology from 1879–1965, covering Native Americans.

Child Development Abstracts and Bibliography. Chicago: University of Chicago Press, quarterly. (HQ 750 .A1 C47)

Abstracts and bibliographies on child development covering the areas of biology, health and medicine, social psychology, and education.

International Bibliography of Social and Cultural Anthropology. New York and London: Routledge, annual. (Z 7161 .I594)

Part of the *International Bibliography of the Social Sciences,* this international, multilanguage bibliography covers materials in more than twenty-five languages and includes author, subject, and place-name indexes.

International Bibliography of Sociology. London and New York: Routledge, annual. (Z 7161 .I594)

Part of the *International Bibliography of the Social Sciences,* this international, multilanguage bibliography covers materials in more than twenty-five languages and includes indexes by author, subject, and place-name.

Inventory of Marriage and Family Literature. Anoka, Minn.: DataTRAQ International, Inc., annual. (HQ 728 .I57)

Annual bibliographical index to journal articles, including indexes of subject, author, and keyword in title.

Men's Studies: A Select and Annotated Interdisciplinary Bibliography, ed. by Eugene R. August. Littleton, Colo.: Libraries Unlimited, 1985. (HQ 1090 .A84)

Annotated bibliography of topics in men's studies in the areas of anthropology, sociology, and psychology.

Sociology: A Guide to Reference and Information Sources. Littleton, Colo.: Libraries Unlimited, 1987. (HM 51 .A29)

A general bibliography of sociology, with separate bibliographies on social science topics such as education, economics, psychology, social work, anthropology, and history.

Women's Studies: A Recommended Core Bibliography. 1980–1985, by Catherine R. Loeb and others. Littleton, Colo.: Libraries Unlimited, 1987. (HQ 1180 .L64)

Supplement to the original 1979 edition, covering significant works on women's studies in the areas of anthropology, sociology, and psychology.

* *Books in Print.* (Z 1215 .P972)

Biographical Sources

Biographical Dictionary of Social Welfare in America, ed. by Walter I. Trattner. New York: Greenwood, 1986. (HV 27 .B57)

Biographies of social workers from colonial times to the present. Includes chronology of significant events in the history of social welfare in the United States.

CD-ROM Data Bases

* PAIS International

Chronologies and Histories

* *Holidays and Anniversaries of the World.* (GT 3930 .H65)
* *New York Times Book of Chronologies.* (D 11 .W47)
* *Timetables of History.* (D 11 .G78)
* *Timetables of Science.* (Q 125 .H557)

Dictionaries and Encyclopedias

Encyclopedia of Crime and Justice, ed. by Sanford H. Kadish. New York: Free Press, 1983. (HV 6017 .E52)

Lengthy signed articles by scholars in the field on broad topics in crime and justice. Includes legal index and glossary.

The Encyclopedia of Marriage, Divorce and the Family, by Margaret DiCanio. New York: Facts on File, 1989. (HQ 9 .D38)

This is a one-volume encyclopedia of sociology focusing on the family. Includes bibliography and index.

Encyclopedia of Social Work. 2 vols. Silver Spring, Md.: National Association of Social Workers, 1987. (HV 35 .S6)

Signed articles by scholars in the field, including biographies and index. Covers economic, political, and social aspects of social work.

Encyclopedia of Sociology. 4 vols. New York: Macmillan, 1991. (HM 17 .E5)

Includes signed articles by scholars in the field and bibliographical references.

Women's Studies Encyclopedia, ed. by Helen Tierney. 2 vols. New York: Greenwood, 1989. (HQ 1115 .W645)

Signed articles by scholars in the field; includes bibliographies and index.

* *Dictionary of the History of Ideas.* (CB 5 .D52)
* *Harper Dictionary of Modern Thought.* (AG 5 .H19)

Directories

American Sociological Association Directory of Graduate Departments of Sociology. American Sociological Association, annual. (HM 9 .A65)

A directory of graduate departments in the United States; includes electronic addresses, a geographical list, and a list by major area of sociological interest.

American Sociological Association Directory of Members, annual. American Sociological Association. (HM 9 .A725)

A directory produced by the professional association for sociologists of its members throughout the United States. Includes electronic addresses, a geographical list, and a list by major area of sociological interest.

* *Encyclopedia of Associations.* (HS 17 .G334)

Guides and Handbooks

The Handbook of Social Psychology, ed. by Gardner Lindzey
and Elliot Aronson. 2 vols. New York: Random House, 1984. (HM
251 .H224)

Extensive signed articles by scholars in the field on broad topics in
sociology, such as theory and methods, special fields of sociology, and
applications.

Periodicals

American Anthropologist
American Sociologist
American Sociological Review
American Journal of Sociology
American Journal of Physical Anthropology
Anthropological Review
Anthropological Quarterly
Anthropological Newsletter
Anthropology and Education Quarterly
Anthropology
Applied Anthropology
Comparative Social Research
Contemporary Sociology
Critical Sociology
Cultural Anthropology
Current Anthropology
Ethnology
International Journal of Comparative Sociology
Journal of Anthropological Research
Journal of Society and Social Welfare
Research in Social Problems and Public Policy
Reviews in Anthropology
Sociological Quarterly
Sociological Inquiry
Sociological Review
Sociology

Statistical Sources

Sourcebook of Criminal Justice Statistics. Washington, D.C.: U.S. Department of Justice, annual. (HV 7245 .N37)

Statistics on the characteristics of the criminal justice system, attitudes toward crime, nature and distribution of known offenses, and persons under correctional supervision.

Statistical Handbook of the American Family. Phoenix, Ariz.: Oryx Press, 1992. (HQ 536 .S727)

A source for statistics on marriage, family life, divorce, children, sexual attitudes, family violence, and the elderly.

Statistical Handbook on Women in America. Phoenix, Ariz.: Oryx Press, 1991. (HQ 1420 .T34)

This statistical source covers demographics, employment, health, and social characteristics concerning women in America.

Uniform Crime Reports: Crime in the United States. Washington, D.C.: U.S. Department of Justice, annual. (HV 6787 .A3)

The Justice Department's annual statistical survey of crime in the United States, with statistics on crimes, persons arrested, and law enforcement. Includes index by crime.

* *American Statistics Index.* (Z 7554 .U5 A46)
* *County and City Data Book.* (HA 202 .A36)
* *State and Metropolitan Area Data Book.* (HA 205 .S72)
* *Statistical Reference Abstracts.* (HA 202 .S7)
* *Statistical Reference Index.* (HA 202 .S7)
* *Statistics Sources.* (HA 36 .S84)

Thesauruses

Finding the Source in Sociology and Anthropology: A Thesaurus-Index to the Reference Collection. New York: Greenwood, 1987. (HM 51 .B78)

A thesaurus of reference terms designed for use when conducting library research in sociology and anthropology.

Thesaurus of Sociological Indexing Terms. 2nd ed. San Diego, Calif.: Sociological Abstracts, Inc., 1989. (Z 691.1 .S63)

This thesaurus has an alphabetical list and a rotated-descriptor list (e.g., deviant behavior–behavior, deviant). Organization gives the main term, a descriptor code, history notes, and scope notes.

SELECT SUBJECT HEADINGS, BREAKDOWNS, AND CALL NUMBERS

Anthropology (GN 1 - GN 890)
Anthropology (General) (GN 1 - GN 47)
Physical Anthropology (GN 49 - GN 296)
Ethnology (GN 301 - GN 673)
Prehistoric Archaeology (GN 700 - GN 890)

Folklore (GR 1 - GR 950)

   Folk Literature (GR 72 - GR 79)
   Folklore Relating to Special Subjects (GR 420 - GR 950)

Manners and Customs (GT 1 - GT 7070)

   Houses. Dwellings (GT 170 - GT 476)
   Customs Relating to Private/Public Life (GT 500 - GT 2370)
   Customs Relating to Special Classes (GT 5320 - GT 6720)

Recreation (GV 1 - GV 1860)

   Outdoor Life (GV 191.2 - GV 200.66)
   Physical Education (GV 201 - GV 555)
   Games and Amusements (GV 1199 - GV 1570)
   Dancing (GV 1580 - GV 1799.3)
   Circuses, Spectacles, Etc. (GV 1800 - GV 1860)

Sociology (HM 1 - HX 970.7)

Sociology (General and Theoretical) (HM 1 - HM 299)

   Civilization. Culture. Progress (HM 101 - HM 121)
   Unity. Solidarity (HM 126)
   Association (HM 131 - HM 134)
   Individualism (HM 136 - HM 146)
   Social Elements (HM 201 - HM 221)

Social Psychology (HM 251 - HM 291)

Social History and Conditions (HN 1 - HN 980)

The Church and Social Problems (HN 30 - HN 40)
Community Centers (HN 41 - HN 46)
By Region (HN 50 - HN 980)

The Family. Marriage. Women (HQ 1 - HQ 2039)

Sexual Life (HQ 12 - HQ 449)
The Family. Marriage. Home (HQ 450 - HQ 471)
Death. Dying (HQ 1073)
Men (HQ 1090)
Women (HQ 1101 - HQ 2030)

Societies: Secret, Benevolent, Etc. (HS 1 - HS 3369)

Secret Societies (HS 101 - HS 330)
Freemasons (HS 351 - HS 929)
Odd Fellows (HS 951 - HS 1179)
Knights of Pythias (HS 1201 - HS 1350)
Other Societies A–Z (HS 1355)
Other Societies by Classes (HS 1501 - HS 2460)
Clubs (HS 2501 - HS 3365)

Communities. Classes. Races (HT 51 - HT 1595)

Communities (HT 51 - HT 65)
Urban Groups (HT 101 - HT 395)
Rural Groups (HT 401 - HT 485)
Classes (HT 601 - HT 1445)
Races (HT 1501 - HT 1595)

Social Pathology. Public Welfare. Criminology (HV 1 - HV 9960)

Charity Organizations and Practice (HV 40 - HV 69)
State Regulation of Charities (HV 70 - HV 72)
By Region (HV 85 - HV 520)
Women and Charity (HV 541)
Charity Fairs (HV 544)
International Social Work (HV 544.5)
Relief (HV 553 - HV 639)

Refugee Problems (HV 640 - HV 645)
Lifesaving (HV 650 - HV 670)
Prevention of Accidents (HV 675 - HV 677)
Free Professional Services (HV 680 - HV 694)
Protection, Assistance, and Relief (HV 697 - HV 1493)
Degeneration (HV 4961 - HV 4995)
Alcoholism (HV 5001 - HV 5720)
Tobacco Habit (HV 5725 - HV 5770)
Drug Habit (HV 5800 - HV 5840)
Criminology (HV 6035 - HV 6197)
Penology (HV 7231 - HV 9920)

Socialism. Communism. Anarchism (HX 1 - HX 970)

Communism/Socialism (HX 519 - HX 550)
Communism: Utopian Socialism (HX 626 - HX 780)
Utopias (HX 806 - HX 811)
Anarchism (HX 821 - HX 970)

EDUCATION

Abstracts and Indexes

Current Index to Journals in Education. Educational Resources Information Center (ERIC). Phoenix, Ariz.: Oryx Press. (LB 5 .C82)

An index by author and subject to contents in educational periodical literature. Indexes more than seven hundred journals. Gives brief abstracts.

Educational Administration Abstracts. Newberry Park, Calif.: Sage Abstracts. (LB 2341 .E3)

These abstracts cover administration, curriculum, teaching, testing, professional preparation, certification, professional development, professional evaluation, and special programs.

Education Index. New York: Wilson. (LB 7 .E23)

Index of articles in English-language periodicals in secondary education, higher education, adult education, and teacher education.

Higher Education Abstracts. Claremont, Calif.: Claremont College, annual. (Z 5814 .P8 C6)

Abstracts topics including students, faculty, administration, and higher education. Abstracts are indexed by author and subject. Most of the abstracting is done by graduate students, who review some one hundred education journals in the process.

Resources in Education. Educational Resources Information Center (ERIC). Washington, D.C.: Department of Education, monthly. (LB 1028 .R4)

ERIC provides indexes and abstracts, by subject, author, and institution, to significant documents in education.

* *Dissertation Abstracts International.* (Z 5055 .U5)
* *Index to Social Science and Humanities Proceedings.* (AI 3 .I53)
* *Public Affairs Information Service: PAIS International.* (Z 7163 .P9)
* *Social Science Citation Index.* (Z 7161 .S65)
* *Social Sciences and Humanities Index.* (AI 3 .R49)
* *Social Sciences Index.* (AI 3 .S62)

Almanacs and Yearbooks

The Condition of Education. Washington, D.C.: Department of Education, annual. (L 112 .N377)

This annual publication by the Department of Education provides data on education in America, covering access to education, curriculum, economic outcomes of education, output of educational institutions, diversity of educational institutions, and human and financial resources of educational institutions.

* *Almanac of the 50 States.* (HA 203 .A5)
* *Book of the States.* (JK 2403 .B62)
* *Information Please Almanac.* (AY 64 .I55)
* *World Almanac and Book of Facts.* (AY 67 .N5 W7)

Anthologies and Collections

Education in the United States: A Documentary History, ed. by Sol Cohen. 5 vols. New York: Random House, 1973. (LA 205 .C53)

An extensive collection of articles and other documents on American education, covering the European heritage in American education, colonial colleges, the profession of education, and other topics. Includes index and bibliography.

Bibliographies

Education: A Guide to Reference and Information Sources, by Lois J. Buttlar. Englewood, Colo.: Libraries Unlimited, 1989. (LA 15 .B87)

General information resources in education and the social sciences, including art, health, language, music, science, history, philosophy, and psychology.

* *Books in Print.* (Z 1215 .P972)

Biographical Sources

Biographical Directory of American Educators, ed. by John F. Ohles. 3 vols. New York: Greenwood, 1978. (LA 2311 .B54)

Signed biographical articles on major American educators throughout history. Appendices include chronologies and indexes by major field, state, and place of birth.

Directory of American Scholars. 18th ed. 4 vols. New York: Bowker, 1982. (LA 2311 .C32)

Emphasis on biographical rather than directory information. Covers more than 37,500 scholars in all fields in the United States and Canada. Gives important dates, degrees, specialties, and awards.

International Who's Who in Education, 3rd ed. Cambridge, England: International Biographical Centre, 1987. (LA 2301 .I57)

Brief biographical citations for educators, including their degrees, specializations, professional associations, the positions they have held, their honors and awards.

CD-ROM Data Bases

ERIC

Dictionaries and Encyclopedias

A Dictionary of Education, ed. by P. J. Hills. London: Routledge & Kegan Paul, 1982. (LB 15 .D4)

Covers major areas such as educational administration, business, curriculum, research, philosophy, and the psychology and sociology of education. International in scope.

The Encyclopedia of Education, ed. by Lee C. Deighton. 10 vols. New York: Free Press, 1971. (LB 15 .E47)

An old standard, with signed articles covering names and subjects in education. Includes index and bibliography.

Encyclopedia of Educational Research, ed. by Harold E. Mitzel. 5th ed. 4 vols. New York: Free Press, 1982. (L 901 .E57)

Signed articles by scholars in the field on broad subjects in education such as academic freedom and tenure, nontraditional higher education, textbooks, and vocational education. Includes bibliographies.

The Encyclopedia of Higher Education, ed. by Burton R. Clark and Guy R. Neave. 4 vols. Oxford: Pergamon Press, 1992. (LB 15 .E49)

An international encyclopedia that covers national systems of education by country, analyzes higher education and society, discusses governance and administration, and explains the various academic disciplines.

World Education Encyclopedia, ed. by George Thomas Kurian. 3 vols. New York: Facts on File, 1988. (LB 15 .W87)

Education country by country. Includes statistics, history of education, constitutional and legal foundations of education, and each country's educational system.

* *Dictionary of the History of Ideas.* (CB 5 .D52)
* *Harper Dictionary of Modern Thought.* (AG 5 .H19)

Directories

The Directory of Financial Aids for Minorities: 1991–1993, by Gail Ann Schlachter. San Carlos, Calif.: Reference Service Press, 1991. (LB 2338 .D56)

Information on scholarships, fellowships, loans, grants, awards, and internships for minorities.

The Directory of Financial Aids for Women: 1991–1992, by Gail Ann Schlachter. San Carlos, Calif.: Reference Service Press, 1991. (LB 2338 .D55)

Information on scholarships, fellowships, loans, grants, awards, and internships for women.

The Handbook of Private Schools. Boston: Porter Sargent, annual. (L 901 .H3)

Information on private schools by region. Includes brief history of the school and information on grades, testing, and tuition.

The International Scholarship Book, by Daniel J. Cassidy. Englewood Cliffs, N.J.: Prentice-Hall, 1990. (LB 2337.2 .C364)

A directory of information on money for college, including dollar amounts, deadlines, rules, and regulations.

The ISS Directory of Overseas Schools: 1991–92. Princeton, N.J.: International Schools Services. (L 900 .I83)

Information on teaching staffs, grade levels, enrollment and capacity, teacher-student ratio, boarding, tuition, history, accreditation, languages, tests, the library, and other aspects of overseas schools.

National Faculty Directory. 3 vols. Detroit: Gale, 1993. (L 901 .N34)

An alphabetical directory of names, addresses, and subject areas of faculty members in American colleges and universities.

Patterson's American Education: 1992. Mount Prospect, Ill.: Educational Directories, Inc., 1992. (L 901 .P3)

Directory of information on middle schools, junior high and high schools, private and parochial schools, by state.

Peterson's Colleges with Programs for Learning Disabled Students. 2nd ed. Princeton, N.J.: Peterson's Guides, 1986. (L 901 .P458)

Programs in more than 900 two- and four-year schools with programs for the learning disabled. Includes information on LD services, staff, fees, admissions, diagnostic testing, tutoring, and counseling.

Peterson's Two Year Colleges: 1993. Princeton, N.J.: Peterson's Guides, 1992. (L 901 .A552)

Directory of information, undergraduate profile, admissions and transfer information, expenses and financial aid, housing, majors, athletics, and student life.

Private and Independent Schools: 1992. 45th ed. Wallingford, Conn.: Bunting and Lyon, 1992. (L 901 .P68)

Directory and biographical information, section on summer programs, and coverage of private and independent elementary and secondary schools in the United States and abroad.

The Scholarship Book, by Daniel J. Cassidy. Englewood Cliffs, N.J.: Prentice-Hall, 1990. (LB 2337.2 .C37)

Information on money for college, including dollar amounts, deadlines, rules, and regulations.

Scholarships, Fellowships and Loans: 1992–93, ed. by Debra M. Kirby. 9th ed. Detroit: Gale, 1992. (LB 2337)

Directory of information on the purpose of various types of financial aid, qualifications for application and award, the selection criteria, funds available, and the application details.

* *Awards, Honors and Prizes.* (AS 8 .A87)
* *Encyclopedia of Associations.* (HS 17 .G334)
* *National Faculty Directory.* (L 901 .N34)

Guides and Handbooks

The Educator's Desk Reference: A Sourcebook of Educational Information and Research, by Melvyn N. Freed and others. New York: Macmillan, 1989. (LB 1027.27 .U6 F74)

Information and reference sources in education. Provides an author's guide to publishing in education. Also covers software for educational research, standardized tests, and national and regional organizations in education.

Periodicals

Academe
American Journal of Education
American School Board Journal
American Teacher
Childhood Education
Chronicle of Higher Education
School and University
Comparative Education
Contemporary Education
Education
Education Digest
Education Week
Education Studies
Education Theory
Harvard Educational Review
Intellect
International Review of Education
Journal of Education
Journal of Educational Method
Journal of Educational Psychology
Journal of Higher Education
Learning
NEA Journal

Peabody Journal of Education
Review of Education
Teacher
Today's Education

Statistical Sources

Digest of Education Statistics. Washington, D.C.: U.S. Department of Education, annual. (L 11 .D48)

Statistical information on elementary, postsecondary, college, vocational, and adult education in America.

State Higher Education Profile. 4th ed. Washington, D.C.: Department of Education, 1992. (LB 2342 .S74)

Statistical data on education in the states, including state rankings, comparison, and analysis.

* *American Statistics Index.* (Z 7554 .U5 A46)
* *County and City Data Book.* (HA 202 .A36)
* *State and Metropolitan Area Data Book.* (HA 205 .S72)
* *Statistical Reference Abstracts.* (HA 202 .S7)
* *Statistical Reference Index.* (HA 202 .S7)
* *Statistics Sources.* (HA 36 .S84)

SELECT SUBJECT HEADINGS, BREAKDOWNS, AND CALL NUMBERS

Education (General) (L 7 - L 991)

Periodicals (L 7 - L 97)
Yearbooks (L 101)
Congresses (L 106 - L 107)
Official Documents, Reports, Etc. (L 111 - L 791)
Educational Exhibitions and Museums (L 797 - L 899)
Directories of Educational Institutions (L 900 - L 991)

History of Education (LA 1 - LA 2396)

General (LA 5 - LA 25)
By Period (LA 31 - LA 133)
Higher Education (LA 173 - LA 186)

United States (LA 201 - LA 396)
Other Regions or Countries (LA 410 - LA 2284)

Theory and Practice of Education (LB 1 - LB 3640)

Primary Education (LB 1501 - LB 1547)
Secondary Education (LB 1603 - LB 1695)
Higher Education (LB 2300 - LB 2430)

Special Aspects of Education (LC 1 - LC 6691)

Social Aspects of Education (LC 65 - LC 245)
Moral and Religious Education (LC 251 - LC 951)
Types of Education (LC 1001 - LC 1099)
Education of Special Classes of Persons (LC 1390 - LC 5158)
Education Extension. Adult Education (LC 5201 - LC 6691)

Individual Institutions: Universities, Colleges, and Schools

United States (LD 13 - LD 7501)
America, Except United States (LE 3 - LE 78)
Europe (LF 14 - LF 5477)
Asia. Africa. Oceania (LG 21 - LG 961)

College and School Magazines and Papers (LH 1 - LH 9)
Student Fraternities and Societies, U.S. (LJ 3 - LJ 75)
Textbooks (LT 6 - LT 501)

POLITICAL SCIENCE

Abstracts and Indexes

Congressional Index. Chicago: Commerce Clearing House. (J 69 .C6)

This loose-leaf service provides an index to and good summaries of bills and resolutions in Congress.

International Political Science Abstracts. Paris: International Political Science Association, quarterly. (JA 36 .I5)

Covers political science methods and theory, political thinkers, institutions, the political process, and international relations.

US Political Science Documents, annual. Pittsburgh, Pa.: University of Pittsburgh. (H 9 .U58)

An abstracting service that provides author, title, source, key subjects, and abstracts to political science documents and journal articles.

* *Congressional Research Service Bill Digest.* (KF 18 .L5)
* *Dictionary of Historic Documents.* (D 9 .K63)
* *Index to Social Science and Humanities Proceedings.* (AI 3 .I53)
* *Public Affairs Information Service: PAIS International.* (Z 7163 .P9)
* *Social Science Citation Index.* (Z 7161 .S65)
* *Social Sciences Index.* (AI 3 .S62)

Almanacs and Yearbooks

The Almanac of American Politics. Washington, D.C.: Congressional Quarterly, annual. (JK 271 .B343)

Congressional Quarterly Almanac. Washington, D.C.: Congressional Quarterly, annual. (JK 1 .C66)

Congressional Roll Call. Washington, D.C.: Congressional Quarterly, annual. (JK 1 .C6635)

The three Congressional Quarterly almanacs listed above provide numerous facts and figures about American politics, America's political leaders, chronology and analysis of votes in the House and Senate, presidential support, party unity and voting participation, and other facts on the American electorate.

International Almanac of Electoral History. Washington, D.C.: Congressional Quarterly, 1991. (JF 1001 .M17)

Election results by country "since the beginning of competitive national elections." Includes brief discussion of each country's electoral history.

Political Handbook of the World, ed. by Arthur S. Banks. New York: CSA Publications, annual. (JF 37 .P6)

Political information on every country, including heads of state, government and organization, political parties, and the media.

* *Almanac of the 50 States.* (HA 203 .A5)
* *Annual Register.* (D 2 .A7)
* *Book of the States.* (JK 2403 .B62)
* *Europa World Yearbook.* (JN 1 .E85)
* *Information Please Almanac.* (AY 64 .I55)
* *Municipal Yearbook.* (JS 344 .C5 A24)
* *Statesman's Yearbook.* (JA 51 .S7)
* *World Almanac and Book of Facts.* (AY 67 .N5 W7)
* *Yearbook of the United Nations.* (JX 1977 .A37)

Anthologies and Collections

Treaties in Force. Washington, D.C.: U.S. Department of State, annual. (JX 235.9 .A35)

A list of all treaties to which the United States is a signatory. Provides a brief description of the treaty currently in effect.

U.S. Treaties and Other International Agreements. Washington, D.C.: U.S. Department of State, annual. (JX 231 .A34)

Full-text documentation of treaties to which the United States is a signatory and other international agreements.

* *Great Documents of Western Civilization.* (CB 245 .V5)
* *Historic Documents.* (E 839.5 .H57)

Atlases

World Atlas of Elections: Voting Patterns in 39 Democracies. London: The Economist, 1987. (JF 1041 .L46)

A visual account of results from the most recent elections held in thirty-nine democracies. Includes statistics, information on party breakdowns, and the electorate.

* *Historical Atlas of U.S. Congressional Districts.* (G 1201 .F9 M3)
* *National Geographic Atlas of the United States.* (G 1201 .S1 N3)
* *Rand McNally Commercial Atlas and Marketing Guide.* (G 1036 .R2)
* *We the People.* (G 1201 .E1 A4)

Bibliographies

ABC Pol Sci: A Bibliography of Contents; Political Science and Government. Santa Barbara, Calif.: ABC-Clio. (Z 7161 .A214)

Reprints of the tables of contents in select periodicals in political science, law, sociology, and economics.

The American Electorate: A Historical Bibliography. Santa Barbara, Calif.: ABC-Clio, 1984. (Z 7164 .R4 A46)

Provides access to references on American voters, voter behavior, and voting trends throughout history.

International Bibliography of Political Science. London and New York: Routledge, annual. (JA 71 .I6)

Part of the *International Bibliography of the Social Sciences,* this international multilanguage bibliography covers materials in political science and includes indexes by author, subject, and place-name.

U.S. Politics and Elections: A Guide to Information Sources, by David J. Maurer. Detroit: Gale, 1978. (Z 1236 .M39)

An annotated bibliography of sources covering over two hundred years of political activity in America.

* *Books in Print.* (Z 1215 .P972)

Biographical Sources

Biographical Directory of the U.S. Congress: 1774– 1989. Washington, D.C.: U.S. Government Printing Office, 1989. (JK 1010 .U5)

A biographical directory of all the members of each session of the U.S. Congress, from its beginnings through 1989.

Biographical Directory of the United States Executive Branch, 1774–1977, ed. by Robert Sobel. Westport, Conn.: Greenwood, 1977. (E 176 .B576)

A reference covering presidents, vice-presidents, and cabinet officers plus a series of chronologies. Shelved not with politics but with American history.

Biographical Dictionary of American Mayors: 1820–1980, ed. by Melvin G. Holli and Peter d'A. Jones. Westport, Conn.: Greenwood, 1981. (E 176 .B5725)

A biographical directory of the elected leaders of cities such as Baltimore, Boston, Chicago, Detroit, Los Angeles, New York, Philadelphia, and San Francisco.

Presidential Also-rans and Running Mates, 1788–1980, by Leslie H. Southwick. Jefferson, N.C.: McFarland, 1984. (E 176.1 .S695)

Who lost as well as who won; a biographical dictionary of those we didn't elect.

Who's Who in American Politics. New York: Bowker, annual. (E 176 .W6424)

Annual reference for biographical data on political figures at the local, state, and national level.

* *Current Biography.* (CT 100 .C8)
* *Dictionary of American Biography.* (E 176 .D56)
* *Who Was Who in America.* (E 176 .W64)
* *Who's Who in America.* (E 663 .W56)

Codes and Rules

* *Code of Federal Regulations.* (JK 416 .C6)
* *Robert's Rules of Order.* (JF 515 .R692)
* *United States Code.* (K 44 .C4)

Dictionaries and Encyclopedias

The American Political Dictionary, by Jack Plano and Milton Greenburg. 8th ed. New York: Holt, Rinehart and Winston, 1989. (JK 9 .P55)

The Blackwell Encyclopedia of Political Institutions, ed. by Vernon Bogdanov. New York: Blackwell, 1987. (JA 61 .B56)

The Blackwell Encyclopedia of Political Thought, ed. by David Miller. New York: Blackwell, 1987. (JA 61 .B57)

The HarperCollins Dictionary of American Government and Politics, by Jay M. Shayfritz. New York: HarperCollins, 1992. (JK 9 .S43)

Safire's Political Dictionary, by William Safire. 3rd ed. New York: Random House, 1978. (JK 9 .S2)

The political science dictionaries listed above are reliable single-volume resources popular in most libraries. As with any resource, an up-to-date political dictionary is required to give you the latest definitions in the current political scene.

Encyclopedia of American Foreign Policy: Studies of the Principal Movements and Ideas. 3 vols. New York: Charles Scribner's Sons, 1978. (JX 1407 .E53)

Signed articles by scholars in the field on the balance of power, colonialism, containment, militarism, sanctions, treaties, and other political variables in foreign policy.

Encyclopedia of American Political History: Studies of the Principal Movements and Ideas, ed. by Jack P. Greene. New York: Charles Scribner's Sons, 1983. (E 183 .E5)

Covers the history of political parties and their platforms as well as political institutions in America.

Encyclopedia of Human Rights, by Edward Lawson. New York: Taylor & Francis, 1991. (JC 571 .E67)

Coverage of subjects and issues in human rights with appendices on the international labor code, United Nations studies and reports on human rights issues, membership of intergovernmental organizations concerned with human rights, glossary, and index.

World Encyclopedia of Political Systems and Parties, ed. by George E. Delury. 2 vols. 2nd ed. New York: Facts on File, 1987. (JF 2011 .W67)

Organized alphabetically by country with each country's article signed by a scholar in the field. Covers government, the electoral system, and political parties.

* *Dictionary of the History of Ideas.* (CB 5 .D52)
* *Harper Dictionary of Modern Thought.* (AG 5 .H19)

Directories

The Almanac of Federal PACs, by Edward Zuckerman. Washington, D.C.: Amward Publishers, annual. (JK 1991 .A744)

Directory of political action committees by subject, covering business, labor, trade, special interests, and PAC contributors.

Congressional Staff Directory. Mt. Vernon, Va.: Congressional Staff Directory, annual. (JK 1012 .C65)

Provides much the same information available in the GPO publication *Official Congressional Directory,* listed below, though it is not as up to date as the *Congressional Yellow Book,* also listed below.

Congressional Yellow Book. Washington, D.C.: Monitor Publishing, quarterly. (JK 1013 .C65)

Provides up to date information on names and position titles as personnel come and go during the political year.

Encyclopedia of Governmental Advisory Organizations: 1992–1993. 8th ed. Detroit: Gale, 1992. (JK 468 .C7 E5)

This directory, which calls itself an encyclopedia, lists organizations by several major subdivisions, including business, economics and labor, education and social welfare, engineering, science, and technology.

Federal Regulatory Directory. Washington, D.C.: Congressional Quarterly. (KF 5406 .A15 F4)

Published since 1969, this directory lists the personnel in regulatory agencies of the federal government and outlines the mission of the agency.

Federal Staff Directory. Mt. Vernon, Va.: Congressional Staff Directory, annual. (JK 723 .E9 F44)

Annual biographical and directory information on the members of the executive branch.

Federal Yellow Book. Washington, D.C.: Monitor Publishing, annual. (JK 6 .F4)

Like the *Congressional Yellow Book,* its federal counterpart is more up to date than other annual directories listed here.

The National Directory of State Agencies. Bethesda, Md.: Cambridge Information Group, 1986. (JK 2443 .N37)

Covers state government administrative agencies and provides information on their administrators and officials.

Public Interest Profiles: 1992–1993. Washington, D.C.: Congressional Quarterly, Inc., 1992. (JK 1118 .P814)

A biographical directory of public interest groups that lobby Congress, including name, subject of lobbying interest, and group indexes. Covers business, economics, consumer groups, and environmental, media, and religious groups. Includes directory of think tanks.

United States Department of State. Washington, D.C.

The State Department publishes the three directories listed below, which are useful in locating current consular offices, diplomats, and foreign service officials.

Diplomatic List, quarterly. (JX 1705 .A22)
Foreign Consular Offices in the United States. (JX 1705 .A28)
Key Officers of Foreign Service Posts. (JX 1705 .A284)

Washington Information Directory. Washington, D.C.: Congressional Quarterly, annual. (F 192.3 .W33)

Congressional Quarterly's *Washington Information Directory* provides brief biographical and directory information on individuals in the executive branch of government.

Washington Representatives. Washington, D.C.: Columbia Books, annual. (JK 1118 .D58)

Another reference to Political Action Committees, which represent trade and professional interests and lobby Congress in the nation's capital.

* *Encyclopedia of Associations.* (HS 17 .G334)

Fact Books

* *Encyclopedia of American Facts and Dates.* (E 174.5 .C3)
* *Facts About the Cities.* (HT 1233 .C385)
* *Facts About the Presidents.* (E 176.1 .K3)
* *Facts About the States.* (E 180 .K4)
* *Facts on File.* (D 410 .F3)
* *Keesing's Record of World Events.* (D 410 .K4)
* *World Fact Book.* (G 122 .U56)

Government Documents

* *Congressional Record.* (J 11 .R2)
* *Federal Register.* (J 1 .A2)
* *Index to Publications of the U.S. Congress.* (KJ 49 .C62)

Guides and Handbooks

A Guide to Manuscripts in the Presidential Libraries, by
Dennis A. Burton. Research Materials Corporation, 1985. (CD
3029.82 .B87)

A catalog of twentieth-century presidential manuscripts in presidential libraries; includes directory information on presidential libraries, a
general description of holdings, and key personnel.

Guide to Congress. (JK 1061 .C6)
Guide to the Presidency. (JK 516 .C57)
Guide to U.S. Elections. (JK 1967 .C662)
Guide to the U.S. Supreme Court. (KF 8742 .W567)

The guides listed above are published periodically by Congressional
Quarterly in Washington, D.C. and contain useful information on each
of the areas of government listed.

Maryland Manual: 1992–93. A Guide to Maryland State
Government. Annapolis, Md.: Maryland State Archives, 1992.
(JK 3831)

Most states, districts, territories, and countries publish some sort of
manual on their political and economic activities on an annual or semiannual basis. It acts as a directory, a history, an encyclopedia, and an
overall public information resource for the jurisdiction. It usually includes notes on the budget, committees, elections, the jurisdictional
constitution, history, and statistics.

* *Guide to the Records of the United States Senate.* (CD 3042 .S46 U54)
* *Guide to the Records of the U.S. House of Representatives.* (CD 3042 .S46
  U54)
* *U.S. Government Manual.* (JK 421 .A32)

Periodicals

American Journal of Political Science
American Political Science Review
Center Magazine
Comparative Political Studies
Congressional Quarterly Weekly Report

Editorial Research Reports (CQ Researcher)
Government and Opposition
Harvard Political Review
International Journal of Politics
Journal of Politics
National Journal
National Political Science Review
Political Quarterly
Political Studies
Political Theory
Polity
PS
Public Administration Review
Public Policy
Review of Politics
Washington Quarterly

Quote Books

* *Dictionary of Biographical Quotation.* (CT 773 .D38)
* *Familiar Quotations.* (PN 6081 .B27)
* *Oxford Dictionary of Modern Quotations.* (PN 6080 .O94)
* *What They Said.* (D 410 .W49)

Statistical Sources

America Votes: A Handbook of Contemporary American Election Statistics, compiled and ed. by R. M. Scammon. New York: Macmillan, annual. (JK 1967 .A8)

The standard reference for election statistics for the states. Loads of statistics and analysis. Referred to by librarians as *Scammon.*

Vital Statistics on Congress, by Norman J. Ornstein and others. Washington, D.C.: American Enterprise Institute, 1984. (JK 1041 .V57)

A statistical reference to the U.S. Congress, its members, their voting patterns, their demographics of representation, and other factors in their political lives.

* *American Statistics Index.* (Z 7554 .U5 A46)
* *Statistical Reference Abstracts.* (HA 202 .S7)
* *Statistical Reference Index.* (HA 202 .S7)
* *County and City Data Book.* (HA 202 .A36)
* *Historical Statistics of the United States.* (HA 202 .B87)
* *State and Metropolitan Area Data Book.* (HA 205 .S72)
* *Statistical Abstract of the United States.* (HC 202)
* *Statistics Sources.* (HA 36 .S84)

SELECT SUBJECT HEADINGS, BREAKDOWNS, AND CALL NUMBERS

Political Science (J 1 - JX 5810)
Official Documents (J 1 - J 909)
General Works (JA 1 - JA 98)

Political Theory (JC 1 - JC 628)

    The Primitive State (JC 20 - JC 50)
    The Ancient State (JC 51 - JC 95)
    The Medieval State (JC 101 - JC 126)
    The Modern State (JC 131 - JC 209)
    Origins of the State (JC 301 - JC 347)
    Forms of the State (JC 348 - JC 499)
    Purpose of the State (JC 501 - JC 561)
    State and Social Groups (JC 541 - JC 561)
    State and Individual (JC 571 - JC 628)

Constitutional History and Administration (JF 1 - JF 2111)

    General Works (JF 8 - JF 37)
    Treatises (JF 45 - JF 195)
    Government (JF 201 - JF 786)
    Political Rights and Guarantees (JF 800 - JF 1191)
    Administration (JF 1321 - JF 1900)
    Civil Service (JF 1410 - JF 1671)
    Territorial Administration (JF 1700)
    Military Government (JF 1800)
    Federal Districts (JF 1900)
    Political Parties (JF 2011 - JF 2111)

Constitutional History and Administration: U.S. (JK 1 - JK 9993)

> General Works (JK 1 - JK 9)
> Constitutional History (JK 11 - JK 277)
> Federal and State Regulations (JK 310 - JK 325)
> Government Administration (JK 401 - JK 446)
> The Executive (JK 511 - JK 611)
> The Departments (JK 631 - JK 893)
> Congress (JK 1001 - JK 1128)
> > Senate (JK 1151 - JK 1271)
> > House of Representatives (JK 1304 - JK 1443)
> The Judiciary (JK 1511 - JK 1598)
> Government Property (JK 1606 - JK 1686)
> Politics. Civil Rights (JK 1711 - JK 1717)
> Naturalization (JK 1800 - JK 1839)
> Suffrage (JK 1846 - JK 1936)
> Electoral Systems (JK 1951 - JK 2246)
> Political Parties (JK 2301 - JK 2391)
> State Government (JK 2408 - JK 9600)

Confederate States (JK 9601 - JK 9995)
British America. Latin America, Etc. (JL)
Europe (JN)
Asia (JQ)
Local Government (JS)
Colonies and Colonization (JV 1 - JV 5299)
Emigration and Immigration (JV 6000 - JV 9500)
International Law (JX)

PRELAW

Abstracts, Digests, and Indexes

Current Law Index. Foster City, Calif.: Information Access Company, quarterly. (K 33 .C87)

Indexes to more than seven hundred law journals in the United States, Canada, the United Kingdom, Ireland, Australia, and New Zealand. Includes coverage of articles, case notes, and book reviews.

Index to Legal Periodicals. New York: Wilson, monthly. (K 9 .N32)

An index to English-language periodical literature in the United States, Canada, Great Britain, Ireland, Australia, and New Zealand found in legal professional journals, academic law journals, and other sources.

Shepard's Acts and Cases by Popular Names: Federal and State. Colorado Springs, Colo.: Shepard's Citations. (KF 80 .S5)

A citation index to legislation and case law that has taken on a name of its own, either during the legislative process or in the popular press, such as the "Brady Bill" or the "Son of Sam Law." Supplemented irregularly.

The United States Law Week. Washington, D.C.: Bureau of National Affairs. (KF 105 .U58)

This two-volume loose-leaf service provides a summary and analysis of current federal agency rulings and a digest of Supreme Court proceedings and opinions. Updated weekly.

* *Congressional Information Service Abstracts.* (KF 49 .C62)
* *Congressional Research Service Bill Digest.* (KF 18 .L5)
* *Dictionary of Historic Documents.* (D 9 .K63)

Almanacs and Yearbooks

The Lawyer's Almanac. Englewood Cliffs, N.J.: Prentice-Hall Law & Business, annual. (KF 190 .L3625)

An almanac covering the legal profession, the judiciary, government departments and agencies, statutory summaries, law firms, legal compensation, and legal education in the United States.

* *Information Please Almanac.* (AY 64 .I55)
* *World Almanac and Book of Facts.* (AY 67 .N5 W7)

Anthologies and Collections

* *Historic Documents.* (E 839.5 .H57)

Bibliographies

American Legal Literature: A Guide to Selected Legal Resources, by Bernard D. Reams and others. Littleton, Colo.: Libraries Unlimited, 1985. (KF 1 .R42)

An annotated bibliography of legal reference materials in selected subjects in the law of the United States.

Bibliographic Guide to Law. Boston: G. K. Hall, annual. (KF 38 .B52)

An annual bibliography of legal materials cataloged by the Library of Congress. Covers United States and international law.

Bowker's Law Books and Serials in Print. New York: Bowker, annual. (KF 1 .L392)

This is Bowker's version of *Books in Print* for the legal literature of the United States. Arranged by author, title, and subject.

Encyclopedia of Legal Information Sources, ed. by Brian L. Baker and Patrick J. Petit. Detroit: Gale, 1992. (KF 1 .E53)

A bibliographic guide with thousands of citations to legal reference resources in hundreds of subjects in the law, covering publications, data-base sources, and legal organizations in the United States.

Legal Looseleafs in Print. (KF 1 .S73)
Legal Newsletters in Print. (KF 1 .L44)

The two bibliographic guides listed above are published annually by Infosources of Teaneck, N.J. They provide a subject and publisher index and list the title, publisher, frequency, circulation, and indexing information on legal loose-leafs and newsletters in the United States.

Biographical Sources

The Justices of the United States Supreme Court: Their Lives and Major Opinions, ed. by Leon Friedman and Fred L. Israel. 4 vols. New York: Chelsea House, 1969. (KF 8744 .F75)

Lengthy biographical essays on the Supreme Court justices and summary and analysis of their major opinions.

Who's Who in American Law. Chicago: Marquis. (KF 372 .W48)

A biographical directory of the nation's lawyers, including information on their schools, publications, and current employment. Published irregularly since 1978.

Codes and Rules

House Ethics Manual, by the Committee on Standards of Official Conduct. Washington, D.C.: Government Printing Office, 1992. (KF 4990 .A354)

This ethics manual provides guidelines for the ethical standards of House members regarding such topics as gifts, travel and entertainment, favors, outside employment, financial disclosure, and campaign practices.

* *Code of Federal Regulations.* (JK 416 .C6)
* *Codes of Professional Responsibility.* (BJ 1725 .C57)
* *Robert's Rules of Order.* (JF 515 .R692)
* *United States Code.* (K 44 .C4)

Dictionaries and Encyclopedias

Ballentine's Law Dictionary With Pronunciations. Rochester, N.Y.: Lawyer's Co-op, 1969. (KF 156 .B3)

Black's Law Dictionary. 6th ed. St. Paul, Minn.: West Publishing Co., 1990. (KF 156 .B53)

The two dictionaries listed above are standard legal desk dictionaries covering terms and phrases in ancient and modern law and in American and English jurisprudence.

Encyclopedia of the American Constitution, ed. by Leonard W. Levy and others. 4 vols. New York: Macmillan, 1986. (KF 4548 .E53)

Contains the Articles of Confederation, the Constitution, a chronology of the Constitution, and cases and subject-area studies in constitutional law.

Directories

The American Bench: Judges of the Nation. Sacramento, Calif.: Foster. (KF 8700 .A19)

Alphabetical by name and organized by state, this directory of judges also provides information on the structure of the courts system and judicial boundaries in the United States.

Directory of Corporate Counsel. 2 vols. Englewood Cliffs, N.J.: Prentice-Hall Law & Business, 1992. (KF 195 .C6 D57)

Directory information for legal firms, biographical data on the individuals who represent it, their job titles, and their area of practice expertise.

* *Martindale-Hubbell Law Directory.* (JK 1517 .M37)

Documents

The Constitution of the United States of America: Analysis and Interpretation. Washington, D.C.: Government Printing Office, biennial. (KF 4527 .L4)

An annotated version of the Constitution printed by the federal government; includes an introduction and historical notes with annotations to the text.

Government Documents

* *Congressional Record.* (J 11 .R2)
* *Federal Register.* (J 1 .A2)
* *Index to Publications of the U.S. Congress.* (KF 49 .C62)

Guides and Handbooks

Effective Legal Research, by Miles Oscar Price and others. 4th ed. Boston: Little, Brown, 1979. (KF 240 .P7)

A classic guide to legal research and legal bibliography; covers the primary reference works in the study of the law.

Legal Research in a Nutshell, by Morris L. Cohen. 4th ed. St. Paul, Minn.: West Publishing Co., 1985. (KF 240 .C54)

A popular guide for law students from West Publishing's Nutshell series; covers the essentials of legal research.

The Oxford Companion to Law, ed. by David M. Walker. New York: Oxford University Press, 1980. (K 48 .W178)

Covers different branches of the law and legal systems in Western countries, mainly those of the United States, Britain, and Canada.

* *Guide to the Records of the U.S. House of Representatives.* (CD 3042 .H86 U55)
* *Guide to the Records of the U.S. Senate.* (CD 3042 .S46 U54)
* *U.S. Government Manual.* (JK 421 .A32)

Law Books

The legal publishing industry in America has long been dominated by a handful of publishers. Surely one of the most successful examples is the West Publishing Company of St. Paul, Minnesota. West Publishing has, for well over a hundred years, produced the essential law books for the national coverage of American law. West Publishing focuses most heavily in the areas of law reporters, law digests, and law encyclopedias.

Law reporters. West's Law Reporters make up the West Publishing Company's national reporter system. Each major set in the national reporter system covers a particular geographical area or legal practice area in the United States. There are seven regional reporters that cover state appellate court decisions and thousands of memorandum decisions. The *Pacific Reporter* covers Washington state, Montana, Oregon, Idaho, Wyoming, California, Nevada, Utah, Arizona, Colorado, New Mexico, Kansas, Oklahoma, Alaska, and Hawaii. The *North Western Reporter* covers North and South Dakota, Minnesota, Nebraska, Iowa, Wisconsin, and Michigan. The *North Eastern Reporter* covers Illinois, Indiana, Ohio, New York, and Massachusetts. The *Southern Reporter* covers Louisiana, Mississippi, Alabama, and Florida. The *South Eastern Reporter* covers West Virginia, Virginia, North and South Carolina, and Georgia. The *Atlantic Reporter* covers Maine, New Hampshire, Vermont, Rhode Island, Connecticut, New Jersey, Pennsylvania, Delaware, and Maryland. The *Supreme Court Reporter* covers all the decisions of the U.S. Supreme Court since 1882. The *Federal Reporter* and the *Federal Supplement* cover U.S. court cases. *West's Bankruptcy Reporter* covers the U.S. Bankruptcy Courts. The *United States Claims Court Reporter* covers all U.S. courts of claims. There are many West reporters for states and for different courts, some of which are so voluminous that libraries don't bother to put call numbers on the volumes; librarians just point to a sign on the wall where the *Federal Reporter* volumes are shelved.

Law digests. West Publishing has a unique research feature called the West Key Number Digests. West's digests and the key number system provide an index to U.S. law as reported in different legal cases. West has prepared Key Number Digests for states, regions like those represented in the national reporter system, and courts, both state and federal. The *American Digest* covers all case law in the U.S. from 1658 to the present. The *U.S. Supreme Court Digest* covers all the U.S. Supreme Court cases. There are also state digests for California, New York, and Illinois, for example, as well as regional digests to complement the Atlantic, Pacific, North Western, South Western, North Eastern, South Eastern, and Southern Reporters.

Legal encyclopedias. Along with its reporters and digests, West publishes legal reference encyclopedias that tie in with the reporters and digests through the key number system. Key numbers are simply numbers assigned by West's editorial staff to certain topics in law. Using West's unique key number system, researchers can reference cases in law reporters, retrieve digests of those cases, and locate encyclopedic references to the legal subjects specific to those cases. Examples of West legal encyclopedias include *Corpus Juris Secundum* and *Words and Phrases.*

On-Line Data Bases

Legislate
Lexis/Nexis
Westlaw

Periodicals

Administrative Law Review
American Jurist
American Lawyer
Georgetown Law Journal

Law Forum
Law and Contemporary Problems
Law and Human Behavior
Legal Times
Harvard Law Review
National Law Journal
U.S. Law Week
University of Chicago Law Review
Yale Law Journal
Virginia Law Review
William & Mary Law Review

Style Books

The Blue Book: A Uniform System of Citation. 15th ed. Cambridge: Harvard Law Review Association, 1991. (KF 245 .B58)

Referred to as "the blue book" for so long that the publisher chose to title it as such. The standard style book for citation to legal authority in the United States.

Thesauruses

Legal Thesaurus, by William C. Burton. New York: Macmillan, 1980. (KF 156 .B856)

This thesaurus of legal terms provides definitions and identifies parts of speech, synonyms, associated legal concepts, foreign phrases and translations, and multiple meanings.

SELECT SUBJECT HEADINGS, BREAKDOWNS, AND CALL NUMBERS

Law (General) (K 1 - K 7720)

Jurisprudence (K 201 - K 487)
Comparative Law (K 520 - K 5582)
Conflict of Laws (K 7000 - K 7720)

Federal Law (Law of the United States) (KF 1 - KF 9827)

General Works (KF 1 - KF 202)
Collections (KF 209 - KF 224)
Persons (KF 465 - KF 553)
Property (KF 560 - KF 720)
Contracts (KF 801 - KF 1241)
Associations (KF 1355 - KF 1480)
Regulation (KF 1600 - KF 2940)
Intellectual Property (KF 2971 - KF 3192)
Social Legislation (KF 3300 - KF 3750)
Public Safety (KF 3941 - KF 3977)
Control of Social Activities (KF 3985 - KF 3995)
Science and the Arts (KF 4270 - KF 4330)
Constitutional Law (KF 4501 - KF 4515)
Public Property (KF 5500 - KF 5865)
Public Finance (KF 6200 - KF 6795)
National Defense (KF 7201 - KF 7755)
Courts. Procedure (KF 8700 - KF 9075)

Law of Individual States (By State) (KFA 1 - KFW 4799)

Law of Individual Cities (By City) (KFX 1 - KFX 9999)

PSYCHOLOGY

Abstracts and Indexes

Abstracts of the Standard Edition of the Complete Psychological Works of Sigmund Freud, ed. by Carrie Lee Rothgeb. International Universities Press, 1973. (BF 173 .F62535)

An author-specific reference source; includes abstracts of Freud's works, with chronological tables to the works and a comprehensive subject index.

Author Index to "Psychological Index" 1894–1935 and Psychological Abstracts 1937–1983. Boston: G. K. Hall; American Psychological Association (BF 1 .P651) and **Cumulative Subject Index to Psychological Abstracts.** Washington, D.C.: American Psychological Association, 1937–83. (BF 1 .P652)

These two indexes come in oversize (folio) volumes with author and title indexes. The earlier volumes of the indexes are mass-produced photocopies of catalog cards for psychology books and articles.

Chicago Psychoanalytic Literature Index. Chicago: Institute for Psychoanalysis, annual. (BF 173 .C452)

Covers 1920 to the present and includes subject indexing of articles, books, and book reviews.

PsycBooks, ed. by Lois Granick. Washington, D.C.: American Psychological Association, annual. (BF 121 .P79)

Abstracts and prints the tables of contents from psychology books each year and organizes them by specific area of psychological inquiry. Abstracts are often taken from the book's preface or dust jacket.

Psychological Abstracts. Washington, D.C.: American Psychological Association, monthly. (BF 1 .P65)

Published since 1927, *PsycAbs* gives "nonevaluative summaries of the world's literature in psychology and related disciplines." The abstracts are indexed, by subject and by author, and numbered.

* *Index to Social Science and Humanities Proceedings.* (AI 3 .I53)
* *Public Affairs Information Service: PAIS International.* (Z 7163 .P9)
* *Social Science Citation Index.* (Z 7161 .S65)
* *Social Sciences and Humanities Index.* (AI 3 .R49)
* *Social Sciences Index.* (AI 3 .S62)

Bibliographies

Author's Guide to Journals in the Behavioral Sciences, by Alvin Y. Wang. Lawrence Erlbaum Associates, Publishers, 1989. (BF 76.8 .W36)

An annotated bibliography of psychology journals; indexes by journal and keyword. Includes list of abstracting and indexing services for psychological topics.

Perception: An Annotated Bibliography, by Kathleen Emmett. New York: Garland, 1976. (BF 311 .E55)

A partially annotated bibliography on the study of perception, with primary concentration on the years 1935–74.

* *Books in Print.* (Z 1215 .P972)

Biographical Sources

Biographical Dictionary of Psychology, by Leonard Zusne. Westport, Conn.: Greenwood, 1984. (BF 109 .A1)

Lists major contributors in the field, their degrees, positions in academia, and their most significant publications.

* *American Men and Women of Science.* (Q 141 .A47)

CD-ROM Data Bases

Medline
Psyclit
PAIS International

Dictionaries and Encyclopedias

The Blackwell Dictionary of Cognitive Reference, ed. by Michael W. Eysenck. New York: Blackwell, 1991. (BF 311 .B535)

A dictionary of signed articles by scholars in the field on cognitive reference and related topics; includes a brief bibliography and index.

Dictionary of Behavioral Assessment Techniques, ed. by Michel Hersen and Alan S. Bellack. London: Pergamon, 1988. (BF 176.5 .D53)

Signed articles with references by scholars in the field; lists psychological tests, their purpose, development, and clinical use.

The Dictionary of Development and Educational Psychology, ed. by Rom Harre and Roger Lamb. New York: Blackwell, 1986. (BF 712.7 .D53)

A name and subject dictionary; signed articles by scholars in the field; includes brief bibliographies and an index.

The Dictionary of Personality and Social Psychology, ed. by Rom Harre and Roger Lamb. New York: Blackwell, 1986. (BF 698 .D527)

A name and subject dictionary; includes signed articles by scholars in the field, brief bibliographies, and an index.

Encyclopedia of Clinical Assessment, ed. by Robert Henley Wood. 2 vols. San Francisco: Jossey-Bass, 1980. (BF 698.4 .E5)

Contains signed articles by scholars in the field on broad topics such as individual development, personality development, and social involvement. Also includes lengthy bibliographies and name and subject indexes.

The Encyclopedia of Human Development and Education: Theory, Research, and Studies, ed. by R. Murray Thomas. London: Pergamon Press, 1990. (BF 713 .E65)

Signed articles by scholars in the field on broad topics such as Piaget's theory of genetic epistemology. Includes bibliographies.

Encyclopedia of Psychology, ed. by Raymond J. Corsini. 4 vols. New York: Wiley, 1984. (BF 31 .E52)

Signed articles by scholars in the field on subjects and names in psychology. Includes brief bibliographies.

The Encyclopedic Dictionary of Psychology, ed. by Rom Harre and Roger Lamb. Cambridge: MIT Press, 1983. (BF 31 .E555)

Signed articles by scholars in the field, brief bibliographies, a glossary, and an index.

Piaget: Dictionary of Terms, preface by Jean Piaget, translated and ed. by Elizabeth Rutschi-Herrmann and Sarah F. Campbell. London: Pergamon, 1973. (BF 11 .A67)

An author-specific dictionary of the terms used in Piaget's writings, with definitions taken from the texts of his works.

* *Dictionary of the History of Ideas.* (CB 5 .D52)
* *Harper Dictionary of Modern Thought.* (AG 5 .H19)

Directories

APA Membership Register. Washington, D.C.: American Psychological Association, annual. (BF 11 .A671)

The annual membership directory of the APA lists more than seventy thousand members, giving membership statistics, a geographical and name index. An appendix lists acronyms and abbreviations used in the directory and in psychology.

* *Encyclopedia of Associations.* (HS 17 .G334)

Guides and Handbooks

Handbook of General Psychology, ed. by Benjamin B. Wolman. Englewood Cliffs, N.J.: Prentice-Hall, 1973. (BF 121 .W63)

An older but classic textbook on psychology, with signed articles by scholars in the field. Includes broad topics such as perception and personality. Includes index.

International Handbook of Psychology, ed. by Albert R. Gilgen and Carol K. Gilgen. Westport, Conn.: Greenwood, 1987. (BF 105 .I57)

Organized by country, this handbook reviews current research and writing in psychology, textbooks, and "future directions" for countries conducting major research in psychology. Includes bibliography for each country and name and subject indexes.

Internship Programs in Professional Psychology: Including Post-Doctoral Training Programs. Association of Psychology Internship Centers, 1990–91. (BF 77 .D57)

Lists pre- and postdoctoral programs by state in the United States and Canada. Includes application requirements, experience available, stipends, and fringe benefits.

The Oxford Companion to the Mind, by Richard L. Gregory. New York: Oxford University Press, 1987. (BF 31 .O94)

A popular one-volume encyclopedia with bibliographies following signed articles. Includes index.

The Psychologist's Companion: A Guide to Scientific Writing for Students and Researchers, by Robert J. Sternberg. New York: Cambridge University Press, 1988. (BF 76.8 .S73)

Presents guidelines for writing research papers in psychology. Illustrates APA guidelines for papers and identifies commonly misused words in psychology. Chapters include "Standards for Evaluating the Psychology Paper" and "Submitting a Paper to a Journal."

Periodicals

American Journal of Psychology
American Psychologist
Behavioral Science
Clinical Psychologist
Contemporary Psychology
Human Behavior
International Journal of Psychology
Journal of Abnormal and Social Psychology
Journal of Abnormal Psychology
Journal of Applied Psychology
Journal of Experimental Psychology
Journal of General Psychology
Journal of Health and Social Behavior
Journal of Personality
Journal of Psychology
Mind

Psychological Bulletin
Psychology Review
Psychology Today

Statistical Sources

* *Statistics Sources.* (HA 36 .S84)

Style Books

Publication Manual of the American Psychological Association. 3rd ed. Washington, D.C.: American Psychological Association, 1983. (BF 76.7 .P83)

The correct style manual to use when writing for the professional and academic community that studies psychology.

Thesauruses

Thesaurus of Psychological Index Terms. 6th ed. Washington, D.C.: American Psychological Society, 1990. (Z 695.1 .P7)

A thesaurus of terms used in indexing periodical literature and documents in the study of psychology.

SELECT SUBJECT HEADINGS, BREAKDOWNS, AND CALL NUMBERS

Psychology   (BF 1 - BF 990)

Periodicals (BF 1 - BF 37)
Philosophy (BF 38 - BF 76)
Study and Teaching (BF 77 - BF 80)
History (BF 81 - BF 149)
Mind and Body (BF 150 - BF 172)
Psychoanalysis (BF 173 - BF 175)
Psychological Tests (BF 176)
Experimental Psychology (BF 180 - BF 204)
Psychotropic Drugs (BF 207 - BF 210)
Sensation (BF 231 - BF 299)

Consciousness (BF 309 - BF 317)
Motivation (BF 501 - BF 504)
Affection (BF 511 - BF 593)
Will (BF 608 - BF 635)
Applied Psychology (BF 636 - BF 637)
New Thought (BF 638 - BF 648)
Comparative Psychology (BF 660 - BF 685)
Psychology of Sex (BF 692)
Differential Psychology (BF 697)
Personality (BF 698)
Genetic Psychology (BF 699 - BF 711)
Developmental Psychology (BF 712 - BF 724)
Class Psychology (BF 725 - BF 789)
Temperament (BF 795 - BF 811)
Character (BF 818 - BF 839)
Physiognomy (BF 839 - BF 861)
Phrenology (BF 866 - BF 885)
Graphology (BF 889 - BF 905)
The Hand (BF 908 - BF 990)

4

Getting the Most from
a College Library

THE COLLEGE LIBRARY is one of the greatest assets on campus, but you can't reap the benefits if you don't get in there and use it. In addition to the different types of information resources we have discussed, there are still other resources in the library that might not be so obvious.

Although we've reviewed hundreds of information resources in previous chapters, we can't neglect the human resources that are abundant in the college library. The following topics include discussions of the various services provided by library faculty and staff members and a few observations about the life of the library.

Reference Services

Those people sitting quietly at the desk marked "Reference" are there to be disturbed, to be interrupted, to be, well, referred to when you have a question that you have tried earnestly to answer yourself but now think you need a little help in answering. Reference librarians are a pretty sharp bunch. They usually have graduate degrees in library and information science. They often have a second master's degree in a particular area of study or a specialization of some kind. If the reference librarian on duty did advanced graduate work in Chaucer and you're writing a paper on olde English, you might really benefit from a quick chat on the subject. Similarly, if the social science reference librarian is a bibliographer in economics and you're an economics major, a few moments of discussion on information resources in economics could be just the thing to put you ahead of the rest of your class. Reference librarians usually have years of experience behind them, an intimate knowledge of the library collection, and an instinct for locating answers to even the most difficult questions. And they are librarians because they love their work. When you are trying to do your best, and you need a little help, ask for guidance at the reference desk.

Departmental Libraries

Some schools have outstanding departments in particular areas of study. They may offer graduate degrees and have an outstanding reputation in terms of faculty and research in those areas. If your college or university has a separate library, for example, in the chemistry department, and you're a chemistry major, you should consider that departmental library your own. Find a well-lit study area with a favorite desk and take up residence.

Departmental libraries have a solid collection of reference materials for that particular academic department's major area of study. Departmental libraries will be staffed by a librarian if they are large enough. When you search your library catalog and come across resources that are right on point for your research, some of those resources may be located in a departmental library. If so, the catalog record will say so, and you may have to go trudging off to another building to find the information resource you want. But if you do, you'll most likely be glad you did and happy to learn about the existence of the departmental library.

Customized Bibliographies

One of the things most large college and university libraries do for their students is to research and write customized bibliographies of works in the library on a variety of topics. This is especially true if the school has a library staff committed to helping students learn the best ways to use the collection. In schools with graduate programs in certain fields, such as art history, chemical engineering, public administration, or social work, prepared bibliographies are often distributed by the office of the academic program itself. These prepared bibliographies may be written by librarians or by the faculty or graduate students of the departments they represent. A prepared bibliography or subject guide may be found in the lobby of the library or in the office of the dean of an academic program. Wherever you find them, they can be extremely useful in identifying library resources that are part of your library's collection or part of a departmental collection and are specific to your area of study.

Library Handbooks

Most colleges prepare a library handbook to help incoming students get some practical acquaintance with the library and the way it works. Though they're usually only a few pages long, a good library handbook will tell you something about the card catalog, the on-line catalog, the classification system used in the library, the types of reference services available, and the hours of library operation. A good library handbook will give you a floor plan of the library and tell you where to find necessities like the computer terminals used to search the library catalog, the photocopiers, and the bathrooms.

Term Paper Support

You're going to have to do a term paper at least once a semester in school. It can be a breeze or it can be a total nightmare. Your college library can help. Librarians know how to do research, how to put the results together in an organized fashion, and how to present the results in a coherent manner. No librarian will write your term paper for you, but the college library may offer term paper seminars or other forms of term paper support when it comes time to research, write, footnote, and cite.

Special Collections

If your library has a special collection, like the papers of a local politician, the manuscript of an author's first novel, a collection of rare books or photographs, or another special library resource, there may be a special place for that resource somewhere in the library. If those resources are extremely valuable or very fragile, they may have somewhat restricted access. They will very likely not be sitting on a shelf in the open stacks. Special collections are dear to the institutions that administer them, and those institutions will often publish a guide to the use of their special collections in order that researchers will be aware of the content and significance of the collection and the rules by which the collection may be used. A little knowledge of the special collections in the library will tell you something about the college library and the college community. The history and records of the college or university you attend will very likely be part of a special collection.

Interlibrary Loan

Interlibrary loan is a service provided by your university library that enables professors and students to borrow books from other libraries. Let's say you're in college in Washington State and the nearest place you can find that has a copy of the book you need for your research is in Washington, D.C. Would you believe you can put in a request to borrow the book and then have the book delivered to you at the college library? This service is not always open to undergraduates, but with some coaxing and a sound, coherent research agenda, you may be able to persuade a librarian to get some things for you that are not part of your college collection. Interlibrary loan takes time, so don't try to arrange it too close to the due date of a project or the end of a semester.

Computers/Audio-Visual Aids/Photocopiers/ Fax Machines

The impact of computers on the college library has been enormous. Computers make many of the research tasks in libraries work so much faster. Of course, some of us still like the old card catalogs, even though we'd probably prefer to use the computerized library catalog when we're in a hurry. If you're between the ages of seventeen and twenty-five, computers and their applications in the home, office, and in school should be nothing new to you. But if you're over thirty-five, and an increasing number of students are, you can probably remember when computers weren't around. The main use of the computer by college library users is in searching the library catalog. But there may be other computer resources also available to you in the college library, such as CD-ROM data bases and on-line data bases.

Many students go to college with their own computers nowadays. This makes the generation before you really green with envy. One of the best things you can do with your own computer when you're in college is hook it up to the college library catalog. The library catalog is a great asset, and you can sometimes take it home with you after the library closes. Via modem you can search the on-line catalog from your home as well as from your dorm. If you're sitting in your dorm room at one o'clock in the morning and decide you want to dial up the library catalog to do some research, you can do that in some schools. That way, you can select the materials you want to look over the next day. If you've got a laptop computer with a modem in it, you can search your library from the beach, as long as you have a phone line.

There are many other useful types of hardware around the library that you should investigate. Audio-visual aids, which include movie projectors, video recorders and players, televisions, record players, tape players, and recorders are there for your use. Microfilm and microfiche readers that will photocopy the contents of the fiche or film you use in your research are also there for your use.

Photocopiers, one of the most useful (when they work) and annoying (when they don't) inventions of the twentieth century, will be found in various places throughout the library, or sometimes in one huge room. Many schools have followed the ideas of the banking industry and made photocopy cards available to students. With a photocopy card, you have a regular credit card to use in the photocopier.

Fax machines, which have actually been around a long time and are finally becoming one of those "how did we ever get along without it" machines, are there for you to use. Think of the joys your parents would get if, at the end of the semester, you faxed them your grades. And of course, the joy of fax if those grades were all A's.

Data-base Services

You will recall from the sections on CD-ROM data bases and on-line data bases that there are plenty of information vendors out there. Remember, CD-ROM data bases are usually free of charge, but on-line data bases can cost money. You will also recall that some on-line data-base vendors market exclusively toward the corporate community and some toward the everyday consumer. Two of the biggies in the corporate vendors department include Lexis/Nexis and Dialog. Two of the most popular consumer on-line services include Prodigy and Compu-

Serve. While you may wish to get some consumer-oriented on-line services for use at home or in the dormitory, some of which will be valuable to you as an undergraduate, you may have reason to ask for reference assistance which demands the use of on-line data bases. Check with your reference librarian to find out what the policy is in your college library. CD-ROM data bases and on-line data bases are definitely the new technology, but in undergraduate school, you're probably going to get the most for your educational hour from the old technology — books.

Community Activities

Library buildings house information resources. I'm sure you figured that out by now. Some of them are built like warehouses, with temperature-controlled rooms full of books from one floor to the next. Some go up several stories. Some are underground. Whatever the architectural dynamics of your college library, it was built to serve a function; it was built to house the collection and to give you a reasonably comfortable place to use it. But there is very likely more space in your library than that designated for bookshelves and computer terminals. Most libraries have offices, a classroom or two, and an exhibit area for the display of special information resources or works of art. Some libraries even have theaters for the presenting of concerts, plays, opera, debates, lectures, and poetry readings. The dynamics of the library building itself, the faculty and staff of the library, and the rest of the university community make the library a living, exciting place. Check out the library bulletin boards or the campus information office. You'll probably be surprised to find a calendar of events for your college library that will keep you busy and entertained during those hours you're not studying.

Work-Study

I include this section because many students work part-time and I can think of no better place for anyone to work than in the college library or a departmental library. If your school offers a degree in nursing, and you're a Nursing major who needs to work to make a few bucks, wouldn't you be better off working in the nursing school library? No. It would be best if you could work as an intern or volunteer in a health care facility of some kind. But the nursing library might be a good second choice, especially if there aren't many health care facilities within your reach on campus. Work-study is a form of financial aid. One of the places you can work if you get financial aid in the form of work-study is the college library. And while I'm not suggesting that you study on the job, no place will ever be more accommodating than the college library when it comes to doing a little homework at work.

Browsing the Collection

Browsing the collection in your college library can be an art, a science, a wonderful and stimulating intellectual journey, or a basic nightmare. Although we have discussed how to do research with library resources by searching author, title, and subject, as well as how to look at the task of research in broad and specific terms, there are instances when browsing can be very rewarding. Now, I know I made some comments earlier about how you had to have a citation to a book and a call number to find it with, so that you wouldn't end up wandering through the stacks until you came across the book that gave you that warm, fuzzy feeling. Well, I still hold to that theory, but there are cases when browsing can be very rewarding, if you do it the right way. Doing it the right way is call "systematic browsing" by librarians. That is, you are browsing the collection, but you're doing it in a systematic way. There's a method to your madness. You can try shelf browsing by isolating a range of call numbers that have proven to be indicative of your area of study. You can browse the library catalog by setting up parameters in an on-line search that gives you only information resources in a designated call number range or only library resources within specific subject headings. Browsing is made much easier in this instance with the help of computerized library catalogs, but shelf browsing can reward you very quickly and unexpectedly with just a glance at an interesting source.

Library Etiquette

Good manners will open a lot of doors for you. And there are customs, rules, expectations, and protocols that we all must follow in different situations. Most libraries have their own list of dos and don'ts. This is my list.

Please do ask a reference librarian for help in locating resources you can't find or in using new or unfamiliar resources. Librarians are in business to help people. Let them help you when you've exhausted your own knowledge and intuition in doing your work. Ask them questions clearly and honestly. Librarians work best with complete, honest questions. If you're completely dumbfounded by something, say so. If you don't know what to look for or how to proceed, say so. Above all, don't try to hide your lack of knowledge by asking an indirect or unhelpful question. Ask a librarian the honest question the first time. The better you ask your question, the better a librarian will be able to help you find an answer.

Please don't ask a reference librarian for directions to the bathroom, how to use the photocopier, how to spell things, and other questions that you should either answer yourself or ask of another library staff member. Ask a reference librarian a reference question.

Please do take notes when doing research, whether on your laptop, on index cards, on the back of your hand, or whatever. Make sure those notes include an appropriate bibliographic citation. For your purposes, and because professors make you cite your sources all the time, your bibliographic citation should include the author, title, place of publication, publisher, year of publication, pages cited, and, for your own future reference, the call number. Get in the habit of writing down citations to information resources using the rules of whatever style book you're supposed to be using. Make sure you put anything by another source in quotes if you use a direct quote. Make sure you identify your sources and distinguish your ideas from the ideas of others.

Please don't ever write in a library book or mark it up in any way. Don't ever alter or damage any type of information resource. Do not put those little yellow stick-on things on book pages. They can rip and tear paper and lift print right off the page. They can damage a book. The same thing applies to paper clips and other adhesive or binding devices. Use a paper bookmark.

Please do check out books and return them promptly. Arrange to have books put on hold or reserve for you if they can't be taken out of the library.

Please don't ever hide books in the library so that you can get to them and no one else can. Sure, it's a problem when you've got two hundred students who need to read the same thing. Professors should put duplicate copies on reserve in this sort of situation. But don't monopolize library materials.

Please do use everything in the library for all it's worth. I mean everything. It's there for you to use in pursuing a quality education, and your tuition dollars are paying for it.

Please don't lose anything. Books go out of print. Information is precious. Many library resources are valuable in numerous ways and cannot be easily replaced. Try to be careful with all library resources. If you use an atlas, which is large and heavy, be very careful with it. If you drop an atlas or almost any other book on the floor, the weight of the book itself may break its spine. Don't open and flatten a book against your desk. This will also break the spine of a book. So will mashing it against the glass on a photocopier. There are some great photocopiers on the market that have an angled photocopy surface to avoid spine damage to books. This is especially important when it comes to brittle books. Many older books were published with low-quality paper that is full of acids. They have been deteriorating since the day the book was purchased. Be especially careful with brittle books and other older, irreplaceable books. Don't treat information resources as if they belong to someone else. Treat them as if they belong to you. After all, your tuition dollars made the investment that bought all those library resources.

Please do follow the rules of the library in the college or university you attend. That way, you'll become a welcome library user.

The Freedom of Information Act

The Freedom of Information Act was passed in 1966 and adopted in 1967. The act has helped individuals and groups in America reach deep into the dark recesses of the government to obtain information. Broadly speaking, the Freedom of Information Act requires agencies of the federal government to release their records to the public upon request, except in circumstances where exemptions exist. Those exemptions include cases in which someone's right to privacy would be infringed upon or the country's national security would be jeopardized.

Both federal and state governments have processes and guidelines by which you can get information through the Freedom of Information Act. It's referred to as an FOIA request and usually submitted in the form of a written request. For instance, if you want to figure out whether or not the FBI has a file on you, just ask in writing. If they do, they'll probably tell you. They might not let you see all of it; there may be huge censored sections in some parts. But if you ask, you'll find out. And if the agency you're requesting information from won't provide it, there are legal remedies for appeal. The media often uses the Freedom of Information Act to gain access to information that is deemed to be within the public interest. You may have to pay for the request. There is often a charge for the costs of searching and reproducing the information requested. If you choose to make a FOIA request, only ask an agency for what you really think might exist and what really applies to your research. Don't abuse the system. But remember, you have the right to request the information.

Endnote

As a student, you have access to a wealth of information, knowledge, and learning. Much of it will come to you from your professors during class. Much more of it is available to you in the college library. But you have to seek it out there and put it to use. Take what professors teach you in class and combine it with an active use of the college library and its resources, and you'll have the ingredients for a highly successful college career. Best of luck!

APPENDIX

A Directory
of Call Numbers Useful to College
Students

Subject–Call Number Index

ACCOUNTING. BOOKKEEPING (HF 5601 - HF 5689)
ACCOUNTS AND BOOKS (HF 5680 - HF 5681)
ACCOUNTS AND DEPOSITS (HG 1660)
ACOUSTICS. SOUND (QC 221 - QC 246)
ADVENTURES, SHIPWRECKS, BURIED TREASURE (G 521 - G 539)
ADVERTISING (HF 5801 - HF 6182)
AERONAUTICS (TL 500 - TL 778)
AESTHETICS OF CITIES (NA 9000 - NA 9425)
AFFECTION (BF 511 - BF 593)
AFRICA (DT 1 - DT 995)
AGRICULTURAL MACHINERY (TJ 1480 - TJ 1496)
AGRICULTURE (HD 1401 - HD 2210)
ALCHEMY (QD 23 - QD 39)
ALCOHOLISM (HV 5001 - HV 5720)
ALGAE. ALGOLOGY (QK 564 - QK 580)
ALGEBRA (QA 150 - QA 299)
ALGEBRAIC GEOMETRY (QA 564 - QA 581)
ALGEBRAIC TOPOLOGY (QA 612)
AMATEUR THEATRICALS (PN 3151 - PN 3171)
AMERICA (E 11 - E 740)
AMERICAN LITERATURE (PS 1 - PS 3576)
ANALYTICAL CHEMISTRY (QD 71 - QD 142)
ANALYTICAL GEOMETRY (QA 551 - QA 563)

ANALYTICAL MECHANICS (QA 801 - QA 939)
ANARCHISM (HX 821 - HX 970)
ANATOMY (QL 801 - QL 950)
ANCIENT HISTORY (D 51 - D 95)
ANCIENT STATE (JC 51 - JC 95)
ANGIOSPERMS (QK 495)
ANGLO-SAXON LITERATURE (PR 1490 - PR 1799)
ANIMAL BEHAVIOR (QL 750 - QL 795)
ANTHROPOLOGY (GN 1 - GN 890)
ANTIBIOTICS (QD 375 - QD 377)
ANTIQUITIES (BQ 221 - BQ 249)
APPLIED OPTICS. LASERS (TA 1501 - TA 1820)
APPLIED PSYCHOLOGY (BF 636 - BF 637)
ARCHAEOLOGY (CC 1 - CC 960)
ARCHAEOLOGY AS A PROFESSION (CC 107 - CC 109)
ARCHITECTURAL DESIGN (NA 2700 - NA 2800)
ARCHITECTURE (NA 1 - NA 9425)
ARCHITECTURE AND THE STATE (NA 100 - NA 130)
ARCHITECTURE AS A PROFESSION (NA 1995 - NA 1997)
ARITHMETIC (QA 101 - QA 145)
AROMATIC COMPOUNDS (QD 327 - QD 341)
ART AND THE STATE (N 8700 - N 9165)
ART AS A PROFESSION (N 8350 - N 8356)
ART MUSEUMS, GALLERIES (N 400 - N 4040)
ART STUDIOS, MATERIALS, ETC. (N 8510 - N 8553)
ARTISTS' MARKS AND MONOGRAMS (N 45)
ARTS AND CRAFTS MOVEMENT (NK 1135 - NK 1149)
ARTS IN GENERAL (NX 1 - NX 820)
ASIA (DS 1 - DS 937)
ASTRONAUTICS (TL 787 - TL 4050)
ASTRONOMICAL INSTRUMENTS (QB 85 - QB 139)
ASTRONOMY (QB 1 - QB 991)
ASTROPHYSICS (QB 460 - QB 466)
ATLASES (G 1000 - G 3122)
ATOMIC PHYSICS (QC 170 - QC 197)
AUDITING (HF 5667)
AUSTRIA (DB 1 - DB 879)
BALANCE OF TRADE (HF 1014)
BALKAN PENINSULA (DR 1 - DR 2285)
BALLET (GV 1786 - GV 1799)
BAND (M 1200 - M 1269)
BANK STOCKS (HG 1723)

BANKING (HG 1501 - HG 3550)
BANKS AND THE STATE (HG 1725 - HG 1778)
BIBLE (BS 1 - BS 2970)
BIOLOGICAL CHEMISTRY (QD 415 - QD 441)
BIOLOGICAL LABORATORIES (QH 320 - QH 323)
BIOLOGY (GENERAL) (QH 301 - QH 705)
BIRDS (QL 671 - QL 699)
BLACK MARKET (HF 5482.6 - HF 5482.65)
BOARDS OF TRADE (HF 294 - HF 343)
BOTANIC, THOMSONIAN, AND ECLECTIC MEDICINE (RV 1 - RV
    431)
BOTANICAL GARDENS (QK 63 - QK 73)
BOTANY (QK 1 - QK 989)
BRIDGE ENGINEERING (TG 1 - TG 470)
BROADCASTING (PN 1990 - PN 1992.92)
BRYOPHYTA (QK 532 - QK 533)
BUDDHISM (BQ 1 - BQ 9800)
BUDDHIST LITERATURE (BQ 1001 - BQ 1045)
BUDDHIST PANTHEON (BQ 4620 - BQ 4905)
BUILDING CONSTRUCTION (TH 1 - TH 9745)
BUSINESS (HF 5001 - HF 6182)
BUSINESS COMMUNICATION (HF 5717 - HF 5746)
BUSINESS CYCLES (HB 3711 - HB 3840)
BUSINESS ETHICS (HF 5387)
BUSINESS MATHEMATICS (HF 5691 - HF 5716)
BUYING (HF 5437 - HF 5444)
CALCULUS (QA 302 - QA 316)
CANADIAN LITERATURE (PS 8001 - PS 8599)
CANVASSING (HF 5446 - HF 5459)
CAPITAL (HB 501)
CARBOHYDRATES (QD 320 - QD 327)
CATECHISMS (BT 1029 - BT 1040)
CHARITY FAIRS (HV 544)
CHARITY ORGANIZATIONS AND PRACTICE (HV 40 - HV 69)
CHEMICAL ENGINEERING (TP 155 - TP 156)
CHEMICAL OCEANOGRAPHY (GC 109 - GC 117)
CHEMICAL TECHNOLOGY (TP 1 - TP 1185)
CHEMISTRY (QD 1 - QD 999)
CHORDATES (QL 605 - QL 739)
CHRISTIAN ANTIQUITIES (BR 130 - BR 133)
CHRISTIAN DENOMINATIONS (BX 1 - BX 9999)
CHRISTIANITY (BR 1 - BR 1725)

CHRISTOLOGY (BT 198 - BT 590)
CHURCH AND SOCIAL PROBLEMS (HN 30 - HN 40)
CHURCH UNITY (BX 1 - BX 9)
CIRCUSES, SPECTACLES, ETC. (GV 1800 - GV 1860)
CIVIL ENGINEERING (GENERAL) (TA 144 - TA 156)
CIVIL SERVICE (JF 1410 - JF 1671)
CIVIL WAR (E 456 - E 655)
CIVILIZATION. CULTURE. PROGRESS (HM 101 - HM 121)
CLASSICAL PHILOLOGY AND LITERATURE (PA)
CLAY INDUSTRIES. CERAMICS. GLASS. CEMENT (TP 785 - TP 888)
CLUBS (HS 2501 - HS 3365)
COLLEGE AND SCHOOL MAGAZINES AND PAPERS (LH 1 - LH 9)
COLLEGE AND SCHOOL THEATRICALS (PN 3175 - PN 3191)
COLONIAL HISTORY (E 186 - E 199)
COLONIES AND COLONIZATION (JV 1 - JV 5299)
COMETS (QB 717 - QB 732)
COMMERCE (HF 1 - HF 6182)
COMMODITIES (HF 1040 - HF 1054)
COMMUNISM/SOCIALISM (HX 519 - HX 550)
COMMUNISM: UTOPIAN SOCIALISM (HX 626 - HX 780)
COMMUNITIES. CLASSES. RACES (HT 51 - HT 1595)
COMMUNITY CENTERS (HN 41 - HN 46)
COMPUTER ENGINEERING (TK 7885 - TK 7895)
COMPUTER SCIENCE (QA 75.5 - QA 76.95)
COMPUTER SOFTWARE (76.75)
CONFEDERATE STATES (JK 9601 - JK 9995)
CONGRESS (JK 1001 - JK 1128)
CONSCIOUSNESS (BF 309 - BF 317)
CONSTITUTIONAL HISTORY (JK 11 - JK 277)
CONSTITUTIONAL LAW (KF 4501 - KF 4515)
CONSUMER EDUCATION (HF 5832)
CONTRACTS (KF 801 - KF 1241)
CORAL ISLANDS AND REEFS (QE 565 - QE 570)
COURTS. PROCEDURE (KF 8700 - KF 9075)
CREATION (BT 695 - BT 748)
CREDIT (HG 3691 - HG 3769)
CREEDS, CONFESSIONS, COVENANTS, ETC. (BT 990 - BT 1010)
CRIMINOLOGY (HV 6035 - HV 6197)
CRYSTALLOGRAPHY (QD 901 - QD 999)
CUSTOMER SERVICE (HF 5415.5)
CUSTOMS ADMINISTRATION (HJ 6603 - HJ 7390)
CUSTOMS RELATING TO PRIVATE/PUBLIC LIFE (GT 500 - GT 2370)

CYTOGAMS (QK 504 - QK 638)
CYTOLOGY (QH 473 - QH 671)
DANCE CRITICISM (GV 1600)
DANCE MUSIC (M 1450)
DANCING (GV 1580 - GV 1799)
DANCING AS A PROFESSION (GV 1597)
DATA PROCESSING (QC 52)
DEATH. DYING (QH 1073)
DECORATION AND ORNAMENT (NK 1160 - NK 1678)
DECORATIVE ARTS (NK 1 - NK 9955)
DEGENERATION (HV 4961 - HV 4995)
DEMOGRAPHY (HB 848 - HB 3697)
DENTISTRY (RL 1 - RL 715)
DERMATOLOGY (RL 1 - RL 803)
DIFFERENTIAL EQUATIONS (QA 370 - QA 387)
DIGITAL COMPUTERS (QA 76.5)
DIPLOMATICS. ARCHIVES. SEALS (CD 1 - CD 6471)
DIRECT MAIL (HF 5856)
DISCOVERY OF AMERICA (E 101 - E 135)
DRAWING. DESIGN. ILLUSTRATION (NC 1 - NC 1940)
DRUG HABIT (HV 5800 - HV 5840)
DUTCH (PF)
DYNAMOELECTRIC MACHINERY (TK 2000 - TK 2891)
EARTHWORK. FOUNDATIONS (TA 715 - TA 787)
EASTERN CHURCHES (BX 100 - BX 189)
EASTERN EUROPE (DJK 1 - DJK 77)
EASTERN HEMISPHERE (D 890 - D 893)
ECCLESIASTICAL THEOLOGY (BV 590 - BV 1652)
ECOLOGY (QH 540 - QH 559)
ECONOMIC GEOGRAPHY (HC 92)
ECONOMIC GROWTH (HD 72 - HD 88)
ECONOMIC HISTORY AND CONDITIONS (HD 1 - HD 9999)
ECONOMIC THEORY (HB 1 - HB 3840)
ECONOMICS AS A SCIENCE (HB 71 - HB 74)
ECONOMICS OF ART (N 8600 - N 8675)
EDUCATION (GENERAL) (L 7 - L 991)
EDUCATION EXTENSION. ADULT EDUCATION (LC 5201 - LC 6691)
EDUCATION OF SPECIAL CLASSES OF PERSONS (LC 1390 - LC 5158)
EDUCATIONAL EXHIBITIONS AND MUSEUMS (L 797 - L 899)
ELECTORAL SYSTEMS (JK 1951 - JK 2246)
ELECTRIC LIGHTING (TK 4125 - TK 4399)
ELECTRICAL ENGINEERING. NUCLEAR ENGINEERING (TK 1 - TK 9971)

ELECTRICITY AND MAGNETISM (QC 501 - QC 766)
ELECTRICITY FOR AMATEURS (TK 9900 - TK 9971)
ELECTRONIC MUSIC (M 1473)
ELECTRONICS (TK 7800 - TK 8360)
EMBRYOLOGY (QL 851 - QL 991)
EMIGRATION AND IMMIGRATION (JV 6000 - JV 9500)
ENGINEERING (GENERAL) (TA 1 - TA 2040)
ENGINEERING ECONOMY (TA 177.4 - TA 185)
ENGINEERING GEOLOGY (TA 705 - TA 710.5)
ENGLISH (PE)
ENGLISH LITERATURE (PR 1 - PR 9680)
ENGLISH LITERATURE: PROVINCIAL/LOCAL. (PR 8309 - PR 9680)
ENGLISH RENAISSANCE (1500–1640) (PR 2199 - PR 3195)
ENGRAVINGS ON GLASS (NE 2690)
ENVIRONMENTAL POLLUTION (TC 172 - TC 196)
ENVIRONMENTAL PROTECTION (TC 169 - TC 171.5)
ENVIRONMENTAL TECHNOLOGY (TD 1 - TD 949)
EPHERMERIDES (QB 7 - QB 14)
ESTUARINE OCEANOGRAPHY (GC 96 - GC 97)
ETCHING AND AQUATINT (NE 1940 - NE 1975)
ETHNOLOGY (GN 301 - GN 673)
EVANGELISM (BV 3750 - BV 3799)
EVOLUTION (QH 359 - QH 390)
EXPERIMENTAL PSYCHOLOGY (BF 180 - BF 204)
FAMILY. MARRIAGE. HOME (HQ 450 - HQ 471)
FEDERAL AND STATE REGULATIONS (JK 310 - JK 325)
FEDERAL DISTRICTS (JF 1900)
FEDERAL LAW (LAW OF THE UNITED STATES) (KF 1 - KF 9827)
FERMENTATION. ALCOHOLIC BEVERAGES (TP 500 - TP 660)
FESTIVALS. CONGRESSES (ML 35 - ML 38)
FICTION AND JUVENILE BELLES LETTRES (PZ 1 - PZ 90)
FICTION IN ENGLISH (PZ 1 - PZ 4)
FIFE (M 1270)
FINANCE (HG 1 - HG 9999)
FINANCE MANAGEMENT (HG 4001 - HG 4280.7)
FINANCIAL INSTITUTIONS (BQ 96 - BQ 99)
FINE ARTS (N 1 - NX 820)
FINNISH (PH)
FISHES (QL 614 - QL 639)
FOLKLORE (GR 1 - GR 950)
FOOD PROCESSING AND MANUFACTURE (TP 368 - TP 456)
FOREIGN EXCHANGE (HG 3810 - HG 4000)

FRANCE (DC 1 - DC 947)
FREEMASONS (HS 351 - HS 929)
FUEL (TP 315 - TP 360)
FUNGI (QK 600 - QK 638)
GAMES AND AMUSEMENTS (GV 1199 - GV 1570)
GAS INDUSTRY (TP 751 - TP 762)
GENEALOGY (CS 1 - CS 3090)
GENETIC PSYCHOLOGY (BF 699 - BF 711)
GENETICS (QH 426 - QH 470)
GEOCHEMISTRY (QE 514 - QE 516)
GEODESY (QB 275 - QB 343)
GEODETIC ASTRONOMY (QB 201 - QB 207)
GEODETIC SURVEYING (QB 301 - QB 328)
GEOGRAPHERS (G 65)
GEOGRAPHICAL DIVISIONS (QE 443 - QE 456)
GEOGRAPHY (G 1 - G 9980)
GEOLOGICAL DIVISIONS (QE 65 - QE 70)
GEOLOGY (QE 1 - QE 999)
GEOMAGNETISM (QC 811 - QC 849)
GEOMETRICAL/MATHEMATICAL CRYSTALLOGRAPHY (QD 911 -
    QD 932)
GEOMETRY (QA 440 - QA 699)
GEOPHYSICS (QC 801 - QC 809)
GERMANY (DD 1 - DD 905)
GLOBES (G 3160 - G 3182)
GOD (BT 98 - BT 180)
GOVERNMENT (JF 201 - JF 786)
GOVERNMENT ADMINISTRATION (JK 401 - JK 446)
GOVERNMENT PROPERTY (JK 1606 - JK 1686)
GRAPHIC ART MATERIALS (NC 850 - NC 915)
GRAPHOLOGY (BF 889 - BF 905)
GRAVITY DETERMINATIONS (QB 330 - QB 343)
GREAT BRITAIN (DA 1 - DA 995)
GREECE (DF 10 - DF 951)
GREETING CARDS, INVITATIONS, ETC. (NC 1860 - NC 1890)
GYMNOSPERMS (QK 494)
GYNECOLOGY AND OBSTETRICS (RG 1 - RG 991)
GYPSIES (DX 101 - DX 301)
HEAT (QC 251 - QC 338.5)
HERALDRY (CR 1 - CR 6305)
HERBARIUMS (QK 75 - QK 89)
HIGHWAY ENGINEERING. ROADS AND PAVEMENTS (TE 1 - TE
    450)

HISTORICAL GEOGRAPHY (G 142)
HISTORY (GENERAL AND OLD WORLD) (D 1 - D 1075)
HISTORY AND PRINCIPLES OF RELIGIONS (BL 660 - BL 2670)
HISTORY OF ARCHAEOLOGY (CC 100 - CC 106)
HISTORY OF CIVILIZATION (CB 3 - CB 481)
HISTORY OF DISCOVERIES (G 200 - G 336)
HISTORY OF DRAWING (NC 50 - NC 376)
HISTORY OF ECONOMICS (HB 75 - HB 130)
HISTORY OF EDUCATION (LA 1 - LA 2396)
HISTORY OF GEOGRAPHY (G 80)
HISTORY OF MEDICINE (R 131 - R 684)
HOMEOPATHY (RX 1 - RX 681)
HOUSE OF REPRESENTATIVES (JK 1304 - JK 1443)
HOUSES. DWELLINGS (GT 170 - GT 476)
HUMAN ANATOMY (QM 1 - QM 981)
HUMAN ENGINEERING (TA 166 - TA 167)
HYBRIDIZATION (QH 421 - QH 425)
HYDRAULIC ENGINEERING (TC 1 - TC 1665)
IGNEOUS ROCKS, VOLCANIC ASH, TUFF, ETC. (QE 461 - QE 462)
ILLUMINATION OF MANUSCRIPTS AND BOOKS (ND 2890 - ND
    3416)
ILLUSTRATION (NC 950 - NC 995)
INCOME (HB 522 - HB 715)
INCOME AND EXPENDITURE (HJ 2005 - HJ 2347)
INDIANS (E 51 - E 99)
INDIVIDUALISM (HM 136 - HM 146)
INDO-EUROPEAN PHILOLOGY (P 501 - P 675)
INDUSTRIAL ENGINEERING (T 55.4 - T 60.8)
INDUSTRIAL PSYCHOLOGY (HF 5548.7 - HF 5548.85)
INDUSTRIAL SAFETY (T 54 - T 55.3)
INDUSTRIAL SANITATION. INDUSTRIAL WASTES (TC 895 - TC 899)
INDUSTRY (HD 2321 - HD 4730.9)
INFLATION (HF 5667)
INORGANIC CHEMISTRY (QD 146 - QD 197)
INSCRIPTIONS. EPIGRAPHY (CN 1 - CN 1355)
INSECTS (QL 461 - QL 599)
INSTRUMENTAL MUSIC (M 1 - M 1490)
INSTRUMENTAL MUSIC FOR CHILDREN (M 1375 - M 1420)
INSTRUMENTAL MUSIC FOR MOTION PICTURES (M 176)
INSTRUMENTAL MUSIC FOR RADIO AND TELEVISION (M 176.5)
INSURANCE (HG 8011 - HG 9999)
INSURANCE OF DEPOSITS (HG 1662)

INTELLECTUAL PROPERTY (KF 2971 - KF 3192)
INTERIOR DECORATION (NK 1700 - NK 3505)
INTERNAL MEDICINE (RC 31 - RC 1245)
INTERNATIONAL LAW (JX)
INVERTEBRATES (QL 362 - QL 599)
INVESTMENT (HG 4501 - HG 6051)
ISLAM (BP 1 - BP 610)
ISLAMIC LITERATURE (BP 87 - BP 89)
ISLAMIC SOCIOLOGY (BP 173.25 - BP 173.45)
ITALY (DG 11 - DG 999)
JAZZ ENSEMBLES (M 1366)
JEWISH THEATER (PN 3035)
JOURNALISM (PN 4699 - PN 5650)
JUDAISM (BM 1 - BM 990)
JUDICIARY (JK 1511 - JK 1598)
JURISPRUDENCE (K 201 - K 487)
KNIGHTS OF PYTHIAS (HS 1201 - HS 1350)
LABOR (HD 4801 - HD 8943)
LAND USE (HD 101 - HD 1395)
LANGUAGE (P 101 - P 157)
LAW (GENERAL) (K 1 - K 7720)
LAW OF INDIVIDUAL CITIES (BY CITY) (KFX 1 - KFX 9999)
LAW OF INDIVIDUAL STATES (BY STATE) (KFA 1 - KFW 4799)
LAWS, REGULATIONS, ETC. (CC 130 - CC 139)
LEXICOGRAPHY (P 761 - P 769)
LIBRETTOS (ML 48 - ML 54.8)
LICHENS (QK 580 - QK 597)
LIFE (QH 501 - QH 531)
LIFE SAVING (HV 650 - HV 670)
LINEAR AND MULTILINEAR ALGEBRA (QA 184 - QA 205)
LIQUIDITY (HG 177)
LITERARY HISTORY (PN 441 - PN 1009.5)
LITERARY HISTORY AND CRITICISM (PR 1 - PR 56)
LITERATURE (GENERAL) (PN 1 - PN 6790)
LITERATURE ON MUSIC FOR CHILDREN (ML 3930)
LOANS (HG 1641 - HG 1643)
LOCAL GOVERNMENT (JS)
LONGITUDE AND LATITUDE (QB 225 - QB 237)
LOTTERIES (HG 6105 - HG 6270.9)
LUMIPRINTS (NE 2685)
MACHINE SHOPS AND MACHINE SHOPS PRACTICE (TJ 1125 - TJ
  1345)

MACHINE THEORY (QA 255 - QA 272)

MAMMALS (QL 700 - QL 739)

MANDOLIN (M 1360)

MANNERS AND CUSTOMS (GT 1 - GT 7070)

MANUSCRIPTS, AUTOGRAPHS, ETC. (ML 93 - ML 97)

MAPS (G 3190 - G 9980)

MARINE POLLUTION (GC 1080 - GC 1581)

MARINE RESOURCES (GC 1000 - GC 1023)

MARINE SEDIMENTS (GC 376 - GC 603)

MARKETING (HF 5410 - HF 5417.5)

MARKETING RESEARCH (HF 5415.2)

MARKETS (HF 5469.7 - HF 5481)

MATHEMATICAL GEOGRAPHY. CARTOGRAPHY (GA 1 - GA 1776)

MATHEMATICAL PHYSICS (QC 19.2 - QC 19.85)

MATHEMATICAL STATISTICS (QA 276 - QA 299)

MATHEMATICS (GENERAL WORKS) (QA 1 - QA 7)

MATHEMATICS FOR NURSES (RT 67)

MECHANICAL DRAWING. ENGINEERING GRAPHICS (T 351 - T 385)

MECHANICAL ENGINEERING AND MACHINERY (TJ 1 - TJ 1570)

MECHANICS OF ENGINEERING (TA 349 - TA 359)

MEDICAL EDUCATION (R 735 - R 847)

MEDICAL PHYSICS (R 895 - R 920)

MEDICINE (GENERAL) (R 5 - R 920)

MEDIEVAL HISTORY (D 111 - D 203)

MEDIEVAL STATE (JC 101 - JC 126)

MEDITERRANEAN REGION (DE 1 - DE 100)

MEN (HQ 1090)

MERGERS (HG 1722)

MESOZOIC (QE 675 - QE 688)

METAL ENGRAVING (NE 1400 - NE 1879)

METALS (QD 171 - QD 197)

METAMORPHIC ROCKS (QE 475 - QE 499)

METEOROLOGY (QC 851 - QC 999)

METEORS (QB 740 - QB 753)

MICROBIOLOGY (QR 1 - QR 500)

MICROSCOPY (QH 201 - QH 278.5)

MILITARY GOVERNMENT (JF 1800)

MIND AND BODY (BF 150 - 172)

MINERALOGY (QE 351 - QE 399)

MINING ENGINEERING. METALLURGY (TN 1 - TN 997)

MINSTREL MUSIC (M 1365)

MODERN HISTORY (D 204 - D 475)
MODERN LANGUAGES. GENERAL. CELTIC (PB)
MODERN STATE (JC 131 - JC 209)
MONEY (HG 201 - HG 1496)
MONOTYPE (PRINTMAKING) (NE 2242 - NE 2246)
MOON (QB 580 - QB 595)
MORAL AND RELIGIOUS EDUCATION (LC 251 - LC 951)
MORPHOLOGY (QL 799)
MOTION PICTURES (PN 1993 - PM 1999)
MOTIVATION (BF 501 - BF 504)
MOTOR VEHICLES (TL 1 - TL 390)
MOTOR VEHICLES. AERONAUTICS. ASTRONAUTICS (TL 1 - TL
    4050)
MUNICIPAL ENGINEERING (TD 159 - TD 167)
MUNICIPAL REFUSE. SOLID WASTES (TC 785 - TC 812.5)
MURAL PAINTING (NE 2550 - ND 2888)
MUSIC (M 1 - M 3)
MUSIC FOR TWO OR MORE SOLO INSTRUMENTS (M 177 - M 990)
MUSIC INSTRUCTION AND STUDY (MT 1 - MT 949)
MUSIC LITERATURE (ML 1 - ML 3930)
MUSIC THEORY (MT 6 - MT 7)
MUSIC WITH COLOR APPARATUS (M 1480)
MUTATIONS (QH 460 - QH 470)
MYTH; COMPARATIVE MYTHOLOGY (BL 300 - BL 325)
NATIONAL DEFENSE (KF 7201 - KF 7755)
NATURAL HISTORY (GENERAL) (QH 1 - QH 278.5)
NATURAL THEOLOGY (BL 175 - BL 290)
NATURALIZATION (JK 1800 - JK 1839)
NATURE CONSERVATION. LANDSCAPE PROTECTION (QH 75 - QH
    77)
NEAR EAST (PN 5359 - PN 5365)
NETHERLANDS (HOLLAND) (DJ 1 - DJ 500)
NETHERLANDS (LOW COUNTRIES) (DH 1 - DH 925)
NEW TESTAMENT (BS 1901 - BS 2970)
NEW ZEALAND (PN 5591 - 5600)
NORMAN PERIOD (PR 1803 - PR 2165)
NORTH AMERICA (E 31 - E 46)
NORTHERN AND SOUTHERN HEMISPHERES (G 912 - G 922)
NORTHERN EUROPE (DL 1 - DL 1180)
NUCLEAR AND PARTICLE PHYSICS (QC 770 - QC 798)
NUCLEAR ENGINEERING. ATOMIC POWER (TK 9001 - TK 9401)
NUMERATION (QA 139 - QA 145)

NUMISMATICS (CJ 1 - CJ 6661)
NURSING (RT 1 - RT 120)
NURSING AS A PROFESSION (RT 82)
NURSING CARE PLANS (RT 49)
NURSING ETHICS (RT 85)
NURSING RECORDS (RT 50)
OCEAN-ATMOSPHERE INTERACTION (GC 181 - GC 190)
OCEANIA (SOUTH SEAS) (DU 1 - DU 950)
OCEANOGRAPHIC RESEARCH (GC 57 - GC 63)
OCEANOGRAPHY (BY REGION) (GC 611 - GC 881)
OCEANOGRAPHY (GC 1 - GC 1581)
OCEANOGRAPHY (GENERAL) (GC 1 - GC 103)
OLD TESTAMENT (BS 701 - BS 1830)
OPHTHALMOLOGY (RE 1 - RE 994)
OPTICS. LIGHT (QC 350 - QC 467)
ORATORY. ELOCUTION, ETC. (PN 4001 - PN 4355)
ORCHESTRA (M 1000 - M 1075)
ORCHESTRA AND ORCHESTRATION (MT 70 - MT 71)
ORGANIC CHEMISTRY (QD 241 - QD 441)
ORGANOMETALLIC CHEMISTRY (QD 410 - QD 412)
ORIGINS OF THE STATE (JC 301 - JC 347)
ORTHODOX EASTERN CHURCH (BX 200 - BX 745)
OTORHINOLARYNGOLOGY (RF 1 - RF 991)
OUTDOOR ADVERTISING (HF 5841)
OUTDOOR LIFE (GV 191.2 - GV 200.66)
PACIFIC ISLANDS (PN 5620)
PAINTING (ND 1 - ND 3416)
PAINTS, PIGMENTS, VARNISHES, ETC. (TP 934 - TP 944)
PALEOBOTANY (QE 901 - QE 999)
PALEONTOLOGY (QE 701 - QE 760)
PALEOZOOLOGY (QE 760 - QE 899)
PASTORAL THEOLOGY (BV 4000 - BV 4470)
PATENTS. TRADEMARKS (T 201 - T 342)
PATHOLOGY (RB 1 - RB 214)
PATRONAGE OF THE ARTS (NX 700 - NX 750)
PEDIATRICS (RJ 1 - RJ 570)
PENOLOGY (HV 7231 - HV 9920)
PERFORMING ARTS AS A PROFESSION (PN 1580)
PERFORMING ARTS. SHOW BUSINESS (PN 1560 - PN 1590)
PERIODICAL AND NEWSPAPER PUBLISHING (PN 4734)
PERSONAL FINANCE (HG 179)
PERSONALITY (BF 698)

PERSONNEL (HF 5500.2 - HF 5506)
PERSONNEL MANAGEMENT (HF 5549 - HF 5549.5)
PERTURBATIONS (QB 361 - QB 410)
PETROLEUM REFINING AND PRODUCTS (TP 690 - TP 692.4)
PETROLOGY (QE 420 - QE 499)
PHARMACY AND MATERIA MEDICA (RS 1 - RS 441)
PHILOSOPHY (B 1 - B 5739)
PHOTOCHEMISTRY (QD 701 - QD 731)
PHRENOLOGY (BF 866 - BF 885)
PHYSICAL AND CHEMICAL PROPERTIES (QH 611 - QH 630)
PHYSICAL AND THEORETICAL CHEMISTRY (QD 450 - QD 999)
PHYSICAL ANTHROPOLOGY (GN 49 - GN 296)
PHYSICAL EDUCATION (GV 201 - GV 555)
PHYSICAL GEOGRAPHY (GB 3 - GB 5030)
PHYSICAL OCEANOGRAPHY (GC 149 - GC 181)
PHYSICAL PROPERTIES OF CRYSTALS (QD 931 - QD 999)
PHYSICS (QC 1 - QC 999)
PHYSIOGNOMY (BF 839 - 861)
PHYSIOLOGICAL PROPERTIES (QH 631 - QH 647)
PHYSIOLOGY (QP 1 - QP 981)
PICTORIAL HUMOR, CARICATURE, ETC. (NC 1300 - NC 1766)
PLANETS (QB 595 - QB 701)
PLANT ANATOMY (QK 640 - QK 707)
PLANT ECOLOGY (QK 900 - QK 977)
PLANT PHYSIOLOGY (QK 710 - QK 899)
PLASMA ENGINEERING (TA 2001 - TA 2040)
POLAR REGIONS (G 575 - G 890)
POLITICAL PARTIES (JK 2301 - JK 2391)
POLITICAL RIGHTS AND GUARANTEES (JF 800 - JF 1191)
POLITICAL SCIENCE (J 1 - JX 5810)
POLITICAL THEORY (JC 1 - JC 628)
POLITICS. CIVIL RIGHTS (JK 1711 - JK 1717)
POLYMERS (QD 380 - QD 388)
POLYMERS, PLASTICS, AND THEIR MANUFACTURE (TP 1080 - TP 1185)
PRACTICAL NURSING (RT 62)
PRECIOUS STONES (QE 392 - QE 399)
PREHISTORIC ARCHAEOLOGY (GN 700 - GN 890)
PRICE (HB 221 - HB 236)
PRIMARY EDUCATION (LB 1501 - LB 1547)
PRIMITIVE STATE (JC 20 - JC 50)
PRINT MEDIA (NE 1 - NE 2890)

PRINTING OF ENGRAVINGS (NE 2800 - NE 2890)
PRINTMAKING AND ENGRAVING (NE 1 - NE 978)
PROBABILITIES (QA 273 - QA 275)
PRODUCTION (HD 28 - HD 69)
PROGRAMMING LANGUAGES (QA 76.7)
PROGRAMS (ML 40 - ML 44)
PROPERTY (KF 560 - KF 720)
PROTESTANTISM (BS 4800 - BS 9999)
PSYCHOANALYSIS (BF 173 - BF 175)
PSYCHOLOGICAL TESTS (BF 176)
PSYCHOLOGY (BF 1 - BF 990)
PSYCHOLOGY OF SEX (BF 692)
PSYCHOTROPIC DRUGS (BF 207 - BF 210)
PTERIDOPHYTA (QK 520 - QK 532)
PUBLIC ACCOUNTING (HJ 9701 - HJ 9995)
PUBLIC CREDIT. DEBTS. LOANS (HJ 8003 - HJ 8899)
PUBLIC FINANCE (HJ 1 - HJ 9995)
PUBLIC FINANCE (KF 6200 - KF 6795)
PUBLIC PROPERTY (KF 5500 - KF 5865)
PUBLIC RELATIONS (HD 59)
PUBLIC SAFETY (KF 3941 - KF 3977)
QUANTUM CHEMISTRY (QD 452 - QD 481)
RACES (HT 1501 - HT 1595)
RADIATION PHYSICS (QC 474 - QC 496.9)
RADIO BROADCASTS (PN 1991 - PN 1991.9)
RAILROAD ENGINEERING AND OPERATION (TF 1 - TF 1620)
RATE OF INTEREST (HG 1621 - HG 1638)
RECREATION (GV 1 - GV 1860)
RELIGION (BL 1 - BL 2790)
RELIGIONS OF THE WORLD (BL 74 - BL 98)
RELIGIOUS ARTS (NX 654 - NX 694)
RELIGIOUS DOCTRINES (BL 425 - BL 490)
RELIGIOUS EDUCATION (BQ 141 - BQ 209)
RELIGIOUS LIFE (BL 624 - BL 627)
RELIGIOUS ORGANIZATIONS (BL 630 - BL 632)
REPRODUCTION (QH 471 - QH 499)
REPTILES AND AMPHIBIANS (QL 640 - QL 669)
REVENUE. TAXATION (HJ 2240 - HJ 3192.7)
ROCKETS (TL 780 - TL 785.8)
ROMAN CATHOLIC CHURCH (BX 800 - BX 4795)
SALINITY (GC 120 - GC 149)
SALVATION (BT 750 - BT 810)

SAMARITANS (BM 900 - BM 990)
SCULPTURE (NB 1 - NB 1952)
SEAFARING LIFE, OCEAN TRAVEL (G 540 - G 550)
SEAWATER (GC 100 - GC 103)
SECONDARY EDUCATION (LB 1603 - LB 1695)
SECRET SOCIETIES (HS 101 - HS 330)
SEDIMENTARY ROCKS (QE 471 - QE 473)
SEDIMENTATION (QE 571 - QE 597)
SENATE (JK 1151 - JK 1271)
SENSATION (BF 231 - BF 299)
SERIGRAPHY (NE 2236 - NE 2240)
SEXUAL LIFE (HQ 12 - HQ 449)
SINGING AND VOICE CULTURE (MT 820 - MT 949)
SOCIAL PATHOLOGY. PUBLIC WELFARE. CRIMINOLOGY (HV 1 -
    HV 9960)
SOCIAL PSYCHOLOGY (HM 251 - HM 291)
SOCIALISM. COMMUNISM. ANARCHISM (HX 1 - HX 970)
SOCIETIES: SECRET, BENEVOLENT, ETC. (HS 1 - HS 3369)
SOCIOLOGY (GENERAL AND THEORETICAL) (HM 1 - HM 299)
SOCIOLOGY (HM 1 - HX 970.7)
SOLAR SYSTEM (QB 501 - QB 991)
SOVIET UNION (DK 1 - DK 873)
SPAIN (DP 1 - DP 402)
SPERMATOPHYTA. PHANEROGAMS (QK 474 - QK 495)
STARS (QB 799 - QB 991)
STATE AND INDIVIDUAL (JC 571 - JC 628)
STATE AND SOCIAL GROUPS (JC 541 - JC 561)
STATE GOVERNMENT (JK 2408 - JK 9600)
STATISTICS (HA 1 - HA 4737)
STEAM ENGINEERING (TJ 268 - TJ 740)
STRATIGRAPHY (QE 640 - QE 699)
STRUCTURAL ENGINEERING (TA 630 - TA 695)
STRUCTURAL GEOLOGY (QE 601 - QE 625)
STUDENT FRATERNITIES AND SOCIETIES, U.S. (LJ 3 - LJ 75)
SUFFRAGE (JK 1846 - JK 1936)
SUN (QB 520 - QB 540)
SURGERY (RD 1 - RD 811)
SURVEYING (TA 501 - TA 625)
SWITZERLAND (DQ 1 - DQ 851)
TABLEAUX, PAGEANTS (PN 3203 - PN 3299)
TARIFF POLICY (HF 1701 - HF 2701)
TAXATION (HJ 3231 - HJ 5957)

TECHNOLOGY (GENERAL) (T 1 - T 995)
TELECOMMUNICATIONS (TK 5101 - TK 6720)
TELEVISION BROADCASTS (PN 1992 - PN 1992.92)
TEXTILE DYEING AND PRINTING (TP 890 - TP 933)
THEATRICAL DANCING (GV 1781 - GV 1785)
THEOLOGY (BP 166)
THEORETICAL ASTRONOMY AND CELESTIAL MECHANICS (QB 349 - QB 480)
THEORY OF NUMBERS (QA 224 - QA 255)
THERAPEUTICS. PHARMACOLOGY (RM 1 - RM 931)
THERMOCHEMISTRY (QD 508 - QD 655)
THRIFT AND SAVING (HG 7920 - HG 7933)
TIME (QB 209 - QB 224)
TOBACCO HABIT (HV 5725 - HV 5770)
TOPOLOGY (QA 611)
TOPONYMY (G 100.5 - G 108.5)
TRANSPORTATION AND COMMUNICATIONS (HE 1 - HE 9900)
TRANSPORTATION ENGINEERING (TA 1001 - TA 1280)
TRAVEL (G 149 - G 180)
TREATISES (JF 45 - JF 195)
TREES AND SHRUBS (QK 474 - QK 495)
TRIGONOMETRY (QA 531 - QA 538)
TRIPITAKA (BQ 1100 - BQ 3340)
TROPICS (G 905 - G 910)
TRUST SERVICES (HG 4301 - HG 4480.9)
TUNNELING. TUNNELS (TA 800 - TA 820)
UNDERWATER EXPLORATION (GC 65 - GC 78)
UNITED STATES (GENERAL) (E 151 - E 740)
UNITED STATES LOCAL HISTORY (F 1 - F 975)
UNIVERSE. SPACE (QB 495 - QB 500)
URBAN GROUPS (HT 101 - HT 395)
UTOPIAS (HX 806 - HX 811)
VALUE (HB 201 - HB 205)
VISUAL ARTS (N 1 - N 9165)
VOCAL MUSIC (M 1 - M 5000)
VOLCANOES AND EARTHQUAKES (QE 521 - QE 545)
VOYAGES AND TRAVELS (GENERAL) (G 149 - G 570)
WAREHOUSING AND STORAGE (HF 5484 - HF 5495)
WATER SUPPLY: DOMESTIC AND INDUSTRIAL (TC 201 - TC 500)
WATERCOLOR PAINTING (ND 1700 - ND 2495)
WEIGHTS AND MEASURES (QC 81 - QC 114)
WELFARE THEORY (HB 846 - HB 846.8)

WHOLESALE TRADE (HF 5419 - HF 5422)
WILL (BF 608 - BF 635)
WOMEN (HQ 1101 - 2030)
WOMEN AUTHORS (PS 147 - PS 152)
WOOD ENGRAVING (NE 1000 - NE 1352)
WORLD WAR I (D 501 - D 680)
WORLD WAR II (D 731 - D 838)
ZOOLOGY (QL 1 - QL 991)

Title–Call Number Index

250 Years of Afro-American Art: An Annotated Bibliography (N 6538 .N5 I35)
ABC Pol Sci (Z 7161 .A214)
Abstracts in Anthropology (GA 1 .A2)
Abstracts of the Psychological Works of Sigmund Freud (BF 173 .F62535)
Academic American Encyclopedia (AE 5 .A23)
Access: The Supplementary Index to Periodicals (AI 3 .A23)
Accountant's Desk Handbook (HF 5635 .A474)
Accountant's Encyclopedia (HF 5635 .P93)
Accountant's Index (Z 7164 .C81 A5)
Accountant's Index: A Bibliography (HG 5635 .A23)
Accounting Articles (Z 7164 .C81 C78)
Accounting Desk Book (HF 5635 .C33)
Accounting Firms and Practitioners (HF 5601 .A8338)
Accounting Handbook (HF 5635 .S586)
Accounting Literature in Non-Accounting Journals (HF 5635 .T36)
Acronyms, Initialisms and Abbreviations Dictionary (P 365 .A28)
Advertising Slogans of America (HF 6135 .S53)
AFI Guide to College Courses in Film and Television (PN 1993.8 .U5 A45)
African American Writers (PS 153 .N5)
AICPA Professional Standards (HG 5667 .A562)
Allusions—Cultural, Literary, Biblical and Historical (PN 43 .A4)
Almanac of American History (E 174.5 .A45)
Almanac of American Politics (JK 271 .B343)
Almanac of Federal PACs (JK 1991 .A744)
Almanac of the 50 States (HA 203 .A5)
Alternative Press Index (AI 3 .A4)
America Votes (JK 1967 .A8)
America: History and Life (E 178 .A48)
America's Corporate Families (HG 4057 .A164)
American Advertising: A Reference Guide (HF 5223 .W54)

American Art Directory (N 50 .A54)

American Artist Directory of Art Schools and Workshops (N 328 .A52)

American Authors: 1600 - 1900 (PS 128 .K96)

American Bench: Judges of the Nation (KF 8700 .A19)

American College of Health Care Executives Directory (RA 977 .A57)

American Electorate: A Historical Bibliography (Z 7164 .R4 A46)

American Engineers of the Nineteenth Century (TA 139 .R7)

American Film Institute Catalog of Motion Pictures (PN 1998 .A57)

American Heritage Dictionary of English Language (PE 1628 .A623)

American Heritage Dictionary of Science (Q 123 .B35)

American Heritage Guide to Archaeology (CC 70 .B7)

American Humanities Index (AI 3 .A7)

American Institute of Physics Handbook (QC 61 .A5)

American Journalism History: Annotated Bibliography (PN 4731 .S56)

American Legal Literature (KF 1 .R42)

American Men and Women of Science (Q 141 .A47)

American Nursing: A Biographical Dictionary (RT 34 .A44)

American Political Dictionary (JK 9 .P55)

American Public Opinion Index (HM 261 .I552)

American Public Opinion Index (HM 261 .A463)

American Sociological Association Directory of Members (HM 9 .A725)

American Sociological Association Directory of Graduate Departments (HM 9 .A65)

American Song: The Complete Musical Theatre Companion (ML 128 .M78 B6)

American Statistics Index (Z 7554 .U5 A46)

American Studies: An Annotated Bibliography (E 169.1 .A486)

American Women Writers (PS 147 .A4)

Animal Behavior Abstracts (QL 750 .A598)

Annotated Bibliography of the History of Data Processing (QA 76.17 .C62)

Annual Bibliography of Victorian Studies (CB 417 .A52)

Annual Register: A Record of World Events (D 2 .A7)

Annual Report of the President (HC 106.5 .A272)

Annual Review of Astronomy and Astrophysics (QB 1 .A2884)

APA Membership Register (BF 11 .A671)

Applied Mechanics Reviews (TA 1 .A6395)

Applied Science and Technology Index (Z 7913 .I7)

Archaeology: A Bibliographic Guide to the Basic Literature (CC 165 .H44)

Architect's Handbook of Professional Practice (NA 2570 .A7)

Architectural Annual (NA 9 .A4)

Architectural Index (NA 9 .A67)

Architecture: A Bibliographic Guide to Basic Reference Works (NA 2520 .E37)

Archives and Manuscript Repositories in the USSR (CD 1711 .G7)
Armchair Traveler (G 465 .A75)
Art and Archaeology Technical Abstracts (AM 1 .A7)
Art and Architecture Thesaurus (Z 695.1 .A7)
Art Books (N 7425 .A66)
Art Books: A Basic Bibliography of Monographs on Artists (N 40 .F73)
Art Index (N 23 .A78)
Art Museums of the World (N 410 .A78)
Art of Literary Research (PR 56 .A68)
Arts and Humanities Citation Index (AI 3 .A63)
Arts in America: A Bibliography (NX 503 .A1)
ASCE Annual Combined Index (TA 1 .A58)
ASCE Publications Information (TA 1 .A58 A53)
Asian American Studies: Annotated Bibliography and Research Guide (E
    184 .O6 K55)
Assessment (RT 48 .A87)
Associated Press Stylebook and Libel Manual (PN 4783 .A8)
Astronomical Almanac (QB 8 .U1)
Astronomy and Astronautics: An Enthusiast's Guide (QB 43.2 .L87)
Astronomy and Astrophysics Encyclopedia (QB 14 .A837)
Atlanta Journal-Constitution Index (AI 21 .A87)
Atlas of Archaeology (CC 165 .A83)
Atlas of Medieval Europe (CB 351 .M293)
Atlas of the Universe (QB 44 .M5425)
Author Index to Psychological Abstracts (BF 1 .P651)
Author's Guide to Journals in Nursing and Related Fields (RT 24 .A97)
Author's Guide to Journals in the Behavioral Sciences (BF 76.8 .W36)
Avery Index to Architectural Periodicals (Z 5945 .C649)
Awards, Honors and Prizes (AS 8 .A87)
Baker's Biographical Dictionary of Musicians (ML 105 .B16)
Ballentine's Law Dictionary With Pronunciations (KF 156 .B3)
Ballet Plot Index (GV 1790 .A1 S77)
Bank and Finance Manual (HG 4961 .M65)
Banker's Almanac and Yearbook (HG 2984 .B3)
Banking Literature Index (HG 1501 .B268)
Beilstein Handbook of Organic Chemistry (QD 251 .B42)
Benét's Reader's Encyclopedia (PN 41 .B4)
Benét's Reader's Encyclopedia of American Literature (PN 41 .B4)
Benn's Media Directory (P 88.8 .B462)
Bernstein's Reverse Dictionary (PE 1591 .B45)
BHA: Bibliography of the History of Art (N 23.3 .B53)
Bible Almanac (BS 635.2 .B4)

Bibliographic Guide to Conference Publications (Z 5051 .B5)
Bibliographic Guide to Dance (GV 1594 .N4)
Bibliographic Guide to Law (KF 38 .B52)
Bibliographic Index (Z 1002 .B595)
Bibliographical Guide to the Study of the Literature of the USA (PS 88 .G6)
Bibliography and Index of Geology (Z 6031 .G41)
Bibliography of Bioethics (R 724 .B42)
Bibliography of Early American Architecture (NA 707 .R6)
Bibliography of Marketing Research Methods (HF 5415.2 .D52)
Bibliography of Philosophical Bibliographies (B 53 .G84)
Biographical Dictionary of Afro-American and African Musicians (ML 105 .S67)
Biographical Dictionary of American Business Leaders (HC 102.5 .A2 I53)
Biographical Dictionary of American Journalism (PN 4781 .B5)
Biographical Dictionary of American Mayors (E 176 .B5725)
Biographical Dictionary of Dance (GV 1785 .A1 C58)
Biographical Dictionary of Psychology (BF 109 .A1)
Biographical Dictionary of Scientists: Engineers and Inventors (TA 139 .B56)
Biographical Dictionary of Scientists: Astronomers (QB 35 .B56)
Biographical Dictionary of Scientists: Mathematicians (QA 28 .B565)
Biographical Dictionary of Social Welfare in America (HV 27 .B57)
Biographical Directory of American Educators (LA 2311 .B54)
Biographical Directory of Negro Ministers (BF 563 .N4 W5)
Biographical Directory of Russian and Soviet Composers (ML 106 .S68 B56)
Biographical Directory of the U.S. Congress (JK 1010 .U5)
Biographical Directory of the United States Executive Branch (E 176 .B576)
Biography Index (Z 5301 .B5)
Biological Abstracts (QH 301 .B37)
Biological and Agricultural Index (QH 301 .B434)
Biology Databook (QH 310 .A392)
Biophysics, Bioengineering and Medical Instrumentation (QH 505 .B473)
Black Media in America: A Resource Guide (P 94.5 .A37 H54)
Black's Law Dictionary (KF 156 .B53)
Black's Medical Dictionary (R 121 .T486)
Blacks in American Films and Television (PN 1995.9 .N4 B58)
Blackwell Dictionary of Cognitive Reference (BF 311 .B535)
Blackwell Dictionary of Historians (D 14 .B58)
Blackwell Encyclopedia of Political Institutions (JA 61 .B56)
Blackwell Encyclopedia of Political Thought (JA 61 .B57)
Blakiston's Gould Medical Dictionary (R 121 .B62)
Blue Book of Building and Construction (HD 9715 .U53 W317)

Blues Who's Who (ML 102 .B6)
Book of Jewish Books: A Reader's Guide to Judaism (BM 561 .B66)
Book of the States (JK 2403 .B62)
Book Review Digest (Z 1219 .C95)
Book Review Index (Z 1035 .A1 B6)
Books in Print (Z 1215 .P972)
Boston Globe Index (AI 21 .B271)
Bowker's Law Books and Serials in Print (KF 1 .L392)
Brands and Their Companies/Companies and Their Brands (T 233 .V4222)
Brewer's Dictionary of Phrase and Fable (PN 43 .B65)
British Archives (CD 1040 .F67)
British Authors Before 1800 (PR 105 .K9)
British Authors of the Nineteenth Century (PR 451 .K8)
British Film Catalog: A Reference Guide (PN 1993.5 .G7 G53)
British Humanities Index (AI 3 .B7)
British Writers (PR 85 .B688)
Broadcast Communications Dictionary (PN 1990.4 .D5)
Buddhism: A Subject Index to Periodical Articles (Z 7860 .Y65)
Builder's Dictionary (NA 31 .B85)
Bulfinch's Mythology (BL 310 .B82)
Business Index (HF 501 .B86)
Business Periodicals Index (Z 7164 .C81 B983)
Business Publication Rates and Data (HF 5905 .S792)
Butler's Lives of the Saints (BX 4654 .B8)
Calendar of Creative Man (NX 447.5 .P38)
Cambridge Ancient History (D 57 .C252)
Cambridge Atlas of Astronomy (QB 65 .G6813)
Cambridge Encyclopedia of Archaeology (CC 165 .C3)
Cambridge Guide to the Museums of Europe (AM 40 .H83)
Cambridge History of the Bible (BS 445 .C26)
Cambridge Medieval History (D 117 .C3)
Canadian Almanac and Directory (AY 414 .C2)
Canadian Books in Print (Z 1365 .S9)
Canadian Encyclopedia (AG 5 .C27)
Catalog of Manuscripts at the National Anthropological Archives (GN 24
    .N34)
Chambers Biographical Dictionary (CT 103 .C4)
Chambers Biological Dictionary (QH 302.2 .C33)
Chambers Science and Technology Dictionary (Q 123 .C482)
Chambers World Gazetteer (G 103.5 .C44)
Chase's Annual Events: The Day-by-Day Directory (D 11.5 .C48)
Chemical Abstracts (QD 1 .A51)

Chemical Engineer's Handbook (TP 151 .C51)
Chicago Manual of Style (Z 253 .U69)
Chicago Psychoanalytic Literature Index (BF 173 .C452)
Chicago Tribune Index (AI 21 .C45)
Child Development Abstracts and Bibliography (HQ 750 .A1 C47)
Children's Literature Review (PN 1009 .A1)
Christian Science Monitor Index (AI 21 .C46)
Chronological Outline of American Literature (PS 92 .R67)
Chronology of the History of Science: 1450–1900 (Q 125 .G39)
Churchill's Illustrated Medical Dictionary (R 121 .I58)
CIBA Collection of Medical Illustrations (QM 25 .N47)
Cities of the World (G 153.4 .C57)
Civil Engineer's Reference Book (TA 151 .C58)
Classified Directory of Artists' Signatures (N 45 .C36)
CLC: Contemporary Literary Criticism (PN 771 .C61)
CMLC: Classical and Medieval Literature Criticism (PN 610 .C53)
Code of Federal Regulations (JK 416 .C6)
Codes of Professional Responsibility (BJ 1725 .C57)
Collier's Encyclopedia (AE 5 .C683)
Columbia Granger's Index to Poetry (PN 1021 .G7)
Columbia Lippincott Gazetteer of the World (G 103 .7)
Combined Retrospective Index to Book Reviews/Scholarly Journals (Z 1035
    .A1 C64)
Combined Retrospective Index to Book Reviews/Humanities (AI 3 .C65)
Combined Retrospective Index to Journals in Sociology (HM 1 .A11 C75)
Communications Abstracts (P 87 .C6)
Communications and the Mass Media: Guide to the Reference Literature (P
    90 .B57)
Companies and Their Brands/Brands and Their Companies (T 233 .V4222)
Comparative Glossary of Accounting Terms (HF 5621 .A24)
Complete Actor's Television Credits, 1948–1988 (PN 1992.4 .A2)
Complete Concordance to the Bible (BS 425 .C65)
Complete Encyclopedia of Television Programs: 1947–1979 (PN 1992.3
    .U5 T46)
Complete Film Dictionary (PN 1993.45 .K66)
Complete Guide to Modern Dance (GV 1783 .M26)
Complete Multilingual Dictionary of Computer Terminology (QA 76.15
    .N37)
Complete Short Stories of Ernest Hemingway (PS 3515 .E37 A15)
Composers Since 1900 (ML 390 .E833)
Comprehensive Biochemistry (QD 415 .F63 C7)
Comprehensive Dissertations Index (Z 5053 .C64)

Comprehensive Inorganic Chemistry (QD 151.2 .C73)
Comprehensive Organic Chemistry (QD 245 .C65)
Comprehensive Organometallic Chemistry (QD 411 .C65)
Computer and Control Abstracts (QA 76.5 .C612)
Computer Abstracts (QA 76.5 .C6126)
Computer Literature Index (QA 76.5 .Q32)
Computer Virus Handbook (QA 76.76 .C68)
Concise Dictionary of Astronomy (QB 14 .M58)
Concise Dictionary of Biology (QH 302.5 .C66)
Concise Dictionary of Chemistry (QD 5 .C66)
Concise Dictionary of Earth Sciences (QE 5 .C66)
Concise Dictionary of Indian Philosophy (B 131 .G67)
Concise Dictionary of Indian Tribes (E 76.2 .L44)
Concise Dictionary of Physics (QC 5 .C66)
Concise Oxford Dictionary of Ballet (GV 1585 .K6313)
Concise Oxford Dictionary of Literary Terms (PN 41 .C67)
Condition of Education (L 112 .N377)
Congressional Index (J 69 .C6)
Congressional Information Service Abstracts (KF 49 .C62)
Congressional Information Service Index (KF 49 .C62)
Congressional Quarterly Almanac (JK 1 .C66)
Congressional Record (J 11 .R)
Congressional Research Service Bill Digest (KF 18 .L5)
Congressional Roll Call (JK 1 .C6635)
Congressional Staff Directory (JK 1012 .C65)
Congressional Yellow Book (JK 1013 .C65)
Constitution of the United States of America (KF 4527 .L4)
Consumer Index to Product Evaluations (TX 335 .C676)
Consumer Magazine and Agri-Media Rates and Data (HF 5905 .S794)
Contemporary American Women Sculptors (NB 212 .W37)
Contemporary Architects (NA 680 .C625)
Contemporary Artists (N 6490 .C65)
Contemporary Authors (PS 129 .C6)
Contemporary Dramatists (PR 737 .C57)
Contemporary Graphic Artists (NC 45 .C6)
Contemporary Novelists (PR 883 .V55)
Contemporary Poets (PN 603 .C6)
Countries and Islands of the World (G 103.5 .W54)
County and City Data Book (HA 202 .A36)
CRC Handbook of Basic Tables for Chemical Analysis (QD 78 .B78)
CRC Handbook of Chemistry and Physics (QD 65 .H5)
CRC Standard Mathematical Tables and Formulae (QA 47 .M315)

Criminal Justice Periodicals Index (HV 8138 .C74)
Criminology and Penology Abstracts (HV 6001 .E9)
Critical Survey of Drama (PN 1625 .C74)
Critical Survey of Literary Theory (PN 45 .C74)
Critical Survey of Long Fiction (PN 3451 .C75)
Critical Survey of Poetry (PN 1111 .C7)
Critical Survey of Short Fiction (PN 3373 .C75)
Cumulative Book Index (Z 1215 .U6)
Cumulative Index to Nursing and Allied Health Literature (Z 6675 .N7 C8)
Cumulative Subject Index to Psychological Abstracts (BF 1 .P652)
Current Biography (CT 100 .C8)
Current Contents: Agriculture, Biology and Environmental Sciences (QH 301 .B374)
Current Contents: Physical, Chemical and Earth Sciences (Q 1 .S322)
Current Contents: Sociological and Behavioral Sciences (Z 5851 .E623)
Current Geographical Publications (Z 6009 .A47)
Current Index to Journals in Education (LB 5 .C82)
Current Law Index (K 33 .C87)
Current Mathematical Publications (QA 1.3)
Cyclopedia of Literary Characters (PN 44 .M34)
Dance Directory (GV 1754 .A1 D3)
Dance Encyclopedia (GV 1585 .C5)
Dance World (GV 1580 .D335)
Dance: An Annotated Bibliography (GV 1594 .F58)
Dancer's Survival Manual (GV 1597 .H67)
Dartnell Public Relations Handbook (HD 59 .D28)
Data Pro Directory of Microcomputer Hardware (QA 76.5 .D253)
Data Pro Directory of Microcomputer Software (QA 76.6 .D37)
Data Pro Directory of Microcomputers (QA 76.5 .D273)
Data Pro Directory of Minicomputers (QA 76.5 .D27)
Data Pro Directory of Software (QA 76 .D322)
Diagnostics (RT 48 .D5)
Dictionary Catalog of the Berg Collection (Z 2011 .N55)
Dictionary Catalog of the Moorland Collection (Z 1361 .N39 H82)
Dictionary of Accounting (HF 5621 .E77)
Dictionary of American Biography (E 176 .D56)
Dictionary of American Composers (ML 106 .U3 B87)
Dictionary of American Literary Characters (PS 374 .C43 D5)
Dictionary of American Nursing Biography (RT 34 .D53)
Dictionary of American Religious Biography (BL 72 .B68)
Dictionary of Angels: Including the Fallen Angels (BL 477 .D3)
Dictionary of Architectural and Building Technology (NA 31 .C63)

Dictionary of Architecture (NA 31 .P4)

Dictionary of Architecture and Building (NA 31 .S84)

Dictionary of Astronomy, Space, and Atmospheric Phenomena (QB 14 .T83)

Dictionary of Behavioral Assessment Techniques (BF 176.5 .D53)

Dictionary of Biographical Quotation (CT 773 .D38)

Dictionary of Botany (QK 9 .L735)

Dictionary of Christian Biography (BR 97 .S65)

Dictionary of Comparative Religion (BL 31 .D54)

Dictionary of Computing (QA 76.15 .D526)

Dictionary of Development and Educational Psychology (BF 712.7 .D53)

Dictionary of Education (LB 15 .D4)

Dictionary of Engineering Acronyms and Abbreviations (TA 11 .E73)

Dictionary of Geological Terms (QE 5 .D55)

Dictionary of Historic Documents (D 9 .K63)

Dictionary of Historical Terms (D 9 .C67)

Dictionary of Human Geography (GF 4 .D52)

Dictionary of Literary Biography (PS 21 .D52)

Dictionary of Literary Terms and Literary Theory (PN 41 .C83)

Dictionary of Mechanical Engineering (TJ 9 .N28)

Dictionary of Medical Eponyms (R 121 .F535)

Dictionary of Medieval Civilization (CB 351 .D24)

Dictionary of Music (ML 100 .D56)

Dictionary of National Biography (DA 28 .D4)

Dictionary of Opera (ML 102 .O6 O8)

Dictionary of Organic Compounds (QD 251 .D69)

Dictionary of Personality and Social Psychology (BF 698 .D527)

Dictionary of Philosophy and Psychology (B 41 .B3)

Dictionary of Philosophy and Religion (B 41 .R43)

Dictionary of Proper Names and Places in the Bible (BS 435 .Q3313)

Dictionary of Scientific Biography (Q 141 .D5)

Dictionary of the Dance (GV 1585 .R3)

Dictionary of the History of Ideas (CB 5 .D52)

Dictionary of the Middle Ages (D 114 .D5)

Dictionary of The Bible (BS 440 .H5)

Dictionary of Toponyms (G 103.5 .V56)

Dictionary of Women Artists (N 43 .P47)

Dictionary of Zoology (QL 9 .L49)

Digest of Education Statistics (L 11 .D48)

Diplomatic List (JX 1705 .A22)

Direct Marketing Market Place (HF 5415.1 .D57)

Direct-Line Distances (G 109 .F 53)

Directory of American Philosophers (B 935 .D5)

Directory of American Scholars (LA 2311 .C32)

Directory of Archive and Manuscript Repositories (CD 3020 .D49)

Directory of Computer Facilities in Higher Education (QA 76.215 .D57)

Directory of Corporate Counsel (KF 195 .C6 D57)

Directory of Departments and Programs of Religious Studies (BL 41 .D46)

Directory of Engineering and Engineering Technology (T 64 .D57)

Directory of Financial Aids for Minorities (LB 2338 .D56)

Directory of Financial Aids for Women (LB 2338 .D55)

Directory of Geoscience Departments (QE 1 .A391)

Directory of History Departments (D 16.3 .G83)

Directory of Management Consultants (HD 69 .C6 D56)

Directory of Medical Specialists (R 712 .A1 D5)

Directory of Museums and Living Displays (AM 1 .H78)

Directory of Music Faculties in Colleges and Universities (ML 13 .D57)

Directory of Online Databases (Z 674.3 .D47)

Directory of Portable Databases (QA 76.9 .D32 D57)

Directory of Published Proceedings (Z 7409 .D56)

Directory of Religious Organizations in the United States (BL 2530 .U6
    D57)

Directory of U.S. Labor Organizations (HD 6504 .A15)

Dissertation Abstracts International (Z 5055 .U5)

Dissertations in History (D 21.3 .K83)

Dorland's Illustrated Medical Dictionary (R 121 .D73)

Dow Jones–Irwin Business and Investment Almanac (HF 5003 .D68)

Dow Jones–Irwin Dictionary of Financial Planning (HG 151 .R52)

Dow Jones–Irwin Guide to Personal Financial Planning (HG 179 .A554)

Dow Jones–Irwin Guide to the Wall Street Journal (HB 3743 .L44)

Drama Criticism (PN 1625 .D72)

Drama Dictionary (PN 1625 .H62)

Drury's Guide to Best Plays (PN 1655 .D78)

Dun's Business Rankings (HG 4057 .A253)

Dun's Regional Business Directory (HG 4058 .W3 D86)

Ecological Abstracts (QH 540 .A66)

Ecology Abstracts (QH 540 .A66)

Editor and Publisher Yearbook (PN 4700 .E4)

Education in the United States: A Documentary History (LA 205 .C53)

Education Index (LB 7 .E23)

Education: A Guide to Reference and Information Sources (LA 15 .B87)

Educational Administration Abstracts (LB 2341 .E3)

Educator's Desk Reference (LB 1027.27 .U6 F74)

Eerdmans Analytical Concordance (BS 425 .W48)

Eerdmans Bible Dictionary (BS 440 .G7613)
Eerdmans Handbook to the Bible (BS 417 .A55)
Effective Legal Research (KF 240 .P7)
Electrical and Electronics Abstracts (TK 7800 .E4383)
Electronic Engineer's Handbook (TK 7825 .E34)
Elements of Style (PN 1408 .S772)
Emily Post's Etiquette (BJ 1853 .P6)
Encyclopaedia Britannica (AE 5 .E363)
Encyclopedia Americana (AE 5 .E333)
Encyclopedia of Accounting Systems (HF 5635 .E54)
Encyclopedia of American Architecture (NA 705 .H86)
Encyclopedia of American Economic History (HC 103 .E52)
Encyclopedia of American Facts and Dates (E 174.5 .C3)
Encyclopedia of American Foreign Policy (JX 1407 .E53)
Encyclopedia of American Journalism (PN 4728 .P35)
Encyclopedia of American Political History (E 183 .E5)
Encyclopedia of American Religions (BT 990 .E58)
Encyclopedia of Architecture (NA 31 .E59)
Encyclopedia of Asian History (DS 31 .E53)
Encyclopedia of Associations (HS 17 .G334)
Encyclopedia of Astronomy (QB 14 .I58)
Encyclopedia of Bioethics (QH 332 .E52)
Encyclopedia of Chemical Technology (TP 9 .E685)
Encyclopedia of Chemistry (QD 5 .E56)
Encyclopedia of Clinical Assessment (BF 698.4 .E5)
Encyclopedia of Computer Science and Technology (QA 76.15 .E5)
Encyclopedia of Continental Women Writers (PN 481 .E5)
Encyclopedia of Crime and Justice (HV 6017 .E52)
Encyclopedia of Dance and Ballet (GV 1585 .E53)
Encyclopedia of Eastern Philosophy and Religion (BL 1005 .L4813)
Encyclopedia of Education (LB 15 .E47)
Encyclopedia of Educational Research (L 901 .E57)
Encyclopedia of Fluid Mechanics (TA 357 .E53)
Encyclopedia of Folk, Country and Western Music (ML 102 .F66)
Encyclopedia of Governmental Advisory Organizations (JK 468 .C7 E5)
Encyclopedia of Health Information Sources (R 129 .E56)
Encyclopedia of Higher Education (LB 15 .E49)
Encyclopedia of Historic Places (D 9 .C29)
Encyclopedia of Human Biology (QP 11 .E53)
Encyclopedia of Human Development and Education (BF 713 .E65)
Encyclopedia of Human Rights (JC 571 .E67)
Encyclopedia of Judaism (BM 50 .E63)

Encyclopedia of Legal Information Sources (KF 1 .E53)
Encyclopedia of Marriage, Divorce and the Family (HQ 9 .D38)
Encyclopedia of Materials Science and Engineering (TA 402 .E53)
Encyclopedia of Mathematics (QA 5 .M3713)
Encyclopedia of Medical Devices and Instrumentation (R 856 .A3 E53)
Encyclopedia of Minerals (QE 355 .R6)
Encyclopedia of Philosophy (B 41 .E5)
Encyclopedia of Physics (QC 5 .E545)
Encyclopedia of Physics (QC 5 .E546)
Encyclopedia of Plant Physiology (QK 711.2 .E5)
Encyclopedia of Psychology (BF 31 .E52)
Encyclopedia of Religion (BL 31 .E46)
Encyclopedia of Religion and Ethics (BF 31 .E4)
Encyclopedia of Social Work (HV 35 .S6)
Encyclopedia of Sociology (HM 17 .E5)
Encyclopedia of Southern Culture (F 209 .E53)
Encyclopedia of Television: Series Plots and Specials, 1937–1984 (PN
    1992.3 .T46)
Encyclopedia of the American Constitution (KF 4548 .E53)
Encyclopedia of the American Religious Experience (BL 2525 .E53)
Encyclopedia of the Musical Theater (ML 102 .M88)
Encyclopedia of the Renaissance (CB 361 .B43)
Encyclopedia of Twentieth Century Journalists (PN 4871 .T34)
Encyclopedia of Ukraine (DK 508 .E613)
Encyclopedia of Unbelief (BL 2705 .E53)
Encyclopedia of World Art (N 31 .E56)
Encyclopedia of World Literature in the 20th Century (PN 771 .E5)
Encyclopedic Dictionary of Mathematics (QA 5 .I8313)
Encyclopedic Dictionary of Physics (QC 5 .E53)
Encyclopedic Dictionary of Psychology (BF 31 .E555)
Encyclopedic Dictionary of Religion (BL 31 .E42)
Energy Information Abstracts Annual (TJ 163.2 .E482)
Energy Research Abstracts (TJ 163.2 .E484)
Engineering Formulas (TA 151 .G4713)
Engineering Index Monthly (Z 5851 .E62)
Environment Abstracts Annual (TD 172 .E5)
Eshbach's Handbook of Engineering Fundamentals (TA 151 .E8)
Essay and General Literature Index (AI 3 .E752)
Ethnic and Racial Images in American Film and Television (PN 1995.9
    .M56 W65)
Europa World Yearbook (JN 1 .E85)
European Authors: 1000 - 1900 (PN 451 .K8)

European Writers (PN 501 .E9)
Everybody's Business: An Almanac (HD 2785 .E88)
Exaltation of Larks (PE 1689 .L5)
Facts About the Cities (HT 123 .C385)
Facts About the Presidents (E 176.1 .K3)
Facts About the States (E 180 .K4)
Facts on File (D 410 .F3)
Facts on File Dictionary of Biology (QH 13 .C66)
Facts on File Dictionary of Chemistry (QD 5 .D26)
Facts on File Dictionary of Health Care Management (RA 393 .R48)
Facts on File Dictionary of Marine Science (GC 9 .F28)
Facts on File Dictionary of Mathematics (QA 5 .G52)
Facts on File Dictionary of Religion (BL 31 .F33)
Facts on File Visual Dictionary (AG 250 .C63)
Familiar Medical Quotations (R 707 .S91 F2)
Familiar Quotations (PN 6081 .B27)
Famous First Facts (AG 5 .K315)
Federal Information Sources in Health and Medicine (R 129 .C45)
Federal Register (J 1 .A2)
Federal Regulatory Directory (KF 5406 .A15 F4)
Federal Staff Directory (JK 723 .E9 F44)
Federal Yellow Book (JK 6 .F4)
Feminist Companion to Literature in English (PR 111 .F45)
Film Index: A Bibliography (PN 1993.45 .W74)
Film Literature Index (Z 5784 .M9 F45)
Film Review (PN 1993 .F624)
Film Review Index: 1882–1985 (PN 1995 .F54)
Film Study: An Analytical Bibliography (PN 1994 .M36)
Financial Mathematics Handbook (HF 5691 .M84)
Finding the Source in Sociology and Anthropology (HM 51 .B78)
Folk Artists Biographical Index (NK 805 .F63)
Folk Tales (GR 153.3 I75)
Foreign Consular Offices in the United States (JX 1705 .A28)
Gallup Poll: Public Opinion Annual (HN 90 .P8 G34)
Gardner's Chemical Synonyms and Trade Names (TP 9 .G286)
General Science Index (Q 1 .G46)
Genetics Abstracts (QH 431 .G322)
Geographical Abstracts (G 1 .G952)
Geological Abstracts (QE 75 .G41)
Geological Society of America Abstracts with Programs (QE 1 .G2143)
Geology for Civil Engineers (QE 33 .M375)
Golden Bough (BL 310 .F7)

Government Reports Annual Index (Z 7916 .B47)
Grants, Fellowships, Prizes of Interest to Historians (D 16.3 .G7)
Gray's Anatomy (QM 23.2 .G731)
Gray's Manual of Botany (QK 117 .G75)
Great Books of the Western World (AC 1 .G7)
Great Composers: 1300–1900 (ML 105 .E944)
Great Documents of Western Civilization (CB 245 .V5)
Great Spanish Films: 1950–1990 (PN 1993.5 .S7 S29)
Greek and Latin Authors: 800 B.C.–A.D. 1000 (PA 31 .G7)
Greek Myths (BL 781 .G65)
Greene's Biographical Encyclopedia of Composers (ML 390 .G85)
Grzimek's Encyclopedia of Mammals (QL 701 .G79)
Guide to American Art Schools (N 328 .W47)
Guide to American Literature (PS 88 .F46)
Guide to Architectural Schools in North America (NA 2105 .G85)
Guide to Chinese Philosophy (B 126 .F8)
Guide to Congress (JK 1061 .C6)
Guide to Information Sources/Geographical Sciences (G 116 .G84)
Guide to Information Sources/Botanical Sciences (QK 45.2 .D38)
Guide to Islam (BP 161.2 .G84)
Guide to Manuscripts in Presidential Libraries (CD 3029.82 .B87)
Guide to Programs in Nursing in Four-Year Colleges (RT 79 .G85)
Guide to Sources in American Journalism History (PN 4731 .G84)
Guide to the Literature of Electrical Engineering (TK 145 .A72)
Guide to the Literature of Art History (N 380 .A75)
Guide to the Presidency (JK 516 .C57)
Guide to the Records/U.S. House (CD 3042 .S46 U54)
Guide to the Records of the U.S. Senate (CD 3042 .S46 U54)
Guide to the Standard Floras of the World (QK 45.2 .F76)
Guide to the U.S. Supreme Court (KF 8742 .W567)
Guide to U.S. Elections (JK 1967 .C662)
Guinness Book of Records (AG 243 .G87)
Halliwell's Filmgoer's Companion (PN 1993.45 .H35)
Handbook of American Popular Literature (PS 169 .P64 H26)
Handbook of Analytical Chemistry (QD 71 .M51)
Handbook of Applied Mathematics (QA 40 .H34)
Handbook of Basic Economic Statistics (HC 101 .H252)
Handbook of Biochemistry and Molecular Biology (QH 345 .H347)
Handbook of Denominations in the United States (BR 516.5 .M38)
Handbook of General Psychology (BF 121 .W63)
Handbook of International Accounting (HF 5686 .I56)
Handbook of Labor Statistics (HD 8064 .A3)

Handbook of Mathematics (QA 40 .B71)
Handbook of Model Accounting Reports and Formats (HF 5635 .V53)
Handbook of Modern Accounting (HF 5635 .H23)
Handbook of Private Schools (L 901 .H3)
Handbook of Social Psychology (HM 251 .H224)
Handbook of Soviet and East European Films (PN 1993.5 .R9 H28)
Handbook of Western Philosophy (B 804 .H17)
Harper Bible Pronunciation Guide (BS 435 .H35)
Harper Dictionary of Modern Thought (AG 5 .H19)
Harper Dictionary of Music (ML 100 .A48)
HarperCollins Dictionary of American Government and Politics (JK 9 .S43)
Harvard Concordance to Shakespeare (PR 2892 .S62)
Hawley's Condensed Chemical Dictionary (QD 5 .C5)
Health United States (RA 407.3 .U58)
Henderson's Dictionary of Biological Terms (QH 302.5 .H65)
Higher Education Abstracts (Z 5814 .P8 C6)
Hispanic American Periodicals Index (F 1401 .H43)
Hispanic Resource Directory (E 184 .S75 S27)
Historic Architecture Sourcebook (NA 31 .H56)
Historic Documents (E 839.5 .H57)
Historical Abstracts (D 299 .H52)
Historical and Cultural Atlas of African Americans (E 185 .A8)
Historical Atlas of the Religions of the World (BL 80.2 .F28)
Historical Atlas of U.S. Congressional Districts (G 1201 .F9 M3)
Historical Dictionary of Data Processing Technology (QA 76.15 .C67)
Historical Periodicals Directory (D 20 .H57)
Historical Statistics of the United States (HA 202 .B87)
Historiography: An Annotated Bibliography (D 13 .H58)
History of Art (N 5300 .J3)
History of Ideas: A Bibliographical Introduction (B 52 .T65)
History of Modern Art (N 6490 .A713)
History of Physics: An International Bibliography (QC 7 .B78)
Holidays and Anniversaries of the World (GT 3930 .H65)
Home Book of Bible Quotations (BS 432 .S667)
Hospital Literature Index (Z 6675 .H76 A5)
Hospital Literature Index (Z 6675 .H76 A5)
House Ethics Manual (KF 4990 .A354)
Houston Post Index (AI 21 .H68)
How to Find Chemical Information (QD 8.5 .M34)
Howard University African/Afro-American Religious Studies (BR 563 .N4)
Humanities Index (AI 3 .H85)
Illustrated Computer Dictionary (QA 76.15 .S67)

Illustrated Dictionary of Electronics (TK 7804 .T87)
Index Islamicus (Z 7835 .M6 L62)
Index Medicus (Z 6660 .I42)
Index of Economic Articles (Z 7164 .E2)
Index of Mathematical Tables (QA 47 .F55)
Index to Artistic Biography (N 40 .H38)
Index to Black Periodicals (AI 3 .04)
Index to Book Reviews in the Humanities (Z 1035 .A1 I63)
Index to IEEE Publications (Z 5832 .I54)
Index to Illustrations of Living Things (QL 46 .M85)
Index to Illustrations of the Natural World (QL 151 .T46)
Index to International Public Opinion (HM 261 .I552)
Index to Legal Periodicals (K 9 .N32)
Index to Maps in Books and Periodicals (GA 105 .A54)
Index to Plays in Periodicals (PN 1721 .K44)
Index to Publications of the United States Congress (KF 49 .C62)
Index to Scientific and Technical Proceedings (Q 101 .I5)
Index to Scientific Reviews (Q 1 .I381)
Index to Social Science and Humanities Proceedings (AI 3 .I53)
Index to U.S. Government Periodicals (Z 1223 .Z9 I5)
Index Translationum (Z 6514 .T7 I42)
Industrial Manual (HG 4961 .M67)
Information Please Almanac (AY 64 I55)
Information Sources in Engineering (T 10.7 .I54)
Information Sources in Physics (QC 21.2 .I53)
Information Sources in the Earth Sciences (QE 26.2 .I53)
Information Sources in the Life Sciences (QH 303.6 .I54)
International Aerospace Abstracts (TL 500 .I57)
International Almanac of Electoral History (JF 1001 .M17)
International Authors and Writers Who's Who (PN 451 .I8)
International Bibliography of Economics (Z 7164 .E2)
International Bibliography of Historical Sciences (Z 6205 .I61)
International Bibliography of Political Science (JA 71 .I6)
International Bibliography of Social and Cultural Anthropology (Z 7161
     .I594)
International Bibliography of Sociology (Z 7161 .I594)t
International Civil Engineering Abstracts (TA 1 .I58)
International Dictionary of Films and Filmmakers (PN 1997.8 .F55)
International Dictionary of Medicine and Biology (R 121 .I58)
International Directory of Arts (N 50 .I6)
International Directory of Company Histories (HD 2721 .D36)
International Directory of Little Magazines (Z 6944 .L5 D5)

International Encyclopedia of Communications (P 87.5 .I5)
International Encyclopedia of Integrated Circuits (TK 7874 .G5)
International Encyclopedia of the Social Sciences (H40 .A215)
International Encyclopedia of Women Composers (ML 105 .C7)
International Handbook of Psychology (BF 105 .I57)
International Index to Film Periodicals (Z 5784 .M9 I49)
International Manual (HG 4509 .M66)
International Marketing Handbook (HF 1416 .I63)
International Monetary Market Yearbook (HG 3853 .F6 I58)
International Motion Picture Almanac (PN 1993.3 .I55)
International Political Science Abstracts (JA 36 .I5)
International Research Centers Directory (Q 179.98 .I58)
International Scholarship Book (LB 2337.2 .C364)
International Standard Bible Encyclopedia (BS 440 .I6)
International Television and Video Almanac (PN 1992.1 .I55)
International Who's Who (CT 120 .I5)
International Who's Who in Education (LA 2301 .I57)
International Who's Who in Music (ML 106 .G7 W45)
Internship Programs in Professional Psychology (BF 77 .D57)
Interpreter's Dictionary of the Bible (BS 440 .I63)
Introduction to Buddhism (BQ 4022 .H37)
Inventory of Marriage and Family Literature (HQ 728 .I57)
Investment Companies (HG 4497.7 .W47)
ISS Directory of Overseas Schools (L 900 .I83)
Jones Average: 1885–1985 (HG 4519 .D59)
Journalist Biographies Master Index (PN 4820 .J68)
Judaism and Christianity (BM 45 .S83)
Justices of the United States Supreme Court (KF 8744 .F75)
Keesing's Record of World Events (D 410 .K4)
Key Officers of Foreign Service Posts (JX 1705 .A284)
Key Sources in Comparative and World Literature (PN 523 .T56)
Kohler's Dictionary for Accountants (HF 5621 .K6)
Landers Film and Video Reviews (PN 1995 .L27)
Lange's Handbook of Chemistry (TP 151 .H23)
Latin American Writers (PQ 7081 .A1 L37)
Lawyer's Almanac (KF 190 .L3625)
LB (Landolt-Bornstein) (QC 61 .L332)
LC: Literature Criticism from 1400 to 1800 (PN 701 .L52)
Legal Looseleafs in Print (KF 1 .S73)
Legal Newsletters in Print (KF 1 .L44)
Legal Research in a Nutshell (KF 240 .C54)
Legal Thesaurus (KF 156 .B856)

Les Brown's Encyclopedia of Television (PN 1992.18 .B7)

Lesly's Handbook of Public Relations and Communications (HM 263 .L46)

Library of Congress: A Guide to Genealogical and Historical Research
   (E 180 .N43)

Library Recommendations for Undergraduate Mathematics (Z 6651 .L697)

Literary History of the United States (PS 88 .L522)

Literary Market Place (PN 161 .L5)

Literary Research Guide (PN 43 .P37)

Logan's Medical and Scientific Abbreviations (R 123 .L8)

Longman Dictionary and Handbook of Poetry (PN 1021 .M94)

Longman Dictionary of Geography: Human and Physical (G 63 .C56)

Los Angeles Times Index (AI 21 .L65)

Macmillan Dictionary of Accounting (HF 5621 .P37)

Macmillan Dictionary of Archaeology (CC 70 .M33)

Macmillan Dictionary of Astronomy (QB 14 .M33)

Macmillan Dictionary of Marketing and Advertising (HF 5412 .M32)

Macmillan Dictionary of Personal Computers and Communications (QA
   76.5 .L682)

Macmillan Dictionary of Physics (QC 5 .L67)

Macmillan Encyclopedia of Architects (NA 40 .M25)

Macmillan Encyclopedia of Computers (QA 76.15 .M33)

Macmillan Film Bibliography (PN 1993.5 .A1 R44)

Madison Avenue Handbook: The Image Makers Source (HF 5805 .M3)

Magill's Bibliography of Literary Criticism (PN 523 .M29)

Magill's Cinema Annual (PN 1993.45 .M33)

Magill's Literary Annual (PN 44 .M332)

Magill's Survey of Cinema: English Language Films (PN 1993.45 .M3)

Magill's Survey of Cinema: Foreign Language Films (PN 1993.45 .M34)

Magill's Survey of Cinema: Silent Films (PN 1995.75 .M25)

Mahon's Industry Guides for Accountants and Auditors (HC 103 .M355)

Mammals of North America (QL 715 .H15)

Man From the U.S.S.R. and Other Plays (PG 3476 .N3 A26)

Management Accounting Research (HF 5635 .C81 K72)

Manual For Writers of Term Papers, etc. (LB 2369 .T8)

Marketing Glossary (HF 5415 .C5414)

Marketing News (HF 5410 .A46)

Marks' Standard Handbook for Mechanical Engineering (TJ 151 .M37)

Martindale-Hubbell Law Directory (JK 1517 .M37)

Maryland Manual (JK 3831)

Mass Media Bibliography: An Annotated Guide (P 90 .B58)

Master's Abstracts International (Z 5055 .U5 A6)

Masterplots (PN 44 .M33)

Masterplots II: American Fiction Series (PN 846 .M37)
Masterplots II: Drama Series (PN 6112.5 .M37)
Masterplots II: Non-fiction (PN 44 .M345)
Masterplots II: Short Story Series (PN 3326 .M27)
Masterplots II: World Fiction Series (PN 3326 .M28)
Materials Handbook (TA 402 .B72)
Mathematical Reviews (QA 1 .M76).
Mathematics Dictionary (QA 5 .J33)
McGraw-Hill Dictionary of Art (N 33 .M23)
McGraw-Hill Dictionary of Earth Sciences (QE 5 .M365)
McGraw-Hill Dictionary of Engineering (TA 9 .M35)
McGraw-Hill Dictionary of Information Technology (QA 76.15 .R68)
McGraw-Hill Dictionary of Mechanical and Design Engineering (TJ 9
   .M395)
McGraw-Hill Dictionary of Physics (QC 5 .M424)
McGraw-Hill Encyclopedia of Ocean and Atmospheric Sciences (GC 9 .M32)
McGraw-Hill Encyclopedia of Science and Technology (Q 121 .M3)
McGraw-Hill Encyclopedia of the Earth Sciences (QE 5 .M29)
McGraw-Hill Encyclopedia of World Drama (PN 1625 .M3)
McGraw-Hill Nursing Dictionary (RT 21 .M33)
McGraw-Hill Personal Computer Programming Encyclopedia (QA 76.6
   .M414)
Measurement of Nursing Outcomes (RT 85.5 .M434)
Mediamark Research Reports (HF 5415.3 .M43)
Medical and Health Care Books and Serials in Print (Z 6658 .65)
Medical and Health Information Directory (R 118.4 .V6 M43)
Medical Word Finder: A Reverse Medical Dictionary (R 121 .H232)
Medieval Studies: A Bibliographical Guide (CB 351 .C76)
Mellor's Comprehensive Treatise (QD 31 .M52)
Men's Studies (HQ 1090 .A84)
Merck Manual of Diagnosis and Therapy (RC 55 .M4)
Metals Handbook (TA 459 .A5)
Meteorological and Geoastrophysical Abstracts (QC 851 .A62)
Metropolitan Museum of Art Library Catalog (Z 881 .N6622)
Microbiology Abstracts (QK 564 .M5)
Microcomputer Index (QA 76.5 .M54)
Miller's Comprehensive GAAS Guide (HF 5667 .M52)
Million Dollar Directory (HC 102 .D8)
Mineralogical Abstracts (QE 351 .M421)
MLA International Bibliography (Z 7006 .M64)
MLA Style Manual (PN 147 .A28)
Modern Accountant's Handbook (HF 5635 .M757)

Modern Catholic Dictionary (BX 841 .H36)

Modern Dance and Ballet on Film and Video: A Catalog (GV 1595 .B68)

Modern Plastics Encyclopedia (TP 986 .A1 M682)

Monarchs, Rulers, Dynasties and Kingdoms of the World (D 107 .T36)

Monthly Catalog of U.S. Government Publications (Z 1223 .A18)

Monthly Checklist of State Publications (Z 1223.5 .A1 U5)

Mosby's Medical, Nursing, and Allied Health Dictionary (R 121 .M89)

Motion Picture Guide (PN 1995 .N346)

MTP Inorganic Chemistry Series (QD 151.2 .I58)

MTP Organic Chemistry Series (QD 251.2 .O69)

MTP Physical Series (QD 453.2 .P57)

Municipal and Government Manual (HG 4931 .M58)

Municipal Yearbook (JS 344 .C5 A24)

Music Index (ML 118 .M84)

Music Reference and Research Materials (ML 113 .D83)

Music: A Guide to the Reference Literature (ML 113 .G85)

Musical America: International Directory of the Performing Arts (ML 12 .M88)

Musicians Since 1900 (Ml 105 .E97)

Mythologies of the World: A Guide to Sources (BL 311 .S63)

Mythology of All Races (BL 25 .M8)

Names and Nicknames of Places and Things (G 105 .N36)

National Directory of Certified Public Accountants (HF 5627 .N26)

National Directory of Corporate Public Affairs (HD 59 .N24)

National Directory of State Agencies (JK 2443 .N37)

National Faculty Directory (L 901 .N34)

National Five Digit Zip Code and Post Office Directory (HE 6361 .N37)

National Geographic Atlas of the World (G 1021 .N38)

National Geographic Historical Atlas of the U.S. (G 1201 .S1 N3)

National Newspaper Index (AI 21 .N325)

National Nursing Directory (RT 25 .U5)

National Union Catalog of Manuscript Collections (Z 6620 .U5 N3)

National Union Catalog: Pre-1956 Imprints (Z 881 .A1 U518)

NCLC: Nineteenth-Century Literary Criticism (PN 761 .N5)

Nelson's Complete Concordance (BS 425 .E4)

New American Dictionary of Music (ML 100 .M857)

New Cambridge Modern History (D 208 .N4)

New Catholic Encyclopedia (BX 841 .N44)

New Grove Dictionary of American Music (ML 101 .U6 N48)

New Grove Dictionary of Jazz (ML 102 .J3 N48)

New Grove Dictionary of Music and Musicians (ML 100 .N48)

New Grove Dictionary of Musical Instruments (ML 102.I5)

New Guide to Modern World Literature (PN 771 .S4)
New Guide to the Diplomatic Archives of Western Europe (CD 1001 .T4)
New Harvard Dictionary of Music (ML 100 .R3)
New Kobbe's Complete Opera Book (MT 95 .K52)
New Oxford Companion to Music (ML 100 .S37)
New Oxford History of Music (ML 160 .N44)
New Publications of the U.S. Geological Survey (QE 75 .A1)
New York Public Library Book of Chronologies (D 11 .W47)
New York Public Library Desk Reference (AG 6 .N49)
New York Times Biographical Service (CT 120 .N45)
New York Times Film Reviews: 1913–1982 (PN 1995 .N4)
New York Times Index (AI 21 .N44)
Nineteenth Century Readers' Guide to Periodical Literature (AI 3 .R496)
NIV Exhaustive Concordance (BS 425 .G62)
Norton Anthology of American Literature (PS 507 .N65)
Norton Anthology of English Literature (PR 1105 .A2)
Notable American Women (CT 3260 .N57)
NTC's Mass Media Dictionary (P 87.5 .E45)
Nurse's Almanac (RT 41 .N85)
Nurse's Legal Handbook (RT 86.7 .N88)
NYPL Dictionary Catalog of the Dance Collection (GV 1593 .N48)
Oceanographic Abstracts (GC 1 .O24)
O'Dwyer's Directory of Public Relations Executives (HD 59 .O353)
O'Dwyer's Directory of Public Relations Firms (HM 263 .O37)
Official Museum Directory (AM 10 .A204)
On the Screen (PN 1994 .F57)
Online Database Search Services Directory (QA 76.55 .O55)
Opera Companies of the World (ML 12 .O63)
Originals: Who's Really Who in Fiction (PN 56.4 .A46)
OTC Manual (HG 4961 .M7237)
Ottemiller's Index to Plays in Collections (PN 1631 .O77)
Oxford Bible Atlas (BS 630 .O96)
Oxford Companion to American Literature (PS 21 .H3)
Oxford Companion to Animal Behavior (QL 751 .O930)
Oxford Companion to Art (N 33 .O9)
Oxford Companion to Canadian Literature (PR 9180.2 .O94)
Oxford Companion to Canadian Theatre (PN 2301 .O94)
Oxford Companion to Children's Literature (PN 1008.5 .C37)
Oxford Companion to Classical Literature (PA 31 .H69)
Oxford Companion to Film (PN 1993.45 .O9)
Oxford Companion to French Literature (PQ 41 .H3)
Oxford Companion to German Literature (PT 41 .G3)

Oxford Companion to Law (K 48 .W178)
Oxford Companion to Medicine (R 121 .O88)
Oxford Companion to Popular Music (ML 102 .P66)
Oxford Companion to Spanish Literature (PQ 6006 .O93)
Oxford Companion to the Decorative Arts (NK 30 .O93)
Oxford Companion to the Mind (BF 31 .O94)
Oxford Companion to the Theatre (PN 2035 .O9)
Oxford Dictionary of Art (N 33 .O93)
Oxford Dictionary of Modern Quotations (PN 6080 .O94)
Oxford Dictionary of Music (ML 100 .K35)
Oxford Dictionary of Saints (BR 1710 .F34)
Oxford English Dictionary (PE 1625 .O87)
Oxford Guide to the English Language (PE 1628 .O87)
Oxford Latin Dictionary (PA 2365 .E5 O9)
Partridge's Concise Dictionary of Slang (PE 3721 .P3)
Passenger and Immigration Lists Index (CS 68 .P363)
Patterson's American Education (L 901 .P3)
Penguin Dictionary of Art and Artists (N 31 .M8)
Penguin Dictionary of Physical Geography (GB 10 .W48)
People's Almanac (AG 106 .P46)
Perception: An Annotated Bibliography (BF 311 .E55)
Peterson's Colleges with Programs for Learning Disabled Students (L 901
    .P458)
Peterson's Two Year Colleges (L 901 .A552)
PH (Handbuch der Physik) (QC 21 .H33)
Philosopher's Index (B 53 .P4)
Philosophy Journals and Serials: An Analytical Guide (B 72 .R72)
Physician's Desk Reference (RS 75 .P5)
Physics Abstracts (Q 1 .S3)
Piaget: Dictionary of Terms (BF 11 .A67)
Piano in Concert (ML 42 .A357)
Place-Name Changes Since 1900: A World Gazetteer (G 103.5 .R66)
Plato Dictionary (B 351 .S7)
Play Index (PN 1631 .P34)
Poetry Criticism (PN 1010 .P449)
Poetry Index Annual (PN 1022 .P6)
Political Handbook of the World (JF 37 .P6)
Pollution Abstracts (TD 172 .P65)
Poole's Index to Periodical Literature (AI 3 .P7)
Popular Music: A Reference Guide (ML 128 .P63 I95)
Post-Feminist Hollywood Actress (PN 1998.2 .S44)
Practical Handbook of Marine Science (GC 11.2 .K46)

Practices (RT 86.7 .P7)
Predicasts F & S Index Europe (HG 1040.9 .E8 F14)
Predicasts F & S Index International (HG 4503 .F8) ⁵
Predicasts F & S Index United States (HG 4961 .F8)
Predicasts Forecasts (HC 101 .P7)
Presidential Also-rans and Running Mates (E 176.1 .S695)
Print Media Production Data (HF 5905 .P7)
Private and Independent Schools (L 901 .P68)
Proceedings in Print (Z 5063 .A2 P7)
Profiles in Belief (BR 510 .P53)
Provinces and Provincial Capitals of the World (G 103.5 .F57)
Pseudonyms and Nicknames Dictionary (CT 120 .P8)
PsycBooks (BF 121 .P79)
Psychological Abstracts (BF 1 .P65)
Psychologist's Companion (BF 76.8 .S73)
Public Affairs Information Service: PAIS International (Z 7163 .P9)
Public Interest Profiles (JK 1118 .P814)
Public Utility Manual (HG 4961 .M7245)
Publication Manual of the American Psychological Association (BF 76.7
    .P83)
Publicity and Public Relations (HD 59 .D68)
Quotable Woman: 1800–1981 (PN 6081.5 .Q6)
Radio: A Reference Guide (PN 1991.3 .U6)
Rand McNally Atlas of the Oceans (G 2800 .R3)
Rand McNally Commercial Atlas and Marketing Guide (G 1036 .R2)
Reader's Adviser: A Layman's Guide to Literature (Z 1035 .R42)
Reader's Digest of Books (PN 44 .K4)
Readers' Guide to Periodical Literature (AI 3 .R48)
Reader's Guide to the Great Religions (BL 80.2 .A35)
Reference Sources in History: An Introductory Guide (D 20 .F74)
Religion and Society in North America (BL 60 .R44)
Religious and Theological Abstracts (BR 1 .R286)
Religious Books: 1876–1982 (BL 48 .R44)
Religious Periodicals Directory (BL 48 .C6)
Repap Media Guide (PN 4888 .P6 M37)
Reports (HF 5415.3 .M43)
Research Guide to Philosophy (B 52 .T5)
Research Guide to Religious Studies (BL 41 .W5)
Resources in Education (LB 1028 .R4)
RILA: International Repertory of the Literature of Art (N 1 .R5)
RILM: Abstracts of Music Literature (ML 1 .I83)
Robert's Rules of Order (JF 515 .R692)

Roget's International Thesaurus (PE 1591)
Safire's Political Dictionary (JK 9 .S2)
Sage Family Studies Abstracts (HQ 536 .S23)
Sage Public Administration Abstracts (JA 1 .S27)
Sage Urban Studies Abstracts (HT 51 .S2)
SC: Shakespearean Criticism (PR 2965 .S43)
Schirmer Guide to Schools of Music (ML 12 .U8)
Scholarship Book (LB 2337.2 .C37)
Scholarships, Fellowships and Loans (LB 2337)
Science Citation Index (Q 1 .S32)
Scientific and Technical Books in Print (Q 100 .S41)
SEC Accounting Rules (HF 5601 .C55)
Serials and Newspapers in Microform (Z 6946 .S47)
Shepard's Acts and Cases by Popular Names (KF 80 .S5)
Short Story Criticism (PN 3373 .S56)
Short Story Index (Z 5917 .S7)
Social Sciences and Humanities Index (AI 3 .R49)
Social Sciences Citation Index (Z 7161 .S65)
Social Sciences Index (AI 3 .S62)
Social Work Research Abstracts (HV 91 .S52)
Sociological Abstracts (HM 1 .S6)
Sociology: A Guide to Reference and Information Sources (HM 51 .A29)
Software Reviews on File (QA 76.75 .S64)
Sourcebook in Geology: 1400–1900 (QE 3 .M298)
Sourcebook of Criminal Justice Statistics (HV 7245 .N37)
Spot Radio Rates and Data (HF 5905 .S74)
Spot Television Rates and Data (HF 5905 .S745)
St. James Encyclopedia of Banking and Finance (HG 151 .M8)
Standard and Poor's 500 Directory (HG 4501 .S366)
Standard and Poor's Corporation Records (HG 4501 .S70)
Standard and Poor's Register (HG 4057 .A4)
Standard Directory of Advertisers. (HF 5805 .S7)
Standard Directory of Advertising Agencies. (HF 5805 .S72)
Standard Directory of Worldwide Marketing. (HF 5804 .S73)
Standard Encyclopedia of the World's Mountains (GB 501 .H8)
Standard Encyclopedia of the World's Oceans and Islands (GB 471 .H9)
Standard Encyclopedia of the World's Rivers and Lakes (GB 1203 .G73)
Standard Handbook for Electrical Engineers (TK 151 .S8)
Standard Handbook of Hazardous Waste Treatment and Disposal (TD 1032 .S73)
Standard Industrial Classification Manual (HF 1042 .A55)
Standard Periodical Directory (Z 6951 .S78)

State and Metropolitan Area Data Book (HA 205 .S72)
State Higher Education Profile (LB 2342 .S74)
Statesman's Yearbook (JA 51 .S7)
Statesman's Yearbook World Gazetteer (G 103.5 .P38)
Statistical Abstract of the United States (HC 202)
Statistical Handbook of the American Family (HQ 536 .S727)
Statistical Handbook on U.S. Hispanics (E 184 .S75 S27)
Statistical Handbook on Women in America (HQ 1420 .T34)
Statistical Record of Black America (E 185.5 .S7)
Statistical Reference Abstracts (HA 202 .S7)
Statistical Reference Index (HA 202 .S7)
Statistics Sources (HA 36 .S84)
Stedman's Medical Dictionary (R 121 .S8)
Stern's Performing Arts Directory (GV 1580 .D247)
Story of the Earth (QE 26.2 .C384)
Structural Engineering Handbook (TA 635 .S77)
Subject Catalog of the Arthur Lakes Library (TN 145 .A77)
Survey of Contemporary Literature (PN 44 .M34)
Survey of Modern Fantasy Literature (PN 56 .F34)
Survey of Science Fiction Literature (PN 3448 .S45)
Sweet's Catalog File (TH 455 .S9)
Symbols: Signs and Their Meaning and Uses in Design (CB 475 .W48)
Taber's Cyclopedic Medical Dictionary (R 121 .T11)
Taxonomic Literature (QK 97 .S7)
TCLC: Twentieth-Century Literary Criticism (PN 771 .C27)
Technical Book Review Index (Z 7913 .T36)
Television News Index and Abstracts (PN 4784 .T4)
Television: A Guide to the Literature (PN 1992.5 .C37)
Textbook of Medicine (RC 46 .T35)
Thames and Hudson Dictionary of Art and Artists (N 31 .T4)
The Biographical Dictionary of Scientists: Physicists (QC 15 .B56)
Theatre World (PN 2277 .N5 A17)
Theological and Religious Reference Materials (BS 511.2 .G67)
Thesaurus of Chemical Products (TP 202 .A83)
Thesaurus of Engineering and Scientific Terms (Z 695.1 .E5)
Thesaurus of Psychological Index Terms (Z 695.1 .P7)
Thesaurus of Sociological Indexing Terms (Z 691.1 .S63)
They Never Said It: A Book of Fake Quotes (PN 6081 .B635)
Thinkers of the Twentieth Century (CT 120 .T45)
Thomas Register (T 12 .T46)
Times Atlas and Encyclopedia of the Sea (G 2800 .T5)
Times of London Index (AI 21 .T51)

Timetables of History (D 11 .G78)

Timetables of Science (Q 125 .H557)

Transportation Manual (HG 4971 .M73)

Treaties in Force (JX 235.9 .A35)

Treatise on Analytical Chemistry (QD 75.2 .K64)

Twentieth Century Authors (PN 451 .K84)

Twentieth-Century American Literature (PS 221 .T834)

U.S. Government Manual (JK 421 .A32)

U.S. Industrial Outlook (HC 106.5 .A17)

U.S. Politics and Elections: Guide to Information Sources (Z 1236 .M39)

U.S. Treaties and Other International Agreements (JX 231 .A34)

Uniform Crime Reports: Crime in the United States (HV 6787 .A3)

Uniform System of Citation (KF 245 .U58)

United States Code (K 44 .C4)

United States Law Week (KF 105 .U58)

UPI Stylebook: A Handbook for Writers and Editors (PN 4783 .U24)

Urdang Dictionary of Current Medical Terms (R 121 .L33)

US Political Science Documents (H 9 .U58)

Use of Mathematical Literature (QA 41.7 .U83)

Van Nostrand Reinhold Dictionary of Information Technology (QA 76.15
.L63)

Van Nostrand's Scientific Encyclopedia (Q 121 .V3)

Visual Dictionary of Art (N 33 .B56)

Vital Statistics on Congress (JK 1041 .V57)

VNR Concise Encyclopedia of Mathematics (QA 40 .V18)

Vocabulary of Jewish Life (BM 50 .H4)

Walker's Mammals of the World (QL 703 .W222)

Ward's Business Directory (HG 4057 .A575)

Washington Information Directory (F 192.3 .W33)

Washington Post Index (AI 21 .W2)

Washington Representatives (JK 1118 .D58)

Water Encyclopedia (TD 351 .V36)

Watergate: Chronology of a Crisis (E 860 .C64)

We The People: Atlas of America's Ethnic Diversity (G 1201 .E1 A4)

Weather Almanac (QC 983 .R83)

Webster's Medical Desk Dictionary (R 121 .W357)

Webster's New Dictionary of Synonyms (PE 1591 .W4)

Webster's New Geographical Dictionary (G 103.5 .W42)

Webster's New World Dictionary of Media and Communications (P 87.5
.W45)

Webster's New World Dictionary of Mathematics (QA 5 .K27)

Webster's Standard American Style Manual (PN 147 .W36)

What They Said: The Yearbook of World Opinion (D 410 .W49)

What's What: A Visual Glossary of the Physical World (AG 250 .B7)

Whitaker's Almanack (AY 754 .W5) Whitaker's Books in Print (Z 2001 .R33)

Whitaker's Books in Print (Z 2001 .R33)

Who Owns Whom (HG 4538 .W423)

Who Was Who (DA 28 .W65)

Who Was Who in America (E 176 .W64)

Who Was Who on Screen (PN 1998 .A2 T73)

Who's Who (DA 28 .W6)

Who's Who Among Black Americans (Z 39.48)

Who's Who in Advertising (HF 6178 .W48)

Who's Who in Africa: Leaders for the 1990s (DT 18 .R35)

Who's Who in America (E 663 .W56)

Who's Who in American Art (N 6536 .W5)

Who's Who in American Film Now (PN 1993.5 .U6)

Who's Who in American Law (KF 372 .W48)

Who's Who in American Nursing (RT 34 .W5)

Who's Who in American Politics (E 176 .W6424)

Who's Who in Art (N 40 .W6)

Who's Who in Computers and Data Processing (QA 76.2 .A1 W5)

Who's Who in Engineering (TA 139 .E37)

Who's Who in Entertainment (PN 1583 .W46)

Who's Who in Finance and Industry (HF 3023 .A2 W5)

Who's Who in Japan (CT 1836 .W47)

Who's Who in the Arab World (D 198.3 .W5)

Who's Who in the East (E 176 .W643)

Who's Who in the Midwest (E 176 .W644)

Who's Who in the New Testament (BS 2430 .B67)

Who's Who in the South and Southwest (E 176 .W645)

Who's Who in the West (F 595 .W64)

Who's Who in the World (CT 120 .W5)

Who's Who of American Women (E 663 .W5)

Who's Who of Emerging Leaders in America (CT 213 .W48)

Wildflowers of the United States (QK 115 .R53)

Woman's Dictionary of Symbols and Sacred Objects (CB 475 .W45)

Woman's Encyclopedia of Myths and Secrets (BL 458 .W34)

Women of Classical Mythology: A Biographical Dictionary (BL 715 .B445)

Women Philosophers: A Bio-critical Sourcebook (B 105 .W6 K47)

Women Religious History Sources (BX 4220 .U6 W65)

Women Studies Abstracts (Z 7962 .W62)

Women's Studies (HQ 1180 .L64)

Women's Studies Encyclopedia (HQ 1115 .W645)
Women's Thesaurus (Z 695.1 .W65)
Working Press of the Nation (PN 4875 .W6)
World Almanac and Book of Facts (AY 67 .N5 W7)
World Atlas of Archaeology (G 1046 .E15 W613)
World Atlas of Elections (JF 1041 .L46)
World Authors: 1950–1970 (PN 451 .W3)
World Authors: 1970–1975 (PN 451 .W67)
World Authors: 1975–1980 (PN 451 .W672)
World Ballet and Dance: An International Yearbook (GV 1580 .W89)
World Bibliography of Bibliographies (Z 1002 .B5684)
World Book Encyclopedia (AE 5 .W55)
World Business Associations (HG 4009 .W675)
World Chronology of Music History (ML 161 .E4)
World Currency Yearbook (HG 219 .P5)
World Directory of Geography (G 64 .O7)
World Education Encyclopedia (LB 15 .W87)
World Encyclopedia of Political Systems and Parties (JF 2011 .W67)
World Fact Book (G 122 .U56)
World Health Statistics Annual (RA 651 .A485)
World Map Directory (GA 300 .W67)
World Nuclear Directory (QC 774.2 .W67)
World Painting Index (ND 45 .H38)
World Philosophy: Essay-Reviews of 225 Major Works (B 29 .W68)
World Press Encyclopedia (PN 4735 .K87)
World Who's Who of Women (HQ 1123 .W65)
Worldcasts (HF 1040 .P74)
Worldmark Encyclopedia of Nations (G 103 .W65)
Writings on American History: A Subject Bibliography of Articles (E 178 .D61)
Yearbook of Astronomy (QB 1 .Y4)
Yearbook of Science and the Future (Q 9 .B78)
Yearbook of the United Nations (JX 1977 .A37)
Zondervan NIV Atlas of the Bible (BS 630 .R37)

BIBLIOGRAPHY

ARBA Guide to Biographical Dictionaries, ed. by Bohdan S. Wynar. Littleton, Colo.: Libraries Unlimited, 1986.

ARBA Guide to Subject Encyclopedias and Dictionaries, ed. by Bohdan S. Wynar. Littleton, Colo.: Libraries Unlimited, 1986.

Books for College Libraries: A Core Collection of 40,000 Titles, by the Association of College and Research Libraries. Chicago: American Library Association, 1986.

Encyclopedia of Librarianship, ed. by Thomas Landau. 3rd ed. London: Bowes & Bowes, 1966.

Guide to Reference Books, ed. by Eugene P. Sheehy. 10th ed. Chicago: American Library Association, 1986.

Harrod's Librarians' Glossary of Terms Used in Librarianship, Documentation and the Book Crafts, by Leonard Montague Harrod. 5th ed. revised and updated by Ray Prytherch. London: Gower, 1983.

The Humanities: A Selective Guide to Information Sources, ed. by Ron Blazek and Elizabeth Aversa. Englewood, Colo.: Libraries Unlimited, 1988.

Information Sources in Science and Technology, ed. by D.C. Hurt. Littleton, Colo.: Libraries Unlimited, 1988.

Introduction to Reference Work: Volume One: Basic Information Sources, by William A. Katz. New York: McGraw-Hill, 1987.

Reference Work in the University Library, by Rolland E. Stevens and Linda C. Smith. Littleton, Colo.: Libraries Unlimited, 1986.

West's Law Finder: A Legal Research Manual. St. Paul, Minn.: West Publishing Company, 1992.

Index